D0473032

TERRORISM TODAY

Terrorism Today, which was first published a year before 9/11, draws directly upon the ideas and words of the gunmen themselves, and lays out with clarity, directness, and detail the ends, ways, and means of the most important terrorist groups. In addition, it makes the case for a better, stronger response to the current global terrorist threat.

This second, revised and updated, edition has been prepared with close attention to what the author terms the new "militant Muslim international". There is also broad coverage of many of the major and minor groups in the communist, anarchist, neo-fascist, and national-separatist milieus, as well as "pro-state" groups. This revised edition contains new material on terrorist finances, technologies and tactics, counterterrorism, and, uniquely, how terror groups end. Taking a global perspective, the book deals not just with the US-led War on Terrorism, but with the interests and actions of several dozen countries and international organizations, to give a complete overview of the terrorist threat. The expanded and updated glossary of terrorist groups completes the new edition, and will be a great aid to students of the subject.

This book will be essential reading for students of terrorism studies, security studies, and politics and international relations, and for students at professional military colleges.

Christopher C. Harmon held the Kim T. Adamson Chair of Insurgency & Terrorism at Marine Corps University from 2005 to 2007, and has taught terrorism courses at five accredited graduate schools. He is the author of two previous books *Statecraft and Power* (1994) and *Terrorism Today* (Cass 2000, first edition).

TERRORISM TODAY

Second Edition

Christopher C. Harmon

Routledge
Taylor & Francis Group

LONDON AND NEW YORK

First edition published in 2000 by Frank Cass Publishers, London

Second edition published in 2008 by Routledge
2 Park Square, Milton Park, Abingdon, Oxon OX14 4RN

Simultaneously published in the USA and Canada
by Routledge
270 Madison Ave, New York, NY 10016

Routledge is an imprint of the Taylor & Francis Group, an informa business

© 2000, 2008 Christopher C. Harmon

Typeset in Times by
HWA Text and Data Management, Tunbridge Wells
Printed and bound in Great Britain by
TJ International Ltd, Padstow, Cornwall

British Library Cataloguing in Publication Data
A catalogue record for this book is available from the British Library

Library of Congress Cataloging-in-Publication Data
A catalog record for this book has been requested

ISBN 10: 0–415–77300–8 (hbk)
ISBN 10: 0–415–77301–6 (pbk)
ISBN 10: 0–203–93358–3 (ebk)

ISBN13: 978–0–415–77300–3 (hbk)
ISBN13: 978–0–415–77301–0 (pbk)
ISBN13: 978–0–203–93358–9 (ebk)

For Laura
and for
Kim T. Adamson, USMC

CONTENTS

ACKNOWLEDGEMENTS

All of the content of this second edition, like the first, is based on open-source information and represents my own analysis and views. Nothing in these pages can be taken to represent the position of the US government, the Department of Defense, the Marine Corps, or the Marine Corps University.

It is of course a considerable honor for any civilian academic to be affiliated with the Corps. My position as inaugural holder of the university's Kim T. Adamson Chair of Insurgency and Terrorism was one of private, not government, employment, and was managed through the Marine Corps University Foundation that assists the Marines' schools. I am thus indebted to both MCU President Donald Gardner and foundation CEO Thomas Draude, both of whom are true gentlemen. The university is accredited by both the Southern Association of Colleges and Schools, on the one hand, and the Joint Staff of the Department of Defense on the other.

The author is appreciative to *The National Interest* for use of some lines about French intelligence and counterterrorism—by Alexis Debat, who wrote "Terrorism and the Fifth Republic" for the Winter 2005/06 issue. Frank Cass, which published the first edition, is now owned by Taylor and Francis; through them I am allowed to reproduce parts of a Red Army Faction document reprinted in the fine Dennis Pluchinsky/Yonah Alexander volume, *Europe's Red Terrorists: The Fighting Communist Organizations*.

I am indebted to these friends for their kindness, and their critical eyes, regarding draft chapters: Paul Guppy, Tom Hastings, Leonard Hill, Jim Phillips, Nick Pratt, Dave Rababye.

FOREWORD

It gives me great pleasure to respond to Christopher C. Harmon's second, revised, and updated edition of his valuable contribution to the Political Violence series.

His book is a model guide to the great variety of non-state organizations that currently employ terror as a political weapon or that have done so in the recent past and the regimes that have sponsored or supported some of these groups. The book does not purport to be a comprehensive guide to the use of terror by states as a weapon of internal repression: That is a subject for another volume, or several volumes, for regime or state terror remains an ever-present and massively lethal part of the global trends in violence.

Christopher Harmon is meticulous in his descriptions of the origins, aims, ideologies or belief-systems, leadership, *modus operandi*, and track records of a huge range of groups. One of his great strengths is his close attention to the history of the non-state groups and the policies of the states that have been attempting to combat and suppress them. He has carefully revised and updated his accounts of the Al Qaeda–linked groups and affiliates and has wisely avoided the mistake of those commentators who have been predicting Al Qaeda's imminent demise ever since the toppling of the Taliban regime in Afghanistan in the fall of 2001. At the same time, he manages to avoid the kind of helpless fatalism of the doom-sayers. He does not offer any trite or simple solutions to the problems that the Al Qaeda network poses for the international community.

It would be well worth publishing this volume in our series for the above reasons alone. However, there is another practical reason that leads me to strongly welcome this book and to commend it to a wider readership both within and beyond academia. In all the understandable flood of interest in the Al Qaeda network, there is a serious danger of loss of perspective. It is crucially important to bear in mind that there are dozens of other active and emerging terrorist groups with entirely different origins, aims, beliefs, leaders, and tactics, which also constitute a significant threat to human rights, security, and economic well-being in their various "enemy" target countries and regions. Governments, police forces, and other agencies concerned with protecting the public in the countries affected need a balanced, comprehensive, and perceptive guide to terrorisms of all kinds.

Chris Harmon's book provides an invaluable and well-researched guidebook to this wider world of contemporary terrorism.

Paul Wilkinson
University of St Andrews

INTRODUCTION TO THE
SECOND EDITION

*Prepare what force you can and cavalry to terrorize the enemies of
God and your enemies.*

Armed with this Koranic verse, Karim Bourti of the Salafist Group for Preaching and
Combat explained his pride in considering himself "a Muslim terrorist." And he says
that he "loves" a model terrorist: "All those who are sincere with Allah support Osama
Bin Laden. Any Muslim who doesn't love Bin Laden has hypocrisy in his heart."

Mr. Bourti spent years organizing international jihad from Paris. An Algerian, he
became a naturalized citizen of France in 2000. Aggressive, Bourti told a journalist
much about his "mission to send young Muslims living in France to get killed abroad."
He collected thousands of Euros and Francs—at mosques, or by phone—which funded
his Salafists. He lectured young men on emulating the courage of those fighting in
Chechnya or Palestine. He praised "martyrdom operations"—which amount to mass
homicide bombings. His personal successes in recruiting included Djamel Herve
Lorseau and Ibrahim Yadel: They trained in the "Al Farouk" camp in Afghanistan run by
Osama Bin Laden; the former died in the Tora Bora region of the White Mountains, and
the latter landed in Guantanamo Bay detention.[1]

Karim Bourti is one archetype of terrorism today: geographically deracinated but
ideological. An Algerian, but plotting against both his own government and that of his
host country. His terror group (GSPC) was a willing subset of the larger transnational
group Al Qaeda, and in early 2007 actually merged with Bin Laden's group. Murderous,
but for "idealistic" reasons. A Muslim who schemes to kill Muslim clerics and politicians.
Living comfortably in an open, liberal democracy but part of a clandestine organization
trying to wreck it. A refugee from a war-torn North African country, now protected by
French police, yet loathing France: it is too secular; it supports the Algerian government;
it sides "too closely with the Americans."[2]

All these violent opinions belong to one Karim Bourti. All were avowed to an
Algerian journalist whom he mistook for an ally. All confirm the profound seriousness
of the global fight against international terrorism. In the years since the first edition of
this book was penned, the world has had Millennium bomb plots; 9-11; devastating
bombings in Ankara, Bali, and Casablanca; and well-orchestrated explosions sequenced
against transit systems in Britain and Spain. In the latter case, the Prime Minister and
government fell.

Today, there are, still at large, many thousands of trainees of Muslim-run terror
camps—from the Sudan in the early 1990s, from Afghanistan in the latter 1990s, and

from Asian locales after 2000 and 2001. The three famous top leaders of Al Qaeda and Taliban are in action, not in chains. And yet, not unreasonably after these hard years, some of the world's good citizens are wearying from it all. Voters and taxpayers may be tired. Some Senators and Members of Parliament who approved strong legislation in the wake of attacks are drifting from their declared positions. Some academics and journalists write indignantly that we have lost our liberties or at least that the democracies face a "crisis of civil liberties." There are American localities in which civil associations or police departments or officials decline or flatly refuse to enforce what provisions of the "Patriot Act" they personally dislike. All the democracies are seeing outspoken people of good will who are baffled by the "war on terrorism" and some have turned harshly on their own because of it.

The Karim Bourtis remind us of who the real enemies are. In saying he is proud to be "a terrorist" he says something deserving attention. We now have decades of experience with terrorism and shelves of journals and books devoted to its study, but there can be muddles where limpid streams should flow. One muddle is the popular belief, ratified by errant academics, that the word *terrorism* is so value-laden, so useless, that it should be avoided in clear discourse. No militant deserves to be labeled "terrorist," and no militant would call himself a "terrorist," it is alleged. This may suggest that we cannot understand the enemy well. Or, it may imply even that, in the words of a lady of the pre–French Revolution salons, "To understand is to forgive."

But that is doubly wrong. First, there can be no acceptable justification for terrorism— the deliberate and systematic murder, maiming, and menacing of the innocent.[3] In any legitimate polity, if a people become permissive to terrorism, they are abandoning moral logic and humanity and are surrendering the field of discourse meant for sane debate and healthy disagreement in politics.[4] The second answer comes when we listen to the killers themselves. They often say—sometimes quietly, sometimes boldly, sometimes in print—that they understand this tool of terrorism, they respect its power, and they rely on it. The terrorists' words belie the notion that terrorism is a meaningless term.

Osama Bin Laden has made a contorted argument that "the Western media establishment…terrorizes" its own consumers: "It implants fear and helplessness in the psyche of the people of Europe and the United States." Personally, Bin Laden usually avoids applications of the word *terrorist* to what his organization does. Yet even Bin Laden, in his video made "three months after the blessed attack against the international infidels…," himself characterizes the 9-11 attacks as "benevolent terrorism" intended to force the U.S. to abandon Israel. In another message—to Taliban leader Mullah Omar, in text found on an Al Qaeda computer in Afghanistan—Bin Laden crowed that "seven out of every 10 Americans suffer psychological problems following the attacks on New York and Washington."[5]

The February 23, 1998 fatwa, now infamous but little attended to at the time by the targeted peoples of the world, was signed by an international range of five Muslim terror leaders, including the Egyptian Al Jihad leader Ayman Al Zawahiri, now the number two in Al Qaeda. The document claimed religious inspiration for this order: "The ruling to kill the Americans and their allies—civilians and military—is an individual duty for every Muslim who can do it in any country…"[6] In propaganda three months later for "The Nuclear Bomb of Islam," Bin Laden issued a declaration that "it is the duty of the Muslims to prepare as much force as possible to terrorize the enemies of God."[7]

Terrorism is also the explicit objective of two different Al Qaeda training manuals discovered in years prior to the 9-11 attacks. The first came in eleven volumes of the early 1990s. With a flood of pages on tradecraft came exhortation to practitioners to assassinate prominent Arab leaders and to kill as many as possible in Western lands (e.g., at gatherings at Christmas-time).The manual recommended that Jewish communities, institutions, clubs, and hospitals can be "carefully chosen and include the largest gatherings so that any strike should cause thousands of deaths." A second manual, some 180 pages, was found in Manchester, England in May 2000. It denounces "apostate" Arab rulers, Jews, and others, repeatedly urges actions to create fear, and advises on poison, explosives, and other weapons to create it. Explicitly mocking "Socratic debates (and) Platonic ideals," the manual demands "the ideals of assassination, bombing, and destruction…" It claims holy text and commentary support this, including this Koranic passage: "…strike terror into the enemies of Allah and your enemies, and others besides whom ye may not know, but whom Allah doth know."[8]

Al Qaeda confreres and allies include many men who are just as outspoken. One is a Syrian-born Londoner named Omar Bakri Muhammad, founder of the city's branch of Hizb Al Tahir (Islamic Liberation Party). He had warned of a big Al Qaeda operation in London a year before the bombing of four subway trains. In an interview with a Portuguese magazine, he extolled terrorism as a tool. "We don't make a distinction between civilians and noncivilians, innocents and nonbelievers. Only between Muslims and nonbelievers. And the life of a nonbeliever has no value…We don't say, 'I'm sorry, it was a mistake.' We say 'You deserved it.' We assume the purpose is to kill as many people as possible, to spread the terror [to] people in the West…Terror is the language of the 21st century. If I want something, I terrorize you to achieve it…"[9]

Rabei Osman Sayed Ahmed, an Egyptian extremist and convict facing trial in Italy in 2006, allegedly kept and shared extensive video and audio files of materials, including a song with the lyrics: "We are terrorists, we want to make it known to the world, from West to East that we are terrorists, because terrorism, as a verse of the Koran says, is a thing approved by God." Another file, a "poem for Jihadists," merely repeated again and again "I am a terrorist; I am a terrorist."[10] Another example is Dr. Yusuf Abdullah Al-Qaradawi, a bank manager and shareholder in Al Taqwa, a bank with a "fundamentalist" posture. Interviewed by the *Palestine Times*, the Doctor advocated operations in which a "Muslim fighter turns himself or herself into a human bomb that casts terror in the hearts of the enemy…" He called for financial and moral support for such acts.[11]

It remains unclear whether, and if so how, Ramzi Ahmed Youssef may have been acting for the new organization of Al Qaeda when he directed the 1993 bombing of the World Trade Center in New York City. That act aimed to topple one of the towers against the other. Though it failed, people were killed; a thousand were injured; in late 2006 came news of thousands of others with respiratory diseases. Yet Youssef has boasted: "Yes, I am a terrorist and I am proud of it."[12]

Hezbollah, or "Party of God," built its reputation on terrorism in the early 1980s, even if now it prefers to pass as parliamentarian in Lebanon—and indeed, some members can.

News reports from Baalbek, Lebanon on July 21, 1987 captured remarkable exhortations to terrorism by crowds of Hezbollah demonstrators. Bearing arms, thousands of Iranian-trained guerrillas and black-clothed women shouted, "The steadfast people cannot be humiliated! Terrorism is the only solution." And, "…tell Mitterand terrorists are everywhere." As then-leader Sheik Subhi Tufeili addressed this crowd, they chanted, "Step up terrorism and war, oh Muslims, destroy our enemies, oh Muslims, remain a terrorist, oh Muslims."[13]

Such open advocacy of attacks on the innocent and unsuspecting are intended to create a general condition of fear. They are part of a political and psychological strategy, one that reaches back long before this current wave of militant Muslim internationalism. When the Brazilian Communist Carlos Marighella wrote his *Minimanual of the Urban Guerrilla* in 1969, he argued for many terrorist acts, including bank robberies to shake "capitalism's nerve system." His book abandons discretion, uses the word *terrorism*, and urges it as a means to effect "irreparable loss against the enemy." Terror acts should be executed with "the greatest cold-bloodedness." "Terrorism is an arm the revolutionary can never relinquish."[14] Marighella died shooting at police. But his manual became celebrated, widely translated, and deeply influential on modern terrorism.

International anarchists of the late nineteenth century were often equally explicit. Some, highly moralistic, such as Russian Prince Alexei Petrovich Kropotkyn, wanted focused attacks on known police torturers or infamous despots. But even he wrote that the boldness and shocking character of acts of "insanity" and "those madmen" would cause ideas to seep into men's minds and win converts. Some anarchists would have settled for the assassination of any and all high-ranking public figures, because it was so destabilizing. Sergey Nechaev's *Catechism of the Revolutionist*, 1869, thus targeted the "cleverest and most energetic figures" in government "to shatter its strength." He warned against pity while praising "merciless destruction." Nikolai Morozov, from Geneva in 1880, published an exhortation to "terroristic revolution." His praise of terrorism included "this advantage that it can act unexpectedly and find means and ways which no one anticipates…All that the terroristic struggle really needs is a small number of people and large material means." Still other anarchists of that era mocked any targeting discrimination and approved of all violence, including petty crime, for the damage that does to any society generally. All acts were "good" if they seemed to help to make government impossible—the strategic end of the anarchists. "More political" nihilists included the famous German Johannes Most, early enthusiast for dynamite, who relished the popular fears created by explosions. He not only preached such attacks for years, he published a newspaper, *Freiheit*, calling for them. One 1884 article by Most was simply titled "Advice for Terrorists."[15]

It is also useful to return to the first uses of the word *terror*. The term *terrorist* first appeared in modern politics in the French Revolution, when it was sometimes applied by revolutionaries to their own actions. They sometimes deemed terrorism "good" when used against enemies of virtue and modernity. As the mood turned against Robespierre and his power-hungry cadre and their downfall arrived in 1794, "terrorist" became a pejorative.[16] But initially it suggested the "good" that strong government could do to ensure the acceptance of revolution. A century and a half later, Lenin's directives and his principle that "the purpose of terror is to terrorize" would illustrate how terrorism can be a tool of states. Another Bolshevik, Leon Trotsky, strongly agreed: His book, *Terrorism and Communism*, makes an elaborate argument for both.

Clearly, many terrorists know what they are, even if we are less sure. Several of today's scholars err in writing that "the terrorist…will *never* acknowledge that he is a terrorist…." That is a myth. And for all the experience of a generation living with terrorism, we retain other such myths. I argued against four considerable untruths in a special chapter of the first edition, not reproduced here; we will hope I have not perpetuated other myths, or created new ones, in the present volume.

This second edition of *Terrorism Today* is akin to its predecessor. It insists on the value of analyzing and quoting the spoken and written words of the terrorists themselves. It strives for currency in the terror acts it mentions or describes, and most endnotes bear post-2000 dates. It is not a chronicle, however, but a search for and analysis of patterns and trends in contemporary terrorism. This volume maintains the arguments, begun in the earlier edition, that terrorism is about power, that it is a strategy, and that it is saturated with politics, even when religious or ecological motives may be at the fore. The present book also continues to argue that terrorism must be opposed, and opposed strongly, with good grand strategy. Such issues as sanctions, renditions, and official political pressures are again addressed in up-to-date form, as are such newer issues as torture. The long counterterrorism chapter deals both with international efforts, such as those by the United Nations, and with U.S. efforts world-wide. A final and wholly new chapter goes beyond the moment to ask "How Terror Groups End." That is a subject on which the academic and professional literature is scarce, yet the question matters deeply to the world during this sixth year of global effort against Al Qaeda.

Christopher C. Harmon
Alexandria, Virginia

Notes

1 Quoted by Mohamed Sifaoui, *Inside Al Qaeda: How I Infiltrated the World's Deadliest Terrorist Organization* (New York: Thunder's Mouth Press, 2003), p. 71. Translation by George Miller is from the French original *Mes 'Freres' Assassins* (Le Cherche Midi, 2003).

2 See Chapter 1, note 1.

3 Ibid., pp. 70–3. "Loathing" is apparently not too strong a word: "Hatred of France is the unifying thread running through the testimonials" of the "jihadi" inmates interviewed by Farhad Khosrokhavar, an eminent French social scientist, for his recent book *When Al Qaeda Talks: Testimonials from Behind Bars* (Paris: Grasset, 2006); that short English statement, and a long description of the book, are in John Rosenthal, "The French Path to Jihad," *Policy Review* 139 (Oct./Nov. 2006), pp. 39–59.

4 Please see Ch. 5 of the first edition of *Terrorism Today*, or the author's article "Terrorism: A Matter for Moral Judgment," *Terrorism and Political Violence* 4: 1 (Spring 1992), pp. 1–21.

5 Bin Laden quotations are from post-9-11 interviews. The first was reported in early November 2001 in the *Washington Times* and the *Chronicle of Higher Education*. The second was quoted in *The Guardian* (UK) of 27 Dec. 2001. The third, a text message, was reported by the *Wall Street Journal*, 30 Dec. 2002.

   In October 2001, Bin Laden told an Al Jazeera reporter that it was unwarranted to charge him with "terrorism." But then he added, "If inciting people to do that is terrorism, and if killing those who kill our sons is terrorism, then let history be witness that we are terrorists."

6 "Text of World Islamic Front's Statement Urging Jihad Against Jews and Crusaders," published in Arabic in *Al-Quds al'Arabi* (London), 23 Feb. 1998, trans. Foreign Broadcast Information Service. The four other signatories are Shaykh Usamah Bin-Mohammad Bin Laden; Abu-Yasir Rifa'I Ahmad Taha, a leader of the [Egyptian] Islamic Group; Shaykh Mir Hamzah, secretary of the Jamiat-ul-Ulema-e-Pakistan; and Fazlul Rahman, emir of the Jihad Movement in Bangladesh.

7 Quoted in the indictment of Osama Bin Laden, Muhammad Atef, et. al. (for East Africa embassy bombings), U.S. District Court, Southern District of New York, 1998, p. 32.

8 "Declaration of Jihad Against the Country's Tyrants: Military Series," an undated manual, found in an Al Qaeda safe house, translated by authorities, and used in trials for bombings. Subsequently published as *The Al Qaeda Training Manual* by the U.S. Air Force Counterproliferation Center, Maxwell Air Force Base, AL, 2004, ed. Jerrold Post. This quotation, from p. 6, appears to be a different translation of the same Koranic passage cited by terrorist Karim Bourti (above).

9 Omar Bakri Muhammad continued: "The word 'terrorism' is not new among Muslims. Muhammad said: 'I am the prophet who laughs when he's killing the enemy.' It is not only a question of killing. It's laughing while we are killing." Quotations from *Publico*, which reappeared in *Harper's* magazine in July 2004. A few of the quoted lines are also in the *Sunday Times* (London), 10 July, 2005. Detailed examination of the man's life and work may be found at: www.jewishvirtuallibrary.org/jsource/biography/Bakri_Muhammad.html. Accessed 4 Sept., 2006.

10 From a 182-page Italian police report obtained by the *New York Times*, 18 Nov., 2005.

11 Steven Emerson, congressional testimony of 2002, citing Sept. 1999 material in the *Palestine Times*.

12 *Washington Post*, 27 Oct., 2005.

13 "France Frustrated in Embassy War with Iran," by Andrew Boroweic, *Washington Times*, 22 July, 1987.

14 Carlos Marighella, *Minimanual of the Urban Guerrilla* [June 1969] (London: International Institute for Strategic Studies, 1971), Adelphi Paper 79. See pp. 36–7 on "Terrorism" and "The War of Nerves." For another edition—with an additional initial section "By Way of Introduction" that also mentions terrorism with approval—see the 39-page version by Pulp Press in Vancouver, Canada, 1974. Translators are given in neither case.

15 All these nineteenth century writings are in Walter Laqueur and Yonah Alexander, *The Terrorism Reader: A Historical Anthology* (New York: Meridian, 1987. This 1978 volume, later revised, is one of the best in our field.

On the similarities between criminality and anarchist activity, see Anna Geifman, *Thou Shalt Kill: Revolutionary Terrorism in Russia, 1894–1917* (Princeton, N.J.: Princeton University Press, 1993). Pages 137, 141, and 146 include self-descriptions of the word *terrorist* by certain anarchists.

16 Walter Laqueur, *The Age of Terrorism* (Boston: Little Brown & Co., 1987), p. 11, citing French dictionaries of the 1790s.

1

POLITICS AND POLICIES

Introduction

"Terrorism is the deliberate and systematic murder, maiming, and menacing of the innocent to inspire fear for political ends." That definition has never been surpassed for clarity and concision. Proffered by analysts in 1979, it remains sound a quarter-century later[1] and better than many alternatives suggested subsequently.

In the latter twentieth century, terrorism became a well-established feature of world politics and conflict. Today as then, terrorism is used by individuals, single-minded small groups, state agents, and broad insurgent movements to seek political and military results judged difficult or impossible to achieve in the usual political forums or on the battlefield against an army. Terrorism is always political, even when it also evinces other motives, such as the religious, the economic, or the social.

Terrorism is about power and political influence. Nothing reveals this as well as the difference between actors' speeches in the film "Munich", released as 2005 closed, and what the perpetrators of the Munich Olympic Games massacre themselves say of that 1972 action. Mohammed Oudeh, whose *nom de guerre* is Abu Daoud, still enjoys speaking about the operation he helped to mastermind for his group Black September. He declared in Cairo, Egypt that he "regrets nothing." He expects Palestinians to "fight as long as it takes Israel to recognize our rights." That interview mirrors others from Gaza City[2] and from Damascus, Syria, his usual safe-haven. And they are consistent with his earlier words, spoken on the twenty-fifth anniversary of the attack: "Munich put the Palestinian cause inside every house."[3]

Abu Daoud's repeated endorsements of terrorism mirror the words of another senior Black September commander, Abu Iyad, who wrote a few years after the action that it was necessary—necessary to put the Palestinian cause before the world. Though he did not think the results perfect, Abu Iyad judged that the "Munich heroes" did attain two of the operation's objectives: World opinion was forced to take note of the Palestinian drama, and the Palestinian people imposed their presence on an international gathering that had sought to exclude them.[4]

"Issa," or Mohammed Massalha, knew the Olympic Village well because he had worked on it as an architect before leading in the hostage-takers and so condemning the place to a different sort of history. "You offered us a showcase," he told German negotiators amid their long talks in the crisis of that September. "Issa" did not survive the mission, but three of the other Palestinian men did. One is alive today and has spoken for the cameras of a documentary film crew. Jamal al Jishey declared: "I'm proud of what I did at Munich, because it helped the Palestinian cause enormously. Before Munich the world had no idea about our struggle, but on that day the name 'Palestine' was repeated all over the world."[5]

These quotations from participants reveal the essence of terrorism as well as any dozen textbooks from the shelves of the social sciences.[6] Deliberation in the act is evident. Abu Iyad calls the operation "meticulously planned": It depended on reconnaissance, efforts of insiders within the Village, and the acquiescence for travel (twice) through communist Yugoslavia, which was an overt patron of the Palestine Liberation Organization, itself the father to Black September.[7] The attack in one German city was part of a systematic Black September campaign on the continent. Earlier targets included Trieste, Italy and Rotterdam, Holland; later attacks brought letter bombs to London, Vienna, Geneva, Paris, and Brussels. Arab targets were also attacked, in accord with the patterns of Palestinian terrorism; Black September murdered not only Jews but Arabs—in Amman, Jordan, before Munich, and in Khartoum, Sudan, afterward. The group's intended audiences were even more diverse: Israel (the enemy nation of the athletes); Germany (democratic, and a NATO member); Europe (over which Palestinian terrorists had ranged widely since 1968, pursuing publicity, glamour, and economic aid); the Arab peoples (with potential allies and recruits in vast numbers); Arab rulers (to be threatened, or encouraged, as appropriate); the United States and other allies of Israel (to be forcefully warned again of the perils of supporting Jerusalem); the nonaligned movement (potential allies, and current ones, such as Belgrade); and the wider world (to whom the terrorists were 'bearers of news').

By attacking unarmed athletes at Munich, the gunmen risked "losing" some of those audiences. Therefore, they disseminated arguments, on site and at a press conference later that fall. Their points may be summarized: Palestine, always wronged, had again been cheated by exclusion from the Olympic Games. The fedayeen had not intended to kill the athletes; it was the Germans who bore responsibility for the bloodbath. Some of the Israeli athletes had, however, served earlier in the state army (a suggestion of their legitimacy as targets.) The Palestinians were offering a reasonable deal: Israeli release of two hundred Palestinian prisoners. But this proffer was rejected. The three Palestinian gunmen who survived the firefight at Fürstenfeldbrook Airport, Munich, were later tortured in a German jail. By such varied and disingenuous arguments, the terrorist spokesmen sought to transfer moral blame for their own actions to German and Israeli shoulders. They had the world's ear: Half a billion people heard and saw television coverage of Munich or its aftermath, and the "production directors" were Black September.

Optimism was the natural accompaniment of the fall of the Warsaw Pact governments, 1989–1991—given those entities' record of fostering transnational terrorism. However, this relative decline in global state-sponsored terrorism and the varieties of post–Cold War politics have not banished the hopes or convictions of many parties that power and progress can be had at pistol-point with the tactics of terrorism. The terrorist method still requires the flaunting of four bedrocks of the Geneva Conventions: that legitimate belligerents must be "commanded by a person responsible for his subordinates; ...

having a fixed distinctive sign recognizable at a distance; …carrying arms openly; [and] conducting their operations in accordance with the laws and customs of war."[8] But hundreds of times a year, every year, small groups and broader insurgencies do precisely what Geneva barred. Usually, they act for calculated reasons, hoping to advance a political or semi-political agenda, enhance their own power, or both. Given that politics and policy are so central to the understanding of terrorists, there is good reason to survey the political objectives of many of the modern-day groups and individuals. The most important types are sketched below.

Anarchism

Anarchists perceive themselves as the "purest" of terrorists, for their politics are the most outside all norms. They live for their overriding commitment to and exultation in the destruction of the state's authority and for the dream of complete freedom. Terrorists of this bent say and write little about whatever political and social forms might follow; many of them expect that political forms will not survive at all. This supposition defies two ancient rules of human behavior: Nature abhors a vacuum, and tyranny is the normal and almost predictable opposite of anarchy. Nihilists to some observers, incomprehensibly violent to most, the anarchists have been more than a passing phenomenon in the modern age. In 1869, Russian thinker Sergey Nechaev published in his pro-terrorist tract, *Catechism of the Revolutionist*, this unrivaled description of the mind and politics of the anarchist:

> Everything in him is absorbed by a single exclusive interest, a single thought, a single passion—the revolution. In the very depths of his being, not only in words but also in deeds, he has broken every tie with the civil order and the entire cultured world, with all its laws, properties, social conventions, and its ethical rules. He is an implacable enemy of this world, and if he continues to live in it, that is only to destroy it more effectively.[9]

The era prior to World War I was most promising for anarchists in the west. Such intellects as Nechaev fostered the proper spirit. Fodor Dostoyevsky struck a contrary and satiric note in his novel *The Possessed*, where a group of anarchists were so unclear in their purposes and so inchoate as a collective that they had real difficulty even in organizing a meeting. But in Russia, revolutionary spirit stirred by anarchists and varieties of communists and others led to the murder of one Tsar in 1881 and the death of another toppled in 1917. As befits its philosophy, the anarchist movement was internationalist in character. Activists in the United States and western Europe murdered President McKinley and five other heads of state in the two decades leading up to the Great War of 1914–18, and they killed or terrorized innumerable others in public places with knives, guns, and homemade bombs.[10]

Forcefully revived in the turbulent and disoriented years of the Vietnam War and given credence by militants, naive persons, and imprudent university professors, anarchism again prospered in the latter third of the twentieth century. Much of the German student movement of the early 1960s and 1970s loved what nineteenth-century anarchists and communists called "propaganda of the deed," and they revealed certain other traits of anarchism; that doctrine became focused into a white-hot beam through a few of its members who went beyond anarchist thought and speech to terrorism. Such groups as June 2 and Baader-Meinhof were the result.

One window into such souls is the 1971 memoir of Michael "Bommi" Baumann, *Terror or Love?* It chronicles a young student's nihilism and his early education in the writings of such communists as Mao Tse Tung, Karl Marx, and Che Guevara; of such celebrated anarchists as Pierre-Joseph Proudhon and Mikhail Bakunin; and of bomb-throwers who published accounts of their own exploits. Tales of destruction thrilled him; he went from mere counter-cultural student organizations and study groups to a 1968 arrest for slashing hundreds of automobile tires. Baumann next moved amongst a drug-using and drug-selling crowd of pranksters and revolutionary agitators called *The Central Committee of the Roaming Hash Rebels*, a small foretaste of today's organizational nexus between political terrorism and narcotics trafficking. Then came his role in the terrorism and anarchism of the June 2 Movement. Baumann's rambling, shoddy volume includes a final chapter revealingly entitled "I Don't Have a Message."[11]

The anarchism of today is a markedly weaker variant. It remains ideologically hazy, a mix of idealism and apparent nihilism, but it lacks the political or lethal punch it had in some former eras. In the same month as 9–11–2001, coincidentally, a new sort of political activist traveled to the "City of Eternal Spring," Cochabamba,[12] Bolivia. According to an anarchist website, AInfos, "People's Global Action" summoned the crowd, which trickled in over time from three dozen foreign countries. Widely differing agendas were on view: antimilitarism, ecology, labor rights, antiglobalist economics and anticapitalism, North-South dialog. "All came from a wide range of political cultures with strategies that range from working within political parties to direct action outside the system (or both)."[13] Serious fissures were evident: There were charges of sexism within the convention and allegations that "Northerners" were dominating "Southerners." In spite of the rampant diversity, the gathering sought "real horizontal solidarity," not only "decentrality and autonomy." They managed several points of agreement, including repudiating capitalism and governments that promote destructive globalism. There was a clear call for less lobbying and more "direct action and civil disobedience." This last wording was key, replacing an older PGA document that had merely favored "non-violent civil disobedience" and "local alternatives by local people."[14]

The September 2001 gathering in Cochabamba has led to little militancy. But what it sought was important: to revive and refresh an older anarchism that had profound effects on the world. "Direct action" was a late nineteenth-century strategy of using violence for provocation and propaganda. This strategy would be in the service of a philosophical and policy end: anarchism—a condition of no government, or at least dramatically reduced levels thereof. A long historical legacy of reflection, argument, and publishing accompanies the discourse and organization at periodic world congresses, such as occurred in Bolivia. The movement has had many philosopher-activists. But it has also had flagrant terrorists, including such early leaders as the German-turned-American Johannes Most, whose journalism helped spread his political message.

Because anarchists are showing few sharp teeth at this moment in history, the attacks publicly linked to anarchism may bear closer scrutiny and may even suggest that some "anarchist" attacks are the work of traditional ideological organizations. For example, the leftist and national-separatist Basque ETA has an ancillary organization of youth, known for anarchistic behavior in smashing up public property in urban centers. First called Jarrai, then Haika, and finally Segi, the group has been forced to change its name to evade legal troubles. Banned today, it has struggled to keep up its "kale borroka," or street violence, taking care to avoid the use of weapons—which makes a great difference when cases go to court. It appears that for the ETA, this youth wing Jarrai-Haika-Segi is an adjunct to their own power and a training ground for hard men and deadly women seeking to become full-fledged Etarras. With such a scheme, ETA hopes to profit from anarchism and national separatism. The group passed a quiet 2006, despite a car bombing at year's end, and has not been active enough to occasion the stories in the press it once had.[15] ETA has been in general decline.

Italy suffered attacks in 2001, none severe, at the Palace of Justice in Venice, two municipal buildings in Catanzaro, a nongovernmental organization in Rome, and a Fiat auto office. Sixty anarchists of "International Solidarity" were arrested for a plot against Milan, where the targets included the cathedral, a disturbing forerunner of the 2002 plot by Al Qaeda's North Africans to blow up Strasbourg cathedral in eastern France. A European Union report noted that these attacks in Italy, announced as "in solidarity with imprisoned anarchists and against prison regimes," also suggest anarchist-leftist militant connections. The website Anarchism-Infos may confirm the connection: At the 'World Social Forum," the anarchists declared, "We have dedicated…much of our effort to the propaganda and to coordinate direct actions with some other more radical left organizations."[16]

Instead of terrorism, some anarchists have chosen to make their demonstrations with clownishness, pranks, peaceful marches, and hot speeches—continuing a pattern in some anarchism of a generation ago. One now finds semiprofessional training groups with revealing names, such as The Ruckus Society, and Co-motion Action, to which demonstrators may pay to learn tactics. None of this need be hurtful. There are also anarchist websites that offer varieties of exhortation and advice—from how to effectively participate in an upcoming street action to short war cries of notably different character, such as "Smash Up Property."

Rioting injured forty-two Londoners and caused property damage of £1 million in a 2000 event. Seattle and Prague have seen large bills for economic damage. Anticapitalism and antiglobalism are unifying political themes of these big-city demonstrations. They have not usually had a lethal edge, and yet at times the threat of killing may be present, both because of older militant heroes of anarchism and because of a zealous minority within today's generally peaceable movement. "One relatively small but vocal and violent protest element" called the Black Bloc has concerned Canadian authorities studying the recent cases in which conferences and demonstrations turned violent. A Canadian Security Intelligence Service report continues: "Considered to be exponents of a virtually defunct philosophy, anarchists received a fillip for their cause in 1995 when the Unabomber's political manifesto was published…many defend the use of violence as the only means to achieve the classic anarchist society based on small independent communities that function without elected leaders."[17]

The American Unabomber remains a link between today's anarchism and today's ecoterrorist movement, as our first edition indicated. There is nothing *necessary* about the relationship between these two movements, yet it has a logic and is convenient to both and thus has its adherents. In America, where there are notably few pure and violent anarchists, there is a broad underground interested in "ecotage" and environmental militancy. This movement is linked to Britain's, and it is integrated by several overtly prodestruction books[18] and by the partisans' faithful attendance to relevant sites on the World Wide Web. Theodore Kaczynski is an intellectual—and perhaps a sociopath— whose very calculated acts of terrorism attacks killed or injured a dozen people in a seventeen-year-long campaign.[19] Today the Montana cabin he made famous sits in an FBI warehouse for criminal evidence, and the manifesto author sits in jail, perhaps permanently. But that most high-tech of modernity's tools, the World Wide Web, carries the full text of his 35,000 word indictment of both technology and society as well as many of his letters and other writings. Dr. Kaczynski's legacy is there, in his writings, not in the few paltry physical possessions of his that were consigned for public auction in August 2006. The Unabomber legacy in politics is in his exhortations on behalf of "wild nature," uncorrupted by man. His contribution to the understanding of strategy lies in an unnoticed, arrogant, brutal line in that lengthy manifesto. After complaining that important writing, including his own, could not easily be placed into print and fully appreciated, another approach is required: "We've had to kill people."[20] Several of his victims perished; Kaczynski was published. Not only did the *New York Times*[21] and the *Washington Post* submit to his will; the Federal Bureau of Investigation suggested they should—in the hope he would be identified by his words, as indeed he was.

Contemporary ecological terrorism incidents and indictments document this virulent movement. It may be more "single-issue advocacy" than philosophical anarchism that differing individuals desire, but incident levels are high, and the militants enjoy support of a lengthening line of 'fellow soldiers.' Websites boast openly of the actions. There have been seven hundred criminal acts by the Animal Liberation Front. The People for Ethical Treatment of Animals has its own long line of violations, property burnings, and acts of sabotage. And it gives funds to combative confreres: Earth Liberation Front has enjoyed PETA help and so has ALF's celebrated fixture—and at times fugitive—Rodney Coronado.[22] For its own part, ELF associates itself with, among other acts, a half-million-dollar fire at a veneer and plywood plant in Glendale, Oregon in 2001 and as much as $50 million in the burning of a five-story apartment complex under construction in California in 2003.[23] A January, 2006 indictment in Oregon lists a "Family" of members from several of these aforementioned groups, united to "influence and affect the conduct of government, commerce, private business, and others in the civilian population by means of force, violence, sabotage, mass destruction, intimidation, and coercion…"[24] The properties targeted included wild horse–holding facilities, U.S. plant and animal inspections stations, a ski facility, meat companies, lumber mills, farms raising wild animal species, and the like. All told, recent eco-attacks in the United States have cost the economy more than $100 million, and several legislators say $200 million is a more accurate tally of the damages.

Violence to property is rarely judged on the same moral plane as violence against human beings. Many ecology militants are careful to avoid the latter. Violence has always fit uneasily into the ecology movement. The seminal work of the movement was Edward Abbey's comical classic, *The Monkey Wrench Gang*, in which a kind of gay

---

Box 1.1 "Industrial society and its future"

Quotations from the "Unabomber Manifesto"

1. The Industrial Revolution and its consequences have been a disaster for the human race. They have greatly increased the life-expectancy of those of us who live in "advanced" countries, but they have destabilized society, have made life unfulfilling, have subjected human beings to indignities, have led to widespread psychological suffering (in the Third World to physical suffering as well) and have inflicted severe damage on the natural world. The continued development of technology will worsen the situation....

166. Therefore two tasks confront those who hate the servitude to which the industrial system is reducing the human race. First, we must work to heighten the social stresses within the system so that a revolution against it becomes possible. Second, it is necessary to develop and propagate an ideology that opposes technology and the industrial society if and when the system becomes sufficiently weakened. And such an ideology will help to assure that, if and when industrial society breaks down, its remnants will be smashed beyond repair, so that the system cannot be reconstituted. The factories should be destroyed, technical books burned, etc....

182, 183. ...We have no illusions about the feasibility of creating a new, ideal form of society. Our goal is only to destroy the existing form of society. But an ideology, in order to gain enthusiastic support, must have a positive ideal as well as a negative one; it must be FOR something as well as AGAINST something. The positive ideal that we propose is Nature. That is, WILD nature...

---

idealism prevails and no one is hurt—except pocketbooks. On the other side, today and in recent decades, is a markedly ugly and inhumane fervor of self-described warriors. One proudly called himself "jihadi." More subtle is the word-choice of medical doctor Jerry Vlasak. A board member of the Animal Defense League, he has declared during 2005—to a Senate hearing on Capitol Hill and to CBS TV cameras—that researchers using animal subjects "should be stopped using whatever means necessary." Pressed as to whether murder might be one such means, Dr. Vlasak replied, "That would be a morally justifiable solution to the problem."[25]

Communism

Not long ago, "Fighting Communist Organizations"[26] received prominence for their actions in newspapers and crime reports and terrorism analyses in Latin America, the United States, and Europe. In those regions, the sons and daughters of Marx, Lenin, Trotsky, and Meinhof have not fared well during the last decade. Communism does hold on in North Korea and by degrees in Vietnam, Laos, and China. But consider Europe's once-numerous states and substate groups. After the fall of the Berlin Wall in 1989, the German "Red Army Faction"—impotent for years already—admitted as much in print, in a remarkable document of 10 April 1992.[27] Communists in such states as Switzerland and Austria may be too few and uninspired; communists in France may be too accustomed to power and sharing power in given locales through the national party. In Britain, doctrinaire communists have not been making a name with violence, and the reluctance deepened once the smell of smoke from 9–11 was hanging in the air. Italy's comrades could not look to strong new Red Brigades. Despite many press stories several years ago, there has been little to the group's presumed "revival" beyond one killing and some flag waving of sorts. By early 2006, several "new Red Brigades" figures had been jailed, and one of them was reportedly confessing, in the old style of the "pentiti."[28]

Two European parties that in past times were seen as ideologically red but also as national separatists have now left behind most of the clothes of communism. Britain's Irish Republican Army Provisionals passed through their "red" ideological phase and moved on; today their best rhetoric is couched in terms of Irish national unity. Several cease-fires and other political alternatives to terrorism are being tried today by the leaders. Another former communist and national separatist, Abdullah Ocalan, founder of the Kurdistan Worker's Party PKK, remains jailed since 1999. The group was stunned by his capture in Africa, but after some five years, remnants regathered to resume limited Kurdish terrorism. They seem to be without orthodox doctrine, holding to anti-Turkish and pro-Kurdish themes. Thus far they have not taken the fight outside Turkey to other countries, as they did so strongly in the 1980s when Communist Internationalism was in the air in Europe.[29]

The communists' picture today has a slightly redder hue in Latin America. The most successful years of communist revolution south of Mexico were followed by authoritarian reaction and then by sweeping democratic change of the latter 1980s and 1990s. The causes of democracy's growth included the strength of foreign allies of embattled governments such as the Salvadoran, and the relative disinterest or inability Cuba manifests in its old dreams of exporting revolution. Many good results of the democratic drive remain. As one example, Chile is a flourishing open society; it had no significant cases of terrorism in 2004; fifteen or twenty years earlier, such incidents were common. Cuba continues as the only Marxist-Leninist regime in the hemisphere. It is as dependent as ever on foreign subsidies, but these come from Venezuela and other states instead of from the Warsaw Pact. There are some reasons to hope, at home in the Castro dynasty. First, there is the warmth emanating from Hugo Chavez's government. Second, there is the return to power in Nicaragua of former comrade Daniel Ortega and his Sandinista Front. Third, one cannot deny the continued growth and power of FARC, the Revolutionary Armed Forces of Colombia; it might be called 'the Hezbollah of this hemisphere.' For Havana, these are pointed answers to the captivating democratic optimism of "the Yankee" and his allies. Cuba remains on the U.S. State Department list of terrorism sponsors, but for undramatic reasons—chiefly because Cuba still harbors fugitive militants from Spain, the United States, and Latin countries.

FARC's activities, from strong bases in Colombia, remind us of terrorism's tendency to go transnational. Bogotá and Belfast both recognized the meaning in the discovery of three alleged IRA Provos in Colombia in August 2001, and neither capital missed the news that one of them, Niall Connolly, was Sinn Fein's open liaison to the Cuban government. A U.S. House of Representatives panel determined that the three Irish militants were training FARC men and women in matters of explosives, part of a liaison reaching back perhaps to 1998.[30] These Irishmen were ultimately convicted and sentenced to 17 years but had by then disappeared.[31] This was only the most remote of FARC's many illegal foreign connections. Hugo Chavez' rank indulgence of Castroite ideology has eased life considerably for FARC guerrillas roaming about certain Venezuelan border regions. Colombian ELN fighters appear inside Venezuela, too. One career diplomat concerned about the FARC and ELN movements notes what "appears to be a more structured relationship. There appears to be more movement of weapons across the frontier into Colombia, and some of it comes from official Venezuelan stockpiles…"[32] Ecuador has its own Colombian guerrillas and sees them as an infestation, not "progressives" from a neighboring state. In 2004, Ecuador caught and extradited Juvenal Ouido Ricardo Palmera, a.k.a. Simon Trinidad, a senior FARC officer and experienced mover of narcotics. Another Colombian was captured the year before in Bolivia: Francisco "Pacho" Cortes was reportedly trying to establish an ELN branch there.

Peru's case, like Chile's, is an example of democracy prevailing over communism and terrorism. Shining Path and Tupac Amaru-MRTA, two groups begun in the classic Castroite era, wrecked parts of Peru in a protracted struggle for power in the 1980s and 1990s, leaving economic ruins and as many as 35,000 dead. Successful government apprehension and prosecution of thousands brought quiet to the country. Democracy, which had begun with difficulty in 1980, appeared to triumph. But politics do not settle like concrete. Former President Alberto Fujimori and his counter-insurgency boss and chief of intelligence, Vladimir Montesinos,[33] are today in custody, while hundreds of convicted undergrounders are getting new opportunities in the courts![34] Even Sendero Luminoso chief Abimael Guzman was given a new trial, although it quickly stalled. In such a way is a country that defeated terrorists reopening itself to them. Court convictions are noble things but never easily had, and when a case has been closed for ten or fifteen years, a court conviction is far harder still. It may be hoped that as releases of guerrillas and terrorists occur, as inevitably some will, Peruvian democracy will be healthy and strong enough to absorb them and suppress any impetus to renewed militancy.

Classic Marxist-Leninist urban parties, given new titles, have run in elections without embarrassment in Eastern Europe. But even when successful, as in Poland, they have shown themselves most unlikely to assume Bolshevik methods. Russia's Vladimir Putin, former KGB man, is a ruthless and disturbing autocrat but not a Stalinist and not a Leninist exporter of revolution. There are in fact few open adherents of these older schools that so readily combined the language and conceptions of political revolution, economic communization, and terrorism at home and abroad for dealing with opponents. Few read Leon Trotsky today or recall the simple confession of pure revolutionary ideology he bared to the world in his 1922 book, *Terrorism and Communism*. He was for both, and proudly. What followers he and Lenin have today tend to put much effort into dissimulation—as the Viet Cong did so brilliantly in their country. They blended populism with Bolshevism and Maoism.

Maoism has become weak in China, even as government's powers still are overwhelmingly strong. Maoism is surely being downplayed in the run-in to the Summer

Olympics of 2008, but there is a deeper pattern of many recent years. It is literally evident in new textbooks reaching the schools in the fall of 2006. Writers "shelved the Marxist template that has dominated... Revolutionary Socialism gets less emphasis than the Industrial Revolution and the information revolution." And Mao is little mentioned.[35] Maoism is defeated in Cambodia, where Khmer Rouge veterans die of age or disease each year, and Communists in office do not advertise their old party links. However, the Little Red Book and the legends of The Great Helmsman do well indeed in two countries adjacent to China: India[36] and Nepal. In both, there are large swaths of countryside now considered red "liberated zones."

Nepal's problem has grown enough to now present a problem to all of Asia. The land-locked country of 25 million is a broken constitutional monarchy. Years of weak government were followed by a palace massacre by a deranged royal. Into this vacuum has moved a classic rural insurgency led by tightly organized, calculating people making free use of terrorism. These indigenous Maoist communists date back to a notable year, 1949. They formed the Communist Party of Nepal then but showed little subsequent promise until the mid-1980s, when they underwent debate, studied Peru's Sendero Luminoso and other Maoist parties, and underwent ideological purification. The Communist Party emerged fighting openly on February 13, 1996. A document of the time, "Theoretical Premises for the Historic Initiation of the People's War," is crowded with telling expressions. The nature of this conflict accords with theory "developed by Mao as the universal and invincible Marxist theory of war." The new movement will destroy feudalism and imperialism to create socialism with "continuous revolution"—eventually attaining communism. In the recent past, these purists have formally denounced any compromise or reform, despising reformists[37] as people whose efforts drain away the raw material for revolution. "Everything is an illusion except state power" and "the principle aim of the armed struggle" is "to capture political power for the people."[38]

The Party leads this struggle, according with classic Leninist and Maoist theory. The nine-man Politburo is led by "Comrade Prachanda" (Pushpa Kamal Dahal) and he defines what the documents obsequiously calls the "Prachanda Path." If one is *not* on the Prachanda Path, he may be badly lost, if not in trouble; only "deviationists" depart from that path. The second-ranking man, Baburam Bhatarai, is an exemplar of how the Party claims its authority—special wisdom from deep study of the socioeconomic and political environments—for he holds a Ph.D. in urban planning. There are at least 5,500 armed guerrillas, 8,000 more in the militias and, hidden beneath those fighters, deep layers of supporters and followers. The militants adeptly use psychological operations, terrorism, and abductions against civilians while turning guerrilla war against security forces. Some six hundred civilians and security force members were killed by the Communists during 2005 alone.[39]

These methods carve out areas of influence. Gradually, in the old pattern, the communists build their shadow governments in the vacuum. This might be termed the "constructive" counterpart to destruction and the killing. In these liberated areas, says Prachanda, "the masses feel that we have power now; we can distribute land, we have collective farming, we can [grant] divorce[s], we...can tax the businessmen, we can manage the forests...." Such terrorism, military action, and administration are together

16

"the basis for the victory of People's War." News accounts testify to the existence of such shadow governments and, in many areas, the corresponding paucity of government officials in most rural areas of Nepal. By late 2006, the Maoists were at work along a second track: work with, and claims to compromise with, other parties as a strategy of dooming forever the constitutional monarchy. "Nepalese Coalition Inks Deal with Maoists," cried a headline of November 2006, amid hopes that a new parliament would be formed during the seven months leading up to June of 2007. Quite properly, U.S. diplomats were insistent that the accords would be fruitless unless the Maoists disarm.[40] The "fight and talk" dual strategy is an old and reliable one, for many revolutionary parties.

Although few countries are as remote, the Nepalese Maoists are alert to the "great spirit of proletarian internationalism" and send delegations to Maoist congregations abroad, as to West Bengal in July of 2001. Documents also laud the fraternal achievements of others abroad. Despite its battered condition since 1992, Sendero Luminoso in Peru is the most praised; the Nepalese explicitly take inspiration from Dr. Abimael Guzman's organization. Nepalese speeches and documents also salute parties, such as one in Kurdistan, and the Nepalese are also part of RIM, the Revolutionary International Movement, a Maoist network of many years' standing. But for obvious political reasons, the Khmer Rouge, discernibly Maoist, are never mentioned in such Nepalese communist documents.

In short, while communism seems passé to much of the educated Western world and shows little appeal in such places as Africa and the Middle East, it still has its adherents. Some find it a better doctrine for providing hope than any they know. Their insurgencies invariably use terrorism, be it deft or heavy-handed, to intimidate opponents and overawe civilians not yet under their power. Some recruits may be optimists; some recruits may be ignorant of the internal history of communist movements, which purge their own with the same ruthlessness that they use seeking state power. However, absent effective democratic government in these outlaying regions of Nepal, India, and the like, communist revolutionaries are not resisted by worthy enemies—well-functioning governments—and so they continue to govern, fight, and flourish.

Neo-fascism

As it manifests itself in the rhetoric and deeds of contemporary terrorists, neo-fascism has important similarities with anarchism and communism. First, all are revolutionary doctrines. Originally, fascism saw itself as profoundly revolutionary—not conservative (as the Left now sees it). The adherents of all three of these revolutionary doctrines despise the "reformists" who would tinker with society and politics to get marginal improvements. They strive for a total remaking of the social order and stand ready to use violence against the innocent to do it. Second, fascism and communism are less opposites than is realized. They are not really opposite ends of a long spectrum but more like the separate ends of a horseshoe, bent well away from the center and bent so far that the two ends nearly come together. The metaphor is reinforced by a certain intermingling of far left and far right. Just as communists and fascists of the 1920s and 1930s sometimes defected to the other's party, there was collusion between left and right in the European terrorist milieu of the 1980s. Third, fascism shares with communism—and doubtless a few anarchists—a hatred of Jews, Israel, and Tel Aviv's policies. A recurring theme of the rhetoric of many contemporary terrorists is distaste for the Jewish faith and Israel. If one more metaphor is permitted, if Osama Bin Laden and any leading European neo-Nazi theoretician were seated together in a train car, after an awkward moment they would default to a shared critique of Jewishness and the need to efface Israel from the map of the world.[41]

In the United States, neo-fascism's actions have notable impact, but their numerical strengths are modest. Moreover, experts who track neo-fascists often combine these with the less ideologically hardened skinheads. The movement has perhaps fragmented, driving up the numbers of hate groups—33 percent in the five years 2000–2005 to just more than 800 groups, according to the Southern Poverty Law Center based in Montgomery, Alabama.[42] They are widely dispersed all over the U.S. map, even if the southern states have more than the northern. The groups involved include the American Nazi Party, Aryan Nations, White Revolution, and National Vanguard. Several of these neo-Nazi outfits have fallen on hard times. Aryan Nations lost its famed compound in Idaho to a civil lawsuit, lost its founding leader, Richard Butler, to natural causes in 2004, and by one account has since lost chief financier Vincent Bertollini to arresting officers.[43] The National Alliance is functioning, but founding leader William Pierce died in 2002.[44] The beneficiary of such setbacks and of continued interest among certain Americans in neo-fascism appears to be the National Socialist Movement. It is adding many chapters, and has representation in well more than one-half the U.S. states. The group was bold enough to do an October 2005 march through a black neighborhood of a city with a black mayor (Toledo, Ohio).[45] The twenty to twenty-five persons marching drew an opposition rally of hundreds that turned violent, despite police efforts. For more than a decade, such shows of strength by avowed anti-racists have been commonplace at the scenes of neo-Nazi or KKK marches in the United Staters.

The spirit of Neo-fascism that William Pierce brought to Hillsboro, West Virginia carries on despite his recent death. Pierce was a talented leader—something the movement worships—but also an active intellect, a former teacher with a doctorate in physics, and the author of the infamous race war novel, *The Turner Diaries* (1978). Pierce went on to pen *The Hunter* (1989), in which a hate-filled sniper suitably named Oscar Yeager "declares war on the enemies of his people," in response to their "treason, race-mixing, homosexuality, and other evils in Washington, D.C with spectacular results,"[46] using bombs, silenced pistols, and garrotes. The prolix professor continued writing up to his death, it would seem; all four articles in the National Alliance periodical "Free Speech" (June 6, 2002 issue) bore his by-line. National Alliance has its book company, which sells many titles and the Pierce novels (under the penname Andrew Macdonald). There is also a flourishing business selling white power music—an international phenomenon in the white racism above-ground. Both forms of propaganda will remain lively, even if the steep attrition in membership is not. There are also card-carrying foreign consumers, such as Stephan Topitz, an Austrian member of the National Alliance convicted in December 2005 for building bombs in his northern Italian home. He had written: "This time we've got to take action against this rabble so that no one will be left—not even the nice Jewish pensioner that lives next door or the sweet Jewish child in the cradle."[47]

The Pierce legacy's guarantor is *The Turner Diaries*. It imagines, and apparently argues for, a race war in America. The story includes a "liberal" government that is in principle and practice despotic; a growing clandestine right-wing revolutionary organization; varieties of terrorism by this group, including truck-bombing a federal building; and prolonged insurgency. Eventually the revolutionary white supremacists win. They follow up civil war with mass terror by the new regime, especially terror against Americans of color, white women who consorted with them, and liberal journalists. Perhaps no other book is so closely associated with neo-fascist crimes in the United States. Robert Matthews was an early admirer and founded his West Coast group, called "The Order," based on the novel's heroes, which itself is a reference back to "The New Order" of which Adolf Hitler spoke so much. That group perished through attrition and a final gun battle between police and Matthews himself on Whidbey Island, Washington. Thus ended his rampages along the West Coast, which included a multimillion dollar robbery, with some of the cash distributed to others in the white power underground.

The legacy of the Pierce novel continued to grow. Timothy McVeigh helped to popularize the book by selling it at gun shows and carrying a copy perennially. After he truck-bombed the federal building in Oklahoma City in 1995, police found a photocopied passage from the novel in his getaway car. Good police work may have preempted a third terrorist and *Turner Diaries* fan. In April 2004, a twenty-year-old Marylander was arrested for discharging an AK-47. Police found masses of explosives, hate literature, including *The Turner Diaries*, a list of liberal gun opponents "marked to die," and a written plan for fifteen men with combat arms to kill 1,500 people at a Democratic caucus. November 2005 then brought conviction for the murder of James Boyd, a Texas black man. It was reported that as he manacled Boyd to a pick up truck, preparing to drag him to death, killer John William King said, "We're going to start *The Turner Diaries* early."[48] A fifth known incident came in February 2006. An eighteen-year-old launched an unprovoked attack inside a gay bar named Puzzles Lounge in New Bedford, Massachusetts. After critically injuring two patrons, he fled the state and committed suicide as police closed in. In his home were a homemade coffin, a Third Reich memorabilia collection, and a copy of *The Turner Diaries*.[49]

Neo-fascism is lively on the European scene. Tens of thousands of members of banned groups are present in Germany and Austria, and there is a presence in other countries as well, especially Russia. St. Petersburg, Moscow, and a town popular with students, Voronezh (300 miles south of Moscow) have all been plagued in recent years with ferocious hate crimes and lethal attacks against foreign students—from China, Vietnam, and other countries, but above all, from black African states. Shaved-head thugs, with a weapon bearing a swastika symbol, shotgunned to death Lanzar Samba, a Senegalese student, in April, 2006. This followed by a month the slashing murder of a nine-year-old girl of African origin, whose crime was to attempt to enter her own home. Mali and Congo have lost students to assaults. An Ethiopian named Taddele Gebre eventually made the *New York Times* for surviving no less than seven racial attacks. Ambassadors for three dozen African countries finally combined to appeal to the Russian government for protection of their students.[50] In April, 2006, a British newspaper sensed "a highly organized campaign of white supremacist terror against foreigners in Russian cities" and noted distribution of a leaflet with tips called "A Manual for Street Terror."[51] At

---

Box 1.2 "Building a New White World"

(From year 2000 literature for a membership drive by American neo-fascists)

The Law of Inequality

Our world is hierarchical. Each of us is a member of the Aryan (or European) race, which, like the other races, developed its special characteristics over many thousands of years during which natural selection not only adapted it to its environment but also advanced it along its evolutionary path…

A Hierarchy of Responsibilities

….Frederick Nietzsche told us that our first responsibility is to help prepare the world for the coming of a higher type of man…

…We have an obligation to our race as a collective agent of progress. Nature has refined and honed the special qualities embodied in the Aryan race…

…Our acceptance of this hierarchy of responsibilities is in contrast to the attitude of the individualists, who do not recognize a responsibility to anyone but themselves; and to that of the humanists, who eschew their racial responsibility.

White Living Space

In spiritually healthier times our ancestors took as theirs those parts of the world suited by climate and terrain to our race; in particular, all of Europe and the temperate zones of the Americas, not to mention Australia and the southern tip of Africa. This was our living area and our breeding area, and it must be so again. After the sickness of "multiculturalism," which is destroying America, Britain, and every other Aryan nation…has been swept away, we must have a racially clean area of the earth for the further development of our people. We must have White schools, White residential neighborhoods and recreation areas, White workplaces, White farms and countryside. We must have no non-Whites in our living space, and we must have open space around us for expansion.

We will do whatever is necessary to achieve this White living space and to keep it White….

---

the same time, anti-Semitism—not unusual in Russia—is a continuous factor in the religious life of Jews. One report on the year 2000 included 18 major cases, such as fire bombings, beatings, and vandalism, and some 64 websites distributing anti-Semitic propaganda or racist literature. Attacks on synagogues or the worshippers inside them occur periodically.

The Russian scene also illustrates a strange but recurrent reality of neo-fascism: Despite its ideological basis in race or nation, it usually has certain international connections. American propaganda printer Gary "Rex" Lauck of Lincoln, Nebraska was for many years a purveyor of literature into European countries, where anti-fascism laws are stiffer than those in the United States. Noted representatives of neo-Nazi groups travel abroad to speak and raise funds. Britain's David Irving, historian and Holocaust-denier, was a fixture on the European continent at conferences. So it is no surprise that America's Ku Klux Klan veteran David Duke has spent several years living in Russia and the Ukraine. His political career in the States flagged, and he has been bedeviled by legal matters, but in front of some Russian audiences he is a hero. Duke lectures and writes and makes postings to his "official" Web site, "David Duke: For Our Heritage and Freedom." One article asks, "Is Russia the Key to White Survival?" Duke also indulges certain Arab and Middle Eastern audiences with his brand of anti-Semitism. This includes ridicule of Israel's security concerns, declaring Tel Aviv to be the greatest of terrorists, and publishing "explanations" of how Israel had advance knowledge of 9–11 and warned Jews working in the World Trade Towers not to go to work that day.[52] Mr. Duke ended 2006 with a public appearance in Tehran where anti-Semites from around the world were gathering for a conference on the holocaust—a fact of history that the new Iranian President Mahmoud Ahmadinejad vocally discounts.

National separatism

Post–Cold War nationalist and national-separatist movements have impressed many countries and distracted capitals worldwide. To examine them in the post-2000 years is to find some that are merely subtle movements: Northern Italian separatism concerns Rome; the "South Tyrol" question lies between Vienna and Rome; the Breton presence in northern France is noticeable in, but no longer a threat to, Paris. Today violence is almost unassociated with these particular movements; it seems remote, or only occasional, and almost unrepresentative. The movements' characters are instead those of cultural pressures, pride in regional language, and attention to what is taught in schools and whether it is politicized. In other regions, the nationalist or nationalist-separatist drive has a bloody edge, which may still threaten to cleave a country. There have been lengthy civil wars in Armenia, Azerbaijan, Bosnia, Kosovo, and Tajikistan since the "new era" opened in 1989 and 1990 in western Eurasia. Ongoing fighting holds our attention in further spots: both Abkhazis and Chechens struggle against Moscow and Russia, for example.

Not all violent nationalist movements yield transnational terrorism, though some do. In the Pacific, Tamils along the northern and eastern coasts of Sri Lanka and led by communist leadership are at war with Colombo, with international effects. India has seen the death of two of its senior politicians, a country as distant as Canada has internal concerns over money raising by the LTTE Tigers, and in August 2006, authorities within the United States broke up an LTTE effort to buy a large store of rifles and some surface-to-air missiles. In Africa, Uganda's Acholi people dominate the membership of the main insurgent group bleeding the country at the appalling rate of some thirty violent deaths per day, and the numbers of displaced are approaching 1.5 million.[53] Kampala and Khartoum have had negotiators meet over this resultant border problems; Sudan is perhaps becoming accountable for having given safe haven to the "Lord's Resistance Army;" Joseph Kony appeared for international negotiations in mid-2006—something he had never done previously. These two widely disparate and geographically separable insurgencies—the LRA and the LTTE—reveal both the local lethality that terror movements may cause and the wider impacts they have on state sovereignty and regional affairs.

Several of the classic nationalist separatist groups can be described as in "strategic pause" today, yielding a peace dividend for their regions. The IRA Provos have stayed serious about a political track—with its Sinn Fein face, negotiating positions, and ballot box—as against the organization's Army Council and Armalite rifle. Both strategic tracks are available to the leadership;[54] top leaders on each track know the other's approaches well or have experience therein; both tracks lead in the same direction: national unification, after expulsion of Britain from Ulster. The Basque ETA, or "Basque Homeland and Liberty," also have declared a unilateral cease-fire. Their political wing has failed, lacking Sinn Fein's skills. And the armed wing of ETA has also failed more than succeeded in recent years. ETA has carried out few clever operations and more car bombings, with unhelpful political effects. Meanwhile, Madrid has managed to arrest several handfuls of operatives, both military and financial, leaving the underground gasping.[55] ETA underwent such repression at the beginning of the 1990s and was in recession for years. It recovered, only to meet this new governmental resistance of 2005 and 2006. Thus, for different reasons, ETA, and especially IRA, have been relatively quiet.

The same *was* true until 2004 of PKK, the Kurdistan Worker's Party. With more than 20 million Kurds in the Diaspora, Abdullah Ocalan and PKK led a nationalist separatist organization that once boasted 30,000 members. The movement was little understood in the Western Hemisphere, where it was less than a peripheral interest;[56] Kurdish militancy was a major interest in Germany, however, as that country was often the locus of PKK bombings. The movement was of major interest to Syria, Iran, and Iraq; all have Kurdish populations and, at times, the governments, or peoples, were aiding Kurdish guerrillas and terrorists. And for Turkey, Kurdish militant nationalism has been a vital interest of state, although not a hard threat to its survival. The insurgency once seemed almost ineradicable and threatened the Republic's delicate balance of democracy, Islam, and NATO membership. But Ocalan was captured and jailed in 1999 and, as our last chapter relates, the movement was nearly helpless and divided for years.[57] It has begun to recover. A new party calling itself *Kongra Gel* controls many of the former members, and terrorism has resumed in a few parts of southern Turkey. Americans and most Europeans have shown no interest in an independent Kurdish state,[58] but the broad demographic base and the inadequacies of governance in Syria and Iraq could be sources of future militant Kurdish nationalism. Thus far, the world ignores this dynamite, concentrating instead on a Palestinian national collective that is only one-fourth the size of the Kurdish Diaspora.

What transfixes the world today is the struggle inside Iraq, a struggle that is part nationalism, part national liberation, part religious. Two hopes of Washington, and of outsiders as well, have been bitterly frustrated: The first was that the removal of the Saddam Hussein regime would not be followed by insurgency; the second was that, given an insurgency, the capture of the dictator in his underground bunker in December 2003 would bring an end to the insurgency. Instead, the insurgency has grown. Rankly dependant on terrorism, terrorism that victimizes many times as many Iraqis as foreigners,

Box 1.3 **Some participants in the Iraqi violence**

There may be 50 different organizations claiming "military" deeds under some banner or another in Iraq today. Their names can be arcane to outsiders but are rich in local or regional lore. A few are named after historical generals of the early Islamic era. Some carry the names of Arab nationalists. Some fight under flags of caliphs or religious figures, according to the International Crisis Group based in Brussels. These include:

- Al Qaida's Organization in Mesopotamia (formerly Monotheism and Jihad)
- Partisans of the Sunna Army
- Voice of Jihad
- Islamic Army in Iraq
- Islamic Front of the Iraqi Resistance
- Victorious Group's Army
- Mujahidin's Army
- Muhammad's Army
- Clans of the People of Iraq
- Islamic Anger Brigades
- Lions of Unification Brigades
- Swords of Justice Brigades

Most of these groups declare their fight to be a response to religious duty. Many claim patriotism. Though some began with overt Baathist Party attachments, these became a minority. At this writing, it is unclear whether the hanging of Saddam Hussein (as 2007 began) will have long-term effects. Further decline of the Baathists' case is the most likely result, but that may be counterbalanced by increasing discussion of U.S. withdrawal.

Concerning the motives of the ostensibly religious groups, International Crisis Group observes: "Religious arguments are founded principally on the nature of the foreign presence, deemed simultaneously an invasion (*Ghazu*), occupation (*Ihtilal*), and crusade (*Harb Salibiya*).... [T]he current insurgency qualifies as a defensive jihad aimed at protecting Muslim territory and broadly viewed by Sunni *Ulama* as a personal duty...as well as a collective duty..."[60]

this insurgency is also remarkably free of any unifying political theory or conception. As the violence grows, the practitioners are seemingly diverse without seeming disorganized. It is many movements, rather than a party. In the language of the new sciences, the insurgency in Iraq is a complex adaptive system.[59] It is home to disciplined militias, embittered Baathists, new members angered by familial losses at Coalition troops' hands, regional volunteers, experienced international terrorist organizations, and would-be suicides who come all the way from Europe. Some in these movements have the direct aid of Iran and of Syria—money, weapons caches, and personne, including Iranian Revolutionary Guards officers have been found within Iraq and during border checks, making the evidence unequivocal. The insurgents and terrorists also possess unnumbered stores of weapons and explosives hidden away within Iraq, which had been involved in two major wars within fifteen years prior to the present insurgency.

In much of man's history, conquest has been the precursor to theft. But coalition forces are repudiating much of humankind's military history by rebuilding Iraq at coalition taxpayers' expense—without using the oil wealth they are helping to restore. And yet the harder the foreigners work, the harder do some 20,000 Iraqis and foreign terrorists work to blow apart the country and even drag it toward civil war. A new and sovereign national government now stands in Baghdad, showing courage, diversity, and moderation. Its security forces are trying to stand but suffer from the corrosion of spies emplaced by insurgent factions and from continuous attrition of terrorist attacks. Army applicants, police academies, and related targets are favorites of the terrorists, but the range of their other targets is breathtaking. Tortured bodies litter Baghdad's streets every day, and popular opinion in Iraq seems divided, as in most revolutionary conditions. Thus, the country stands, but uneasily; whether it can hold its balance until 2008, or 2010, is not yet clear.

Religion

The Iraqi insurgency, being a mixture of nationalism and religion, is a fair point of transition between those two sections of the present chapter. Nothing is more striking in world politics today than the rise of religiously minded militancy and international terrorism. 1979 was the signal year: a conventional dictatorship in Iran gave way to a hot-blooded politicoreligious mix of mullahs and new political faces, and soon Tehran became a terrorism exporter.[61] Elsewhere in the world, some religious terror groups were present but did not often make news beyond state borders. Indian Sikhs staged a few spectaculars, including bombing an airliner in flight in the 1980s. Militant Christian sects, such as Aryan Nations and branches of "Identity Christians," made headlines in the United States but then suffered some of the decline evident generally in the far right wing's political debacle of the Oklahoma City federal building bombing. Meanwhile, aided by Iran, Hezbollah, Hamas, and the Palestine Islamic Jihad all flourished.

These intimations of the future were instructive. In a wise 1993 monograph for the U.S. Army's think-tank in Carlisle Barracks Pennsylvania, Dr. Steve Metz described *The Future of Insurgency* as one increasingly dominated by religious groups on the one hand and by criminal groups on the other. Another study, made a decade later by a troika of scholars, including Leonard Weinberg, measured "Terrorist Group Formation" and showed a sharp rise in new violent groups with religious foundations. This coincided with a relative decline in freshly starting groups with traditional political ideologies, such as racism, nationalism, and communism.[62]

Our era has become one of religious terrorism; yet the gathering evidence and experience of several decades has left its "typology" unsettled. During the "Global War on Terrorism," philosopher Francis Fukuyama and historian of Islam Douglas Streusand and others have propounded the conception of "Islamofascism." Their argument is that the new terrorists of 9–11–01 and 3–11–04 and 7–7–05[63] are political-religious totalitarians for whom state power is to be all-encompassing and integrated from the

24

top. This is at full variance from keeping powers of government explicitly limited and separated in branches, in the ways described in *The Federalist* papers and observable in modern democracies. The new terrorists are bent on power and political rule, not some "personal spiritual struggle" as implied by another legitimate use of the word *jihad*. Finally, the new terrorists are eager to commit mass murder as a means to reach power; they do not limit themselves to overt and covert political and religious work. By the fall of 2006, the U.S. President and Secretary of Defense had combined the concepts of Islamic militancy and fascism in speeches, provoking commentary and criticism in the press. An interview with famed film writer Hanif Kureishi (*My Beautiful Laundrette*; *My Son the Fanatic*) featured his approving use of the word.[64]

And yet, if one looks closely, the idealism and religion and political content of such modern transnational terrorists also has a mix of another element, the one of which Dr. Metz wrote: the criminal. Many "religious" groups are also deeply engaged in criminal activities. Being revolutionaries and would-be founders of a new state, they are entirely untroubled by law breaking in the foreign countries in which they operate and think they must respond only to "a higher law." And the proceeds of crime go to finance their political, social, and religious work (see Ch. 3). Thus, Hezbollah shows flaming religious idealism and a lesser Lebanese nationalism, but it is also deeply engaged in smuggling. One locus of this is the "Tri Borders" area linking Paraguay, Brazil, and Argentina; another locus is the United States, where cigarette smuggling and other activities have yielded large cash inflows. Hamas and the Palestine Islamic Jihad used fraud, phony academics, and window-front deceptions in Florida to turn university offices into collection points for monies for jihad in the Levant. The August 2006 airline bombers of Pakistani and British origins appear to have drawn finances from a well-known charity, claiming a thousand offices in Pakistan alone, Jamaat ul Dawa,[65] which had already been discolored by the stains of earlier funding of other killers of an Islamic bent. The Taliban, thought to be so religious that it can be shocked by the sight of a woman's legs and driven to dynamite statues that could represent deities, is deeply engaged in heroin trade,[66] one of the lowest paths humans know to self-enslavement. Al Qaeda's use of Islamic charities has now corroded and embarrassed the long-revered Muslim tradition of *zakat*, or charitable giving. And in Europe, Algerians supporting Al Qaeda have become infamous for credit card fraud and older forms of robbery. The point is underscored by the fact that many individual terrorists actually began life as petty criminals; the cases include Al Qaeda men Abu Musab al Zarqawi (Jordanian) and Jose Padilla (former Chicago gang member).

2006 will be a year that later historians recognize for dramatic progress by religiously inspired political movements. Hamas stunned the world with electoral success in areas controlled by the secular Palestine Authority, which Yasser Arafat and the PLO's Fatah organization had controlled. The group now is to govern, yet declines to abandon either terrorism or its doctrinaire rejection of Israel's existence. Then, a few months later, Hezbollah, composed of Lebanese Shias with intimate ties to the Iranian mullahs, stunned Israel by snatching two IDF troopers and then holding its own in a full-scale Summer War in Lebanon in July and August.[67] This further success for a well-entrenched political and guerrilla force was new encouragement to the region's religiopolitical activists, such as the Muslim Brotherhood.[68] The year was also one of continuities for other religiously inspired groups. The Taliban, quiescent after 2001, continued its revival in Afghanistan and Pakistan, its chief, Mullah Mohammad Omar, "Commander of the Faithful,"[69] still uncaught despite worldwide efforts by the lone superpower. Other allies of Al Qaeda continued to flourish as well—from Jemaah Islamiah in Indonesia to the several Salafist groups of Northern Africa who operate in the wider Mediterranean region, including Western Europe.

Thanks to Mohamed Sifaoui,[70] a courageous television journalist, the post-9–11 world has an insider's account of Al Qaeda's Algerians, a religious terror group with an international reach. The "Salafist Group for Preaching and Combat" is named for one of the main schools of Muslim faith, but its origins are less lofty. GSPC split away from the earlier, and still extant, terror organization GIA, or Armed Islamic Group, around 1997. Founder and leader Hassan Hattab had openly criticized GIA for murdering civilians, but to his own record of attacks on Algerian security forces he soon added civilian targets: a Berber singer named Matoub Lounes; a group of European tourists; and the like. Hattab is believed dead, as is his successor, Nabil Sahraoui,[71] who publicly pledged, "We strongly and fully support Osama Bin Laden's jihad against the heretic America." The group of several hundred operates in North Africa but also on the European continent, where one can avoid the prisons of Tunisia or Algeria and exploit the well-known tolerance of the West Europeans. Such activities as theirs, however, have been forcing a change in such tolerance and a new kind of unpleasant political attitude.

The Salafists for 'Preaching and Combat' do both; that is, the group does not merely preach and raise funds for orphans; it also used gas cylinder bombs and nail bombs to wreck high-speed French rail lines and blow up underground Metro stations. GSPC's Karim Bourti and other midlevel operatives also recruited men for other dimensions of their international enterprise. Second- and third-generation Muslims with French citizenship, some still in an existential mix about their French location and their North African origins, could sometimes be found and engaged. The recruits include Djamel Herve Loiseau, who perished in Tora Bora, Afghanistan during the now-legendary battle there as Bin Laden's people were uprooted from their bunker complex and forced to die or retreat into Pakistan. The French Muslim recruits to GSPC also included Ibrahim Yadel, who ended up imprisoned at Guantanamo Bay, Cuba. "I stir people up" declared recruiter Karim Bourti. "I encourage them to join the jihad. It's important for Islam." He was a liaison.[72] GSPC's Karim lectures young men on the fighting in Chechnya, Palestine, and other Muslim struggles and prompts them to commit to fighting abroad for the cause.

When the Algerian infiltrator and covert journalist asked him why he too did not go fight, Karim had a reasonable reply: "It was the theologians who stopped me. They said to me, 'You have mastered two languages [Arabic and French]; you must stay in France." Karim did so, continuing to call for preaching and for combat, exposing much of his thought and work to journalist Sifaoui in the explicit hope that the latter would "show the actions of Al Qaeda in a positive light." The television journalist became a confidant, but ultimately he used his film and audiotapes to devastating public effect, in both a television special and a book-length account, *Inside Al Qaeda*. [73] The latter includes the revelation that Karim Bourti was proud of the appellation "terrorist" and quoted a Quaranic verse that said essentially "Prepare what force you can and cavalry to terrorize the enemies of God and your enemies."[74]

The utter seriousness of the Salafists Group for Call and Combat about exporting religious revolution of violent kinds was underscored for Italians by arrests in their country during November 2005. Naples carabinieri grabbed three suspects from GSPC: Yamine Bouhrama, Khaled Serai, and Johamed Larbi. Bouhrama had been in training camps in three remarkable places: Georgia, Chechnya, and Afghanistan. As disturbing, for police, were their alleged contacts with North Africans in London arrested for manufacturing the plant derivative ricin, potentially a weapon of mass destruction. The three arrested also had contacts with militants in France, Norway, Bosnia, and Britain.[75] July 2006 brought further arrests, this time a cell based in Vicenza and Padua. Paramilitary police arrested four suspects from the GSPC, charging them with financing and recruiting new militants and with acquiring false documents to further the process.[76]

GSPC successfully overtook many of the West European assets of the now-weaker Armed Islamic Group, according to the U.S. State Department. The newer organization also has members in Canada, a country that has seen all too many militant imports from Algeria. In North Africa, GSPC has been operating in parts of northern Mali, Mauritania, and Niger, called the Pan-Sahel. This has prompted unusual collaboration between the region's governments and further, equally unusual collaboration between Algerians and Americans. At least one case of bilateral counter-terrorist success is now part of the thin bilateral relationship between Algiers and Washington. And the Algerians have made their own assaults on the group within their own borders. Two terrorists were killed in 2004 operations. A third, Abderazak al-Para,[77] who had directed the large European hostage operation, was captured. In 2006, two dozen members surrendered at the town of Tipaza, Algeria. However, GIA has had still harsher luck at the hands of Algerian security forces, making GSPC still the largest and most active of the transnational Algerian terror groups.[78] That is significant, for innumerable Algerians have been involved abroad, ever since civil war ignited in that country in 1992.

It is unclear whether an important plot against the U.S. embassy in France involved the Salafist GSPC or other Al Qaeda operatives. France discovered the danger and opened a case, literally one day before 9–11–01. Ringleader Djamel Beghal fully and freely admits to training in Afghanistan. Before some authorities, he additionally confessed to working closely with Abu Zubeida, a top Bin Laden operations aide. The early 2005 trail of his group was a revealing look at Algerian operations in Western Europe—including connections to the Netherlands, Spain, Germany, and the United Kingdom. This "Beghal network" was based in Corbeil-Essonnes, France, and most were caught in France. One individual escaped but was quickly picked up in Britain: Kamel Daoudi. The young Algerian man worked at a cyber café in Paris; he was perfect for serving Al Qaeda as a communications expert and did so, according to reports. He was also articulate, and later wrote three long-hand letters in French from his jail cell. They tell the tale of his evolution so well that they were reprinted at length in the *New York Times* and offered on several educational or political websites, including Islamweb.net (in its "Kids' Corner").[79] Kamel Daoudi describes his happy days growing up in Paris, playing in the *Jardin des Plantes*, and some early success in school. But he was also stung by his classmates' racial discrimination. As he developed expertise in languages, he hoped to be the next archeological "Indiana Jones." A subsequent ambition grew to be an aeronautical engineer and thus serve Algeria, but this too he abandoned as he

---

Box 1.4 USA–Canada and terror groups' border crossings

Jama' at al Fuqra

The Lahore (Pakistan)-based sect is reported to have formed communities in Hancock and Brooklyn, New York; Buena Vista, Colorado; Red Barn, Virginia; and other U.S. sites. Counterparts in Canada are in British Colombia and Ontario. Purported members have been convicted for murder, arson, and other crimes. In an Ontario bombing of a Hindu temple, the cell combined Texan and Canadian members. Money raised or laundered in Canada has gone back into the organization in Lahore. This group was being studied by journalist Daniel Pearl when he was captured and beheaded. At least two reported members have been high-profile terrorists: Clement Rodney Hampton-el, and Richard Reid.[81]

Palestinians

Gazi Ibrahim Abu Mezer (or "Mezar") and Lafi Taisir Khalil were West Bank residents. They apparently entered the United States on false documents, lived briefly in North Carolina, and went back and forth across the Canadian border several times—Abu Mezer was caught three times by U.S. authorities, deported north twice, and released the third time by a U.S. judge. The two moved into an apartment in Brooklyn, New York in mid-1997 and prepared a suicide vest with nail bombs for an attack on subway riders. An associate betrayed them to police, and a shoot-out followed. Both were convicted and jailed in the United States. The two toyed with authorities on both sides of the border. They were never proven to be part of any group, despite reported connections to Fatah, Hamas, or al Zawahiri's Egyptian "Al Jihad."[82]

Armed Islamic Group

An Algerian group linked to Al Qaeda, GIA hatched the "Millenium Plot" of December 1999. A Canadian woman acted as transporter and aided the two Algerians: Bouabine Chanchi, who trained in a Bin Laden camp in Afghanistan, and Ahmed Ressam, caught with 130 pounds of explosives driving across the Canadian border into Washington State and headed for Los Angeles International Airport. Investigations also show that Al Qaeda was raising money in Canada.[83]

Al Qaeda

The Osama Bin Laden group is raising cash in Canada and has agents there as well, in part to prepare attacks on the United States (see above). Al Qaeda agent and Syrian citizen Nabil al-Marabh once tried to enter the United States with a false Canadian passport, hiding in a tractor-trailer at Niagara Falls. Caught and deported, he was released by the Canadians, only to again cross the southern border. Washington is said to suspect that this Al Qaeda agent may even have

---

provided falsified documents to the 9–11 hijackers. Al Marabh's associates include Raed Hijazi, convicted of terrorism in Jordan; he says he met Marabh in Afghanistan in 1994.

Hezbollah

This organization of pro-Iranian Lebanese has successfully raised large sums of cash in Canada for export to the fighters. Others have done the same in the United States, and there may be connections. For example, when a large and successful cigarette-smuggling ring financing Hezbollah was broken in the United States, key evidence came from Canadian wiretaps on a Hezbollah operative in Canada.[84] Dearborn, Michigan is very close to Canada, and Dearborn's Middle Eastern community is reported to include many Hezbollah supporters and activists—not merely politically interested Muslims who would not condone terrorism.

Other groups

In 1999, a U.S. immigration commissioner testified openly that Canada had been used as a "portal to the United States" by Hamas, the Irish IRA, the Tamil Tigers, and various Sikh separatists. In this period, Canadian authorities publicly discussed the presence and operations of up to fifty terrorist groups in Canada.[85]

became politicized. Being in engineering school at the University of Paris began to feel inappropriate.

> ...I started to worry about religious and political questions. The context of the time was the war in Algeria, where they were about to set up a regime based on Islamic law. The West hated us because we were Arabs and Muslims. France did everything possible to ensure that Algeria would not be an Islamic state....So I reviewed everything that I had learned and put all of my knowledge into a new perspective. I then understood the only person worth devoting my life to was Allah.... This glorious battle will not stop until the law of Allah has been re-established and applied by a just and honest caliph.... My ideological commitment is total and the reward of glory for the relentless battle is to be called a terrorist. I accept the name of terrorist if it is used to mean that I terrorize a one-sided system of iniquitous power and a perversity that comes in many forms...My fight will only end in my death or in my madness.[80]

Pro-state terrorism

A final type of terrorism cannot always be reliably deemed "right-wing." Its purpose is to maintain the power of a state—whatever its ideology—or to preserve[86] advantages held by particular groups. Most often, pro-state terrorism involves illegal clandestine violence against revolutionaries attempting to change those power relations or undermine the state. Pro-state terrorism is as important in contemporary world politics today as are the subversive varieties. From death squads in Central America seeking to suppress communist revolution to Loyalists in Northern Ireland who would hold on to British governmental ties, these groups seek to assure the survival of the political status quo and protect their own powers within it. The "deliberate and systematic murder, maiming, and menacing of the innocent..." is as crudely effective and as morally troubling when the policy end is strengthening, rather than replacing, the political status quo. This is especially true when the state that is supported by illegal armed parties is unworthy of its citizens. And most despotisms are indeed utterly unworthy.

Modern political figures, such as Robespierre and Lenin, were seminal thinkers about, and skillful practitioners of, terrorism aimed to undergird their own regimes. They have spawned many heirs. In the 1960s and 1970s, some Latin American countries unwilling or unable to institute healthy political changes illegally used state powers to frighten classes of their own citizens into submission. Usually without Leninist efficiency, these illegal partners of government combined inside political support, intelligence from police and other official sources, sometimes army modes of transportation and weaponry, and anti-communist passion—the latter being in abundance in these largely Catholic populations. The results included nocturnal house invasions, morning body counts along stream beds and rural paths, courts that reliably supported prosecutors, and vigils by relatives and defense lawyers for what became known as "the disappeared." In Guatemala alone, endless insurgency and pro-state terrorism combined to kill 100,000 people and make 40,000 others "disappear."[87] The wider political legacy has been two-fold: More states than not successfully repressed insurgency and sometimes terrorism as well, and more countries than not still shudder over the struggle even now as, freed from dictatorship, they join the ranks of the democracies.

Spain was a healthy democracy with a mild Socialist Party government in the 1980s. However, between 1983 and 1987, certain members of government undertook the killing of terrorists of ETA. Grupos Antiterrorists de Liberacion, or GAL, was formed by Spanish police and Interior Ministry people, acting undercover or with aliases, and by contract thugs of various nationalities. These pro-state assassins doubtless believed they were "retaliating" against known terrorists, especially those they could not reach but who were hiding in France. However, the hit squads of GAL killed twenty-seven persons, and some of them were innocent of ETA activity. When journalists and a Madrid magistrate exposed the death squads' organization and finance by the Spanish state, the otherwise strong 1992 reelection prospects of Felipe Gonzalez were crushed. Spain's "dirty war" of the mid-1980s was a major issue of politics by the end of the 1990s, with trials ongoing for persons who had tried to turn terrorism against its ETA initiators.[88]

Far less clear are relations between the Loyalist terrorists of Northern Ireland and the British government that has been in charge there directly since the "troubles" became urgent in 1969. "Orangemen"—Protestants of the six counties of Ulster—have among them militias that have killed with frequency. After the 1985 Anglo-Irish Agreement prompted their fears that the status quo would change, Loyalists ratcheted up activity; their killings jumped to five times the earlier levels, or about forty deaths a year.[89] In the late 1990s, Loyalists were killing as many persons a year as are Nationalist groups, such as the IRA.[90] A study of Loyalists who join militias finds the numbers are highest when Protestants have the most cause to fear a united Ireland, as when Sinn Fein's

Gerry Adams was negotiating directly with Tory Prime Minister John Major. At present, neither side truly expects full unification of the North and the South in Ireland.

That Irish and British police frequently arrest and convict Loyalist terrorists indicates two things. One is that the government does not endorse the Loyalist crimes, even if radical Irish Nationalists find such a conclusion inconceivable.[91] Second, there are simple practical problems with all "pro-state" terrorism, beginning with credibility and legitimacy. If citizens fear political revolution or change, they tend to look to their own government as their guarantor if it has legitimacy, not to any paramilitary. The state, even when under attack, may not need or want the "help" of pro-state terrorism, and any association with terrorists undermines its own political legitimacy and thus its efforts against revolution. A related problem is manpower. In a credible state, convinced right-wingers probably support the government and may already work for it, as in the civil service or by legally bearing arms in the police or army. They may simply wish to serve the state in that capacity rather than becoming involved logistically or personally with pro-state terrorists. Thus, argues one analyst of northern Ireland's troubles, the most likely sources of Loyalist militia manpower are not government, police, or military personnel but those who have been refused entry to such organizations or have retired from them.[92]

Conclusion

The phenomenon of terrorism grows out of political purposes. These are usually crystallized in policy statements that can be found in the organizations' charters, formal statements, and communiqués. Though the words may not always be honest or may not be coherent, let alone persuasive, they exist and, with their accompanying acts of terrorism, demand to be understood. The declared policies serve various group needs, including appeals to a wider audience, public justification of crimes against the innocent, and internal purposes, such as recruitment and indoctrination. The groups' objectives vary widely, but all have a strong political component, even the contemporary religious groups. From the political foundations there arise other opportunities and problems for terror groups; subsequent chapters address the strategies with which they advance their political goals, operate, acquire funds, and the like.

Transnational terrorism sponsored by state governments is well known as a strong component of the terrorism phenomenon of today. As foregoing sections on anarchism, communism, and religion suggested, individuals and substate groups may have very different political motives for fostering international attacks. The same is true of states. What Lenin was doing with early Bolshevik foreign policy had a later, long echo in the first decades of the Guavarist and Castroite regime in Cuba, and one of the many commonalities was shared ideology. Yet, under Mommar Qaddafi, Saddam Hussein, and Hafez al Asad, the states of Libya, Iraq, and Syria sponsored international terrorism, far less for pan-Arabism or any other ideology than for immediate purposes of state: silencing dissidents, intimidating a neighbor, and the like. Iran, since its religious and political revolution of 1979, has used international terrorism for ideological and other important reasons of state, usually with skill and good success. Tehran has long been, and remains, the globe's preeminent sponsor of transnational violence.[93] We will continue to address the purposes, strategies, and practices of state terrorism and state-sponsored terrorists but without singling them out as a category distinct from all others. For while they are political, they are of innumerable political types.

Notes

1 Adopted by The Jonathan Institute in Jerusalem in a 1979 conference on international terrorism. Many papers and publications by conferees followed, including two books edited by Benjamin Netanyahu: *International Terrorism: Challenge and Response* (New Brunswick, NJ: Transaction Books, 1981), and *Terrorism: How the West Can Win* (New York: Farrar, Straus, Giroux, 1986); see p. 9 of the latter for the definition I am using in *Terrorism Today*.

   Though this does not remove gray areas from the challenge of defining terrorism, it clarifies much of what is white and much of what is black. One must not demand more of a definition than the nature of its subject allows. The definitional challenge can be and often is overstated in the social science community; we would run head-on into similar difficulties if we demanded a perfect and inviolable definition of "war."

   The best-known book on this problem of definitions is Alex P. Schmid, *Political Terrorism* (New Brunswick: Transaction Books, 1983).

2 Reuters News Agency story by Nidal al-Mughrabi, "Palestinian Rips 'Munich,'" *Washington Times*, Dec. 28, 2005.

3 News reports of 2005 and 2006, and an AP report of Sept 5, 1997.

4 Abu Iyad, *My Home, My Land: A Narrative of the Palestinian Struggle* [1978], with Eric Rouleau; trans. L. B. Koseoglu (New York: Times Books, 1981), p. 112.

5 Director Kevin Macdonald and producer Arthur Cohn made "One Day in September," a year 2000 film by Passion Pictures.

6 Consistent with our first edition of 2000, we seek in the present volume to draw as much as possible on the words, ideas, and documents of terrorists themselves. The many good reasons to do so were underscored by wide disinterest in the pre-9-11-01 fatwas by Al Qaeda.

7 On Yugoslav aid to international terrorism, see "Why Abbas Chose Yugoslavia," *Wall Street Journal*, Oct. 23, 1985, and "A Look at the Yugoslav-Libya Link," *Wall Street Journal* (Euro. ed.), June 6, 1986, by Rep. James A. Courter, formerly of the U.S. House Armed Services Committee. I had the honor to be his aide and draftsman for some such work.

8 Part I, Article 4 of the "Geneva Convention Relative to the Treatment of Prisoners of War of August 12, 1949."

9 Sergey Nechaev, *Catechism of the Revolutionist* (1869), repr. in Walter Laqueur and Yonah Alexander, eds., *The Terrorism Reader: A Historical Anthology*, 2nd ed. (New York: Meridian, 1987), p. 68.

   There are many ways that terror groups break ties with the civil and cultured world. Violent evil acts are one sort—such as a revolutionary's administration of 'justice" by killing a victim of a show trial in a public square of a rural village. Appalling rituals, as during initiation, are another means; the Mau Mau in Kenya in the 1950s were exemplars. The effect is to break the participant's bonds with society, making any "retreat" and return seem impossible.

10 Anarchists killed President Carnot of France in 1894; Premier Canovas of Spain in 1897; Empress Elizabeth of Austria in 1898; King Humbert of Italy in 1900; President McKinley of the United States in 1901; and Premier Canalejas of Spain in 1912. Their less successful attempts included four aimed at assassination of heads of state in Europe in 1878 alone. Barbara W. Tuchman, *The Proud Tower* (New York: Macmillan, 1966), p. 63. See also James Joll, *The Anarchists* (New York: The Universal Library, 1966), p. 129, etc.

11 Michael Baumann, *Terror or Love?* (1971; New York: Grove Press, 1979), p. 48. Other pages of related interest include 27, 34, 50–56, and see the references to Franz Fanon, Mao, and others.

12 Cochabamba (and Santa Cruz) Bolivia are also identified as suffering from bank robberies from which perhaps some money may be flowing into guerrilla activities. See the pair of

articles by Martin Arostegui in the *Washington Times*, Dec.12 and 30, 2006. He describes nascent efforts to revive MRTA and Shining Path, the Peruvian terrorist groups, and mentions a newly-formed Bolivarian Continental Coordinator (CCB) to support leftist militants in South America.

13 Manifesto of Dec. 8, 2001, "We Are Everywhere! People's Global Action (PGA) Meeting in Cochabamba, Bolivia," *A – Infos News Service*, www.ainfos.ca, courtesy of Mr. Zachary Ainsworth.

14 A-Infos News Service is "A multi-lingual news service by, for, and about anarchists" with an address at Chiapaslink@yahoo.com; these quotations are from "We Are Everywhere!" op. cit.

15 Council of the European Union report from Brussels, Jan.21, 2002, and Spanish papers from the "4th Section of the Penal Court" on "Verdict No. 27/05," June 20, 2005, and other documents available in English on www.ehwatch.org/docs/conclusions.eng.rtf Accessed Aug. 29, 2006.

16 "Anarchist Meeting in Porto Alegre, Rio Grande du Sul, Brazil," Dec.13, 2001. The possibility of Anarchism's link to leftists, such as the Red Brigades, is also discussed by Steve Wright and Bruce Lindsay in *Arena Magazine*, Dec.1, 2001.

17 "Anti-Globalization—A Spreading Phenomenon," Report # 2000/08, Canadian Security Intelligence Service, Aug. 22, 2000, p. 4 of 11, *www.csis-scrs.gc.ca/eng/miscdocs/200008e. html*

18 Dave Foreman, *Confessions of an Eco-Warrior* (New York: Harmony Books, 1991). But the older, gentler book popular among ecologists is Edward Abbey, *The Monkey Wrench Gang* (New York: Avon Books, 1976). Abbey penned a successor: *Hayduke Lives!* (Boston, MA: Little, Brown and Co., 1990).

19 There is a chart of his attacks (at p. 144) in Chris Waits and Dave Shors, *Unabomber: The Secret Life of Ted Kaczynski* (Helena, MT: Helena Independent Record & Montana Magazine, 1999). As my views are much determined by study of the bombings and the 35,000 word manifesto, it is valuable to supplement this with the conclusion of the two authors who studied his many journals. "In Ted's journals he said he made a conscious effort to overcome his middle-class inhibitions, becoming free to commit crimes without the burden of guilt. He deprogrammed society's norms and the training of his early years. He then reprogrammed his mind so he felt satisfaction from violence, even murder, acts that seemed to cleanse his mind and ease the hatred temporarily;" p. 264.

20 The Unabomber [Theodore Kaczynski] Manifesto, "Industrial Society and its Future," Sept.19, 1995, in the *Washington Post*.

21 The *Times* helped pay for the 8-page insert which was then printed only in the *Post*.

22 *Washington Times*, Aug. 22, 2005.

23 ELF's initials were on a 12-foot banner at the scene that said "If you build it, we will burn it." On that evening, Rodney Coronado was giving a speech in the same state; *AnimalRights. net* declared this a coincidence in a posting of Sept. 16, 2003, accessed Aug. 20, 2006. In interviews that day, Coronado defended the attack and distinguished it from "terrorism" which he says "kills people."

24 Some believe there is hard difference in the strategies of ALF and ELF. That is not clear to the present author, and it is unsupported by the lengthy indictment in at least once case, that against "The Family"; filing by Karin J. Immergut, U.S. Attorney for the District of Oregon, Jan. 19, 2006. Of course, activists can be members of multiple groups.

25 *Los Angeles Times*, Nov. 13, 2005. In a classic fashion of militant advocacy within open democracies, Vlasak also says he *personally* would not hurt others to defend "beings." And he denies membership in the Animal Defense League—although he is married to its co-leader and he often passes out its communiqués.

26 *Europe's Red Terrorists: Fighting Communist Organizations* is a fine book of documents eds. Yonah Alexander and Dennis Pluchinsky (London: Frank Cass, 1992).

27 The RAF's words are displayed in an inset within ch. 6, following.

28 Estimates of membership of "the new Red Brigades" are hard to find; one occurred in *Le Figaro* of June 26, 2003: 100–50. The older movement had thousands of hard-core supporters and many hundreds of armed men and women.

29 The "Kurdistan Freedom Hawks" or TAK now claim some of the headlines after violent acts, as with two bombings in the resort town of Cesme on the Aegean coast in 2005. Their relationship to PKK remnants or Kongra Gel is unclear.

30 On the FARC-IRA relationship, see *Jane's Intelligence Review*, Sept. 2002, 24–25, as well as "Summary of Investigation of IRA Links to FARC Narco-Terrorists in Colombia," an April 24, 2001 report by staff of the House International Relations Committee; www.house. gov/international_relations/findings.htm , accessed May 13, 2002.

31 Press on the complicated proceedings includes the *Washington Times* of Dec. 17, 2004.

32 Thomas A. Shannon, assistant secretary of state for Western Hemisphere affairs, U.S. Dept. of State, speaking to the *Washington Times*, May 17, 2006. The lead paragraph reads: "Venezuela has allowed its intelligence service to become a clone of Cuba's while it shelters groups with ties to Middle East terrorists and allows weapons from its official stockpiles to reach Colombian guerrillas, a senior U.S. official said yesterday."

33 See, for example, "Montesinos: Blind Ambition," a document collection by The National Security Archive, on the Wweb site: www.gwu.edu The editor discusses, among other factors, state terror by the Peruvian Army Intelligence Service and a government-run death squad called "Grupo Colina."

34 American news outlets have been oddly silent about this quiet revolution in Peru. *The Washington Post* had one report, and mention was made in the State Dept.'s *Country Reports on Terrorism: 2004* (Wash. D.C.: Government Printing Office [hereafter, GPO], April 2005). On Dec. 23, 2005, the *Washington Times* reported on rising banditry based on the cocoa trade, noting how some former Maoists were now out for the money.

35 *New York Times*, Sept. 1, 2006, front page story.

36 See "India's Ragtag Band of Maoists Takes Root Among Rural Poor," *Washington Post*, May 13, 2006. *The Economist* has an Aug. 19, 2006 report at pp. 38–40.

37 Terrorists' contempt for, and concern over, reformers is an important fact but one rarely described in books about terrorism. Rightly fearing that reforms could weaken the impetus for revolution and violence, terrorists often strike at "liberals" and "reformers" before more obvious targets, such as senior generals, secret police chiefs, or conservative politicians. One sees such hatred of reformers in, for example, the *El Diario* interviews that Sendero Luminoso chief Abimael Guzman gave to that party paper in July 1988.

38 Denouncing "reactionary forces" in the countryside, such as capitalists and landowners, the manifesto of 1996 says, "Our armed struggle will be conducted by taking agrarian revolution as the axis and relying on the laboring masses, particularly the poor peasants..." A communist reporter who met with the General Secretary in 1996 announces, in his interview notes, that the Party "is applying Mao's strategy of a protracted people's war—establishing base areas in the countryside and aiming to surround the cities, seize nationwide power..." *Revolutionary Worker* 1043, Feb. 20, 2000.

39 U.S. Dept. of State, *Country Reports on Terrorism: 2005* (Wash. D.C.: GPO, April 2006).

40 The *Washington Times* continues to offer some of the best regular U.S. news coverage of the revolution in Nepal; this story was by Chitra Tiwari, Nov. 11, 2006.

41 See ch. 5 of our first edition of *Terrorism Today* as to "Right and Left: Extremists but not Enemies," pp. 198–201.

42 Southern Poverty Law Center's emphasis on numbers of groups (however small) makes it difficult to determine how many individuals they think to be involved. This characteristic of their reports is notable in the Spring 2006 issue of their *Intelligence Report*, and a lengthy *Washington Post* story using their data and appearing April 19, 2005.

43 *Intelligence Report* of the Southern Poverty Law Center (Summer, 2006), pp. 4–5.

44 The current Chairman of the National Alliance is Eric Gliebe.

45 *SPLC Report*, of the Southern Poverty Law Center 36: 2 (June, 2006), p. 3.

46 From a publicity note on the National Vanguard Books website, *www.natvan.com/cgi-bin/ webc.cgi/st_prod.html* accessed Oct. 14, 2002. Oddly, the tactics in the Washington-based novel were akin to those used by Washington-area sniper John Allen Mohammed, terrorizing the city and environs in Oct. 2002. But Mohammed was a black with ill-defined links to a black separatist organization, while his victims were of several races.

47 *Intelligence Report* 121 (Spring 2006), p. 71.

48 Now on death row for more than 7 years, King denies he was even in the murder vehicle and blames its owner Shawn Berry and brother Lewis Berry for the murder; *Washington Times*, Aug. 21, 2006.

49 The Maryland arrest is noted in *Intelligence Report* (Summer 2004), found at *www.splcenter. org/intel/intelreport/article.jsp?sid=310* on 8 Aug. 2006. The Massachusetts case is covered in the print edition of *Intelligence Report* (Spring 2006). The other incidents linked to the book were separately reported. For example, ABC News on April 18, 1996 reported that McVeigh had *The Turner Diaries* among his possessions, and the broadcaster ran film of McVeigh's sister saying, "I think it was one of his favorite readings."

50 *New York Times*, May 3 and 6, 2002.

51 *The Independent* (London), April 8, 2006; Russian skinheads "espouse a mixture of nationalism and fascism."

52 See for example David Duke's articles still up on his Web site: "One Year Later: 911," "Israeli Terrorism and Sept. 11," and "The Big Lie—The True Reason Behind the Attack."

53 Human rights sources, 2006 congressional testimony by Nina Shea, and the Dept. of State, *Country Reports on Terrorism: 2005*, in its brief on "Lord's Resistance Army."

54 It may be a minority viewpoint, but I place no faith in the elaborate and over-publicized process of recent years in which the IRA allegedly "put its arms beyond use" or surrendered them. Some of the inspectors were not to be trusted, but the larger problem is that only the Provos know how many weapons they actually had. Turning in many can still leave many hidden.

55 For example, 56 ETA suspects went on trial in Madrid in late 2005; *New York Times*, Nov. 22, 2005.

56 In this paragraph, I am using Donald E. Neuchterlein's useful separation of "national interests" into categories of peripheral, major, vital, and survival. His rubrics are a fine alternative to the bad habit of loosely referring to all interests as "vital national interests." *America Overcommitted: United States National Interests in the 1980s* (Lexington, KY: University of Kentucky Press, 1985).

57 My resources on PKK include Ihsan Bal & Sedat Laciner, "The Challenge of Revolutionary Terrorism to Turkish Democracy, 1960-80"; *Terrorism and Political Violence*, vol 13 # 4 (Winter 2001), pp. 90–115; and many essays by Dr. Michael Radu of the Foreign Policy Research Institute in Philadelphia, some of which appear in his new book, *Dilemmas of Democracy Dictatorship: Place, Time, and Ideology in Global Perspective* (New Brunswick, NJ: Transaction Publishers, 2006).

58 During and just after the second Iraq war, when the character of Iraqi governance was a primary one in Washington, there were seemingly no public discussions of prospects for a Kurdish state or autonomous area. A conversation with one U.S. Defense Dept. political appointee made it clear that even mention of the subject was deemed in poor taste.

59 I owe to General P. K. Van Riper and Dr. Chris Bassford my introduction to the "new sciences." One may with utility think of Al Qaeda as a "complex adaptive system."

60 The quoted material is from "In Their Own Words: Recalling the Iraqi Insurgency," Middle East Reports No. 50, Feb. 15, 2006, by the International Crisis Group.

61 Our first edition required a half-dozen pages—all developed from public and available sources—to describe the main ways in which Iran exports terrorism. On March 20, 2006, the author gathered with James Phillips and Ken Katzman at the Heritage Foundation to broadcast a panel discussion of Iran's elaborate and heavy involvements in the region, including the ongoing insurgency in Iraq. Now, as this second edition is completed, Iran has scored a victory with its aid to Hezbollah in the Summer War of 2006. A new U.S. congressional

report complains that officials had been underestimating Iran's disturbing international activities. And important Iranian Revolutionary Guard figures have been discovered in Iraq, helping the underground.

62 Steven Metz, *The Future of Insurgency* (Carlisle Barracks PA: Strategic Studies Institute, Dec. 1993). Ami Pedahzur, William Eubank, and Leonard Weinberg, "The War on Terrorism and the Decline of Terrorist Group Formation: A Research Note, *Terrorism and Political Violence* 14: 3 (Autumn 2002), 141–7.

63 By popular numerical shorthand, the New York attacks became known by "9-11-01," the Madrid train attacks by "3-11-04," and the London tube bombings by "7-7-05." In these cases, the perpetrators' motives are believed strongly similar.

64 Notes on the controversy: Critics of the terms *Islamofascism* or *Islamic fascism* include a few who evidently have not studied fascism. What many critics dread is any connecting of a great religion with a sick political ideology of 20th century Europe. Americans and Europeans often refer to "their" own neo-fascists and neo-Nazis of today—as I do in this chapter—which fact should remind us that the term *fascist* is not merely a new weapon for the "clash of civilizations."

Streusand, a historian of Islam with a doctorate from the University of Chicago, teaches at Marine Corps University, Quantico VA, and co-authored a 2006 article on language and militant Islam. *Washington Post* columnist David Ignatius offered mixed views on the term *Islamofascism* as applicable to today's terrorism. Film director Hanif Kureishi used the term twice and approvingly in a *National Public Radio* interview of Aug. 22, 2006 WAMU (Wash. DC).

65 See the organization's website, as well as the *Washington Post* of Aug. 15, 2006.

66 The many witnesses to this include U.S. Gen. James Jones, who directed NATO's forces in Afghanistan and Europe until mid-2006 and briefings by the general and by Afghan officials on our Afghanistan trip of late Feb. 2006. See also the general's subsequent remarks to *Forbes* magazine Aug. 17, 2006.

67 For example, the *Financial Times* has carried the commentary of an estimable critic of the Middle East and Islam, Oliver Roy, on Aug. 18, 2006: "The perceived victory of Hezbollah in Lebanon may be short term but has highlighted some new and important developments. For the first time, the Israel Defense Forces were unable to prevail in an all-out war. More significantly, the winner this time is a Shia Muslim, non-state, armed movement supported by Syria and Iran. In Israel's previous wars, from 1948 to 1982, the challengers were Sunni Arabs."

68 For example, a thoughtful Egyptian's perspective appeared in op-ed pages of the *New York Times*, Aug.20, 2006.

69 An authoritative description of the Taliban leader Mullah Mohammad Omar is by Ahmad Rashid, *Taliban,* rev. ed. (New Haven CN: Yale University Press, 2001). A journalistic portrait was by Robert Marquand, *Christian Science Monitor*, Oct. 10, 2001. Marquand's report on this man intimately linked to Al Qaeda and Muslim fanaticism opens with a story of a Pakistani trying to dissuade the Taliban ruler from blowing up 1,700-year-old statues of Buddha: "Mullah Omar replied by describing a dream he'd had about a 'mountain falling down on him.' Before it hit him, Allah appeared, asking Omar why he did nothing to get rid of the false idols." The Pakistani closed his attaché case and left, shoulders sagging, as "There was nothing left to say." The Taliban's destruction of age-old art continued in Afghanistan.

70 Mohamed Sifaoui, *Inside Al Qaeda: How I Infiltrated the World's Deadliest Terrorist Organization*, trans. George Miller (New York: Thunder's Mouth Press, 2004).

71 *New York Times*, June 21, 2004. The Algerian Army caught and killed a number of GSPC members that season, including Sahraoui.

72 "Al Qaeda link to July 7 Sought; Recruiter Eyed in British Blasts," by Massoud Ansari for the London *Sunday Telegraph*, repr. *Washington Times*, July 10, 2006. The news story was prompted by the first anniversary of the plots and by a new Al Zawahiri videotape release in which Al Qaeda claimed to have trained the British subway bombers.

73 See especially Sifoui's book, p. 71.

74 Ibid., pp. 71–6. The verse the GSPC man quoted is one other terrorists have cited as well; see my Introduction for many further examples of this arrogance and accuracy by the terrorists themselves.

75 *Sunday Times* (Johannesburg, So. Africa), Nov. 17, 2005.

76 Associated Press/*Newsday*, July 21, 2006. For this and other "clippings" the author thanks staff at the George Marshall Center for European Security Studies, Garmish, Germany.

77 Al Para is a code name, said to derive from Algerian paratroop service, for the terrorist Amari Saifi.

78 Al Jazeera on Aug. 20, 2006 quotes an Algerian minister to the effect that some 800 Islamic militants may be at large within his country; that presumably refers to armed full-time members and to both major groups, GSPC and its "father," GIA. Detailed coverage of the Salafist Group for Preaching and Combat may be found in the Jamestown Foundation's *Terrorism Monitor* for 7 Jan. and Nov. 4, 2004.

79 Elaine Sciolino analyzed and edited the script for the *New York Times*, Sept. 23, 2002. Reprint (without any attribution) occurred on Islamweb.net, viewed 20 Aug. 2006. Further stories on Kamel Daoudi include *BBC News*, Oct. 5, 2001, and *Asia Times*, Feb. 19, 2005.

80 *New York Times*, ibid.

81 Larry Martinez, "Jama' at al Fuqra: a.k.a. Society of the Impoverished," *Journal of Counterterrorism & Homeland Security International*, vol. 8 no. 3 (2002), pp. 36–8. *New York Times*, Jan. 3, 2002. Harvey Kushner calls the two "Freelancers" but then later notes "possible links" to Hamas; *Terrorism in America* (Springfield, IL: Charles C Thomas Pub., 1998), pp. 143–4; 190.

82 *The Standard* (St Catharines, Canada), Sept. 28 and Oct. 2, 2001. FBI, *Terrorism in the United States: 1997* (Wash. D.C.: GPO, n.d.), p. 5, with a follow-up note in the 1999 annual. Kushner, op. cit., pp. 47–8.

83 *New York Times*, Dec. 3, 2001; *Insight*, Dec. 17, 2001.

84 For a report on Hezbollah fund-raising in Canada, see the *Los Angeles Times*, March 29, 1997.

85 Testimony of Michael A. Pearson, executive associate commissioner for field operations, Immigration & Naturalization Service, USA, Hearing before the Subcom. On Immigration and Claims, Judiciary Comm., U.S. House of Reps., April 14, 1999; *www.house.gov/judiciary/pear0414.htm*. See also *Los Angeles Times*, March 29, 1997: "While it is little remarked upon in Canada, authorities have known for years of fund-raising and other activities that go on here in support of Muslim radicals and other violent groups, anti-terrorism experts said…"

86 The term *preservationist* is that of Bard O'Neill, author of *Insurgency & Terrorism:Inside Modern Revolutionary Warfare* (Washington DC: Brassey's., 1990, pp. 20–1, repr. Potomac Books, 2005). It is a useful term, whereas "preservationist" terrorism by Northern Irish militias is intended as "pro-state" violence, Serb terrorism or Ku Klux Klan terrorism today is intended to preserve advantages for an ethnic group but is not "pro-state" because it contravenes the governments' interests in Bosnia and the United States, respectively.

87 *New York Times*, Dec. 30, 1996. Though violence in Guatemala diminished greatly since the phased 1996–97 peace accord, terrorism lingered on as a specter. A Roman Catholic bishop who supervised a 1,400-page study of human rights abuses during the long internal struggle was murdered two days after publishing his report in 1998.

88 Peter Taylor, *States of Terror: Democracy and Political Violence* (London: BBC Books, 1993), pp. 98--104. See also the detailed *New York Times* articles of Feb. 12–14, 1997.

89 Steve Bruce, 'Loyalists in Northern Ireland: Further Thoughts on Pro-State Terror', *Terrorism and Political Violence* 5: 4 (Winter 1993), 252.

90 Though the Nationalists (IRA, INLA, etc.) have killed more than the Loyalists, the latter have been "making up for lost time." In the 14 months before June 1994, police brought 138 charges against Protestant paramilitaries and 83 against Catholic organizations, such as IRA.

91 For example, the New York weekly *The Irish People* headlines suspicions of cooperation between anyone in government or security forces, on the one hand, and "Orange"/Loyalist militias on the other.

92 The analysis in this paragraph is largely derived from Steve Bruce, 'The Problem of 'Pro-State' Terrorism: Loyalist Paramilitaries in Northern Ireland', *Terrorism and Political Violence* 4: 1 (Spring 1992), 67–88.

93 This fact was underscored in the early days of 2007 when Iranian officials were discovered in Iraq directly helping the insurgents. The Iranians included several officers of the Revolutionary Guards, which have a long history of training and helping foreign militants.

2

STRATEGIES OF
TERRORIST GROUPS

Introduction

Strategy is the considered application of means to advance one's ends. Terrorists, far from being "mindless," as American politicians sometimes say, are disturbingly calculating about the means they use. Military analysts often describe terrorism as less than a strategy and merely as a tactic, but depending on circumstances and the terrorists' intentions, it can be either. In the post-1945 world, terrorism has been a strategy central to a score of revolutionary movements. The groups' documents, communiqués, and testimonials—given to the press or spoken in court—reveal choices made to use terror. States, as well, continue to use terror as a weapon against foreign entities, émigrés, and others they deem enemies. The many consequences of those deliberate choices to employ terrorism range from the most general and ambiguous, through the devastatingly inhumane and destructive, to the decidedly political, and other effects on contemporary life.

At least five terrorist strategies are so common around the globe that they deserve explicit enumeration and analysis.[1] They are, or many of them are, self-consciously and commonly used in tandem, making their separation for analytical purposes slightly artificial. They all meld violence and propaganda in some form to gain public effect. As Abimael Guzman, the Sendero Luminoso ideologist, once himself rightly declared, revolutionary strategies normally include both *destruction* and some forms of *construction*.[2] That is, the terrorists' actions yield not just damage to targets but some form of progress for the militants in their drive for greater power. Rarely is terrorism merely nihilist; it ordinarily aims at strategic objectives.

The first strategy is to create or further a sense of societal dislocation, fear, and even anarchy. The Chinese military thinker Sun Tzu saw that creating "disorder" is as useful as, or more useful than, the destruction of enemy forces. This strategy is most commonly used by revolutionaries, but it can also work for pro-state terrorists: Bombings and other crimes provoke public fears and thus enhance public support for further law enforcement measures, or even dictatorship. Adolf Hitler is believed to have successfully manipulated public fears by burning the *Reichstag,* or national government building, in 1933 when he was already Chancellor, to blame the act on German communists, win votes in impending elections, and legitimate a planned crackdown against opponents of the Nazis.

An original use of the strategy—a hybrid of the revolutionary and the anti-revolutionary—was sketched in print by the modern Brazilian terrorist and theoretician, Carlos Marighella. His pulp-paper *Minimanual of the Urban Guerrilla* was found in a hundred safe houses in the late twentieth century and was translated into many foreign languages. Marighella realized that terrorism does not merely undermine public confidence in government; it forces government into a reactive posture: as repression increases, the government angers its own populace, driving neutrals toward the revolutionaries. Marighella imagines an inevitable sequence in which terrorist chaos leads to intensified repression by the government, which fails to stop terrorism but begins a new cycle of *decreasing* public support for the status quo and the government and *enhanced* public support for the terrorists. "The people refuse to collaborate with the authorities, and the general sentiment is that the government is unjust, incapable of solving problems, and resorts purely and simply to the physical liquidation of its opponents." In such ways is a normal political situation translated into a violent, chaotic, and then military one.[3]

This "crackdown" model—as we might call it—outlived its author. In the 1990s, some analysts understood Italian right-wing terrorist bombings as an attempt to use fear to create greater authoritarian controls. In an altogether different setting, the same principle lay behind this propaganda effort: a 1993 Hamas leaflet listing several dozen political objectives demanded that the faithful embarrass Yasser Arafat's Palestine Authority (PA), which was arresting members of religiously motivated Palestinian organizations, such as Hamas. It was hoped that the "program of confrontation" would be so effective that it would force redeployment of Israeli security personnel into areas handed over to Arafat! The bald exhortation of the leaflet was thus for: "Escalating operations in order to force the occupation to reoccupy other areas and impose a security siege on areas under the PA's control."[4] Manipulating public opinion and building electoral strength were central to Hamas' defeat of Arafat loyalists in polling of January 2006. Now they are arresting Fatah members on occasion, shooting them on others, and building their own security forces to better rival that of Fatah's.[5]

Such a strange sequence of anarchy, "crackdown," and then revolution is not the aim of all terror groups, of course. Some do less planning; some groups have far more direct plans; there are groups with very limited goals that do not include taking the full powers of state. What does seem nearly universal is that the destruction by terror groups is in their minds a necessary part of their own effort at construction of sorts. Terrorists look to "positive" dimensions of their actions. For example, violence is intended to forcefully draw the polity's attention to a "neglected" issue. The hope, justified by terrorists' general success, is that a public shocked by a terrorist act or campaign will come to feel attention *should* be paid. The public often does respond, even if it does not fully believe the propaganda circulated at the time of the action by the terrorists. Recent public issues to be heated up by terrorist acts include those as different as "animal liberation" and mass murders of Armenians in pre-modern Turkey. Agitation and violence on such an issue can spread chaos while also building a terror group's profile in public eyes.

The second terrorist strategy to be explored in this chapter is more focused than the creation of anarchy: It is to discredit, diminish, or destroy a particular government and replace it with another. Attacks on officials—tax collectors, judges, policemen, county or village officials, persons responsible for elections—undermine the prestige and efficiency of government. They can result in the reduction of services or closure of regional or rural offices or implicit acquiescence of "no go" areas in the country where the government's writ no longer counts—"gray areas," as they may be called. Government is ordinarily weakened by this process, but if it strikes back with harsh force, making inroads against terrorism, it may also discredit itself in national eyes. States engaged in 2006 in rough counterinsurgency efforts—and lambasted for it by influential critics and human rights monitors—include Nepal, Israel, Egypt, India, Pakistan, and Turkey.

The "positive" effects of political strategies for the terror groups are many and diverse. Political work lends legitimacy to a group or doctrine suspicious to the public because of reliance on violence. Political strategies are internally important to the group because, after all, the terrorism is in support of some urgent political program. The terrorist group's prestige, size, and effectiveness are often enhanced proportionally to how the government is damaged. Each terrorist action creates a platform from which to appeal to the public about objectives. With time and effort, even an unusual ideology or foreign political conception can gain credibility.[6] In the struggle, with all its sessions of planning, cooperation, and physical confrontations with enemies, new leaders with considered ideas about a revolutionary government may emerge. Thus, the long period of covert and overt revolutionary activity became for such leaders as Yasser Arafat and Daniel Ortega a sort of journeyman's years, when they exercised authority over an ever-growing segment of the nation, gaining experience and credibility. In due time, both led and dominated their respective states.[7] Ortega later dared to risk his Sandinista Party's despotic hold on power by holding elections in 1990. He lost and, in subsequent elections, he also lost. Then in November 2006, the old combatant gained enough political ground to become president.

Some contemporary terror-using groups opt for a gradual or partial, overt role in state political power. To get it they use violence but also respected and pacific forums of debate; they compete in local elections; they are open to participation in coalition governments. The IRA's political wing Sinn Fein and Lebanon's Hezbollah have often won seats in the national parliaments and many more in local or district electoral bodies. There have been few academic studies of the phenomenon of terror groups and political parties,[8] but more are forthcoming now that Hamas shocked the Middle Eastern world with its electoral success of January 2006.

Economic strategy, a third aspect of terrorism, was badly neglected by contemporary political science until 9-11. This disinterest is no reflection of the true damage. Terror's economic effects are varied and sometimes enormous. General social effects of dislocation are dramatically enhanced by such common terrorist tactics as taking over public highways to "tax" commercial users; arson campaigns against large corporations; sabotage of oil pipelines; bombings and extortion that increase insurance prices and operating costs; protracted efforts to disrupt the export of manufactured goods or agricultural crops; bank robberies; and campaigns against tourist facilities that garner much of some nations' foreign incomes. Such efforts are intended to directly harm the property owner and perhaps also to harm the government, which immediately experiences losses in tax revenues, declines in foreign investment, and additional expenses for everything from fire trucks to police.

The Farabundo Marti National Liberation Front in El Salvador and Sendero Luminoso in Peru[9] were examples of groups with overt and devastating economic strategies for waging rural war and terrorism. Today in their footsteps has come the highly successful "Communist Party of Nepal (Maoist)." Not far away are other Maoists—less organized and less ideological—within India, where a movement beginning in the village of Naxalbari[10] in West Bengal has continued, and grown, in the subsequent half-century. September 2004 brought the fusion of two important Indian groups into a new entity, the Communist Party of India (Maoist). These "Naxalites" have a program of organized rural terrorism, and they stepped up their violence in early 2006 with mass hostage taking and a number of throat slittings. In mid-July of that year, they made a deadly assault on a village that had dared to defend itself with citizen militiamen.[11] Their efforts to weaken India while enhancing their own authority in "liberated zones" have killed nearly 1,000 Indians and displaced fifty times as many.[12]

As the Naxalite example suggests, economic strategies yield positive advantages to the terrorists. Groups with strategic reasons to oppose existing international trade patterns can enforce limited self-sufficiency on areas they control. Cutting roads and power lines can do the same and serve also as "propaganda of the deed." Terrorizing merchants and carrying out arson attacks on multinational companies can advance a communist economic program and also support extortion efforts. Bank thefts, as explained by Carlos Marighella, not only harm capitalism's "nerve centers" but garner large funds to pay for anticapitalist attacks. International narcotics exports—whether by North Korea or by revolutionary political groups—undermine the health and productivity of capitalist and democratic countries, where the drugs feed destructive personal habits. Such sales are more lucrative than virtually any other known manner of feeding terrorists' coffers. One could not understand the PLO of the 1980s, or the Kurdistan Worker's Party of the 1990s, without understanding the economic benefits of narcoterrorism.[13] Today, remnants of Taliban (in and near Afghanistan) are among the largest beneficiaries of illicit drug exports; in 2005 alone, two different indictments in a U.S. federal court connected heroin reaching the U.S. market with known Taliban contacts.[14]

Military damage is a fourth way in which terrorists advance their overall object. Depending on the group, the rendering of damage to the state's military forces or infrastructure is usually of secondary or tertiary interest; terrorists prefer undefended, nonmilitary targets. However, as Al Qaeda's fiery attack on the Pentagon and bombings of American military personnel in the Middle East indicate, terrorists may have a marked impact on nations' armies. In peacetime, terrorists' pinprick attacks undermine readiness and spread fear among military ranks. That was the purpose of twenty years of bombings and murders at NATO installations in Western Europe, the targets including barracks, weapons depots, and oil pipelines. Terrorists may thin the ranks of national police forces, which have or can have both peace and wartime roles. That was clearly a strategy the Basque ETA "Etarras" employed against the Spanish Guardia Civil and it explains the scores of attacks Iraqi insurgents make annually on police recruits and army recruit depots.

If events escalate from "low-intensity conflict" into open war, terrorists are in prime position to be proxy forces for an external power or an indigenous political organization. The U.S. Ambassador for Counterterrorism in 2005–2006, Henry Crumpton,[15] is among the British and American leaders to state that Iran is exporting bomb components and bombing techniques into Iraq while enhancing its bilateral ties to Shia militia forces in Iraq. It has long been evident that Iran exerts very direct control over the Lebanese Hezbollah, despite the likelihood that some of those militiamen have their own intentions or are moved by nationalism. Nonetheless, all find themselves advancing Iranian state purposes by indirectly weakening the Lebanese state's armed forces. Sometimes Hezbollah fights those very Lebanese forces in bloody street battles. Sikh militias and terrorists in northwestern India may or may not wish to serve the interests of Pakistan, but they do so by distracting and tying down innumerable Indian national police and military personnel, who are continuously bled with classic "bite and flee"[16] guerrilla tactics. Various militias of today make a continuous low-level battleground of parts of a giant world state, India.[17]

The "positive" effects for the movement using terrorism are many. Military-style operations by terrorists provide battle experience, draw recruits, capture weaponry, develop expertise in logistics, and may draw in foreign support. Depending on dogma and doctrine, today's terrorist leaders may anticipate that terrorism can be combined with clandestine organization and guerrilla combat experience to develop from an underground into a truly national military capability. That is in fact the Maoist model of the development of protracted guerrilla war—from low-level violence and propaganda, to a second phase of mixed or "mobile" warfare featuring formal military units, and ultimately to a third, rather conventional phase of operations by regular armies.[18] These phases conform to a strategic defensive, a strategic stalemate, and a strategic offensive. Mao's model was followed with minor variants by Hanoi in the Vietnam wars and by Abimael Guzman's Sendero Luminoso in Peru. The model is perceptible—but not explicitly followed—by Sri Lanka's Tamil "Tigers." The LTTE advanced through formative stages of violence: They began with propaganda and terrorism, moved into tactically impressive guerrilla attacks, and learned to conduct conventional military operations.[19] Under self-imposed wraps of a "peace offensive," the Tigers remained in the middle stage of strategic stalemate from 2002 through 2005, armed and ready but with most guns silent. By 2006 they were back on limited offensives. Colombo is not strong enough to destroy this highly developed military threat to the state.

Fifth and finally, terrorism is often done for international effect. Consider examples of assassination. Killing a foreign arms broker may be one government's way to deter future arms sales to dissidents or enemies. Once this was a state strategy of France; in the late 1950s, when the FLN was waging war against French control of Algeria, French secret agents appear to have sought out and killed certain of the Europeans supplying arms to the FLN. Israel may sometimes follow such a strategy, and not only in the famous "Wrath of God" operations against Palestinian operatives living openly in Western Europe. Israeli hit men allegedly went to Brussels in March 1990 and killed Gerald Bull, the expert in long-range "super gun" development. Bull was building two fearsome tubes for the Iraqis that could have dropped ordinance onto Israel, as well as Iran. Such state killings might also serve as warnings to foreign governments, a form of political and military deterrence, against countries that would make international military sales to violent substate groups.[20]

Assassination is also a common tool of substate groups. This is an important indicator that terrorism is not always "promiscuous" or "indiscriminate," despite the insistence of some definitions. One of the Muslim fanatics who killed Egypt's President Anwar Sadat in 1981 wrote later that "Terror is a means to confront God's enemies."[21] The same killing was also a strategic blow to the Camp David Peace Accords of 1978 that subdued tensions between Cairo and Jerusalem. Now, self-proclaimed "jihadis" rail against Sadat's successor, Hosni Mubarak. A "moderate" figure to most outsiders, he is resented by some at home for his long grip on national power, and he is deeply hated by extremists claiming faith in Islam, in part owing to his ready use of jails to confine opponents. Mubarak is among the named "apostates" damned and threatened in the opening pages of the Al Qaeda's training manual found in Manchester, England.[22] That manual's emphasis on assassination is elaborate and detailed, as in lessons 10, 14, 15, and 16.[23] The context, set in the manual's initial pages, makes it clear that this tactic is in service of a larger strategy of creating strife and prompting Islamicist revolution.

An assassination is selective, but each such act is designed to do much more than destroy one victim. In the case of the self-declared warriors for Allah, each attack is a testament to the power of religion, and the assassin's personal risk proves his or her faith has triumphed over concern for liberty or life. Each killing raises the flag of action and calls to others to follow and commit their own acts. It adds to the social polarization that occurs with terrorism, compelling citizens to declare themselves one way or the other on the issue of secular governance or life under the *Sharia,* law guided by the Koran. The perpetrator might also expect his acts to draw political support from persons in government or pull in financial support from abroad. He may wish to prove himself so as to rise in the organization. He may wish to pay a debt, for training or schooling or cash payment, to a state, such as Iran or Sudan, for advancing Muslim revolutions. In one of the more revealing passages in audiotapes made after 9-11-2001, Osama Bin Laden proclaims that with these attacks every Muslim must now choose—he must be for the jihad, or against it.[24] Such appeals are personal—for recruitment—and strategic—meant for a whole world.

Having thus introduced the destructive and constructive dimensions of the five most common strategies employed by contemporary terrorism, it is now appropriate to further discuss each and how they work together.

Spreading chaos

The world's terrorist groups can ordinarily be successful in the first of all common objectives: causing chaos. If one excludes the ongoing Iraq war—and of course, some analysts might not—the number of transnational terrorist incidents worldwide is not rising.[25] However, all acts have their individual and collective impacts, and the destructiveness of certain acts is now greater, on average, than was the damage of the typical attack fifteen or twenty years ago. One might say there is a higher "lethality index" but not higher overall numbers, for most countries of the world. The United States suffered virtually no terror attacks in the five years after 9-11-01. Many other countries were as fortunate.

Attacks on aircraft and their passengers are one illustration of the mix of continuity and change that characterizes modern terrorism. Even more than a city bus, an aircraft in flight is the darkly perfect "box" in which to manipulate, terrify, or kill unarmed civilians. No escape seems possible. Any bold action—even one misfired bullet from one air marshal—risks plunging a fragile aircraft into the ground. Radio, cell phones, satellites, personal computers, text messagers, transponders, and on-board recorders guarantee that the sky box theater of terrorism will be heard and felt, "live" or later, by audiences of millions. Temptations being so great, terrorists took to the skies, especially in the latter 1960s. The world became habituated to the hijacking of passenger airliners in the early 1970s and then wondered in the 1980s whether it had seen the passing of this form of terrorism. So makers of chaos turned to deadlier means: blowing up airliners. The secular Palestinian Abu Nidal did this on the ground when circumstances suited, but terrorists are assured of higher fatality rates if the operation is done in flight.

A Canadian airliner disappeared beneath the surface of the Atlantic at night in 1985, taking 328 victims, probably murdered to attract attention to the cause of Sikhs fighting in India. A UTA airliner was destroyed over Chad in September 1989; a French judge indicted four Libyan officials for the act that killed 171, including seven Americans, and Paris demands compensation.[26] Pan Am 103 blew up over Scotland in December 1988, apparently to satisfy Libya, or both Libya and Iran (Tehran had lost a passenger liner that flew too near a U.S. warship in the Persian Gulf). In a stunning pre-9/11 action, suicide killers of the Algerian "Armed Islamic Group" (GIA) loaded an Air France liner with tons of extra aviation fuel and placed twenty sticks of dynamite in the cockpit; the plan was to explode their plane over Paris or crash it into the Eiffel Tower. French commandos interrupted this December 1994 operation before it could flamboyantly murder hundreds inside and outside the jet.[27] More recently, Al Qaeda missile men came very close to shooting down an Israeli contract carrier full of tourists leaving Kenya in November, 2002.

Most of these incidents killed many times more citizens of a given state than it had lost soldiers in fighting in the first Gulf War, even if each act was less disruptive than such a war. The personal and political damage is indeed widespread. Ill effects radiate out like spokes from the hub and include unease even in one's home, fear of travel, disinclination to attend public events, distrust of one's own government because of its inability to protect citizens, and perhaps racialist dread of foreign peoples who support or are alleged to support international terrorists.

Hijackings, complete with lists of political demands read over the media, yield one sort of disorientation and despair. When explosions go entirely unclaimed, this yields another kind of fear. Some cases involve multiple claims, furthering confusion and complicating discussion of retaliation. There are bombings—such as the truck bombing of the AMIA Jewish community center in Argentina in July of 1994—which are not conveniently accompanied by a claim of credit.[28] Instead of indignation that may be directed at a known lethal enemy, the public faces the fear of knowing only that terrorists have struck and may do so again, for reasons unknown. As terror attacks grow more lethal and employ new and hideous means, such as gas, radioactivity, and biological weapons, the general fears they cause may increase. There is both wonder and fear in the fact that, five and six years after anthrax attacks on the U.S. Capitol, authorities cannot say who the perpetrators were.

It is occasionally argued that terrorism does not ultimately succeed. One slender book to appear with notable swiftness after 9-11 claims that terrorism "never" succeeds.[29] These are fatuous assurances. At best, we should say that terrorism *alone* does not gain authority to govern...and that is but a limited truth.[30] Terrorism is rarely employed by itself, without other accompanying strategies for gaining power. Calculating militants usually have additional means. The Bolshevik, Castroite, Sandinista, and Palestinian revolutions are among the many that used terrorism to help to create fundamental change and place in power Vladimir Lenin, Fidel and Raul Castro, Daniel and Humberto Ortega, and Yasser Arafat. The PLO managed its terrorism campaigns brilliantly, running a full political program to influence the thinking world while running ugly operations to shock the world under such cover names as "Black September." When Abu Daoud was arrested on (other) murder charges in Jordan, the Presidium of the Supreme Court of the Soviet Union supported him by formally requesting a "humane act" to free this "prominent leader in the Palestine resistance movement…" Many other states and entities supported Palestinian terrorism as a form of political struggle. Today there is a "statelet" for the Palestinians; even the U.S. government initially helped pay its bills. Abu Daoud, for his part, continues boasting about his past terrorism successes in fresh interviews in Egypt and Syria.[31]

Though terrorism holds out promise as a strategy for taking power, it serves still better for something far easier—destroying the power of others.[32] Terrorism's role in unsuccessful but devastating revolutions and in other political crises has been, and will be, immense. Consider how the life of Paris has been rent. "Carlos the Jackal" killed in Paris a generation ago. A 1986 campaign was conducted by the Lebanese Armed Revolutionary Faction, linked to Syria and the East bloc services.[33] The City of Light was recovering...until a bombing campaign by Algerians of the Armed Islamic Group shattered the peace again during 1995. Algerian immigrants and gunmen in the ranks of the Salafist Group for Preaching and Combat hung like a pall over France in the years just before and after the millennium year of 2000. Mohamed Sifaoui, driven from his journalist's office in Algiers by terrorism, moved to Paris later and found GSPC active there. Infiltrating the group, Mr. Sifaoui garnered stunning video and interview footage of this ally of Al Qaeda and uncovered some of its operations beyond France.[34] Still another round of violence awaited Paris: that of the unemployed, angry, and militant of North Africa, who burned thousands of automobiles and rioted for weeks in the fall of 2005. It remains to be discovered what if any roles the active terror groups had among these thousands of protesters. However, clearly the recent history of Paris shows how fierce, small, and violent groups can bring chaos to civilized communities. There are scores of similar examples from scores of other countries. Contemporary terrorism has a very high capacity for achieving its broadest and most typical first strategic objective, the wrecking of normalcy and political order.

Box 2.1 Osama Bin Laden's media strategies

The Al Qaeda organization's mastery of media is now apparent. Publications emerge in varied form, take diverse approaches to audiences, are usually well composed, and are often timed for particular events in the West, such as election, or anniversaries of Al Qaeda actions. One successful Al Qaeda dimension, As Sahab, has had a U.S. Muslim in the production lead. The terrorists also use their media to transmit secret messages—an art called steganography—as by imbedding a message within a "normal" video.[35]

In 2002, a text purportedly written and released by Bin Laden himself added to the growing literature and found new ways to articulate the terrorist group's ongoing struggle on the world stage. The "Statement from Shaykh Usama Bin Ladin, May God Protect him, and Al-Qa'ida Organization" appeared on an internet site called Al-Qal'ah on October 14, 2002 and was translated and released by the U.S. Foreign Broadcast Information Service. One paragraph of the long statement is of particular interest for its direct appeal to allies, and potential allies, in global media:

"There is the group of the media people and writers who have a prominent impact on and a big role in directing the battle, breaking the enemy's morale, and boosting the [Islamic] nation's morale. The time has come for the media to occupy its rightful position and play its required role in confronting this vicious campaign and the declared Crusade with all its visual, audio, and written organs. The media men—whether they are writers, journalists, analysts, or correspondents—should rise to the level of responsibility and the event and play their required role of enlightening the nation. revealing the truth about the enemy, and exposing his schemes and ploys. They should stand as one rank regardless of their affiliations; the enemy today does not differentiate between one group and another. His aim is to destroy everything that has anything to do with Arabism and Islam."

Discrediting and destroying existing government

A second strategy of most terror groups is related but less broad: it is to discredit, diminish, or destroy a particular government, ruining its legitimacy and authority so as to replace it with a revolutionary government. The anticipated new government may be left, right, religious, or other. This strategy is worked out with diverse kinds of effort. Two of the most common are use of political propaganda and use of political front groups.

Vladimir Lenin believed that operating a newspaper was a multifaceted way of making political inroads. "A newspaper is not only a collective propagandist and a collective agitator, it is also a collective organizer," he noted in *What Is To Be Done*. Today his newspaper, *Iskra* ("Spark"), is forgotten; even its famous successor *Pravda* ("Truth") went broke in 1996, but Lenin's point was sound. The Algerian FLN found that their paper, *El Moujahideed*, with such good writers as Frantz Fanon, could sell even better outside Algeria than inside; it was one of the many ways in which the Front reached the Algerian Diaspora in France, among other audiences. A decade later, in the

United States, the Weather Underground was aware that selling their paper, *Prairie Fire*, on the streets was a way for cadre to prove commitment, make contacts with prospective recruits, and also generate a little money for the Weathermen.

It is for such reasons, and for the content of the news, that dozens of terrorist groups today publish periodicals. For example, the IRA's *An Phoblacht* ("Republican News") is available from 58 Parnell Square in Dublin;[36] it sells throughout Europe, can be purchased in New York, and is available on the Internet. Its stories, in turn, may be rewritten or reprinted by editors of such sympathetic news organs as *The Irish People*, the New York City–based weekly, or more mainstream newspapers.[37]

The American "Unabomber" well understood the modern power of computers, the World Wide Web, satellites, and other forms of very modern communications, but he also kept faith in what newspapers could do. In his famous and famously long Manifesto, which his terrorism compelled two U.S. newspapers to publish, Dr. Theodore Kaczynski openly explained his method of combining violence and the printed word:

> ... freedom of the press is of very little use to the average citizen as an individual.... If we had never done anything violent and had submitted the present writings to a publisher, they probably would not have been accepted. If they had been accepted and published, they probably would not have attracted many readers, because it's more fun to watch the entertainment put out by the media than to read a sober essay. Even if these writings had had many readers, most of these readers would soon have forgotten what they had read as their minds were flooded by the mass of material to which the media expose them. In order to get our message before the public with some chance of making a lasting impression, we've had to kill people.[38]

Where security is tight or where the climate of opinion or laws circumscribe overt activism, terror groups may be restricted to quiet distribution of leaflets and press releases. This has been an activity of many terror groups with supporters inside the United States, including the Lebanese Hezbollah.[39] In Palestine, printed propaganda handouts helped the *intifada* from its beginning. As one example, in a March 1994 incident, Fatah Hawks loyal to Yasser Arafat were distributing propaganda by car in a Gaza refugee camp when they became embroiled in a firefight with undercover Israeli troops that left six Hawks dead.[40] Others distributing leaflets in the region include Kach and Kahane Lives, the right-wing Jewish organizations founded, respectively, by an American rabbi and by his son. Kach press releases that threatened Arabs with expulsion and promoted violence had appeared in the months prior to the 1994 Hebron mosque rampage by Kach activist Baruch Goldstein, who murdered thirty-nine worshippers in a few moments with a Galil automatic rifle.[41] At one time, the elder Kahane had run for parliament, in addition to his other political activities; later, stained by terrorism, both Kahane groups were banned in Israel and remain banned. Meir Kahane and his son Binyamin have been murdered in separate instances of 1990 and 2000.[42]

Like the newspaper and the leaflet, radio is a traditional means of propaganda that terrorists still employ. Frantz Fanon was exhilarated by radio's power and wrote an essay about the French and FLN struggle for control of the airwaves. Algerian revolutionaries had broadcasters in Tunis, Cairo, and other cities, and even though they might be jammed, reporting reaching the Berber and Arab peoples within Algeria was electric in its effects. The communist Czech government allowed Red Brigadists who had slipped behind the Iron Curtain to make propaganda broadcasts back into Italy. Rome mounted no violent response and rarely even complained in public. It is thus no surprise that a typical group of the 1980s and 1990s—the Kurdistan Workers Party, or PKK—would seek and acquire broadcasting privileges from several locales, especially Damascus; such help is an important aspect of state sponsorship of transnational terrorism. Hezbollah for its part manages radio "Voice of the Oppressed," which beams out of the Bekaa Valley.[43]

Video arts, thought to be the most powerful of media, are increasingly important to terrorists as to others in the world. Lebanon's Hezbollah is an innovator in managing its own TV station, Al Manar. This has prospered, succeeded, and grown, and the company has added other forms of media. Al Manar is a potent entity. Sometimes it enjoys itself with such tricks as continuously rerunning loops of tape showing a guerrilla success in ambushing Israeli Defense Force troops. Based in Beirut, the station employs Saudi-based "Arabsat" space media. And through late 2004 it was also beaming via French-based "Eutelstat;" France then banned that avenue to Al Manar. 2005 found Hezbollah lobbying Paris for lifting the ban.[44] The United States also sought to limit Hezbollah's impact by placing its station on its Terrorist Exclusion List, which does affect cable carriers and the activities of Al Manar personnel. However, Hezbollah TV has been reaching as many as 10,000,000 viewers worldwide. [45]

Al Qaeda is successful in its skilled and steady use of independent outlets, stations run by friendly governments, and the voracious demand of the open market for its carefully prepared videos of ten to forty-five minutes' length. These have displayed the faces and talents of, among others, Saudi exile Osama Bin Laden, Egyptian surgeon Ayman Al Zawahiri, and skilled colleagues in their As-Sahab production cell—especially "Azzam the American," Adam Gadahn, a former Californian and now the first U.S. citizen in half a century to be charged with treason.[46] The team creates and places Al Qaeda videos with such TV outlets as Al Jazeera, based in Qatar, but with reporters and staff at work worldwide. Al Qaeda keeps open its options and has enjoyed good fortune on the World Wide Web. Two propaganda videos—each portraying one of the top leaders—appeared on the same day in April 2006 on the Web; from there, TV stations snatched them up and screened them for viewers. In September 2006, after a White House suggestion that Bin Laden was less visible than before, As Sahab put a new, long video into circulation within a few days. Its footage allegedly included the leader with several of the 9-11 hijackers, a media first.

Other Muslim militants are eager to be as Web-savvy as Al Qaeda; this is the most glamorous new form of terrorist propaganda. Recent studies locate as many as 5,000 terrorist sites, though many of these are temporary, and they may close down or relocate when pressed by scrutiny of researchers and state agents in intelligence and law enforcement. A striking illustration of the success in Web activity is Abu Musab Zarqawi. Around 1995, he was languishing in a Jordanian jail; by 2005, the headlines about him included: "Zarqawi Goes From 'Zero to 60' on Use of Web." One key to his success is the talent of Younis Tsouli, who used the Web name "Irhabi 007," meaning Terrorist 007; with this Londoner's technical help and the labors of others, Zarqawi's repute rose until it elicited such hosannas as this by Evan Kohlmann of GlobalTerrorAlert.com: "I would call him [Zarqawi] the Alexander Graham Bell of terrorist propaganda."[47] The militant died in a Coalition surgical air strike during 2006. He had become one of those leading, self-proclaimed "jihadis" who felt that while they lost a primary base area—Afghanistan—they could relocate to cyberspace and to Iraq, entrenching well in both venues.[48] Today the International Crisis Group and other authorities studying Iraq find the quality and number of insurgent and terrorist videos to be rising steadily.

A second form of political action, more complex than propaganda, is the use of front groups. This was famously successful for the "National Liberation Front" set up by the Vietnamese communists. Less successful practitioners have included the Manuel Rodriguez Patriotic Front (MRPF), founded as an arm of Chile's communist party but purporting to be an array of democratic forces, patriotic and nationalistic. The Front lingered on into the latter 1990s, but its strategy of combining terrorism and political efforts was weakened badly by the Party's internal divisions, by Chile's democratic and economic successes, and by Chilean counterterrorist work.[49] In Corsica, meanwhile, it appears that A Cuncolta Nazionalista has been a political veil over the terror bombings by FLNC, the Corsican National Liberation Front.

Sinn Fein ("Ourselves Alone") has fronted, and presumably still fronts for, Irish Republican Army "Provisionals." The connections between them were underscored by memoirs of defector Sean O'Callaghan, who served in Sinn Fein and IRA hierarchies simultaneously. The "republicans" have a powerful strategy of combining bullets and ballots. Sinn Fein has the ability to effectively communicate the IRA's views and negotiating positions while softening its hard edges. Before 9-11, the front could easily and publicly solicit financial aid in Ireland and America. At home it wielded limited powers of local government, and any attempt to suppress Sinn Fein's voice could be met with greater violence from the IRA.[50]

A Spanish Basque political party, Herri Batasuna (HB), devoted decades to being political cover for ETA. It was a persistent, sometimes influential, helpmate. Among its more frustrating years was 1992, when important arrests badly injured the ETA organization on both sides of the border with France.[51] Though the armed underground most needed support, their political front was itself in disarray. HB chief Inaki Ensaolo had been questioning the "effectiveness of the armed struggle in light of the steady weakening of ETA's military potential and lack of social support." Polls of Basques increasingly showed that they thought ETA terrorism was failing. A majority of Basque political parties signed an extraordinary document that said as much: The Anjuria Enea Pact condemned the strategy of terrorism as a means of achieving Basque autonomy, but *Herri Batasuna* could not condemn its own. HB's troubles had grown by 1997, and subsequent mass public demonstrations by voters opposed ETA violence. The front group collapsed, reappearing later as "Batasuna." However, Madrid's strategy of granting the Basques semi-autonomy worked better than ETA's strategy of terrorism and front group work. Suddenly, in early 2006, ETA announced a cease-fire.[52]

Calls for peace can well signify dispiritedness and perhaps defeat, as in the case of the Basque "Etarras," but it can also be a prudent temporizing maneuver, another form of "fight and talk." The astute use of the open palm, extended to shake hands, can be coordinated with the fighting arm—whose strength encourages an opponent to take the negotiation offer. We are familiar with the lengthening pause for peace that has quieted

---

Box 2.2 Batasuna: Fronting for ETA

Sophisticated violent groups often create, or work with, a political organization that renders aid and "cover." Herri Batasuna was for years such a helpmate to the Basque terrorists of ETA, Euzkadi to Askatasuna, Basque Fatherland and Liberty. The linkage was, however, apparent to the Spanish courts, so Herri Batasuna was proscribed. Re-emerging as "Batasuna"—an unimaginative new name—it was again banned by Spain's Supreme Court in 2002. Today, both the ETA killers and the Batasuna politicos are in trouble, even existential trouble.

Spain granted Basque and other regions limited autonomy from Madrid. From the early 1990s, citizens of the Basque lands have shown less and less fervor for the shootings, robberies, extortion letters, and car bombs with which ETA presses its demands for a fully separate homeland.

By 2004, those favoring the violent road to power were distinctly unpopular. Late that year, for example, Batasuna spokesman Arnaldo Otegi said that before peace could commence, there must be a public referendum on the future of the Basque lands. Mainstream political figures rejected such a sequence, wanted the immediate end of violence, and so responded critically. A student in Madrid shared his similar displeasure with Batasuna leaders with a foreign reporter: "… [O]ut of eight of us [discussing this] not one person thought they would explicitly condemn violence. How can they? Their party has always depended on terrorists."

The furthest Mr. Otegi would go toward nonviolence was to promise that Batasuna would "take the conflict away from the streets to a negotiation and dialogue table." Gerry Adams may be able to manage this in Northern Ireland; Batasuna's leaders seem unable, even though Sinn Fein has reportedly been advising the Basque front on negotiation strategies.

If Basque militant leaders cannot navigate the difficult waters of overt advocacy of violence in a successful democratic society, their followers are also lagging visibly further and further behind. Popular support for ETA tactics continues to wane. And there is a third problem: expert Spanish law enforcement. During 2004, at least a hundred ETA suspects were arrested in Spain and France, and 2006 brought many more arrests, as of cell members specializing in financing the revolution. Today, prospects are no better than a few years ago when the Popular Party's Secretary General chose these public words about his rivals: ETA is weaker "than at any point ever in its history. And since Batasuna and ETA are synonymous, Batasuna too is in terrible shape."[54]

Ulster. There are other variants. Among the more novel is the round of negotiations witnessed several years ago between the Colombian government and the communist Revolutionary Armed Front of Colombia, FARC. Over several weeks, negotiators for the two sides traveled through Western Europe, holding each session in a new town and hoping that the publicity, profusion of good will, and abundance of external influences would prod these antagonists into solving their mutual Colombian problems. This was a boon for the terrorist side, to be treated as nearly equal to the men and women serving a

Colombian government duly elected by millions of citizens. Such public performances can only have two results: Either the terrorists extract certain concessions or they go back into the field with renewed legitimacy and a crown of reasonableness. As legitimacy is a central goal in all terrorist political effort, neither of these results can be favorable.

In guerrilla and terrorist politics, fronts are, and will remain, common. Analysts may expect to find them in the Iraqi insurgency, for example.[53]

Economic damage

Economic and property damage is a third major strategy of terrorism. Though there have been very few formal studies of this dimension of terrorism, its significance is evident. Bombs and fires may, at once, attract popular attention, yield cover stories in the press, render property damage, kill the innocent, deprive society and the economy of the victims' labor and intellectual capital, place a government on the defensive psychologically or politically, and force expenditures that governments, corporations, and insurance companies would not ever wish. All this—and not just politics or religion—leads terrorists to stage major attacks. An example is the July 2006 near-simultaneous bombings of multiple trains in Mumbai, west-central India. The detonations killed or wounded nearly 1,000 people but was as well taken to be an economic strike by Muslims against a region predominantly Hindu and notably wealthy.

Al Qaeda is an economic war exemplar. Property destruction is a primary element of the grand strategy of this global terrorist organization. The American targets of the coordinated attacks of 9-11-2001 were more than economic, as much as they were political and military. The group has since turned terrorism against America's political partners, such as Australia and the United Kingdom, in accordance with Osama Bin Laden's pledge in videotape of October 2004.[55] However, the United Kingdom is also among the United States's most important business partners. Bin Laden, the wealthy former Saudi businessman, may take his richest satisfaction in making economic war. His February, 1998 *fatwa* included the unfounded directive to Muslims to "comply with God's order to kill the Americans and plunder their money wherever and whenever they find it."[56] Bin Laden's October, 2002 letter "To the Americans" maintained the theme, twice charging that Arab governments "steal" the wealth of the *umma* (Muslim community) and sell it to Americans "at paltry prices…This theft is indeed the biggest theft ever witnessed by mankind in the history of the world." And, "If people steal our wealth, then we have the right to destroy their economy."[57] Two years on, in October, 2004, the Saudi exile thrilled himself with the hope that 9-11 and its aftermath lost for the United States, "according to the lowest estimate—more than 500 billion dollars." He portrays ongoing fighting in Afghanistan and Iraq as part of the "bleed until bankruptcy plan" he has for the world "Mujihideen."[58]

Communists, whose ideology wraps totalitarian bindings around economics, politics, and social movement, have always understood how a noncommunist political order can be shaken—even shaken into ruins and dust—by repeated, prolonged attacks on the economy. An example of such a protracted campaign—"sabotage of the dictatorship's war economy"—came in the 1980s in El Salvador from the alliance of five guerrilla parties in the FMLN. Over many years, the insurgents employed most imaginable antieconomy tactics, from machine gunning crop-dusting planes to dynamiting bridges to burning cash crops to systematically destroying nearly all the country's locomotives to cutting roads and thus isolating rich crop-exporting regions. In the words of a reporter, the FMLN rendered "massive physical damage and reduced export earnings (and) turned El Salvador into an economic basket case dependent on the American dole." However, continued U.S. aid, intense effort by millions of noncommunist Salvadorans, and indigenous leaders helped the country and the state to survive.[59]

One may now study communist economic terrorism to the south of El Salvador, in Colombia. Kidnapping for political and financial purposes is almost a national industry, given the persistent efforts of the two main communist groups, FARC and the ELN. There are also regular bank heists—"expropriations" in the parlance of the perpetrators, who deem capitalism illegitimate and think it their right or duty to "steal from the thieves." There are regular interruptions of highway traffic; commercial truck drivers lose cargoes or vehicles; private automobiles are emptied of passengers and all are robbed in actions called "revolutionary taxation." The overall national effect, apart from its furtherance of a general sense of insecurity and dislocation, is to reduce commercial intercourse, escalate law enforcement costs, and bring down tax receipts by governments. Such industries as mines and private interests as small as cattle ranches or agricultural centers are bilked on a recognized schedule by agents of guerrilla organizations; the victims face arson or murder if the fruit of their labor is not shared on demand. The peculiar local phrase for the extortion of cattle ranchers is "vaccination"—a wry suggestion that regular payments are the rancher's inoculation against death.

So large are the Colombian guerrillas' economic operations that they have turned from keepers of ledgers to computer operators to track their illicit wealth. The two largest "guerrilla" entities rank economically among the top 50 Colombian corporations. Today FARC alone garners $600 million a year just from narcotics. All the terrorists' takings are a direct loss to the national economy. To them are added the costs of extra security, as well as millions in extorted payments to the well-organized revolutionaries. Colombia's national stresses include narcotics, political corruption, violent attacks on the judiciary, and the counterinsurgency war; all these have connections to the terrorism problem; terrorism and its economic strategies and effects are thus as insidious as any other Colombian problem.[60]

The economic damage that terrorists do can be analyzed in ways that leave aside the ideology of the threatening groups. Staggering sums must be expended each year on private security for persons, corporations, and events. Consider the variety of countries bidding to host Olympic Games. In 1984, in Los Angeles, security cost $100 million—seemingly a fantastic amount. However, several plots were evaded, and the games proceeded flawlessly. In 1988, Seoul met the expensive and dangerous challenge of sponsoring the Summer Olympics in a country often showing political stress fractures and under threat by a hostile and jealous northern neighbor. After the 1987 downing of the Korean Air Lines flight, there were no further terrorist acts. The 1992 Olympics took place in Spain surrounded by worries that included explicit ETA threats. Madrid and Barcelona oversaw security efforts that began years in advance, included many foreign specialists, and easily broke all cost records at some $350 million. Hoping to match the peacefulness of all these host cities, Atlanta and the United States spent almost as much in 1996. Government marshaled up 16,000 police, supplemented by a large FBI force and more than 1,000 military personnel. New technologies for crowd observation and control were deployed. Yet a right-wing zealot, Eric Rudolph, marred the peace by a pipe bomb attack in Olympic Park. By 2000, and 2004, the Summer Games host cities of Sydney and Athens, respectively, needed no coaching. Both planned for security years in advance, made elaborate use of foreign help from such states as Israel and the United States deemed good at security, and poured money freely into personnel and infrastructure that would protect their games. Both summer events passed smoothly. The games of 2000 and 2004 were triumphs for those involved; both were appalling in their economic waste. Australia spent hundreds of millions it would have preferred to devote to social, defense, and other matters. Greece exceeded $1 billion in spending on security for the Games.[61] The Chinese are closely studying these challenges already.

Military damage

Contemporary terrorists' strategies *may* include a military one; that is our fourth concern in this chapter. Some groups deliberately avoid this path. The Armenian Secret Army for the Liberation of Armenia (ASALA) virtually never attacked military targets in the United States or Europe or Lebanon, despite its many violent operations in those places in the 1980s. Greece's communists of Revolutionary Organization 17 November managed a few peacetime assassinations of civilian defense officials or attaches. There are also right-wing terrorist groups, such as the British Loyalist types in Northern Ireland, who rarely tangle with security forces or conduct serious military operations, perhaps for the reason that they may see themselves as odd allies of the security forces as against Irish revolutionaries.[62]

A second category of terror organizations may be said to have "mixed" objectives: They target both civilian and military personnel and installations. This they justify by their "total war" mentality and its conviction that "there are no innocents"—a nihilistic assertion traceable in terrorism back to nineteenth-century anarchists. Carrying out *some* military attacks also assures them of martial credibility, and it fosters hopes of growth out of relative impotence as a minority. ELN—the National Liberation Army—in Colombia exemplifies such a group. Its several thousand members' activities can readily be described as insurgency, or terrorism, as they are in fact both. They would seek state power if they had the operational reach and the depth in personnel. Other examples of terror groups whose targeting reveals "mixed objectives" include Al Qaeda and Zarqawi's Al Qaeda chapter in Iraq. Terrorism is about power, and attacks on military targets are an unequivocal expression of the drive for power.

Third, there are terror organizations that have or seek to have broad popular strengths as a full-blooded insurgency. They explicitly aim, as Mao's Chinese did, to grow into a conventional power and ultimately take control of the state so as to rule. Maoists saw that conception work in China in the two decades that began in 1930; they are hoping it is working today in the full-fledged insurgency that Nepalese communists began in 1996, which has killed hundreds of security forces and hundreds of Nepalese civilians. More traditional Marxist-Leninists, such as the LTTE "Tigers," have similar plans. Already in command of capacious political and military forces, LTTE is strongly contesting

Colombo's authority in both realms. The analyst should not assume that a group using terror aims to grow but, in fact, most such groups do so plan. The most disturbing thing about Abimael Guzman's Sendero Luminoso was its broad power in 1985 or 1990; almost as disturbing was the Chairman's five-phase strategic plan,[63] which enjoyed fabulous successes right up until his arrest in late 1992.

"Terrorism" and "guerrilla war" *may* merge in variant forms, at times, in practice, even if the former attacks are deliberately done to innocents and the latter are against military units or targets (i.e., "unconventional warfare"). Terrorist practitioners draw heavily on the ideas and literature of practiced guerrilla commanders. Mao Tse Tung once wrote that guerrillas "may be compared to innumerable gnats, which, by biting a giant both in front and in rear, ultimately exhaust him."[64] "Bite and flee" was a favored Italian Red Brigades slogan of the 1970s. One student of terrorism of that era added his own variant, naming his book *The War of the Flea*. Tactically, both terrorist and guerrilla tend to favor the pin-prick attack, always with surprise, and normally with escape plans. However, an odd wrinkle in modern practice, the suicide bombing, has reduced by far the general need of the latter skill, at least among "religious" terrorists. Their "bite and flee" ways spare them from fully meeting their better-armed state adversaries. They work to refine the strategy of exhaustion, by which stealth, intelligence, and swiftness make them ineradicable and a continuous drain on the strengths of the government.

Terrorists today have evolved many ways of attacking the military strengths of the state without daring to muster all their personnel on any one battlefield. They may compromise the intelligence services, both to spare themselves difficulties or to plan assassinations; this was an innovation of the old IRA's gifted Michael Collins (d. 1923). They can assassinate defense officials and senior military officers, expecting to disturb the military structure or kill individual linchpins of it; this occurs in Iraq, as in small arms murder of a respected Sixth Iraqi Army Division commander, Mubdar Haatim Hazya al Dulaimi, on March 6, 2006 in Baghdad.[65] Terrorists may attack infrastructure, such as exposed weapons systems, or bases, or defense industry labs. Limiting the operational mobility of armed forces is possible for insurgents with the manpower to lay bombs in roads, snipe at convoys, or lay in wait for riverine patrols. Even years after 9-11-01 and despite prodigious Pakistani efforts against al Qaeda, there remain "no go" areas in that country's western border areas near Afghanistan; in such places, the Pakistani Army can hardly operate, let alone capture such terrorists as Osama Bin Laden.

Destruction of small parts of a state's armed forces is another clear goal of the military uses of terror. Consider how Sri Lankan Tamil Tigers have killed Navy personnel with their adept operations on the water and below it. Yet other "military" strikes by terrorists aim to drive a wedge between one country and its ally. Muslim radicals have done this by threatening Spain and blowing up trains entering Madrid; this had the obvious and embarrassing effect of forcing that Iberian power to evacuate from Iraq.[66] It is a common aim, but one often too ambitious, to force the ultimate evacuation of the occupier or otherwise defeat the state's force. This has been an objective of terrorism against U.S. forces in Vietnam, the Philippines, and Somalia. Al Qaeda rhetoric regularly trumpets the first and last cases as proof of American weakness. Iraq today is witness to all these military strategies by terrorist groups. The insurgency there is inchoate in many respects, yet it is clear that the diverse groups do have in mind some common operational objectives. Indeed, one think tank finds it disturbing to see how parallel the opposition efforts have become recently.[67]

To enhance their own legitimacy and to magnify the effect of armed attacks by suggesting that more of the same is to be expected, terror groups clothe themselves in martial language and titles. Thus have tiny groups of past years made the press as the Sikh "Dashmesh Regiment" and the Californian "Symbionese Liberation Army"—only to soon disappear in a way in which no "army" could. The Japanese Red Army was a stronger and persistent threat, but even the indulgences of North Korea have not kept it vital. With the arrest of leader Fusako Shigenobu in November, 2000 and a disbandment pledge of April the next year, the JRA can probably be considered finished.

"Peacetime" bombings at NATO bases, USO clubs, and barracks wounded scores of American service personnel, and occasionally killed, in the 1970s. In June 1996, a terrorist truck bombing—of the Khobar Towers residence at an Air Force base in Saudi Arabia—killed nineteen and wounded some 500. A federal court ruled in December, 2006 that the peacetime deployment, at the local government's wish, was not one to be confused with war and the attack was therefore to be considered an act of terror.[68]

Another democracy to absorb high casualties from terrorism amid its security forces is Spain. ETA Basques have a proclivity for hitting the national police force, the Guardia Civil.[69] And in El Salvador during the many years of political violence there, leftist guerrillas killed army and police personnel as freely as they attacked civilians; in only six months of 1981, 2,000 security forces died in violent encounters,[70] a traumatic experience for any nation and a pervasive tragedy for a country as small as El Salvador. The bomb-targeting of Iraqi candidates for police services since 2003 has followed the same logic, to fearsome degrees.

Armed conflicts between groups using terrorism and guerrilla attacks on a nation's police and military forces serve the useful purpose of dispersing and tying down the state's armed personnel. Traditional guerrilla strategy is to "appear everywhere and be nowhere," giving the smaller armed force moments of numerical advantage. In both the guerrilla war and terrorist environments, the effect of this strategy on the state is to require it to deploy forces widely and visibly to reassure the populace and to keep security forces in a high state of readiness, which is exhausting. The overall effect may be studied in Germany in the late 1970s and Northern Ireland during much of the late twentieth century. Not only do the deployments tire the state; the overall effect is to make a liberal democracy appear to be its precise opposite: an armed camp. As theorist and communist Carlos Marighella well knew, terror group propagandists then use that public sense to effect. German radicals of the 1970s and 1980s occasionally exulted in the "police state" effect, claiming they successfully "exposed the latent fascism" of the republic. In such ways does the terrorists' fourth strategy support the second: A sometime military approach helps the substate violent group to discredit a particular government.

The current Iraq war shows how defense budgets can be drained by requirements for continuous surveillance, patrolling, and training for counterterrorism action. Government spends less on desirable social programs, costing it political appeal. Foreign borders may be less well protected. Ultimately, a national armed force intended to resist foreign neighbors may be entirely distorted in its purpose and preparation, twisting inward on the nation as an agent of repression. Every battalion that Pakistan deploys against dissidents today is distracted from service on the Indian border or from training for conventional conflict. In Colombia, by the mid-1990s, internal security had so deteriorated because of FARC and ELN insurgents that British Petroleum Exploration contracted with the Colombian Ministry of Defense to underwrite an army battalion of 650 men to ensure its oil operations minimal protection.[71] FARC and ELN make enough attacks on the regular Colombian armed forces to require a national effort by the Army to keep control.

An altogether different effect of military damage by terrorists is to weaken a state to prepare it for assault by an outside power. This might occur by chance; as internal violence goes on, an external power moves to take advantage. Or it can be part of a foreign design, a "softening attack" instigated from abroad. The prospect that indigenous Euroterrorists might indeed act in loose conjunction with the Warsaw Pact must have been pondered by NATO defense planners in the mid-1980s. Fuel pipelines were attacked in Belgium and Germany, military bases and trains were bombed; and there were incidents of known and suspected Warsaw Pact reconnaissance of critical bridges, theater nuclear missiles, and the like. In 1986, German and Italian communist terrorists opened new and lethal campaigns against the America-sponsored Strategic Defense Initiative. Several European laboratories, researchers, and officials associated with SDI were bombed, shot up, or burned out. Any doubts about the terrorists' strategic purposes were voided by leaflets they published to mark the murders. Any doubts about Soviet state views of these events should be weighed alongside the ongoing Soviet propaganda offensive against SDI at that time.[72]

Less successfully, Iraq made efforts during the First Gulf War to concert terrorism against the countries that sent armies to defend Kuwait and Saudi Arabia. Saddam Hussein repeatedly called for worldwide attacks by terrorists, expecting to divide the coalition, weaken the will of its belligerents, and inhibit military deployments. And some terrorists friendly to Iraq responded—or acted on their own. There were some 300 international terrorist attacks in the first two months of 1991 (as many as occurred in all of 1996). An unapologetic Iraqi ally, Yasser Arafat, directed or permitted the occurrence of Palestinian attacks on two U.S. soldiers in Jidda, Saudi Arabia, according to one report.[73] In Yemen and in Germany, there was automatic weapons fire at the U.S. embassies; in the latter case, the Red Army Faction took credit. In Turkey, a vital staging area of logistics heads and air bases and a full partner in NATO, Dev Sol and other terrorists hit Western targets. A U.S. customs agent was killed at Incirlik air base, and there were bombings of an American consulate and the Turkish-American Association in Adana. In Athens, the 17 November Organization carried out seven bombings in just four days in January, 1991; they were "acting in solidarity with the people of Iraq."[74] In Manila, an Iraqi diplomat's sons were found to possess bomb-related chemicals in their home and were detained. Another diplomat was killed while trying to place a bomb at the U.S. Cultural Center in Manila. And there was at least one plan for killing the U.S. Commander-in-Chief, George Bush—by a pro-Iraqi individual in the United States. That he was arrested before he could carry out the attack[75] was symbolic, for the net effects of all the terrorists' worldwide efforts were dramatically limited. Counterterrorism and cooperation between governments of unparalleled intensity thwarted Hussein's terrorism strategy.

Internationalization of the cause

The next common strategy of contemporary terrorism, the fifth to be detailed here, is international action and the internationalization of the cause. To commit terror acts abroad may simply be more convenient than doing so at home amid police opposition and probing intelligence personnel. International terrorism is virtually guaranteed publicity—a prime political objective. However inhumane their results, actions in another country may inspire groups there or inspire other foreigners to cooperate or to carry out further militant acts of their own. Some see this pattern in militant Muslim attacks today. The history of leftist Euroterrorism of the 1970s is one of mutual inspiration and internationalist ends. One of the patterns of the same continent in the following two decades is international activity by neo-fascists—not attacks in foreign countries but the seeking of transnational support: ideological, logistical, and financial.

By definition, most contemporary religious terror groups are "universalistic" in their appeal; they think internationally by nature. To religious extremists it is somewhat unnatural to draw a boundary between two states (e.g., Libya and Egypt) or to worry about preserving such regimes when neither is "legitimate," let alone holy and inspiring to Muslims. Mohammed's armies and preachers once conquered all of northern Africa and crossed the Straits of Gibraltar to Spain and France. The contemporary descendants of these imperialists want to make another crossing in our era.[76] History is not the only angle of inspiration for some self-described "Jihadis." "The Project," a widely circulated document, is among the more current indicators of hope for creating a new caliphate.[77] So too are certain speeches by Osama Bin Laden and Ayman Al Zawahiri.

However, hot adherents of Islam are also interested in probing into Asia's Muslim communities that were no part, or barely part, of the last Baghdad-based caliphate. Indonesia is an important locale of power already; witness the strength of Jemaah Islamiya, the bombers of Christian churches there in 2000, of Bali tourist targets in 2002, and of a Marriott hotel and the Australian Embassy in Jakarta in 2003 and 2004, respectively. Apostles of terrorism in Indonesia also gaze abroad toward allies or potential adherents in the southern Philippines and Thailand, where southern separatism percolates year after year and costs thousands of casualties.[78] Iran's state agents and semi-independent foundations have probed for political and spiritual footholds in the southern states of the former Soviet Union. Nor can the United States be ignored as a recruiting ground, even if no nation was more foreign to the caliphates. America is home to merely 6 million Muslims, most of whom disdain terrorism, but no country so large and influential can be ignored, and so innumerable small institutions have been founded in the States to spread Islam. These include the black American Muslim group al Fuqra, responsible for crimes that include violent acts in the United States yet loyal to a cleric in Pakistan. No nation so wealthy as the United States can be ignored by fundraisers, which is why Illinois and Texas and Florida and Virginia and North Carolina have discovered offices or individuals raising dollars—from tens of thousands to a million or more in some cases—for such foreign militants as Al Qaeda, Hezbollah, Hamas, or the Palestine Islamic Jihad. An astounding example, up through 2002, was the SAAR Foundation. With Saudi money, several key Iraqi operatives, and a laughably little office in Herndon, Virginia, SAAR handled millions of dollars worth of funds transactions for partisan political and hostile groups, including Al Qaeda.[79]

Before 9-11, our first edition detailed some of the way in which Northwestern Europe had become an operations base and outlet for the new Muslim radicalism mixing politics and religion and violence. Rich in media centers, substantial and diverse in its populations, and influential in such world forums as the United Nations, the northwestern European states are also home to residents of Muslim faith and to nonresidents and illegal aliens of both pacific and malevolent intent. Algerians, Egyptians, Kurds, and others propagate the Muslim faith among their ethnic and religious confreres—in Spain, Germany, and Belgium, all of which had cells operationally related to the 9-11 hijackers. Sweden and Finland are less-than-willing havens for undergrounders. For example, Stockholm and London have been outlet cities for *An Ansar*, the pro-Armed Islamic Group (GIA) paper that in 1995 was opposing French governmental support for the secular regime in Algeria and describing this French involvement as "suicidal." One *An Ansar* graphic showed the Eiffel Tower in Paris exploding, while GIA was issuing a leaflet threatening France with "military strikes in the very heart of its great cities."[80] Explosions of that time aboard French commuter trains and targets in Paris underscored the danger in these published threats, as did vivid memories of the GIA-sponsored effort only months before to blow up a passenger airliner over Paris or fly it into the Eiffel Tower.[81]

France is roiled today not only by Muslim activism. With its proud traditions of offering a home to many kinds of émigrés, France is also dealing with an embarrassing presence of violent Iranian exiles who oppose the mullahs' regime in Tehran. MEQ, or People's Mujahedin-e Khalq, is a secular, Marxist nationalist force with a long record of terrorism and a headquarters in France at varying times, including today. Maryam Rajavi is perfectly placed there, in a valley north of Paris, to conduct interviews, plan her state visits to the United Kingdom and the Continent, and carry out worldwide propaganda. This access is vital; her group boasts several thousand guerrillas and armed militants, trained and blooded but geographically remote—mostly confined within the new Iraq. MEQ publicity, however, cannot be confined. A reader of English-language or U.S.-based newspapers during 2005 and 2006 could be surprised by the expense and numbers of oversized advertisements MEK placed to "Support Freedom in Iran," or "Condemn Tehran's Meddling in Iraqi Elections." In an example of November 2005, the group published a broadsheet—"35,000 Iranians Rally in Brussels"—for causes including "Removal of Terror Tag" from their People's Mujahedin Organization. That demonstration was outside European Union headquarters, and MEQ claimed that 260 European lawmakers were in support. Some Europeans—and certainly the U.S. State Department—officially list this group as terrorist in character. Once generously endowed by Iraq, it subsists now on the Iranian Diaspora and various front companies.[82] Federal judges in California crushed an MEQ effort at raising money there in late 2004.[83] However, the Rajavi group has been able to use addresses or offices in London, Brussels, and other European cities.[84]

Neo-fascists' internationalism is limited by its racial and ideological nature, but even proponents of a world view dominated by spiritual and political attachments to "the homeland" can see advantages to internationalist action. German and Austrian neo-fascist leaders sometimes travel to Latin America to raise funds or visit living relics of the World War II years. The activists also travel within Europe, enhancing their contacts in the white-power scene and thus burnishing their image among comrades and followers

Box 2.3 Imad Mugniyah, a much-wanted man

The man presumed to be the head of intelligence for Hezbollah is one of the world's half-dozen most influential terrorists. The following 15 quotations are gleaned from a few specialized publications that have recognized the significance of Haji Imad Fayez Mugniyah. Some of their statements of fact are not verifiable by the present author.

> Born in the Lebanese village of Tir Dibba on July 12, 1962, Mugniyah was the eldest of four children .... He joined Force 17, Yasser Arafat's personal security guard in Beirut .... [He] spent his days and nights running with armed colleagues 'sniping at Christians' [and] perfected one of his signature attacks: truck bombs boosted by bottles of butane gas ....
>
> Robert Baer, *See No Evil*, 2002; Kenneth R. Timmerman, *Countdown to Crisis*, 2005

> When Arafat left Beirut in 1982, Mugniyah and his Force 17 comrades fell under the command of the Iranian Revolutionary Guards ... About September 26, 1983, Iran's embassy in Syria received an order from Tehran to take a 'spectacular action' against the U.S. Marines who were in Beirut. Mugniyah was put in charge ...
>
> Timmerman, op. cit.

> Imad Mugniyah was a central figure in the taking of Western hostages in Beirut in the mid-1980s. Most were claimed by Hezbollah under the code name of Islamic Jihad. The reason for seizing the hostages was not just hatred of the United States; they had specific demands as well: ... release of the 17 prisoners convicted of bombing the American and French embassies in Kuwait. One of those prisoners was a Lebanese by the name of Mustafa Badreddin, the brother-in-law and cousin of Imad Mugniyah, a militia leader with a growing reputation ... Failure to bring his brother-in-law home would involve a loss of face among Beirut's competing gangs. Secondly, Mugniyah's wife had made it a point of honor ... thirdly ... Badreddin and Mugniyah were former partners who had worked together on a number of operations.
>
> Gavin Hewitt, *Terry Waite and Ollie North*, 1991

> In the June 1985 hijacking of TWA 847—and thus the death of U.S. diver Robert Stethem—Mugniyah appears to have been in command. He may even have been among those of the second party who boarded the hijacked plane as it sat in Beirut. Investigators reportedly identified a set of his fingerprints in one of the lavatories of the aircraft.
>
> Timmerman, op. cit.

On an occasion after the TWA hijacking, according to a press report, intelligence discovered Imad Mugniyah on the southern coast of France. Marine Oliver North of the National Security Council wanted him seized. The White House approached the French government instead—but to no avail. After top-level White House debate, it was decided that a unilateral "snatch" would be too damaging to relations with Paris.

Past press reports

The Iranians have picked two men to take over the leadership of Hezbollah and its armed wing, Islamic Jihad. One is Aqal Hamieth, former security chief of Amal ... The second chief is Imad Mugniyah. According to some Middle East sources, Mugniyah controls many of the western hostages now being held in Lebanon.

Foreign Report (The Economist), 12 November, 1987

In April 1988, Shiite gunmen hijacked a Kuwait Airways Boeing 747 and took hostages, including members of the Kuwaiti royal family. The PLO chairman and the Egyptian foreign minister accused Iran of being behind the plot, in which several hostages were shot. Kuwait's independent *al-Qabas* newspaper reported Wednesday that the alleged kidnapper, Imad Mugniyah, was believed to have boarded the plane when it landed in Mashhad, Iran. Mugniyah was identified as one of the security chiefs in Beirut for Hezbollah, or Party of God, which is believed to be the umbrella organization for pro-Iranian groups holding foreign hostages in Lebanon.

Charles Campbell's A.P. story printed 15 April, 1988.

In the mid-1990s, the FBI discovered that Mugniyah was on a plane that was scheduled to make a stop in Saudi Arabia. But the ... Saudis blocked American efforts to grab him.

Timmerman, op. cit.

From 1991 to 1996, Sudan was host to Iranian Revolutionary Guards and many international terrorists, including Osama Bin Laden, other members of Al Qaeda, and the integral force of al-Jihad, Egyptians whom Dr. Zawahiri had led into al Qaeda's ranks. Testifying later in federal court in the Southern District of New York, one of these Egyptian terrorists disclosed: "I was aware of certain contacts between al Qaeda and al Jihad organization, on one side, and Iran and Hezbollah on the other side. I arranged security for a meeting in the Sudan between Mugniyah, Hezbollah's chief, and Bin Laden."

Ali Mohamed, 20 October 2000

Box 2.3 continued

In the Persian Gulf, in late July, 1996, American warships, a full complement of military hardware, and nearly 4,000 Marines, sailors, and SEALS, were praying they could pull off the mission of their lives. They had been assigned to grab the man, who … had killed more Americans than any other terrorist. His name is Imad Mugniyah, and U.S. intelligence believed they had tracked him … aboard a merchant ship, the *Ibn Tufail*. Marine commander John Garrett helped plan this top-secret mission. … [S]ays long time CIA agent Bob Baer, who has chased Mugniyah for years, "Mugniyah is probably the most intelligent, most capable operative we've ever run across, including the KGB …" [But] the mission was called off … they couldn't verify that the target was still on board the vessel, says Garrett.

CBS News, 1 May 2002

[Intelligence indicated] … Tehran had appointed Mugniyah as its point man for operational contacts with Bin Laden's men. The reports showed that, in October and November 2000, Mugniyah coordinated travel between Saudi Arabia, Beirut, and Iran for eight to ten of the 'muscle hijackers'—the terrorists whose job on 9/11 was to seize control of the planes and force the passengers into submission. Then in January 2001, in a bunker just south of Tehran, protected by elite Revolutionary Guard security men, Mugniyah met with Ali Akbar Nateq-Nouri, a top advisor to Iran's Supreme Leader Ayatollah Ali Khamenei. With him were Iranian intelligence officials involved in planning overseas terrorist operations. The guest of honor was … Dr. Ayman al-Zawahiri, the top deputy to Osama Bin Laden.

Timmerman, op. cit.

In early October [2001], a European intelligence official adds, fugitive Lebanese terrorist Imad Mugniyah met in Mashad with a senior Iranian intelligence officer and an Iraqi identified as a top deputy to Saddam Hussein in charge of intelligence matters, apparently to discuss cooperation with Bin Laden and the Taliban in Afghanistan … The Lebanese born Mugniyah reports directly to Iranian military intelligence and lives in Iran, according to U.S. and European intelligence reports.

Kenneth Timmerman, *Insight*, 3 December, 2001

Demonstrating Mugniyah's operational maturity, Hamid Zakiri, a defector from the [Revolutionary] Guards' al–Quds Force, argued that Mugniyah himself facilitated the escape of senior al-Qaeda personnel to Iran after September 11 [2001]. This included some of Osama Bin Laden's close family members.

Asharq al-Awsat,11 August 2006, quoted in *Terrorism Monitor*, 8 September, 2006

> With the dawn of the new century, Mugniyah acquired some maturity as a terrorist archetype. His elevation to such maturity is witnessed by his accompanying Iranian President Mahmoud Ahmadinejad to Damascus to meet with Syria's President Bashar al-Assad earlier this year to discuss security issues for both states.
>
> *The Times* (London), 23 April 2006, quoted in *Terrorism Monitor*, op. cit.
>
> Before this Spring 2006 event, Imad Mugniyah had not appeared openly in public for twenty years.
>
> (CCH)[85]

at home. Austria, Belgium, Britain, and Germany see foreign neo-fascist traffic, as do the Scandinavian countries. An American from Nebraska, Gary "Rex" Lauck, has published bales of neo-fascist propaganda for the European markets and served as the "NSDAP-Overseas Organization." His internationalist appeals have included calls to skinheads to join with him as fellow "members of the great world-historical Aryan racial movement."[86] Lauck ran out of luck in Denmark, where he was arrested, deported to Germany for violations of its stiff anti-fascist laws, and jailed for four years.[87]

Racialists interested in "white power" have moved beyond old-fashioned printing and mailings. They are additionally finding reading and reinforcement on the Internet, a symbol of the new information age and the new global environment. The Web is almost free, and it is much more difficult to police than printed matter or political rallies. American right wingers are using websites of confreres in Europe and in Canada, where Ernst Zundel and other propagandists have lived. American neo-fascist Milton John Kleim Jr. authored a "National Socialism Primer" on the Internet. In the mid-1990s, he published the on-line essay, "On Tactics and Strategy for USENET," which has been widely cited and can still be accessed (as of late 2006). Kleim exhorts politicized readers to exploit the opportunity to establish a Web page for a few hundred dollars and thus reach tens of millions of Internet users. He begins:

> USENET offers enormous opportunity for the Aryan Resistance to disseminate our message to the unaware and the ignorant. It is the only relatively uncensored (so far) free-forum mass medium which we have available. The State cannot yet stop us from "advertising" our ideas and organizations on USENET, but I can assure you, this will not always be the case. NOW is the time to grasp the WEAPON which is the NET and wield it skillfully and wisely while you may still do so freely.

The neo-Nazi argued for action by volunteer "Cyber guerillas," good use of foreign and foreign-language newsgroups, an understanding of how messages should be "tailored" to receiving groups, and said moreover, "We MUST move out beyond our present domain, and take up positions on 'mainstream' groups."[88] True to form, Milton John Kleim, Jr. may be found on the Web today reviewing books on the Amazon.com site. Samples of his postings include five stars' worth of praise for a new Microsoft Windows text, disdainful references to a paperback on "the cult of art in Nazi Germany," harsh words for Daniel Jonah Goldhagen's volume on ordinary Germans and *Hitler's Willing Executioners*, and a salute to the "Awesome quality" of a DVD entitled "Adolf and Eva" with its edited home movies taken by Eva Braun, the Fuhrer's mistress.[89] In such ways does one U.S. resident reach out internationally on the World Wide Web.

It is a tenet of communism, especially its Trotskyite and Leninist forms, that to succeed, the revolution must be international in scope. The newer communist groups fit most, but not all, of the old internationalist communist patterns. Shining Path has a Peruvian focus, primitive localist economic ideas, only cursory contacts with other armed groups outside Peru, and a surprisingly open disdain for established communist governments, such as those of China and the USSR of the 1980s. Sendero ridiculed them as bureaucratic and unrevolutionary. Despite all this, the striking fact is that by the early 1990s, Sendero had an impressive international network. There was the Committee for the Defense of Human Rights in Peru; a Belgian outlet for publishing the different lingual versions of Shining Path's newspaper, *El Diario Internacional*; and marketing leader Abimael Guzman's writings. In Spain, Great Britain, and Switzerland, there were supporting groups. London was headquarters for the Revolutionary Internationalist Movement (RIM), a front for Sendero and other world Maoist groups.

Another forum popular for militant internationalism is the United Nations. Winning explicit endorsement by the UN's political and cultural bodies can offer valuable political strengths, access to international media, and economic support. Examples of insurgents who achieved success within the UN at the same time as they conducted (1) guerrilla war and (2) mutilations and murders of Algerian and European civilians are the Algerians of the National Liberation Front, who thus turned from rebels to rulers in 1962. Another example is Yasser Arafat's Palestinians, who admired the FLN and also used the UN to nail down repeated endorsements of the PLO as the "sole legitimate representative of the Palestinian people," a prelude to the PLO's later acquisition of recognized governmental powers.

The United States is almost as popular a forum as the United Nations. Certainly the United States lacks the UN's neutrality, but it does remain a key to Security Council decisions. There is as well the Americans' wide-open media market. The United States is home to thousands of universities and political action organizations that might be coaxed to take an interest in a foreign people's troubles. Congress is a diverse and many-centered power to which foreign organizations would like to connect themselves, in one way or another. Organizations with records as terrorists have proven able to sometimes successfully cultivate individual American Congressmen or caucus groups.

Conclusion

The foregoing are five of the strategies by which contemporary terrorist groups and insurgents have pursued or are pursuing their goals. Some of these means, such as the creation of political front groups, demand unusual sophistication. All demand deliberation and skills. The most successful groups calibrate their use of terrorism to suit the political and social environs, and they use multiple means and alter their approach to suit changes caused by the environment, governmental interference, or good or bad fortune. In short, successful terror groups have a conception of "grand strategy" and pursue their aims in multiple ways.

The ability to study, deliberate well, and decide is something above and beyond mere charismatic leadership or the impulse to act boldly. Strategy requires judgment. And it is a telling fact of the terrorist demographic that leadership ranks tend to be educated, and often highly so; this ensures their ability to deliberate, study, and decide with more than minimal sophistication; sometimes it allows them to "play" outsiders in ways that are embarrassing. One intimation of deliberative character of many of today's terror group leaders is the striking presence in many of their *vitae* of master's and doctoral degrees. A study of "the Central Staff of the global Salafi jihad" claims that 20 percent of those have doctorates.[90] The second man in the Communist Party of Nepal (Maoist) holds such a diploma, in urban planning, from a sound university in India. He understands something of human organizations and is thus more adept at the reorganizations his party is pressing on the Nepalese. Shining Path's leader Abimael Guzman—now jailed but likely to get a new trial—has one doctorate in law and another in philosophy. He also visited Mao's China, so when he lectures on Maoist stages of armed struggle or prepares to argue with a prosecutor, he knows of what he speaks. The ranks of the PLO leaders of the 1970s–1990s were full of university degree holders, and more than a few had the master's. When Abu Abbas bantered in recent years with reporters in Saddam Hussein's Iraq, his literacy did not spare him from being considered a killer, but he could attempt to charm with quips about his graduate work in Shakespeare, and he understood public relations.[91] A central core of the Red Brigades leadership of the 1970s emerged from the Sociology Department of the University of Trento, where some of them were faculty, not students. They did not just engage in "struggle"; they understood it and so brought Italy closer to dissolution than at any time since 1943.

It is evident why the best definitions of terrorism include such words as "calculated" and "deliberate" and "aimed towards political ends."

Notes

1 This chapter's structure and argument follow the author's "Five Strategies of Terrorism," *Small Wars and Insurgencies* 12: 3 (Autumn 2001), 39–66. That essay is itself akin to ch. 2 of our year-2000 edition. The author offers his appreciation to Alan O'Day for subsequently including the *Small Wars* version in his edited volumes in The International Library of Essays on Terrorism: vol. 2, *Dimensions of Terrorism* (Aldershot, U.K.: Ashgate, 2004), pp. 275–302. Many facts, observations, and endnotes are new for this 2006 writing.

2 "Comrade Gonzalo" said this to his party newspaper *El Diario* in a rare and famous day-long interview, the text of which the paper reprinted and sold widely in July, 1988. The Peruvian government confiscated what copies they could and Sendero's presses as well. The organization relocated some propaganda operations abroad. My own copy of the *El Diario* interviews is a 1991 reprint, in English translation, by a Communist support group in Berkeley, CA.

3 Carlos Marighella, *Minimanual of the Urban Guerrilla*. Undated. The many reprints include that of the Adelphi Papers, no. 79 (London: International Institute for Strategic Studies), August, 1971, p. 40.

4 "Hamas 1993 Plan to Torpedo Gaza-Jerico Accord", *Al-Aqsa* (Jerico), Jan.1, 1995, repr. by Joint Publications Research Service (JPRS), Jan. 19, 1995, pp. 20–1.

5 World news of early January 2007 included innumerable reports on Hamas-Fatah violence, some of it lethal. Unfortunately, this is not unexpected from two organizations whose rise depended heavily on terrorism.

Some say cynically that "terrorism" is a mere label and that "terrorists" are morally indistinguishable from other belligerents; the appellation merely is dropped after they gain power. But the Hamas-Fatah fratricide of 2006–2007 reminds us otherwise; when terrorists gain state power, their prevailing instinct is naturally to continue using terror.

6 What facts of Nepalese traditional culture make Maoist communism attractive there? Almost none, and the legacy of Beijing's conquests can only make the clash of civilizations worse. And yet, with skill and persistence, the propagandists and operatives of the Maoist Nepalese have been rewarded with power in many parts of the country.

7 Mr. Arafat should be credited with creating the Palestine Authority, a proto-state; he died in 2004.

8 Leonard B. Weinberg's *Political Parties and Terrorist Groups* (London: Frank Cass, 1992) was a small but ground-breaking study of this problem; I do not know of a successor.

9 In Peru, the economic destruction by Shining Path/Sendero Luminoso up through 1992 was enormous. It helped provoke the *autogolpe* that increased President A. Fujimori's power but cost Peru dearly in foreign confidence and foreign investment. On the "constructive" side— and Shining Path does attempt to manifest one—the ideology favors a return to precapitalistic farming practices, self-reliance, and little to no trade with surrounding communities. So attacks on roads and dynamite attacks against the national power grids are useful blows against infrastructure and represent a step in the affected area toward Sendero's economic program of autarky. But after 1992 SL authority in the countryside virtually collapsed.

10 See for example "A Saga of Revolutionary Heroism, Supreme Sacrifice and Absolute Determination," a time-line mentioning the May 25 1967 founding action, published on the website of the Communist Party of India (Marxist-Leninist), accessed July 23, 2006. Note that there is a difference between this party and the Maoists discussed in the text. A more detailed and worthy account of the Sept. 2004 creation of CPI(M) is at the South Asia Terrorism Portal: www.satp.org/satporgtp/countries/india/terroristoutfits/CPIM.htm

11 Self-defense militias have sometimes been among the several most useful countermeasures against insurgency or revolutionary terrorism, and yet there has been little recent literature on the pros and cons of organizing, training, arming, and leading such militias.

12 *New York Times*, April 30, 2006.

13 U.S. governmental reports and Congressional hearings on terrorism and on narcotics are useful, and see Dr. Rachel Ehrenfeld, *Narco-Terrorism: How Governments Around the World Have Used the Drug Trade to Finance and Further Terrorist Activities* (New York: Basic Books, 1990).

14 There are two important 2005 indictments of Taliban drug traffickers in the Southern District Court of New York. Debate continues, however, over Taliban's ally Al Qaeda: One newspaper reports that even the U.S. government disagrees about this, with the Defense Department seeing an Al Qaeda connection to the opium trade and the Central Intelligence Agency denying that the evidence merits such a conclusion.

15 April 28, 2006 remarks at the State Department during release of the annual *Country Reports on Terrorism: 2005* (Wash. D.C.: GPO, April 2006). Administration officials' remarks about Iran's aid to the Iraqi insurgency have become more and more certain—a pattern we observed earlier in declarations about Syria's role in the Iraq insurgency.

Mr. Crumpton's departure in early 2007 is unfortunate; he is one of the best-qualified men to have held this State Department job. He had a career in counterterror work, mostly at CIA but including a stint at FBI. He was sworn in as Ambassador and Coordinator for Counterterrorism on August 2, 2005.

16 Guerrillas "may be compared to innumerable gnats, which, by biting a giant both in front and in rear, ultimately exhaust him." Fleet Marine Force Reference Publication 12–8, *Mao Tse-Tung on Guerrilla Warfare* (Wash. D.C.: Headquarters, U.S. Marine Corps, Dept. of the Navy, April, 1989), p. 54.

17 As 2006 turned into 2007, there were several reports of new lethal political violence in Assam, for example.

18 This formula is from Mao's writings of the 1920s and 1930s, but its three phases are frequently garbled or misstated in American books and articles, both civilian and military. Part of the difficulty comes from Communist Vietnamese writing; certain influential figures argued for a neo-Maoist four-phased approach for their own revolution.

19 Mao Tse-Tung, *Selected Military Writings of Mao Tse-Tung*, 2nd ed. (Peking: Foreign Languages Press, 1963), pp. 181–2, 244–8, 279–80. Mao rarely wrote of terrorism, but the aforementioned pages well express his thesis that a small revolutionary group can develop into one that challenges, and eventually overcomes, a state army and political apparatus. Shining Path and several other groups of today are adherents of Mao.

20 *Foreign Report* (London), May 24, 1990. Under construction were two "superguns"—made to use various propellants, including rocket fuel—on the model of the uncompleted German V-3, circa 1945.

21 This quotation from Talaat Fouad Kassem's Pakistani-based journal, *Al Murabitoun*, is one of many examples showing that some political murderers have no fear of the appellation "terrorist." Other illustrations are in the 'Introduction' to this present edition.

22 Reportedly work of the late 1990s, the manual was found in May 2000 in the home of Anas al-Liby, an Al Qaeda operative living in England. Now *Military Studies in the Jihad Against the Tyrants* (The Al Qaeda Training Manual) has been published by the U.S. Air Force Counterproliferation Center, Maxwell Air Force Base, Alabama (August, 2004). The editor, Jerrold M. Post of The George Washington University, was an expert witness at a trial of Al Qaeda suspects in the 1998 East Africa embassy bombings.

23 Ibid.

24 On questions of recruitment into militant Islam, one of the best sources is Marc Sageman, *Understanding Terror Networks* (Philadelphia: University of Pennsylvania Press, 2004).

25 The point is worth underscoring because citizens often reveal a feeling that terrorism is becoming more common. In fact, it became common in the early 1970s and has remained so.

26 Libya agreed to pay for bombing the UTA flight but, as of mid-2006, has not yet done so.

27 Col. Andrew N. Pratt (USMC ret.) has often taught this case study to officers in his counterterrorism program at the George C. Marshall Center in Garmish, Bavaria, as I observed there in 1999. As there is little published literature in English on the events, Pratt recommends as sound and accessible "Anatomy of a Hijack," Thomas Sancton's long dispatch from Paris in *Time Magazine*, Jan. 9, 1995. *Terrorism Today* (2000) noted this important GIA action and the skilled French response.

28 This point was made in a guest editorial in the *Los Angeles Times*, Aug. 18, 1996. In late October 2006, Argentina formally charged former President A. H. Rafsanjani, other top Iranian officials, and Hezbollah intelligence chief Imad Mugniyah with the bombing, which murdered or injured almost 400 people.

29 The moderate and significant contention has been that of Dr. Walter Laqueur, author of many worthy and influential writings on terrorism and extremism. But one should avoid the incompetent argument of Caleb Carr, *The Lessons of Terror: A History of Warfare Against Civilians: Why It has Failed and Why it Will Fail Again* (New York: Random House, January 2002).

30 One case of violence undirected by intelligent political effort is that of Che Guevara, a hero of the Cuban insurrection, when he moved on to Bolivia. Unable to win influence in the countryside with armed actions, he wrote in his diary: "Until now, the peasants have not been mobilized, but through terrorism and intimidation, we will win them." Instead, he was killed by government special forces. Cited by Georgie Anne Geyer, "Long Shadows Cast by Che," *Washington Times*, Oct. 7, 1997.

31 Roberta Goren, *The Soviet Union and Terrorism* (London: George Allen & Unwin, 1984), pp. 116, 130, 140. For Abu Daoud's recent interviews, see the wire services of late 2005 and 2006.

32 A vivid example is the "Unabomber" manifesto, appearing in the *Washington Post* Sept. 19, 1995 and then on the Internet: "We have no illusions about the feasibility of creating a new, ideal form of society. Our goal is only to destroy the existing form of society." This part of paragraph 182 does not reveal, however, that even the Unabomber had a "positive" intention: the manifesto makes it clear that he hopes by killing to draw attention to his views on technology and nature and to help to spawn a revolution that will destroy the former and thus enhance the latter. He does not detail post-revolutionary political life—if there is to be such.

33 *Foreign Report*, Sept. 25, 1986.

34 Mohamed Sifaoui, *Inside Al Qaeda: How I Infiltrated the World's Deadliest Terrorist Organization*, trans. George Miller (New York: Thunder's Mouth Press, 2004). At p. 52, Sifaoui calls "willfully insane" the *Canal Plus* TV documentary released in France suggesting that the 1995 attacks were actually the work of the Algerian secret service, with French complicity. On the contrary, Sifaoui says the two terrorists, properly accused, were Boualem Bensaid and Smain Ait Ali Belkachem, working for Djamel Zitouni, then leader of the Algerian revolutionaries of GIA.

The financier of many of the 1995 attacks is believed to be Rashid Ramda, in British custody for a decade and finally transferred to French authorities on Dec. 1, 2004, according to The U.S. State Dept., *Country Reports on Terrorism: 2005* (Washington, D.C.: GPO, April 2006), p. 99.

35 This art has characterized Al Qaeda operations for years, according to experts interviewed by the press. It was confirmed for me in an early January 2007 interview with a former military intelligence officer who recently discovered an embedded message on an Al Qaeda website.

36 According to the newspaper's website, there is also a business and finance office on Fitzwilliam Square in Dublin. But #58 Parnell Square has long been an important locus of *An Phoblacht* activity, and it is an address to which financial contributions may be sent. Some Sinn Fein offices are also at 58 Parnell Square.

37 Their close link is described by Jack Holland in *The American Connection* (New York: Viking/Penguin, 1987).

38 Paragraph 96 of "Industrial Society & Its Future," known as the Unabomber Manifesto, op. cit.

39 It has been the main activity in the United States, according to former CIA counterterrorism official Vincent Cannistraro, quoted by Paul Wilkinson, "Hezballah: A Critical Appraisal," *Jane's Intelligence Review* (August 1993), p. 370. Money raising is also a function for the U.S.–based cadres now.

40 The printed appeal was characteristic of leaflets: Its availability was a limited show of political strength, and its text made specific arguments, such as calling on local residents "to respect orders issued by the Hawks", and warning Palestinians that "some renegade gangs were using the name of the Hawks to commit robberies." Paraphrase by the *Washington Post*, March 29, 1994.

41 *Washington Post*, March 1, 1994.

42 Meir Kahane was shot by a Muslim in New York City in 1990. His son Binyamin, and Binyamin's wife were killed in the Middle East by the al Aqsa Martyrs on the last day of 2000.

43 *Foreign Report*, Sept. 17, 1992; Aug. 1, 1996. "Hezbollah Gets Radio Up…," Arabic News.com, Oct. 16, 1997, accessed on Nov. 7, 2006 at www.arabicnews.com/ansub/Daily/Day/971016/1997101622.html In 2005, Spain removed Hezbollah TV from its carriers to Latin America, and the next Spring, in 2006, France and Spain withdrew Hezbollah's al-Nour radio from carriers reaching into markets in Europe, Asia, and South America. The U.S. Treasury designated the Lebanese Media Group, al-Nour radio, and al-Manar television as "terrorist entities;" Foundation for the Defense of Democracies, June 29, 2005 and April 6, 2006, accessed on Nov. 7, 2006 at www.defenddemocracy.

44 U.S. Dept. of State, *Country Reports on Terrorism: 2005* (Washington, DC: GPO, April 2006), p. 98.

45 *New York Times*, Dec. 14, 2004; U.S. Dept. of State, *Country Reports on Terrorism: 2004* (Washington, D.C.: GPO, 2005), p. 100. There is a book about the station (which I have not seen): *Beacon of Hatred*, by Avi Jorisch. I can recommend, for details on Hezbollah media, Ron Schleifer, "Psychological Operations: A New Variation on an Age Old Art: Hezbollah versus Israel," *Studies in Conflict & Terrorism*, 29: 1 (2006), 1-19.

46 Articles on Adam Gadahn include the Michael Martinez article in the *Chicago Tribune* on Oct. 30, 2006, and that of Henry Schuster, "In Pakistan, Signs of Al Qaeda All Around," CNN, Sept. 7, 2006. Accessed on Nov. 7, 2006 at: www.cnn.com/2006/WORLD/asiapcf/09/05/tracking.terror/

47 Quoted in the *New York Times*, June 9, 2006.

48 The *Washington Post* has reported well on Muslim terrorists' use of the Web. Several phrases in my text here, including the headline and the reference to moving from physical space to cyberspace, come from the fine three-part series by Steve Coll and Susan B. Glasser, Aug. 7–9, 2005. Scholar Gabriel Weimann is perhaps the leading authority of the Muslim radicals' Web activities for propaganda purposes; his book is entitled *Terror on the Internet: The New Arena; The New Challenges* (Washington, DC: U.S. Institute of Peace, March 2006). His earlier USIP paper (Special Report No. 116; March 2004) was the basis for various lectures, and I profited from hearing two he gave in Washington.

49 The Communist Party of Chile used "what we call 'the veil'...It is disguised communism, that is, through the PPD [Parties for Democracy], [and] the MIDA [Allendist Leftist Democratic Movement]...Not even the Lautaro Youth Movement members know they are not autonomous...Members believe they are members of the Lautaro Youth Movement and nothing else. "Commandante Miguel" in an interview by *La Tercera de la Hora*, in Santiago, Aug. 1, 1992, repr. *JPRS: Terrorism*, Aug. 13, 1992. This case is old; the pattern is timeless.

50 Adrian Guelke and Jim Smyth, "The Ballot Bomb: Terrorism and the Electoral Process in Northern Ireland", *Political Parties and Terrorist Groups*, Leonard Weinberg, ed. (London: Frank Cass, 1992), p. 122. This book was the first to so directly analyze the relations of various organized political parties and fronts with terror groups.

51 1992 was an important year for French-Spanish cooperation in arresting ETA. As 2006 began, more than 150 Basque terrorists were in French jails. More than 500 more were in Spanish jails.

52 One car bomb at year's end was blamed on ETA, and in the midst of allegations by Basque partisans that Madrid is abandoning the preace process.

53 In Iraq today, according to two scholars, there is good evidence that the Iraqi Islamic Party and the Association of Muslim Scholars are effectively "fronting" for insurgents. They share core objectives, publicize their demands, and the like. See Michael Eisenstadt and Jeffrey White, "Assessing Iraq's Sunni Arab Insurgency," policy paper 50 (Washington, DC: Washington Institute for Neareast Policy, Dec. 18, 2005),

54 *BBC News* of Nov. 14, 2004; http://news.bbc.co.uk/go/pr/fr/-/1/hi/world/europe/4011895.stm See as well the May 27, 2005 issue of *Spain Herald* (Madrid), "Batasuna Leader Arnaldo Otegi jailed as Alleged ETA Boss;" www.spainherald.com/833.html. Both were accessed April 30, 2006, and elmundo.es (Madrid), accessed on Nov. 7, 2006 at www.elmundo.es/elmundo/2006/03/22/espana/1143031408.html, transl. by Google. The January 2007 *Smithsonian* story adds the note about Sinn Fein-Batasuna discussions.

55 In a videotaped speech with Arabic subtitles, Bin Laden declared that "Your security is in your own hands. And every state that doesn't play with our security has automatically guaranteed its own security." He noted arrogantly that this is why he had not attacked Sweden. A full translated text was accessed Dec. 12, 2005 at http://english.aljazeera.net/NR/exeres/79C6AF22-98FB-4A1C-B21F-2BC36E87F61F.htm

56 "Text of World Islamic Front's Statement Urging Jihad Against Jews and Crusaders," in Al Quds al- Arabi, in Arabic (London), Feb. 23, 1998; trans. *JPRS*.

57 "To the Americans," on Oct. 6, 2002, transl. *The Observer* (London), Nov. 24, 2002, from the Al-Qala'h website on Oct. 14; reprinted in *Messages to the World: The Statements of Osama Bin Laden*, ed. Bruce Lawrence (London: Verso, 2005), pp. 160–72. The speech includes many other invocations to economic war and praise of the damage to the U.S. economy on 9-11. One of these Bin Laden quotations also appears in the U.S. Army's *A Military Guide to Terrorism in the Twenty-First Century*, 2nd ed. (Fort Monroe, VA: TRADOC, Aug. 15, 2005), p. 2/9.

58 Oct. 2004 speech, op. cit. Certain other radical Muslim organizations anticipated, or share, Al Qaeda's desire to solicit funds for economic war. See for example ch. 2 on "Economic Jihad" of the excellent new book by Matthew Levitt: *Hamas: Politics, Charity, and Terrorism in the Service of Jihad* (New Haven, CN: Yale University Press, 2006).

59 William Montalbano, "Strategy of Destruction by Rebels in El Salvador Risky," *Los Angeles Times*, May 29, 1983. The Radio Venceremos broadcast quoted above was on Feb. 19, 1985, cited in *Foreign Broadcast Information Service (FBIS): Central America* that day, p. 8. Another broadcast that August included announcement of a reopening of commercial traffic and boasted that, in the guerrilla ban now ending, "The FMLN has dealt one of its hardest blows on the country's shaky war economy," Radio Venceremos said.

60 June 1998 brought election to the presidency of Andres Pastrana. Today, President Uribe is doing a far better job at assuring Colombia's security.

61 The Winter Games also passed calmly in Turin, Italy, in February 2006, but the state of Italy mobilized 9,000 police and expended large sums to effect the safety of the 2,500 athletes and hundreds of thousands of spectators; *U.S. News & World Report*, Jan. 9, 2006, p. 15. I am grateful to Lt. Col Avanulas Smiley of the U.S. Army, and Mr. Tom Hastings, formerly of the State Dept., for telephone interviews on Olympics security.

62 This is a tentative suggestion, because, as a general statement about world terrorism, one may say that left and right usually devote much more attention to smashing moderates and the middle ground than they do attacking each other; please see ch. 5 of our first edition.

63 An accessible summary of Sendero's strategic five-phase plan is in Gordon H. McCormick, *From the Sierra to the Cities: The Urban Campaign of the Shining Path*, R-4150 USDP (Santa Monica, CA: RAND, 1992), p. 23. The phases were to be agitation and armed propaganda; an opening campaign against the socioeconomic system; generalized guerrilla struggle; conquest and expansion of support bases together with strengthening the guerrilla forces; and fifth and final, civil war, capture of the cities from the countryside, and the collapse of state power.

64 Mao, *Guerrilla Warfare*, op. cit., p. 54.

65 *Washington Post*, 7 March 2006. A Sunni Arab sheik, victim Dulaimi was highly-regarded as a general, "destined to be a senior leader of all the armed forces," by one account.

66 This was widely noted at the time and is remarkable proof of how effective terrorism can be. Such fears, troubles within the alliance, and reductions or withdrawals of contingents from Iraq were also featured in an excellent *Washington Post* story by Peter Baker on May 17, 2006.

67 *In Their Own Words: Reading the Iraqi Insurgency*, Middle East Report 50 (Brussels: International Crisis Group, Feb. 15, 2006).

68 *Estate of Michael Heiser et. al. vs Islamic Republic of Iran*, Judge Royce C. Lamberth, U.S. District Court for the District of Colombia, Dec. 22, 2006.

69 ETA also hits the usual terrorist targets: judges, prison officials, local politicians. See the Dept. of State, *Patterns of Global Terrorism: 1997* (Washington, DC: GPO, 1998), 17.

70 An estimate by the Salvadoran rebels themselves which others deem reliable, according to the *Los Angeles Times*, Jan.1, 1982.

71 *New York Times*, Aug. 22, 1996.

72 German laser research and other labs and industries were attacked, and then followed the murders of Karl-Heinz Beckurts, Director of Research at Siemens Company, an SDI contractor, and Gerold von Braunmuhl of the Foreign Ministry, a principal advisor on talks with the United States on strategic defense. Communiqués in both murder cases by

the Red Army Faction identified the motive: "great responsibility" for SDI-related "secret negotiations" and research. Then in Italy, the Air Force general and Defense Ministry officer most closely associated with Italian support for "Star Wars" development, Licio Giorgieri, was murdered by the Red Brigades, who left a 14-page leaflet titled,: "No to Italian adhesion to star wars-- Italy out of NATO". It seems relevant that at this time England underwent a wave of nine deaths of talented scientists, some of them doing defense work. See James A Courter of the US House Armed Services Committee, "Warfare in Peacetime", an address to the International Churchill Society, Dallas, TX, Oct. 31, 1987, *Proceedings of the International Churchill Society: 1987* (Hopkinton, NH: ICS, 1989).

73 William Safire, *New York Times*, May 27, 1991.

74 Paraphrase by a Greek official, in the *New York Times*, Jan. 30, 1991.

75 *Providence Sunday Journal* (RI), Jan. 20, 1991; see also ch. 6 of our first edition.

76 These remarks are about violent expansionists, not typical Muslims of the twenty-first century.

77 See the work of Australian scholar David Kilcullen. Marc Sageman also emphasizes the terrorists' determination to create a new transnational and Muslim polity.

78 Violent plots by Muslims have often been uncovered in Australia, too, but these seem less aimed to recruit than they are directed at punishing Canberra for its roles in the global war on terrorism. Al Qaeda has several times explicitly threatened Australia for this reason. For example," We warned Australia beforehand not to take part in the war in Afghanistan, as well as about its disgraceful attempts to separate East Timor, but it ignored the warning until it woke up to the sound of explosions in Bali;" Bin Laden's audiotaped message "To the Allies of America," Nov. 12, 2002, in Lawrence, op. cit., pp 173--5.

79 Anonymous [Rita Katz], *Terrorist Hunter: The Extraordinary Story of a Woman Who Went Undercover to Infiltrate the Radical Islamic Groups Operating in America* (New York: Ecco/ HarperCollins, 2003).

80 *Washington Post*, Oct. 18, 1995.

81 In December, 1994, four GIA men hijacked an Air France jet in Algeria. Three hostages were killed. The drama ended on the ground in Marseilles, when commandos stormed the plane, saved the other 167 passengers, and killed all four hijackers.

82 See for example the ads in the *Washington Times* of Nov. 22 and Dec. 30, 2005, or the *International Herald Tribune* that Oct. 12th. The *New York Times* profiled Maryam Rajavi in exile in Auvers-sur-Oise, Sept. 24, 2005, 40 years after the group's founding by her present husband and coleader, Massoud Rajavi. Other portraits of the group include the pages in *Extremist Groups: An International Compilation of Terrorist Organizations, Violent Political Groups, and Issue-Oriented Militant Movements*, eds. Richard H. Ward et. al. (Huntsville, TX: Office of International Criminal Justice and the Institute for the Study of Violent Groups, Sam Houston State University, 2002), pp. 625–32. Fooled by the group's anti-Iranian rhetoric, American Congressmen have often supported letters or initiatives arranged by the People's Mujahedin-e Khalq, but the Department of State has long listed them as a terrorist organization.

83 MEK, sometimes called MEQ, had collected money in airports in California and sued to perpetuate that right despite the State Department's listing of the group as an illegal terror organization. A judge in Los Angeles ruled for them, but on Dec. 20, 2004, a three-judge federal panel based in San Francisco ruled that not only was the ban on money-raising legal, there is no legal right for an accused group to contest its designation. David Kravets, in an A.P. wire story of Dec. 21, 2004. The article—like scores of others in recent years—quotes Georgetown University's David Cole as opposed to such counterterrorism rulings.

84 An impressive article on U.S. policy toward the Iranians of MEK by Major Adam Strickland, USMC, is slated for publication by *The Intelligencer*, the journal of the Association of Former Intelligence Officers, during 2007.

85 I have standardized the spelling of Mr. Mugniyah's name from the varied sources above. Fuller citations on the books used appear in the bibliography. The July 1996 incident was well described in the later *CBS News* item, according to a military officer who was aboard,

and directed me to the news story. "Ali Muhamad" is Ali Abdel Suud Mohammed Mustafa, whom Sageman describes as the trainer of Bin Laden's personal bodyguards who had served in both the Egyptian and American armies.

I once attended a formal banquet at which a very-high-ranking U.S. intelligence officer declared repeatedly that his organization was in close pursuit of Mugniyah and would catch him. The speaker warmed to his subject and teetered between a noble promise, and a boast. With Mughniya still at large, we recall Winston Churchill's praise, after World War II, for the code-breakers at Bletchley Park who did almost unbelievably good work and were never exposed. He compared them to the wise hen that laid golden eggs but never cackled…until afterward.

86 Quoted by the Anti-Defamation League, "The Skinhead International: A Worldwide Survey of Neo-Nazi Skinheads", from the Internet, March 21, 1996. *WAR,* the American magazine of the White Aryan Resistance, features "WAR's International News," intended to "generate a loose international network that acts as an 'Amnesty International for white prisoners of war,'" according to Helene Loow, "Racist Violence...", op. cit., 156.

87 Lauck, who has been called the "Farm Belt Fuhrer," was jailed from 1996 to 1999 and was also involved in subsequent legal differences with the German Interior Ministry re. intellectual property right. See for example BBC News Jan. 25, 2002, accessed on Nov. 8, 2006 at news.bbc.co.uk/1/hi/world/Europe/1782103.stm

88 "On Tactics and Strategy for USENET," an essay by Milton John Kleim, Jr., may be found under a German heading "Nazi-Propaganda im Internet" at www.burks.de/tactic.html as of Nov. 8, 2006.

89 "Reviews Written by Milton John Kleim, Jr. (Mendocino County, California, USA)," accessed Nov. 8, 2006 at www.mazonn.com/gp/cdp/member-reviews/A239CTI637LR7N

90 Sageman, *Understanding Terror Networks*, p. 75.

91 See "Propaganda at Pistol Point: The Use and Abuse of Education by Leftist Terrorists," *Political Communication: An International Journal*, 9: 1 (Jan–Mar. 1992), pp. 15–30.

3

OPERATIONS

Funding terror

Terrorist funding is an organized, diversified, and sometimes complex dimension of groups' operations. The subject was usually ignored by academics, news periodicals,[1] and policy makers before the World Trade Center thundered into dust one day in September 2001. Since that attack, the importance of terrorist financing and economics has been apparent. That said, it will always remain far less important than the loss of almost 3,000 souls from Mexico, Ivory Coast, Japan, Israel, Portugal, Britain, Colombia, the Philippines, the United States, and several dozen other countries.

One evident way to assess terrorism's impact is through economic damage figures. The comptroller for New York estimated shortly after 9-11 that when judged together, all the costs to the city and population could become $100 billion. Subsequent estimates would differ, depending on methodology; many are lower, and some are higher than $100 billion. Overall bills for the nationwide impact include the temporary fall in the stock markets and many other enormous bills. Osama Bin Laden made a remarkable, belabored series of calculations—which took two pages of interview text to propound— settling on a figure of "no less than $1 trillion by the lowest estimate, due to these successful and blessed attacks." The editor (in English) of his collected messages and videos, Dr. Bruce Lawrence, arrived at his own figure of $1.2 trillion.[2]

The damage is clearly part of an economic strategy of Al Qaeda and other groups, as indicated in chapter 2, previously. Another, altogether different way to address the relationship between terrorism and money is to study the groups' expenditures. This would reveal much about their priorities, perhaps their politics, and certainly their operational style. A third approach could frame the topic according to sources of income based on activity: kidnapping, the narcotics trade, extortion, and the like. Our method here will be to analyze six kinds of human sources for terrorism's income. Most reflect a mix of legitimacy and illegitimacy. In that, terrorist economics shares a characteristic ambiguity often present in other terrorist functions—as when Hamas functions as both terrorist organization and governing party in the Palestine Authority.

The six resources, in order of discussion, are as follows: (1) terrorist groups themselves—that is, members' activities that generate funds directly; (2) individual donors, who may or may not consider themselves "members" of a group; (3) ethnic diasporas; these include many more nonmembers than members, but both categories may give, sometimes under compulsion; (4) aid organizations and charities, which may be the creatures of terror groups or merely helpmates, witting or unwitting; (5) companies, whether official, semiofficial, or semilegitimate; their proceeds end up directly in terrorists' hands; and (6) states. Their role in terrorism has been neglected since the Cold War but, in some cases, their importance to terrorist financing is enormous.

The groups themselves

A disturbing fact about the 9-11-01 attacks is their remarkably low cost to the terrorists. Citizens victimized by the day's high death tallies, and subsequent years' economic and tax bills, were amazed to read that the hijackings cost as little as one half-million dollars. This suggests that terrorism is highly efficient, if one balances economic losses to society against terror group expenses. In fact, a pessimist could paint an even darker picture. Terror operations are not merely cost-efficient; they often *make* money: Terrorism can be a highly profitable business.

Police discoveries of a decade and a half ago in Colombia included computer diskettes in a safe house of the National Liberation Army (ELN). These revealed the entire portfolio of a wealthy organization; one could tell with exactness how much this Castroite and criminal group was taking in from extortion at mines, cattle rustling, narcotics trafficking, straight robberies, and other activities. ELN is far less wealthy than FARC, the Revolutionary Armed Forces of Colombia. Estimates of 1992 showed that the smaller of the communist groups had enough income to rank it forty-fifth among Colombia's legitimate corporations; the larger, FARC, ranked at twenty-third. Not long thereafter, the state's Inter-Institutional Committee for the Study of Finances of the Subversives decided that the lucrative range of their activities means that "the subversives have sufficient funds…to stop committing crimes right now and to subsist 20 years doing nothing." By 2005, the picture was even rosier for the FARC. The authoritative *Jane's Intelligence Review* noted that FARC had such cash surpluses that it was frequently burying the money underground.[3]

Counterfeiting, sales of self-produced products, receipts for political publications, books and music, and many other sources of income help to fill terrorist coffers around the world today. Some schemes are imaginative. The Maoists of Khmer Rouge used to illegally harvest Cambodian hardwood in their native land and sell it across the border in Thailand. Lebanese agents of Hezbollah made a small fortune by buying and reselling cases of cigarettes within the United States, working the marginal advantages of different state taxes.[4] Some terrorists go beyond "imaginative" to bump up against the bizarre: Aum Shinrikyo guru Shoko Asahara was so venerated by followers that he could sell them vials of his blood and his bath water.[5]

Robbery, one of the Colombian communists' methods, is a terrorist commonplace. Sunni Muslim terrorists of Al Gama'a in Egypt have practiced robbery, preying on Coptic Christians and exploiting the latter's modest success. Al Gama'a has stolen frequently from the Copts' jewelry stores and other establishments. Such actions paid for Al Gama'a operations without directly challenging fellow Muslims. To take a very different organization, the Irish Republican Army Provos have for decades funded some operations with robbery. Post offices were one easy mark, as defector Sean O'Callaghan writes in his memoir. Some "hauls" have proven too ambitious and thus dangerous even when apparently successful; a bank theft of late 2004 attracted harsh scrutiny for its method—hostage taking—and for its yield—almost $50 million in British pounds. This robbery, together with the murder of Robert McCartney in January 2005, combined into a public relations fiasco for the Provos. "Loyalists" conduct their own organized crime. A British task force estimated in 2002 that almost half the identifiable criminal gangs in northern Ireland have some link, "current or historic," to Loyalist or Republican militants.[6]

Kidnapping is another classic terrorist operation that may make far more revenue than it costs to execute. Spectacular successes marked the earliest days of the terrorism business, especially in Latin America. Ransoms there in corporate cases climbed—from $1 million for a Fiat executive and $2 million for a British executive of Arrow Steel to $3 million for a Firestone Tires executive, and ever-upward. One imagined something of a record was set when Argentina's ERP got $14.2 million for an Exxon officer, but this was untrue; Marxist-Leninist rivals from the Montoneros received $60 million for the sons of the chairman of the Boro Bunge y Born commercial empire.[7] The practice did not become widely known within the United States, but it did in Western Europe. Then, by the end of the 1990s, most kidnappings in Latin America and Western Europe were criminal and nonpolitical.[8] And the same is true now, especially in Mexico, plagued by amateur and cut-rate kidnappers who specialize in quick-turn-around cases rather than old-style protracted theater starring unwilling political victims. Colombia is an exception. Political kidnapping in Colombia rivals the purely commercial in its numbers. Its associated agonies are many—for the society, for the victim's family and friends, and above all for the victim. There are now some 3,000 captives with their lives on hold, including former Member of Parliament Ingrid Betancourt, authoress of the 2001 book *Until Death Do Us Part: My Struggle to Reclaim Colombia*.[9]

Illegal narcotics are, for certain groups, the most lucrative source of terrorist wealth. After all, Americans, Europeans, and other consumers are driving a world market so large that if a mere fraction of production and trading can be dominated by terrorists, it yields them great returns for their violent purposes. FARC and ELN in Colombia are heavily involved. Their practices vary but, according to time and place, have included protecting growers, growing, processing, shipping to other Latin processors, and facilitation of foreign sales, as by protecting airstrips. As long ago as 1982, government agents in southern Colombia battled FARC guerrillas to capture an airstrip, seven airplanes, base areas and laboratories, and cocaine weighing nearly 14 tons. Two decades later, a U.S. House subcommittee reported that knowledgeable Colombians thought FARC alone could be making $2 million *a day* in narcotics during 2002. Colombian and foreign estimates are of growth in revenue, not recession. No less than fifty different leaders of FARC now stand indicted on U.S. criminal charges alone, for exporting at least $25 billion in cocaine to the United States and other countries. FARC supplies half the world market in coke. Recent authoritative figures reflect FARC drug income as not less than $600 million a year.[10]

All manner of terrorist groups have now been linked to narcotics trafficking. In older days, the nationalist or communist Palestinians of the PLO; Lebanese militias made up of Christians or Muslims; and such Latin communist groups as Colombia's M-19 were so engaged.[11] Though neo-fascist groups have not drawn attention in this way, some "pro-state" terrorists, such as Colombia's AUC, have. The "Self Defense Militias" long

Box 3.1 Field notes from Afghanistan

Narcotics have become an essential fund source for certain contemporary terror groups. Among these: Taliban, the madrassa "students" who ruled Afghanistan briefly and are now fighting to reclaim power. Apart from preaching, clandestine organization, political influence operations, and frequent terrorism against Afghans, Taliban is encouraging, and drawing large revenues from, the opium and heroin trades. I learned more on a visit in late February, 2006, arranged by Joseph Murphy and other Marine Corps associates.

Among my papers: a decree by Hamid Karzai, "The President of the Islamic Republic of Afghanistan," ordering "surrender of Baz Mohammad, an accused in the case of smuggling of Narcotics, to the Judicial authorities of the United States government, which is in keeping with the 1988 United Nations treaty against the unauthorized transfer of Narcotics and Psychotropic drugs..." The Baz Mohammad Organization is one of two just indicted in federal court in New York for importing Afghan heroin into the U.S.... while in business with Taliban.

Roger Lane, British Royal Marine, was one of my teaching colleagues at the US Marines' Command & Staff College. He has two stars now but has to worry over problems of narcotics. The production is worth $600 million at the farm gate, he tells us in his office. Worse, there is 4–8 years of inventory hidden away, much of it in desert hides. Worse, some police are corrupt: "We've heard of auctions of senior police appointments" to coalitions of drug businessmen.

What can be done? Eradication? Buy-up programs? Crop substitution?

Our visiting team discusses options as the days and evenings and briefings slide by. Afghans eradicated only a few hundred acres in 2005! 2006 will see much more than that, the Deputy Minister for Narcotics assures us. He asks for patience: "Our ministry was new in 2004."

Uniformed briefers from our Coalition side make it clear: our troops don't do the eradication—the Coalition declines that work—our policy is protect eradicators but not do eradication ourselves. We don't need the trouble with the populace. When Afghan government teams come to plow under the poppy, farmers lead their families out into the fields and lie down in front of the govt.'s tractors.

Human nature is vulnerable to the big profits. But "There's no one reason for growing," General Lane had told us. "My analysis and reading indicates that as many as twenty reasons are common for farmers to plant poppy."

The New York Times reported as I left the States that Taliban brazenly circulates leaflets in areas it dominates which instruct farmers to plant poppy. And an Afghan aid official tells us "Some farmers are given money from abroad, by foreigners, to start up poppy crop...It's only business." Those US indictments show how the system works: Taliban provides the heroin dealers and farmers with crop security, heroin labs, transportation routes, and protect the farmers. Taliban makes millions this way...they did it when in power, up 'til 2001, and they do it now as "sub-state actors."

Helmand and other provinces lie close to international borders with Pakistan, Iran and Tajikistan. Most labs are in borderlands, for ease of export. General James Jones of EUCOM tells us that "The Black Sea is a notorious route for bulk shipments." His staffer briefs U.S. policy on Afghan drugs, naming 5 pillars: eradication; interdiction; alternative livelihoods; public information; a judicial system that prosecutes.

Ministers agree: the Taliban leaders direct this insurgency from a safe haven in Quetta, Pakistan.

led by Carlos Castano were ultimately deriving as much as 80 percent of their operating income from the drug trade, his autobiography admitted. Today, most AUC units are breaking apart or formally demobilizing; Castano has not been seen since 2004 and is presumed dead. Irish "Loyalists"—another form of "pro-state terrorist"—also deal drugs, especially cannabis and ecstasy.[12]

National separatist groups have often been found deeply involved in narcotics dealing or in "taxation" of that trade when others engage in it. The European groups most involved have included the Kosovo Liberation Army, which moved heroin and cocaine,[13] and the longer-established Kurdistan Worker's Party, or PKK. It is unclear whether the practice continues now that PKK has been reconstituted as Kongra Gel.[14] Recently, the new "religious" terrorists have repeatedly been found to be deeply engaged in the criminal drug trade. Taliban insurgents, on the offensive in Afghanistan today, have links directly into U.S. heroin markets, for example.[15] Algerian radical Islamists are involved in drug dealing for reasons they take to be political and religious. Al Qaeda may not be profiting from narcotrafficking—evidence against them appears thin—but its business skills in so many other fields make drug dealing unnecessary for Al Qaeda's survival.

Just as "puritanical" communists of decades past were willing to traffic in narcotics even if they would never allow their legal sale and use, modern self-proclaimed "jihadis" are proving willing to be traffickers—just not users. The Taliban and the Algerians are merely the beginning. According to reporter David Kaplan, the Moroccans who operated widely in the Mediterranean world to arrange the savage Madrid train bombings of 11 March, 2004 were "major drug dealers" who, when arrested or otherwise discovered, yielded up to authorities some $2 million in narcotics! Kaplan pieces together a larger pattern:

"Similar reports of drug-dealing Jihadists are coming out of France and Italy. In Milan, Islamists peddle heroin on the streets...and then hand off 80 percent of the take to their cell leader, according to Italy's *L'Espresso* magazine....As early as 1993...French authorities warned that dope sales in suburban Muslim slums had fallen under the control of gangs led by Afghan war veterans with ties to Algerian terrorists....investigators believe Jihadists have penetrated as much as a third of the $12.5 billion Moroccan hashish trade—the world's largest..."[16]

Individuals

Individual donors are a second important source for terror groups. Frequently such persons have no formal membership in the terror group but, for various reasons, they elect to give of their wealth. This may be the result of extortion, pressure by people with family or national ties, simple idealism, or other reasons. Many other sorts of individuals have knowingly handled terrorist money.

As January 2007 commenced, a case typical of new U.S. struggles with Muslim terror was ongoing before a Chicago federal judge. The case involves a U.S. citizen of Palestinian descent; his presumed accomplice who, like many others in terrorism, is highly educated; evidence that hundreds of thousands of dollars were moved from the relatively wealthy United States to the poorer environment of Palestine; dispute over whether the chief suspect is a principle figure in Hamas' American operations or merely a charitable patsy; possible use of a charity as a front and as a form of moral court defense; complaints of torture; and an indignant declaration by a spokesman of the Council on American-Islamic Relations that the suspect should be admired as "a symbol of a larger Palestinian struggle"—rather than as a terrorist. This case against Muhammad Salah, and a former university professor from Virginia named Abdelhaleem Ashqar, is one of many of recent years involving Americans charged with direct financing of murderous struggles in distant lands.[17]

Wealthy individual donors came to light in the post-9-11 months when analysts of Al Qaeda documents found in Bosnia read of a "Golden Chain" of Saudis and other Sunnis who had been giving generously. They were funding jihad quietly or covertly while carrying on with their own public, business, and private lives. A Council on Foreign Relations study then found that "Individuals and charities based in Saudi Arabia" have long been Al Qaeda's top money source. In Indonesia, for example, Al Qaeda ally Jemaah Islamiya received $73,000 on one occasion from a Saudi sheik.

Such cases are the latest in a lengthy line of earlier donors and earlier terrorists. Examinations of Palestine Liberation Organization funding disclose gifts from wealthy men of business or public life. They acted out of nationalism, other forms of idealism, or fear of the gunmen who metaphorically "stood behind" the gracious or smiling collector. Italian publishing house heir Giangiacomo Feltrinelli began writing checks liberally in the late 1960s for the Communist International, as some called the network of loosely associated revolutionaries using terrorism in Europe. Beneficiaries included the Proletarian Action Group and the Red Brigades, who were staging hundreds of attacks a year in Italy by the early 1970s. More recently, the *New York Times* has interviewed American Charles F. Feeney, who made a fortune running duty-free shops at airports, about his donations to Sinn Fein, the political front for the IRA Provos.[18] Some $280,000 in gifts was reported, likely making Mr. Feeney the largest registered individual donor in the United States. Such aid was not then illegal; indeed, during the Clinton Administration, Sinn Fein fund raisers openly collected in the United States, and Gerry Adams himself repeatedly was a guest at the White House.[19]

The ethnic diasporas

A third important source of terrorists' funds is national or ethnic diasporas. These are harder to "tap" quietly for funds, but they also enjoy certain advantages over individuals: their breadth and their promise of fostering public political solidarity. In a globalized world, ethnic diasporas are convenient, assessable, and often renewable. Sometimes they seem unlinked to terrorism: This author knows of no evidence that the thousands of Chinese immigrants lodged in South West Canada are funding violent transnational political groups.[20] Nor do ethnic Basques living in Nevada—where there is a considerable community—seem to fund ETA terrorists. However, within the United States, Lebanese, Arabs, and Irish are in fact collecting and giving, sometimes to very disturbing recipients.

Outside Ireland, "the diaspora has always been interested in what was going on in Ireland," said a professor mildly, when interviewed for a news story[21] on the large sums Sinn Fein and other activists have garnered in the United States. Americans from Boston and New York are often more candid; the eastward, transatlantic flow of arms, explosives, and dollars into the hands of Irish paramilitaries is widely known in America. This long pattern of donations—so remarkable to any social scientist and so infuriating to any British government—began in the 1860s and continued sporadically up through present days.[22] Openly registered funds are popular: Northern Irish Relief (NORAID) and Friends of Sinn Fein are each logged as lobbyists with the U.S. Department of Justice. NORAID's receipts have been small in all recent years, but "Friends" raised nearly $400,000 within a mere six months of one year, 1999.

However, 9-11 was hard on fronts and charities tied to political militants; ambiguities one might have winked at became ambiguities that disturbed people. Meanwhile, underground there are doubtless still other running fund streams. And one route well above ground was noted by Michael Kraft, a recently retired U.S. State Department authority on terrorism. With the price of air tickets between Ireland and the USA so low, sometimes it has well served the Irish militants to place their U.S. cash in the hands of couriers and have them fly it to its destination aboard normal commercial flights headed east.[23]

The United States has few Tamil citizens and no previous experience in handling Tamil Tigers of the LTTE; their fund-raising in North America has been Canada's concern.[24] An August 2006 indictment is the basis for a dozen arrests and a serious U.S. court case. Between Washington State, New Jersey, New York, and also Canada, Tamil agents traveled about in pursuit of a major weapons deal. Their urgency was apparent; 2006 was the year in which the cease-fire in Sri Lanka broke down, and by summer terrorist violence and guerrilla war were escalating. The promised transaction—some $900,000 for rifles and Russian surface-to-air missiles—proved to be a government "sting." It is unclear whether Canadian weapons might have moved to Sri Lankan rebel hands in recent years, but the flow of Canadian dollars is well known. The largest part of the Tamil diaspora, of course, lives in India, in the province of Tamil Nadu, across the Palk Strait from Sri Lanka. The diaspora to the north has been notorious for supplying aid, recruits, safe haven, and weapons to the Tamil Tigers, especially in the 1980s when India's government foolishly encouraged such assistance.[25] Today, what aid flows south is more private than public, and all clandestine. Blood is thicker than water, and the strait will hardly stop ethnic brethren from sharing each others' concerns and fights.

Latin America's "tri-border" area linking Argentina, Paraguay, and Brazil was not well known when our first edition appeared in 2000; diverse reports, and government actions, have now made it infamous. In the area live surprisingly large Lebanese- and Arabic-speaking populations, many settling there in the years after civil wars began tearing Lebanon apart several decades ago. Authorities largely tolerated Hezbollah fund raising, at least until recently. Smuggling, legitimate business, and perhaps extortion are among the ways in which Lebanese activists so far from home acquire currency for shipping back to zealous Shia in the "old country." The matter is especially serious, given broad suspicion of the area with respect to two massive and lethal explosions against Jewish and Israeli targets in 1992 and 1994. An estimated 20,000 Arabs live in the tri-border area, and some 7,500 of the retailers are of Arab origin.

One man alleged to be the ringleader for Hezbollah, Assad Ahmad Barakat, may have moved as much as $50 million from the region into Hezbollah hands, according to a local prosecutor. Several years later, by the end of 2006, the U.S. Treasury was imposing sharp bans on various individuals and entities in the tri-border area, including Barakat, declared to be "a major financial artery to Hezbollah," according to the director of the department's Office of Foreign Assets Control.[26] Lebanon's ambassador to Argentina and Paraguay once admitted to knowing of large transfers but replied that the money is for "humanitarian aid for orphans of Muslims killed in action."[27] The quip underscores a firm rule, evident long before the Summer War of 2006 proved it again: Lebanese diplomats consistently defend Hezbollah as a "legitimate resistance organization." In reality, it is a rival to Beirut and state authority, and Lebanon's government has acquiesced to what it cannot manage or rule.

Another such "carrefour"[28] of world transit received emphasis in our first edition seven years ago. West Europe is attractive for financing and indeed all aspects of logistics for transnational terrorism, given the presence of commercial transport, E-links, banking, and business connections. This makes the region a good geopolitical bridge for terrorist operatives, and among those to make use of it—before Al Qaeda—have been the Kurdish terrorists of PKK. In the 1990s, Dutch police tracking extortion and other fund raising by the Kurdistan Worker's Party testified to a flow of millions of guilders into the group's coffers. A senior German state security specialist suggested that some $12 million a year was reaching PKK hands from racketeering operations among Kurds in his country. And across the Channel in the United Kingdom, British police estimated that millions were gathered in "shakedowns" of Kurdish immigrants living there.[29] Little wonder that Abdullah Ocalan's organization could boast of 30,000 members and field guerrilla forces that in some tactical situations could bloody segments of the Turkish Armed Forces.

Aid organizations and charities

A fourth lens through which to examine terrorist financing is the aid organization or charity. The innovative, pronounced pattern by which Al Qaeda managed monies through such institutions is now well known. This has probably damaged some charity work around the globe. Muslim suspects in select court cases involving aid agencies may no longer enjoy the respect that charity work once gave; some defendants may

Box 3.2 Elusive operations: the funding of the LTTE of Sri Lanka

Shipping line

Organized by logistics wizard Kumaran Pathmanabha, a.k.a. "KP," and under commercial covers, the Tamil Tigers of LTTE operate ships registered in places as distant from Sri Lanka as Honduras and in Singapore, Thailand, and the like.

Small boats

A veritable fleet of small craft in and near Sri Lanka and southern India ferry goods for sale, weapons for use, and personnel. The Palk Strait makes easy shipments to and from southern India, where there are innumerable Tamil supporters of the Sri Lankan LTTE.

Donations

Donations from the 50 million Tamils in the Indian state of Tamil Nadu were actively encouraged by such Indian politicians as M.G. Ramuchandran, himself a generous donor. This official policy changed when Rajiv Gandhi was assassinated by the LTTE. Doubtless many living in India do still give, if more quietly. Ironically, when India intervened militarily against the Tigers, their propaganda then used this 'heroic national fight' as a basis for appealing for more money from Tamils.

The wider Tamil Diaspora

For a decade and a half, at least, LTTE has attracted and "worked" ethnic Tamils abroad for contributions. Fund collectors sometimes show disturbing familiarity with their income levels—and thus their capability to pay. Toronto, Canada ("Little Jaffna") may be the richest source, but Tamil communities also pay in the United States, Britain, France, Norway, Germany, and Sweden, according to Mr. Norayan Swamy. Malaysian authorities a decade ago reported that a large number of the country's 2,000,000 Tamils were contributing, "some voluntarily and others forcibly, to the LTTE and to fund Tiger terrorism in Sri Lanka."

Bank robberies

Many LTTE cadres have committed such thefts "for the revolution." Banks as targets have both operational-financial utility for leftist terrorists and political importance, as Carlos Marighella wrote in a famous terrorism handbook of a generation ago. LTTE once blew up the country's central bank in Colombo. As yet, no single LTTE heist has been as grand as one achieved by former Tamil rivals, militants of TELO; they stole five suitcases of rupees, the largest bank robbery in the country's history.

Box 3.2 continued

Narcotics

Historically, ethnic Tamils have been prominent among Europe's drug smugglers, and it appears that LTTE partakes in this commerce. The London *Times* uncovered an LTTE network moving heroin throughout Europe and North America over two years preceding August 1987.

Overt offices

At varying times and places, the Tigers' political fronts have been able to encourage donations. Anton and Adele Balasinghams orchestrated some such work among London Tamils in the early 1980s. Later, until 1991, Kittu—a battle veteran with an amputated leg—popularized the Tigers' cause, gave interviews, and supervised fund collection "from a plush office in the heart of the city." Madras, India had an office at that time for LTTE also.

Mass media and the web

Velupillai Prabhakaran, the magnetic leader of LTTE, once resisted all interview opportunities. However, reportedly, he has determined they are good for reaching expatriots. Occasionally he does such appearances. His Tigers and their allies also create videos used to raise money and recruits. Tamil artwork, propaganda, and violent incident reports are among the "eye candy" on websites that help to pay for operations. See for example www.eelam.com and www.ltteps.org

Revolutionary taxes and liberated zones

More than a terrorist group, the Liberation Tigers are a full-fledged overt and covert guerrilla army that controls large swaths of land, especially on coastal areas in the northwest, north, and east of the island. When possible, Prabhakaran's administrators tax transactions. These include purchases from LTTE stores, sales of such crops as rice to LTTE dealers, and even official permission slips to travel to non-LTTE-controlled territory in Sri Lanka. For example, one might pay the Tigers 20 rupees for a form to travel within Sri Lanka and a further 200 rupees to guarantee one's return.[30]

even feel shadowed by ongoing anger against Al Qaeda. Few things are as morally ugly as terrorism—the deliberate assault on the innocent to promote a political program; funding such acts by diverting money from charity, effectively robbing those in need, will be seen by many jurors and critics as running only a step or two behind actually perpetrating the violence.

Some terrorists may manage to penetrate a charity and twist it to group ends. In other cases they may found the charity with the very intention of using it as cover for money transfer and other banking operations. Either way, terrorism has been able to possess a generous and appealing face, which is in fact a mask.

No sooner had news broken in August 2006 of the joint British and Pakistani preemption of a plot to bomb ten airliners passing over the Atlantic than came the follow-on: The banker to the plotters may well have been a "religious charity." Jamat ud Dawa was already in disrepute for reportedly pressing the same agenda as Lashkar e Taiba,[31] which fights for Sunni control over Kashmir by flagrant terrorism—not just guerrilla war against Indian troops. 2006 also brought convictions for another sizeable group of LET adherents in a conspiracy that the press called "the Virginia jihad." About a dozen men in northern Virginia came together for paramilitary training that included exercises on a military base, paint ball games, inspirational talks, and religious studies with a local imam. Among those convicted in court was Ali Asad Chandia, a teacher at a Muslim school in College Park, Maryland, sentenced to 15 years for material support to the fight in Kashmir. His actions included service as a driver for Mohammed Ajmal Khan, a senior military leader for Lashkar e Taiba, and giving him safe haven when Khan was in the United States in 2002 and 2003.[32]

Just outside Washington, DC, where United Airlines flight 93 was headed when it crashed on a farm on September 11, 2001, quiet offices and individuals had worked for years funding operations by Osama Bin Laden and his many allies. Principals for the "Safa Group" living in Falls Church, Virginia and other communities orchestrated money-making efforts by the Saar Foundation, and the Wafa Humanitarian Organization. Records seized in 2002 show that another charity, the Benevolence International Foundation, was assisting Al Qaeda and allied terrorists in Bosnia-Herzegovina, Chechnya, Georgia, Pakistan, Afghanistan, and the Philippines.[33] Meanwhile in Pakistan, from an airfield in Karachi, the Al Akktar Trust International funded not only Al Qaeda, but other Pakistani-based gunmen, to include Said Memon, believed central to such terrorism acts as beheading American journalist Daniel Pearl.[34]

The Global Relief Foundation, based in Bridgeview, Illinois, was apparently an Al Qaeda front. It had revenues of more than $5 million in the year of 9-11, using it not only to aid Muslims around the world but for the promotion of violence. One Global Relief Foundation publication described as "jewels" the words of Abdullah Azzam, the Palestinian who cofounded Al Qaeda with Osama Bin Laden. Azzam "produced a new theory for saving the [Islamic] nation from disgrace," it said. Other Foundation publications praised violent struggle, as in a 1995 appeal for donations "for equipping the raiders, for the purchase of ammunition and food." Various American connections to the "charity" and its international operations finally caught the government's eye. For example, a foreign affiliate's chief was in communications with Bin Laden's personal secretary, Wadi Hage, who lived in Texas and was convicted of a role in Al Qaeda's 1998 embassy bombings in Eastern Africa. October 2002 found the U.S. Treasury closing down the Bridgeview office.[35]

Violent Palestinians of Hamas have their own beneficent allies with kindly faces. Over long years of building support, politicking, and money raising before coming to power in January 2006, the "Islamic Resistance Movement" or Hamas profited politically from alliances with aid agencies, hospitals, universities, and social associations. In one limited sense, charities and political organizations are two forms of institutions that seek to manage human affairs; Hamas was doubly engaged. Its aid programs in Palestine were expansive, costing millions every year. So too did their infrastructure of political fronts, schools and scholarship programs, guerrilla camps, suicide belt bomb factories, and a dozen other things Hamas felt it needed. Hamas' expenses are some $50 million a year. Approximately half of that is garnered through its "charities" and aid agencies;[36] much of the other half comes from Tehran. The Holy Land Foundation,[37] based in Richardson, Texas, was designated in 1994 by Hamas leaders to be the primary fund-raising entity for its supply, according to FBI studies. Holy Land levied an incredible $13 million in 2000 alone and sent some of it on to violent groups, such as Hamas. Sometimes, money passed to charities managed by Hamas. In another case, Holy Land's monies went to Hamas through an intermediary, the Sanabil Association for Relief and Development, a Lebanese charity.[38] Money being fungible, Hamas can spend it on guns or spend it on butter.[39] Either would have useful political effects. It is striking to consider what even a portion of $13 million could provide in real charity in impoverished Palestine.

Other fund-raisers for Palestine were lodged in Tampa, Florida. Many of them supported a rival to Hamas, the Palestine Islamic Jihad. The PIJ had as many as 40% of its leaders operating from Tampa at one point, according to a U.S. prosecutor.[40] The best cover was not a charity but a university—another exemplar of authenticity and idealism. WISE, or World and Islamic Studies Enterprise,[41] was an institute set up at the University of South Florida to serve as a propaganda and fund-raising arm for the PIJ. Its two leading lights were college professors. Ramadan Abdallah Shallah served on the board of WISE and taught college until suddenly disappearing into the Middle East; he surfaced as the new secretary-general for the PIJ in Damascus, Syria. His neighbor and colleague at the University of South Florida, Sami al Arian,[42] was also suspected and carried on a long defensive battle in which he loudly and repeatedly claimed academic privilege and denounced his critics as anti-Muslim. He too was proven guilty of terrorism—not by admissions but by a U.S. court in 2006. These same two men were involved with "ICP"—a fund-raising entity. In classic "front" fashion, it went under two different names: It was legally registered as the "Islamic Concern Project, Inc.," but Professor Sami often spoke of it publicly as the "Islamic Committee for Palestine." What is the larger picture of PIJ finance? It gets nearly all its money from Iran, according to a senior and recently retired Israeli general of the intelligence services. However, no smart subversive organization is entirely single-sourced. PIJ was able to garner revenues for years within the United States, right "in the belly of the beast."

Semi-official companies

Semi-legitimate commercial covers and corporations are an economically useful and often reliable form of funding terrorism. The corporate operations work as political fronts do: They disguise terror organizations but in economic ways, and they do not merely offer disguise; corporate covers directly facilitate logistics and may well make profits while doing so. Shipping companies and banks are among the common intermediaries for, and purveyors of, terrorist business, but the sophisticated terrorist group moves beyond those in a search for legitimacy and expanded opportunity. In the United States in recent years, the militant Muslim international has been found to draw money from investments of many kinds; sales of cars; cigarettes; houses; and the like.[43]

Import-export firms are unfortunately ready-made to facilitate transnational terrorism. It was Kintex, a firm based in Sofia, Bulgaria, that placed a Turk named Mehmet Ali Agca in St. Peter's Square on the crucial day in May 1981 to shoot Pope John Paul II.[44] That operational requirement—and indeed, any mention of the Bulgarian role—seemed forgotten in 2005 when Agca was released from Turkish jail amid journalistic buzz, but it was essential to the mission's success in badly wounding the Pontiff. Meanwhile, during the Cold War, the Abu Nidal Organization, a splinter and enemy of the PLO, ran import-export outfits in Warsaw and East Berlin. The SAS in Poland was created by Nidal's financial steward, Samir Najm al Din, a Palestinian from Iraq. Not far away, Zibado in East Germany moved arms—some for mere commercial reasons and doubtless others for Abu Nidal Organization terrorist operations in Europe. Zibado's cover was commerce in other things, from pianos to animals to frozen fish. It is unclear how profitable this cover entity was, and it does not greatly matter; the main purpose was at a lower level, underneath the table.[45]

A later example of such firms that cover terrorism is the Darkazanli Import-Export Company, based in Hamburg, Germany.[46] Syrian-born Mamoun Darkazanli and his firm offered connections to other Al Qaeda lieutenants. One was Wadi al-Hage, the U.S. citizen living in Arlington, Texas and a central figure in Bin Laden's American underworld. Hage was using the Darkazanli Import-Export Company in Hamburg for his own business address before he helped to orchestrate lethal 1998 terror bombings in East Africa (some perpetrators of which are still missing). Another "businessman" helped by this company was Mamdouh Mahmud Salim, a Sudanese engineer who sought out and acquired electronic equipment for Al Qaeda. These two were also connected to each other, as cosignors on a Deutsche Bank account.[47]

Banks are of course themselves a natural and common partner to terror networks.[48] The legacy of the BCCI, with its account holders, such as Abu Nidal, remains fresh in the memory of the world business community. Dubai Islamic Bank, in the United Arab Emirates, was shut down in the United States owing to its Al Qaeda connections. The Al Taqwa bank is another Al Qaeda tool that moved money in and out of the UAE—as well as in Kuwait, Switzerland, and the Bahamas. Founded by the Muslim Brotherhood in 1988 with the explicit purpose of helping fundamentalists to compete with Western banks, it served Al Qaeda too, by skimming money off each transaction and by transferring money between foreign companies.[49] Hamas also enjoyed help from Al Taqwa and did not cramp its operating style with only one such affiliation. It created its own bank, the Al Aqsa Islamic Bank, in 1997, about a decade after the Palestinian group was founded and helped to commence *Intifada I*. Al Aqsa evaded Israeli sanctions by opening joint projects with Citigroup, reportedly; these expanded until an operative could deposit money into an Al Aqsa account in Europe, as an example, and another could withdraw the sum through a Citibank chapter in Israel.[50] Citibank was doubtless embarrassed and surprised by this Hamas activity, which illustrates a related pattern: Banks that are merely used by terrorists may be very distinguishable from the minority of institutions specifically created to finance and facilitate illegal operations. Yet both kinds have their place in terrorism today.

State financiers and sponsors

States are important entities in facilitating today's transnational terrorism, and yet their roles have often been neglected in post–Cold War analyses,[51] especially owing to strong current interest in "networks" and "flat" terror organizations. Of the known practitioners of state-sponsored terror today, Iran, Syria, and North Korea are the most evident examples of financing of terrorists and illegal activities. They damage the international community in this manner.

A generation ago, one valuable study distinguished twelve different types of state involvement in transnational terrorism. One of these was financial support. Some four others on the list carry clear financial ramifications or qualify as forms of state aid: provision of safe-haven; training support; supply of weapons and other logistics; and potential for provision of nuclear or biological technologies.[52] The latter is especially important in the new millennium: Many terrorists might be willing to commit massive mayhem, but most of those would require state assistance to acquire and use certain weapons of mass destruction.

From the point of view of the willing capital, state sponsorship of terrorism can be relatively inexpensive, relying as it may on existing state structures. A state can thus aim for large effects with small investment and prepare ready assurances for purposes of deniability. For their own purposes, states already have, own, or deal with weapons manufacturers; major banks (public and private); secret communications channels; diplomatic pouches that are rarely if ever inspected; and such convenient meeting sites as foreign embassies, state safe houses, and the like. Some governments are willing to use such assets to kill defectors or loud-mouthed refugees, a specialty of Saddam Hussein's Iraq before it expired in 2003 and of the mullahs' Iran. Or, disdaining extreme secrecy and discrimination, states sometimes conduct broad intimidation campaigns in which personnel, vehicles, side arms, identification, and communications are deployed, semi-secretly, to contain public opposition or weaken trade unions or hostile political factions. Anti-communist regimes, such as Guatemala's, have done this in recent memory. Islam A. Karimai's Uzbekistan has been doing it in 2004 and 2005, in addition to widespread torture of political captives.[53]

Syria has been intimidating Lebanese opponents of its occupation of Lebanon (ended in late 2005) and killing some who resisted their intimidation. The stunning 2004 car bombing of former Lebanese Prime Minister Rafiq Hariri, which also killed twenty-two other innocent people February 14, 2005 in Beirut, appears to have been a Syrian operation, according to elaborate investigations by the United Nations still incomplete at this writing. Detlev Mehlis, and then Serge Brammertz, were detailed by a Security Council committee to investigate the horrific murder after Lebanon's own inquiry appeared to be useless at best. The report, which Secretary General Kofi Annan transmitted in June 2006, is reportedly a powerful case study of the ease with which organized state institutions may swing into the terrorism business when so directed. Syrian intelligence operatives, Syrian offices in two countries, and other "prepaid state assets" of Damascus were deployed to effect the murder, it appears. Of unusual interest was evidence pointing to Syrian use of two existing terrorist organizations, the PFLP-GC and the group Albash, as working directly with Syria in the operation—in pre-attack reconnaissance, for example.[54]

Iran has a full range of similar "prepaid" national assets and prolonged experience in deploying them. Our first edition required five pages to sketch these structures; nothing fundamental has changed.[55] To begin with semi-official levels, government-sponsored foundations may call for a killing, as the Fifteenth Khordad Foundation did in novelist Salman Rushdie's case. There maybe other useful government fronts. Recipients of Iranian largesse, such as Palestine Islamic Jihad and Hamas and Hezbollah, may take actions they know Tehran will approve. The Revolutionary Guard operates inside and outside of Iran, training international terrorists. The capital is home to representatives of many foreign groups and foreign embassies and other means of communication, suasion, and logistical coordination. Diplomatic meetings may cover for more lethal matters, as needed. MOIS, the Ministry of Intelligence and Internal Security, has many resources and is backed by a wealthy state with aggressive intentions and a hatred for Israel that is naked and raw, under President Mahmoud Ahmadinejad. Finally, there are loyal allies, such as Syria. Fundamental differences between hyperreligious Iranian governors and secular Syrian governors have not kept Tehran and Damascus apart in the support for anti-Israeli and anti-Western terrorism. New evidence of many of these relationships, and their lethal effects, emerged in federal court in December 2006 in Washington DC.[56]

The funding that Iran extends directly to terrorists is profoundly important. One of the world's two or three most effective guerrilla armies and terrorist organizations is Hezbollah, and its logistical depth and sophistication are indebted to continuous financing by Tehran. The *Foreign Report* of the *Economist* reported frequently on "How Iran Helps Hezbollah" in the 1980s.[57] During the 1990s, estimates of Iranian aid to Hezbollah ran between $30 million and $40 million, with some as high as $70 million. Iran admitted to aid, as did the recipients. A year before the Summer War of 2006, one columnist described aid from Iran to Hezbollah as "more than $100 million a year." Such an estimate seemed extreme; now it is perhaps average; other estimates go much higher. Observers note the impressive weaponry and infrastructure Hezbollah displayed against Israel, including such feats as clandestine creation of an immense underground bunker system within sight of a UN observation post and the Israeli border with Lebanon.[58] Within six months of the war's end, it appeared to a senior Israeli intelligence official that Hezbollah's stores of rockets were replenished fully. Iran's aid is massive and continuous, and it is also illegal, making Tehran responsible for the group's international transgressions, to include its kidnapping of two Israeli soldiers[59] on July 12, 2006, beginning an international war.[60]

Hamas—ethnically Palestinian and Sunni in religion—could be deemed too different from the Shia ruling Persia to merit aid, but Tehran has no such limit to its patronage. Hamas bankers and gunmen are subsidized with several tens of millions of dollars a year from Tehran, according to Canadian and Palestinian sources and estimates used in U.S. federal court prosecutions after Hamas murders of U.S. citizens. The organization's wealth is also aided greatly by donations from mosques and wealthy benefactors and cells in such distant places as the United States that, considered globally, add millions each year. Other states have also helped Hamas: Syria, Libya, Sudan, Qatar, and Yemen.[61]

A third recipient of Tehran's help is the PIJ (Palestine Islamic Jihad). Its finances may break one of the few rules in the terrorist underworld: Few groups subsist on only one source of income. However, PIJ gets all its money from Tehran, according to a recently retired Israeli two-star general and intelligence expert. Support was confirmed by Tehran in late 2005 when it agreed to pay families of suicide bombers $5,000.[62] In short, Iran is pouring cash into the hands of three of the Middle East's most active terror organizations. The undersecretary in charge of U.S. Treasury intelligence, Stuart Levey, says of Iran that they are the central banker of terror…a country that has terrorism as a line item in its budget.[63] The breadth of Hamas and Hezbollah operations in politics, social work, education, and the like and in violence is a testament to this foreign capital's interests, not merely the interest of the Palestinians.

North Korea offers a further example of a state's financing of terrorism.[64] Its practices differ from Iran's. Unblessed with Tehran's economic assets, Pyongyang actually uses its diplomats, other officials, and party structure to conduct black market operations to earn the foreign money its clandestine operations expend. Russia, Egypt, India, and Venezuela are among the countries affected by this commerce and attendant abuse of diplomatic privilege. Dozens of diplomats have been arrested for smuggling, around the world. An account by Raphael Perl of the Congressional Research Service (U.S.) details the regime's efforts through a Communist Party office, "Bureau 39," with the express purpose of raising money abroad to pay for North Korean operations and even for military concerns at home. Production and export of heroin and methamphetamine, other smuggling, and counterfeiting are all branches of this activity.[65] An emerging book by Korea specialist Bruce Bechtol dismisses the analytical option that this is "corruption"; he places Bureau 39's building in the capital and hard beside the personal office of "Dear Leader" Kim Jong-Il. Dr. Bechtol finds the government to be perhaps the only one on earth that so directly organizes its diplomats, certain military personnel, and other state apparatus for the obvious purpose of engaging in illegal international commerce.

Drug production and export by North Korea became evident during the 1980s. The work has been growing. By the mid-1990s, opium production reached forty tons a year, and then in 1996 this was supplemented by large-scale methamphetamine manufacture, aimed at markets in Thailand, Japan, and the Philippines. Illicit drug exports were bringing Pyongyang some $70 million by 1997, with no subsequent abatement in the decade since. In December 2000 and July 2002, Taiwan made two huge drug busts of North Korean cargo ships carrying heroin. Another such ship came into Australian waters in April 2003, apparently looking for contacts and an off-load. The Australian Navy estimates that $48 million worth of heroin was aboard the ship, though much was thrown overboard and went unrecovered. In 2004, there were two major busts of North Korean diplomats caught moving narcotics in Egypt and Turkey.[66]

Apart from illegal drugs, the regime has two other main sources of hard currency: arms exports—especially rockets—and counterfeiting. Counterfeiting has become a North Korean specialty and, in several cases, its product is clearly tied to radical political groups. U.S. currency is normally the preferred matter for copying; agents working abroad in Peru, Germany, Macao and other countries have located $45 million in U.S. $100 bills counterfeited by North Korea. Japanese Red Army hijacker Yoshimi Tanaka, carrying a genuine official North Korean passport and driving a North Korean Embassy automobile, was nabbed in Thailand in 1996 with $7 million in counterfeit U.S. currency. Interpol had been on alert for this man for seven years.[67] Four Japanese Red Army hijackers from a 1970 incident still live in North Korea as well.[68]

Unembarrassed by such setbacks, anemic economically, and still utterly unhelped by globalization and legitimate trade prospects, Pyongyang forges on. In late 2005, a perfect post–Cold War triptych was detailed in world newspapers: (1) high-quality $100 bill counterfeits made by North Korea (2) were linked to the illegal Marxist-Leninist Irish Workers Party leader Sean Garland, arrested Oct. 7, 2005 in Belfast, and (3) a Chinese organized crime network shipping North Korean counterfeit bills into the United States. So well known a Nationalist activist that he is featured in several IRA songs, Mr. Garland now is accused of meeting North Korean agents in Warsaw, Moscow, and Minsk as he traveled about. He is said to have been "placing" the forged notes in East Europe and also the United Kingdom.[69] So if North Korea has not carried out an international terrorist outrage in recent years, it does perhaps continue to liaise with revolutionaries, as the Irish and Japanese cases indicate.

Conclusions

Terrorists today enjoy many of the advantages of globalization, even if some legacy groups no longer have the Soviet bloc support of an earlier era. International finance can be tapped for ill almost as readily as for good. Violent political organizations are showing skill and creativity in making transfers, investments, and withdrawals. They favor diversified methods of generating income…or at least avoid being dependent on a sole source. If terrorists' purposes differ greatly from those of organized crime, they may resemble them in certain methods and in illegality. As indicated in the foregoing survey of many prominent financial players on the terrorism scene, it is vital for successful clandestine groups of the modern day to have accountants and financial planners and large numbers of couriers. It is less vital, but all too common, for them to have complicit banks and even state agents.

Notes

1 The author came to this realization in an amusing way in 1996 when circulating his draft article backed by long research but carrying a light title: "More Bucks for the Bang: How Terrorists Raise Revenue." Two U.S. monthly magazines were offered the article; both delayed replying; both eventually declined to print the manuscript. Later the author was <u>un</u>amused to see the manuscript's concept, framework, and even some material appear under

another byline, published overseas in English. One moral in the story is that interest in terror financing was very low within the United States ...until 9-11-01. Then, major newspapers and journals took the greatest interest, because of the damage and because of the efforts the U.S. government put into criminalizing, tracking, and punishing such terrorist economic activity.

2 "Terror for Terror," an interview of Oct. 21, 2001 by Taysir Alluni, in *Messages to the World: The Statements of Osama Bin Laden*, ed. and trans. by Bruce Lawrence (New York: Verso, 2005), pp. 111–2.

3 Many early 1990s articles from Colombia's press were translated and published by the Foreign Broadcast Information Service (FBIS; e.g., an interview with a former FARC guerrilla in *El Tiempo* [Santa Fe de Bogotá], July 15, 1993). The Dec.8, 1992 *Christian Science Monitor* reported ELN was making about $200 million a year, emphasizing extortion and robbery. On July 17, 1995, *Cambio 16* (Santa Fe de Bogotá; trans. FBIS on same date) related that the insurgents were generating 1.344 billion pesos per day. *Jane's Intelligence Review* reported dramatic increases in FARC income as of Sept. 2005.

4 One cell was based in Charlotte, NC and was led by Mohammed Hammoud, convicted in 2003 for his success. Another Hezbollah member, Mahmoud Kourani of Dearborn, MI, was convicted in March 2005 of fund raising and recruiting; his brother was Hezbollah's chief of military security in southern Lebanon. CNN, Jan. 16, 2004; *Washington Times*, staff editorial of May 20, 2005; *Free Press* (Detroit), March 29, 2006. Still others from Hezbollah were arrested in the United States trying to buy night vision goggles—a notable fact given that Israel found Hezbollah to have British models in Lebanon in the war of 2006.

5 Aum sold more conventional items—such as computers and health food products—and probably derived the greatest part of its revenues from the donations of members entering the cult. *Washington Post*, Nov. 1, 1995, and Andrew Marshall and David Kaplan, *The Cult at the End of the World* (New York: Crown Publishers, 1996).

6 *Jane's Intelligence Review*, Sept. 2002, p. 26.

7 Christopher Dobson and Ronald Payne, *The Terrorists*, 2nd ed. (New York: Facts on File, 1982), pp. 90–1. This duo cowrote many other books and helped to initiate serious study of terrorism.

8 Kevin Whitelaw, "Your Money or Your Life," *U.S. News & World Report*, March 22, 1999, pp. 34–41.

9 Published in 2001 in Colombia and France as *The Rage in my Heart*, and then in the United States as *Until Death Do Us Part: My Struggle to Reclaim Colombia*, trans. Steven Rendall (New York: Ecco/HarperCollins, 2002). Ingrid Betancourt was kidnapped in 2002 by FARC and is presumed alive today. Among the press stories about her is that by Nora Boustany, *Washington Post*, Oct. 8, 2003, and the press release *News From France*, released by the French Embassy in Washington, DC, Nov. 3, 2004.

10 Older reports were of some $40 million a year in FARC drug income, and then $50 million, and up. As late as 1984, the *New York Times* pointedly declined to attribute much drug income to FARC. I wrote to the paper that year on the matter and also published "How to Fund Communist-Guerrilla Revolutionaries: Deal Drugs," for Public Research, Syndicated (e.g., *Los Angeles Herald Examiner*, Aug 1, 1984). The dollar estimates continued rising and have had wide media coverage. The *New York Times* of March 4, 2001 covered a Colombian army operation that uncovered notebooks documenting FARC's links to drugs-for-guns trading on a major level, especially via Brazil and a FARC front working the Brazilian border territory. The U.S. House of Representatives' Committee on International Relations report appeared April 24, 2001 as "Summary of Investigation of IRA Links to FARC Narco-Terrorists in Colombia." For the (current) estimate of $600 million a year in drug income, see "Colombian Report Shows FARC is World's Richest Insurgent Group," *Jane's Intelligence Review*, Sept. 2005, pp. 12–7. For FARC members indicted in the United States, see the Department of Justice press release of March 22, 2006.

11 A good book on the evidence of the 1970s and 1980s was by Israeli criminologist Dr. Rachel Ehrenfeld, *NarcoTerrorism* (New York: Basic Books, 1990). In 2002 she published *Funding*

Evil, of which there was later a second edition. Syria's income from narcotics trade in the Bekaa Valley, which it controlled, was detailed by the *Los Angeles Times* Jan. 26, 1992; government agents—not just private individuals—were said to be profiting.

12 *Jane's Intelligence Review*, Sept. 2002, p. 28. The Irish Republican Army has also dealt drugs. "Provos" sometimes punish or kill drug dealers and publicize their actions, but that should not be understood to be done from puritanical motives (recall how city-dominating organized crime is known for punishing pickpockets and other thieves it does not control.) "IRA Uses Murder to Stamp Authority on Drug Trade," *The Times* (London), Dec. 21, 1995; courtesy of Dr. Harold W. Rood.

13 "Drugs Money Linked to the Kosovo Rebels," *The Times* (London), March 24, 1999; Jerry Seper, "KLA Finances Fight with Heroin Sales," *Washington Times*, May 13, 1999.

14 Official American caution on this was signaled by Asa Hutchinson, head of the Drug Enforcement Administration, testifying before Congress April 24, 2002. He said only that "Historic DEA information indicates that the PKK members are involved in the taxation of drug shipments and the protection of drug traffickers throughout the Southeastern Region of Turkey and other areas of operation." www.dea.gov/pubs/cngrtestr/ct042402.html

15 Two indictments opening cases in the Southern District of New York during 2005 show links from Taliban and Afghan heroin to U.S. consumers. Drug kingpin Baz Mohammad, based in Pakistan, boasted to gang members that his export of heroin to the United States was a "jihad" in which Americans pay for drugs that kill them. One may read these indictments or, for example, see the press release from the U.S. Attorney for the Southern District of New York on Oct. 24, 2005.

16 David E. Kaplan, "The New Business of Terror," *U.S. News & World Report*, Dec. 5, 2005. Kaplan is also coauthor of an admirable book on the Aum Shinrikyo terror cult.

17 *Turkishpress.com* reports that Mr. Salah has already been convicted of another charge, in a civil case over a Hamas shooting of American David Boim at a Jerusalem bus stop; see the dispatch from Chicago by AFP at http://archive.turkishpress.com/news.asp?id=147203 as well as the *Chicago Sun-Times* for Jan. 10, 2007 and the *Chicago Tribune* for Jan. 9, 2007.

18 *New York Times*, Jan. 23, 1997. See also the *Times'* Maureen Dowd's indulgent story on Mr. Feeney in the *International Herald Tribune*, Nov. 27, 1997. Feeney says he carefully monitored how the money was spent—on nonviolent activities. Yet money is fungible, and a donor might also argue that his own position is identical to that of the Clinton Administration: Sinn Fein (rather than IRA) merited support in the hope that the peace process would work.

IRA's interweaving of its Army Council and its politicians in Sinn Fein is one of the more successful "front" operations of modern times, as ch. 2 above suggests. Evidence for this includes the membership in both the political front and the Army Council of defector Sean O'Callaghan, who wrote a memoir *The Informer*, as well as such popular press articles as that in *National Review*, Jan. 27, 1997. Another example: One of the three IRA men who were reportedly teaching techniques to FARC in Colombia was Niall Connolly, the registered Sinn Fein representative in Havana of some years. The Dublin government is normally discrete about the Sinn Fein—IRA Provos reality, but in February 2005, Irish Justice Minister Michael McDowell flatly declared that Gerry Adams, Martin McGuinness, and Martin Ferris of Sinn Fein's leadership are also members of the 7-man Army Council. He was supported by Foreign Minister Dermot Ahern. This remarkable news was largely ignored; the *Washington Post* put the story back on p. 16 on Feb. 21, 2005.

19 Such Sinn Fein visits were widely reported in the American press and the "Irish republican" press, and in November 2006 I confirmed the White House traffic with a U.S. Ambassador who was involved.

20 Conversely, it is likely that the mainland Chinese government is very suspicious that such overseas émigrés may send money to the minority of Uigars—western Chinese Muslims— who are involved in political activism and campaigns of small bombings.

21 *New York Times*, March 18, 2001, speaking with a professor of Irish studies at Boston College.

22 Jack Holland, author of several books, has tracked two centuries of traffic from the U.S. East Coast across the Atlantic to Eire and Ulster; *The American Connection: U.S. Guns, Money, and Influence in Northern Ireland* (New York: Viking Penguin, 1987).

23 Compare the *New York Times* story on "Irish charm" seducing hundreds of thousands of dollars from American pockets, published just before terrorists destroyed the World Trade Center, and the *Wall Street Journal*'s article two weeks after that attack, called "Irish Nationalists May Feel U.S.'s Funding Squeeze." The article dates are March 18 and Sept. 27, 2001.

24 Somini Sengupta, "Canada's Tamils Work for a Homeland From Afar," *New York Times*, July 16, 2000.

25 The official Indian aid ended about 1991 when Rajiv Gandhi was assassinated by the LTTE. The Tigers' superb logistics network is discussed in the books of M. R. Narayan Swamy: *Tigers of Lanka: From Boys to Guerrillas* (Colombo: Vijitha Yapa Publications, 2004) and *Inside an Elusive Mind: Prabhakaran* (New Delhi: Konark Publishers, 2003). On the Lebanese terror organization's fund-raising in Canada, see the *Los Angeles Times*, March 2,9 1997 as well as post-9-11 literature.

26 A.P. story by Jeannine Aversa, Dec. 6, 2006, courtesy of Mr. Larry Cosgriff.

27 Blanca Madani, "Hezbollah's Global Finance Network: The Triple Frontier," *Middle East Intelligence Bulletin* 4: 1 (Jan. 2002).

28 French for "cross roads."

29 Press reports of the 1990s sourced to intelligence, and recent comments by an American observer of Kurdish militancy in Germany.

30 Sources for this inset include the LTTE websites www.eelam.com and www.ltteps.org; Daily News (Colombo), March 28, 1996, trans. FBIS June 5, 1996; the World Socialist Web site's April 2001 "First-Hand Report From LTTE-Controlled Territory in Sri Lanka;" the books of M. R. Narayan Swamy; and Richard H. Ward, *Extremist Groups: An International Compilation of Terrorist Organizations, Violent Political Groups, and Issue-Oriented Militant Movements*, 2nd. ed. (Huntsville, TX: Office of International Criminal Justice and the Institute for the Study of Violent Groups, Sam Houston State University, 2002). I have had the honor of working in the classroom with several first-rate Sri Lankan military officers, including Mohan De Zoysa of the Air Force.

31 The two organizations had the same headquarters in Muridke near Lahore Pakistan. *Washington Post*, Oct. 16, 2005 and June 7, 2006; "In the Spotlight: Lashkar-i-Taiba ("Army of the Pure"), CDI Terrorism Project, www.cdi.org/terrorism/lt-pr.cfm; and see the charity's own Web site: Jama'at-ud-Da'awah Pakistan, at http://jamatuddawa.org/Englsih2/index.htm

32 *Washington Times*, Aug. 26, 2006.

33 *New York Times*, May 1, 2002.

34 The 38-year-old reporter was in Pakistan, covering a terrorism story and seeking to interview Sheik Mubarak Ali Shah Gilani (or 'Jilani'), founding leader of Al Fuqra, meaning "The Impoverished." The sect has several dozen American cells, in New York, Virginia, Colorado, and the like, and it raises money and sends it to Pakistan. The State Attorney General for Colorado had a brief on the group posted on its Web site for many years: "Information Regarding Colorado's Investigation and Prosecution of Members of Jamaat ul Fukra," www.ago.state.co.us/Reports/fukra.stm Killings, assaults, or weapons violations have been attributed to certain al Fuqra members. However, the man convicted in abducting Pearl is a British Muslim, Ahmed Omar Sheikh.

35 *Washington Post*, Oct. 19, 2002.

36 Estimates of Matthew Levitt, a former Treasury officer, his work on Hamas' budget references figures from such sources as the FBI and the governments of Jordan and Israel; *Hamas: Politics, Charity, and Terrorism in the Service of Jihad* (New Haven, CN: Yale University Press, 2006), p. 54.

37 On the deportation of Abdel Jabber Hamdan—for involvement in Holy Land's fraud, filmed meetings with Hamas leaders, and the like—see the *New York Times*, Feb. 9, 2005.

38 *Wall Street Journal*, Dec. 5, 2001. The FBI said that Shukri Abu Baker, CEO of Holy Land, was identified by many witnesses as a member of Hamas. U.S. authorities also said a bank, Al Aqsa Bank, was the pawn of Hamas, and a U.S partner, Citibank, then cut off its business relations.

39 An illustration of the fungibility of money for Hamas was reported by newsman Joshua Mitnick. "Palestinians lined up outside of Gaza mosques Friday to hand over money and jewelry. Contributions ranged from hundreds of dollars to 22 cents, the value of one Israeli shekel. The A.P. reported that Hamas raised $3 million in the one-day campaign, but a fund-raising official from Gaza's Jabaliya refugee camp said the figure was half as much. Though many Gazans expressed hope that the money would go to Hamas' orphanages and schools, the Jabaliya fund-raiser—who called himself Abu Jankal—said the funds would go to Hamas' military wing." *Washington Times*, April 15, 2004.

40 A.P., May 26, 2005.

41 Anonymous [Rita Katz], *Terrorist Hunter* (New York: HarperCollins/Ecco, 2003), ch. 4.

42 Ibid. There were many reports on Sami al Arian when he was charged and more when he was convicted (on one charge, in 2006). Other stories mentioned him when discussing wider Islamist funding issues, e.g. in the Oct. 20, 2003 *Wall Street Journal*.

43 *New York Times*, Sept. 19, 2002.

44 Paul Henze, *The Plot to Kill the Pope* (New York: Charles Scribner's, 1983); Claire Sterling, *The Time of the Assassins* (New York: Holt, Rinehart, & Winston, 1983).

45 Patrick Seale, *Abu Nidal: A Gun for Hire: The Secret Life of the World's Most Notorious Arab Terrorist* (New York: Random House, 1992); see also *Insight* magazine, Jan. 21, 1991.

46 Our first edition (2000, ch. 3) called attention to the role of German and Low Country-towns and cities in the logistical operations of international terrorists. This became significant in the 9-11 investigations, which found the key cells operating from Hamburg and from Spain. Belgium also emerged (in some U.S. press) for its criminal networks providing false passports.

47 Steven Emerson, Executive Director of The Investigative Project, "Fund-Raising Methods and Procedures for International Terrorist Organizations," testimony before the House Committee on Financial Services, Subcommittee on Oversight and Investigations, Feb. 12, 2002, pp. 13–4.

48 Terrorists have their banking problems; honest people may have others: The banking principle of "interest" is awkward, within Islam and respect for the sharia. Special efforts have to be made by devout Muslims to comply with religious codes while banking; see for example the *New York Times* for Feb. 8, 2005, "Among Islamic Banks, A Shortage of Scholars."

49 President George W. Bush, speaking at Treasury, Nov. 7, 2001; Emerson testimony, ibid., p. 19.

50 Emerson, op. cit., p. 21. Citibank backed out fast when it discovered the Hamas scam.

51 Laurie Mylroie, a Washington-area resident with a Harvard Ph.D. and many publications, strives to remedy this analytical deficiency in contemporary terrorist studies and news reporting.

52 Defense Systems, Inc. study quoted by John W. Murphy, *State Support of International Terrorism* (Boulder, CO: Westview Press, 1989), pp. 31–3.

53 *New York Times*, Oct. 26, 2005.

54 A UN–supervised report was first completed as a draft Oct. 2005; apparently there have been further versions. The UN News Center supplies limited information on the contents of the report, but journalists have clearly examined it at length and reported on the connections of the plot to Syria. The second leading investigator met with Bashar al Asad on April 25, 2006 as part of his inquiries. Then-Secretary General Kofi Annan met with Asad in August 2006.

55 *Terrorism Today*, 1st ed., pp. 117–21.

56 *Estates of Michael Heiser, Millard Campbell, et. al, versus Islamic Republic of Iran*, et. al, U.S. District Court for the District of Columbia, decision of Dec. 22, 2006, Judge Royce C. Lamberth.

57 That headline is from the Dec. 7, 1985 edition of *Foreign Report*, once the best single English-language publication on terrorist operations. Today it is owned by Jane's Publications.

58 I am obliged to Major Robert Kaminski for relevant articles from *Jane's Intelligence Review*, Nov. 2006, and Andrew Exum's paper "Hezbollah at War: A Military Assessment," *Policy Focus 63* (Dec. 2006), from the Washington Institute for Near East Policy.

59 Ehud Goldwasser and Eldad Regev were seized July 12, 2006. Even Hezbollah's leader admitted by the end of August that this was the proximate cause of the war.

60 Estimates were offered by many, including Dr. Rachel Ehrenfeld, who continues to write on the subject regularly. However, generally discussion of the financial aid largely died away in the 1990s and did not return to the *mainstream* media until Hezbollah started war with Israel in July 2006. F. Michael Maloof's useful and unusual column on "more than $100 million" was done for News World Communications, Aug. 26, 2005.

61 Matthew Levitt, *Hamas*, ch. 7.

62 *Washington Post*, Oct. 27, 2005.

63 AP story in the *Washington Times*, Aug. 29, 2006.

64 One forthcoming source on this is by an intelligence expert and Korea specialist, Bruce Bechtol, *Red Rogue: The Persistent Challenge of North Korea* (Wash. D.C.: Potomac Books, July 2007); see esp. ch. 6.

65 Recent reports by Raphael Perl for the Congressional Research Service and a 2006 telephone interview with Mr. Perl. Bruce Bechtol reported to an international conference on Korean development (at the James A. Baker Institute for Public Policy at Rice University, November 2005) that illegal drug sale profits for North Korea total at least $500 million and possibly as much as three times that much, while counterfeiting profits run some $50 million.

66 It is startling how often Pyongyang's officials get arrested for black-marketeering. When I commented on seeing many incidents in the press of the 1980s, a U.S. colonel offered his own story of being on an embassy assignment in Denmark and seeing just such North Korean behavior there; Stanley G. Pratt, USMC, in Newport R.I., 1988 or 1989.

67 *Kyodo* (Tokyo) in English, March 28, 1996, trans. FBIS June 5, 1996.

68 U.S. Department of State, *Country Reports on Terrorism: 2005* (Washington, DC: GPO, 2006), p. 114.

69 Washington-based reporter Bill Gertz first broke this story in a book, according to the London *Times*. Then reports in that paper on Oct 9 and 10 prompted by Garland's arrest in Belfast were followed by new stories by Gertz in the *Washington Times* Oct. 11 and 12 and Dec. 2, 2005 and by Jay Soloman's story in the *Wall Street Journal*. Earlier arrests (Aug. 2005) had been made due to appearance of such counterfeit in Los Angeles and Newark areas.

   For another dimension of Irish militancy and smuggling, see "Terror International," in *The Weekly Telegraph* (London), May 5–6, 2002.

4

TECHNOLOGIES AND TACTICS

Introduction

Weapons of mass destruction are not the most proximate threat from terrorists. In our first edition, we resisted the trend—widespread in Washington and also in counterterrorism literature—of focusing on weapons of mass destruction (WMD). Instead, our argument was, and remains, a three-part proposition. Low-tech threats are the most proximate and acute; they continue to serve terror groups well. The high-tech WMD threats are important and of enormous consequence should any one of them be realized. However, they are difficult to arrange and handle, for terrorists. State aid might well be required, especially for a nuclear bomb, and only one or two states today might be so daring. The middle range, the "mid-tech threat," was deemed the most promising for terrorists. "A group with professional skills and a medium-grade conventional weapon"[1] could itself manage to inflict wide-scale economic destruction, political damage, or mass casualties.

In the unpredicted events of Sept. 11, 2001, conventional, mid-grade technology was hijacked for terrorist use. The novel Al Qaeda plot made a fresh twist in an old pattern stretching back several decades: devastating damage done by rather conventional instruments. Most deaths, in point of fact, have come from wrecking air liners and from explosives. The latter are often of banal types, such as TNT, or even homemade concoctions involving fertilizer. It was fertilizer mix that "pancaked" the seven-floor federal building in Oklahoma City in 1995 and blew apart a section of Manchester in 1996. The New York World Trade Towers were attacked the first time with a bomb stirred together in a warehouse, and then terrorists plotted to collapse New York traffic tunnels with a chemical home brew. The el-Ghriba Tunisia synagogue explosion of April 2002 was done with a truckload of natural gas, which burned alive local Jews and also a dozen visiting German tourists.[2]

The low-tech threats

On December 8, 2005 two bicyclists peddled along the street in Netrokona, Bangladesh, strapped up with bombs. They rode into a crowd; one detonated, killing six and wounding dozens.[4] Theirs were personal contributions to a growing campaign of that year to unsettle the Asian democracy with small bombs. They arrived in a way that is

Box 4.1 Children of the "Army of the Lord"

The "Lord's Resistance Army" in Uganda is a living display of at least four characteristics of contemporary terrorism: (1) a mix of fanaticism, religion, and politics;
(2) practice of torture and murder to create a wider state of fear; (3) the "child
warrior," that simplest of weapons; and (4) the political-military organizational
form called *the militia*.

Uganda, tyrannized through the 1970s by Idi Amin, now has a more acceptable
government under President Yoweri Museveni. Though moderate, it is not strong,
and in the gaps between the capital and the countryside, or between governance
and anarchy, armed and privately directed organizations may appear. In Uganda's
case, the most destructive militia today is the Lord's Resistance Army.

A self-described voodoo priestess named Alice Lakwena initiated the organization
under the banner of the "Holy Spirit Movement." Her theology, as described
by an interviewer, is a "mish-mash of traditional beliefs and her own take on
fundamentalist Christianity." She told her young followers of the 1980s that they'd
be invulnerable in battle and led them into "holy war" against the Ugandan army.
They were crushed; she escaped into Kenya and still lives there in a refugee
camp.

Lakwena's nephew, another autocratic and self-described supernatural, Joseph
Kony, assumed control and renamed the effort the LRA. It has astonished
observers and opponents with its range of abuses of civilians—normally it avoids
engagements with the Ugandan army. Murder and torture are common inflictions
on the areas it can reach. To take one case among many, a village was attacked;
adults were forced to be porters to carry their own goods out into the bush; then
these same villagers were executed by LRA. Mutilation is a common LRA tactic
to terrify. Also, the thousands of killed, wounded, or tortured include World Food
Program volunteers.

Though the problem of "child warriors" is common in Africa, Latin America, and
Asia, the Lord's Resistance Army is an archetype. As many as 20,000 children
have been kidnapped by this group over the last two decades. Most personnel
are in fact young, stolen from their homes and villages, propagandized, and
treated as property. Some are forced to kill others, to "blood" them and make it
unlikely they would ever return home. Boys are made into undertrained guerrilla
fighters, or porters. Girls are usually sex slaves, cooks, or designated "wives" for
the male leaders.

Kony's militia aspires to hold power (at some level) within Uganda, to champion its
own ethnic group, the Acholi people, as against the government in Kampala and
perhaps to overthrow the national regime. Alice Lakwena declares her aspiration

to return to Uganda from exile. In the meantime, most of their victims are Acholi, and most of the killings are done with remarkably simple personal weapons.

Joseph Kony and four commanders were indicted in October 2005 by the International Criminal court at The Hague.[3] LRA leaders are also engaged in negotiations with international intermediaries.

remarkably common in contemporary terrorism and yet usually goes without remark: on a bicycle. Frequently these are armed attacks. The shooters track their victim carefully or coordinate with others who help; once they have fired, they might quickly escape. U.S. citizens Jaime Raul and Jorge A. Orjuela were murdered in this way by gunmen riding a motorcycle in Cali, Colombia. An authority on the Tamil Tigers of Sri Lanka has noted that this assassination method has been a standard in use by killers from LTTE.[5] The approach on bicycle from behind can be perfectly stealthy; an approach from the front permits better identification of the victim. Either way, in a sluggish sea of wide four-wheeled vehicles, the killers often slip between them to escape.

The trusty and cheap two-wheeler is equally useful for transport of a bomb. A week after the combination attack by cyclists in Bangladesh, a bomb detonated alongside the Economics Ministry, near parliament, in Athens, Greece. It caused extensive damage. The bomb arrived aboard a motorcycle, which was left leaning up against the building.[6] Recent years have seen many variants on such bombings via bicycle, moped, and motorcycle. They have come in India and Pakistan and in Europe. One of the most politically significant attacks in recent French history was a small bomb carried in the side bag of a two-wheeler, left leaned up against a building, where it detonated. This was all that was technically required for attacking the Rue Copernic synagogue in Paris in 1980, but the political effects were enormous and ugly, and some analysts wrongly imagined that they had seen the beginning of a whole new era of neo-fascism in Europe.[7]

Small bombs remain a staple of terror attacks worldwide. They can be simple to build, and for the uninitiated, technical advice abounds on the Internet or books and pamphlets and magazines. High-school children may learn to make them as quickly as adults. For example, in the state of Maryland, dozens of pipe bombs and other incendiaries are recovered, or detonated, every year. The American "Unabomber," Theodore Kaczynski, overcommitted to environmentalism, relied on not only simple parts but wooden boxes to house his "infernal machines" (as nineteenth-century writers described bombs). All the political force of a thousand pamphlets is imagined to be contained in the black powder of a modest bomb. Bombs guarantee attention—even when they do not ignite. The further advantage of the small bomb is how quickly it may be replicated for cross-city or cross-country campaigns. Many terror groups are enamored with carrying out a range of attacks, at once or in succession, to harass, broaden the ripples of palpable fear, and prove that they cannot be dismissed as a mere crank individual. Groups prove they are more than that by "demonstration" bombings involving multiple small devices. This was done by Puerto Rican terrorists on the island in the 1980s, and by Corsicans on their island in the 1990s. Their numbers for a single day's work have been eclipsed by

Muslim extremists in Bangladesh, who on August 17, 2005 detonated several hundred bombs. "Only" two people died amid all the noise; clearly it was publicity that was the terrorists' goal. These terrorists were after immediate and public effects that the Anarchists of nineteenth-century Europe and Russia would instantly recognize.

The scores of attacks intensified Bangladeshi police activity and, by December 2005, they had collected an instructive display of what a terror organization might use to make production-line, modest bombs intended to maim and bleed their victims. Supplies found included ammonium nitrate; gunpowder; wire of many sorts; lead; electric circuits and fuses; batteries; iron balls; bombs; soldering machines; scales; wristwatches; and nearly 5,000 electric detonators. Dhaka's *Daily Star* reported with satisfaction these recoveries from the "hornet's nests" and noted the collection of a thousand books on jihad, as well as CDs and press clippings on militancy. The arrests focused on personnel of Jama'at ul Mujahideen Bangladesh, most importantly Ataur Rahman or "Sunny," the alleged number 2 figure and military commander.[8]

On the same December day in 2005 on which suicide bicyclists attacked a crowd in Bangladesh, a Palestinian stabbed an Israeli in the West Bank of the Jordon River. His personal weapon, in this obscure incident of terrorism, was the knife. The knife was in fact the preferred weapon of the famous Shiite "Assassins" of the eleventh through thirteenth centuries: They wanted to get close to the enemy and be certain of his identity and his death; they did not care to escape. So too was the knife a preferred weapon of Hamas when that new group began attacks at the end of 1987. Hamas would graduate into explosives and later expand the use of the suicide bombing within the Middle East, but the allure and power of the knife remain. The terrible swath that it ripped in a human being's throat was coldly called 'Le Grand Sourire', or the big smile, by Algerians who saw it left by National Liberation Front killers during their war to expel France. The tactic returned to that country in a new round of bloodshed in the 1990s, when fundamentalists Islamicists of FIS and GIA terrorizing villagers in rural areas made near-civil war with security forces. The knife was the weapon that the Sunni "Army of Jhangui" (LeJ)[9] used in the videotaped decapitation of reporter Daniel Pearl in February 2002. That "model" act came into wide use in Iraq in 2003 and 2004, where terrorists also make electronic copies of the film of the beheadings for sale at low prices to the public.[10]

Such beheadings seem intended to touch on a tradition of rendering justice with the sword, or invoke certain Koranic passages, or suggest the practice of sacrificing animals. Such conclusions imply deliberation and explicit terrorism; such conclusions are resisted by many experts on Islam; yet, these intellectual and psychological implications do occur to those seeing the photographs. References to sword, Koran, and animal sacrifice are forcefully brought to the attentions of any who actually read the screed giving last-minute advice to the 9-11 hijackers. "The Last Night" is a stunning document of some four pages invoking mental preparation for taking over the aircraft, prayers of diverse kinds, and anticipation of heaven with its beautiful women and other companions. Three passages compare the coming action (by the "muscle men" with their box cutters) to a holy sacrifice of animals with a knife (e.g., "God said: 'Strike above the neck, and strike at all of their extremities'").[11] These sentences also dissuade the men from causing unnecessary pain to the victim—an illustration of the perverse moralism often evident in terrorist declarations and communications. It seems apparent that this new emphasis on beheadings among terrorists in S.W. Asia and the Middle East has effectively combined four things: the simplest of weapons, the ubiquitous video camera[12] and World Wide Web, and the most complex sorts of psychological and political effects as desired by the terrorists.

The lowliest and most un-innovative attack of modern terrorism is surely the simple shooting. These attacks have the advantages of being swift, discriminate, often very lethal, and remarkably inexpensive. Filipino New People's Army "Sparrows" perfected the art of shooting a policeman once or twice from behind and then taking his revolver before disappearing by foot into the street crowds. The gunman thus collected a victim and a well-maintained, loaded firearm all within seconds.[13] Shootings for explicit political purposes take place each week, if not more often, somewhere in the world. Sometimes, especially in Iraq today, terrorists use security force uniforms—to be able to get close to their intended victims. The illegal gunmen may also ride, if that is more convenient, as Sri Lankan LTTE "Tigers" often do, on bicycle. Where cars are more available or convenient, they suffice as well. In an all-too-technically easy case that long bedeviled the Saudi police, a recruiter for militant Islamic groups named Mohammed Abdel-Rahman Muhammad al-Suwailmi managed to shoot five policemen from his car in drive-by attacks. He was eventually caught at the end of 2005.[14] The next obvious upgrade has arrived: In November 2006, the military in Iraq found some forty automobiles modified to allow snipers to fire unseen from within the trunk. This devilishly simple and effective method had for many terrible weeks during 2002 protected a two-man team of Washington, DC area sniper-murderers.[15]

One of the only things cheaper than a few bullets is a match; there is as well the plastic pocket lighter. With good cause, the ancient Chinese theorist Sun Tzu devoted one of his chapters in the short book, *The Art of War*, to fire and its grave potential for war. Ancient history in the West is similarly rich with illustrations of how fire can be used to dazzle, disorient, damage, or destroy—all of which may be among the purposes of today's terrorists. A skilled arsonist often escapes manhunts for years; an unskilled or uncaring one may strike with far less preparation and equipment than can most attackers in terrorism or war. During 2005, the absolute monarchy in Swaziland, with its southern African population of 1.2 million, was shaken by a firebombing campaign. Blamed on a small opposition "Democratic Movement," the gasoline and pipe bombs have struck the homes of government officials, police, and government offices.[16] Every chart of terrorist incidents and methods, year on year and around the globe, reserves a bold column or two for tracking the tactics of arson and firebombing.

Ecoterrorism remains a high-level problem in England, the United States and other countries, and the most common attacks on U.S. properties are with fire. Meat packing plants, refrigerated trucks, buildings attached to industrial-style farms, and other assets have been burned frequently in the United States. The perpetrators are brazen. Theodore Kaczynski, haunted by a desire to live amid "wild nature," explained in a 35,000 word manifesto why he felt compelled to kill. Most of his successors in the American ecological movement do not kill and would not kill, but some of them do burn property. With Unabomber-like diligence, their acts are chronicled by unknown hands at Web sites maintained by such groups as the Earth Liberation Front and People for the Ethical Treatment of Animals. Their strategy is political, psychological, and economic; their

Box 4.2 Death tallies of "low intensity conflicts"

The figures below reflect selected conflicts and estimated totals for all deaths from all political causes (not only terrorism) for a given recent period, with a comment on trends or status in late 2006.

Afghanistan	7,000	2004–2006	sharply escalating terrorism and insurgency as Taliban drives to reclaim national power
Algeria	150,000	since 1992	abated notably after 1999 accords with some parties; only scattered fighting and terrorism in 2005 and 2006
Bangladesh	600	after 2001	several impressive recent arrests are unlikely to top the Islamicist movement
Basque lands	1,000	since 1968	arrests and political weakness led to unilateral cease-fire by ETA in 2006
Colombia	63,000	since 1963	the Western Hemisphere's worst insurgencies, but matched by a stronger state
Chechnya	15,000	since 1999	following several bad years, 1994–1996, much quieter
Corsica	100+	since 1975	recent years are quiet ones
Darfur-Sudan	200,000	2003–05	only Janjaweed militias engaging in genocide
India	23,000	2000–04 only	terrorism deaths only; does not fully reflect all of India's ongoing insurgencies
Iraq	30,000	2003–05 only	civilian dead, after Saddam's removal; currently high rates of killing
Kashmir	67,000	unclear	also the cause of much violence outside Kashmir
Kurdish insurgency	40,000	since 1984	a five-year cease fire ended June 2004, so violence has returned in Turkey
Pakistan	1,200	2002–04 only	appears to exclude Waziristan campaign with its military and civilian losses as well as violence since 2004 in Balouchistan

Palestine	4,000	2000–05 only	excludes the 2006 war
Philippines	15,000+	since 1968	mixed status and some peace talks (separatist, South)
Philippines	40,000	since 1969	a spate of acts after peace talks collapsed (NPA insurg.) in 2004; but now mostly quiet
Nepal	13,000	since 1996	Maoist insurgency in a strategic pause in 2007
Sri Lanka	69,000	since 1975	LTTE called off cease-fire of Feb.2002; more than 1,000 dead in 2006 alone.
Thailand	2,000	after 2003	Malay-Muslim insurgency, southern provinces
Uganda	200,000	since 1987	21 violent deaths a day in Acholi area of the North.

means include modest implements to start or accelerate fire. Such methods serve as well for ambitious anticapitalists and anti-imperialists who attack foreign companies on their home soil. These actions alienate no one with bloodshed; they are simple to effect; they can easily be accompanied by a claim to a news agency, guaranteeing credit. In the Western Hemisphere, the most common site for arson may well be Colombia, where the ELN and FARC routinely burn oil installations and related targets. In other parts of Latin America, arson was once common at U.S.-owned sites; that problem has dwindled with the strength of the Marxist-Leninist groups in those countries.

The mid-tech threat

The second major level of threat—less common than the first but also markedly more dangerous—is attack by a group, small or large, with professional skills or weapons of medium-tech quality or power, or all of these attributes.

Bombs, for instance, are not always a low-tech weapon; they have also been built and used at advanced levels of sophistication by certain skilled terror organizations. The IRA Provos are among those with dedicated master bomb makers in their ranks. After mastering the art of homemade mortars, used often in attacks in the United Kingdom, they apparently went to Colombia to teach this black art to FARC. A number of Irish suspects have been seen or arrested there. FARC already possessed great skill at using propane gas tanks—of cooking size for homemakers—as the basis for bombs slung into military bases or civilian targets, with considerable results. No doubt there is a forthcoming new technique in airplane bombing, as the combination of plastique and altimeter fusing has been too well known to security personnel for several decades. One prospect was suggested by the year 2006 scare over flights originating in Britain, with their ugly prospect of self-proclaimed "jihadis" smuggling aboard separate chemicals to be combined into an explosive mix at the crime scene in the air.

In Baghdad, in 2004, military-style "shaped charges" were introduced and joined the other forms of street fighting and urban warfare. Some British and American intelligence sources declared that Iran is providing these weapons. The bomb's force on detonation is directed instead of dispersed in 360 degrees. On one day, for example, a shaped charge was brought down a highway hidden on a bicycle, and pedaled into a place often patrolled by military convoys. An alert U.S. Marine warned over radio that the rider of the bike suddenly disappeared, so following Marines in an armored personnel carrier made a wide berth around it. However, somewhere close by, a waiting triggerman moved his finger on a detonator at the right moment, and the explosion reached across the highway to the deviating vehicle and penetrated its considerable side armor.[17] This shaped charge "upgrade" has counterparts in a half-dozen new varieties of detonators for old-style explosives. Bombs in Iraq and elsewhere today may be set off by things as simple as an egg timer or a rigged wrist watch but as innovative as a garage-door opener, a car door opener, a cell phone, pager, electric eye, infrared beams, or radio signal.[18]

The many contemporary variants on the act of bombing include both tactical and technical innovations. The bomb's central place in grim forms of political influence fighting is presently underscored by two strong new patterns, fresh developments with little to no parallel in the widespread terrorism of the 1970s or the Anarchist attacks of a century ago. One is the suicide bomb. The other is double-bombings.

Today's sophisticated suicide bomb's origins may lie in a very-low-tech phenomenon of Khomeini's Iran. It was in a desperate war with Iraq when the methods of psychological shock and suicide appeared to offer salvation. At least 10,000 children were rushed into various battles, some into the forefront of infantry attacks, and some into mine fields where they were human mine detectors. A survivor of this bizarre military "campaign" describes actions the children took: "Because donkeys are too stubborn to do it....We fought by throwing ourselves in front of the tanks, by leaping on the mines, by taking on the enemy with a stick or a rifle. We tried and tried, but we didn't become martyrs." Initially, the Iranian children were given many weeks of training; this dwindled for a coldly logical reason: Commanders saw that elaborate training would be wasted, as few would survive contact with Iraqi lines. Initially the children were given metal keys to wear around the neck, symbolic keys to paradise; later the keys would be made of plastic. A German journalist writing a history of the suicide bomb notes how Tehran publicized these practices of using children and portrayed their deaths without embarrassment.[19]

Such mass suicides soon gave way to real terrorist accomplishment with the vehicle bomb. This required but one "friendly" death, yet it can yield hundreds of "enemy" casualties. In Lebanon, these vehicle bombs arrived driven by men of Hezbollah, Iran's fierce and talented Shia proxy force. In Lebanon and Kuwait, embassies and military barracks of France and the United States collapsed before Hezbollah's precision attacks using suicides driving vehicle bombs. After 1983, there were others. It was a car bomb that murdered 23 Lebanese, including a former prime minister, when his convoy passed through a Beirut street in February 2005, and then it was a car bomb that murdered a newspaper editor in that city ten months later. Both targets were Lebanese men who had strongly criticized the Syrian occupation of their country.[20] Reports suggest both bombs may have been made in Syria or by Syrians. That was also the case with the truck bomb that Hezbollah drove into the U.S. barracks in Beirut in 1983.

Gradually the practice of suicide bombing (on foot, on a bicycle, or in a vehicle) emigrated to the Palestinians. Hamas required much deliberation and specific clerical decrees to allow adherents to kill themselves. The Koran's injunctions against destroying one's own life had to be separated decisively from its praise for dying while in righteous attack, and much has emerged about these internal debates. Secular Palestinian groups were initially reluctant to permit suicide bombings by their cadres, but they came to see too many headlines stolen away by more religious rivals. Yasser Arafat's Fatah self-consciously and deliberately opened a new wing, the Al Aqsa Martyrs Brigade, to recruit and manage those who would commit mass homicide and die in the act. The important fact about contemporary Palestinian terrorism is that it is operationally sophisticated. There is an elaborate method of recruitment and indoctrination, frequently, and then, in the attack, the individual-victim is often "supported" by one or more back-up triggermen. In short, there is one bomb but redundant systems for detonating it. This was also true in the 2002 Bali attack.[21]

Secularly motivated suicide attacks—rather than religious—have been influential in Sri Lanka. Velupillai Prabhakaran has led his LTTE Tiger organization since 1976. He might have come to the suicide attack concept by watching the news later from the Middle East. There was the LTTE tradition of wearing a cyanide capsule around the neck in battle with the expectation that it must be bitten if capture loomed. However, suicide attacks are very different, and the date of the LTTE's first is much celebrated in the movement as July 5, 1987. Thus LTTE followed Hezbollah. After the introduction of such tactics came the development of special units dedicated to self-destroying attacks, normally against military targets, such as Sri Lankan army or navy units.[22] The ideology of Marxism-Leninism, with a mix of nationalism, sufficed as intellectual grounding for these very dedicated personnel. A powerful 1998 movie produced in India, Santosh Sivan's "The Terrorist," suggests the training and psychological preparation undergone by willing cadre. They are isolated, indoctrinated, and given special favors, including a "last night" banquet with Prabhakaran himself. Then, as in the Middle East, they attain heroic status and literally become icons, the stuff of pride and posters, legends and leaflets.

The Sri Lankan navy has repeatedly been attacked by such suicide commandos, beginning in 1984. The attacks often succeed—showing how a combination of human will power and modest, mid-grade technologies may cripple or sink a modern warship.[23] A recent academic paper by a Sri Lankan naval officer[24] details the several specific types of Tamil craft the Tigers have made for taking on the government navy, and nearly all are for suicide attacks. LTTE has a special breaching craft, for example, designed to blow a hole in the hull of a Navy ship so that a second Tiger boat can pass through it immediately and cause a second blast within, killing sailors and perhaps sinking the ship. To succeed with such attacks requires the most careful preparation and, in the attack, flexibility and luck; thus, the missions are unusual and entrusted only to the elite. The LTTE thus successfully blends classic terrorism with classic guerilla warfare. In older times, for a military man, the euphemism "suicide mission" usually meant "exceedingly dangerous" but involved no desire to die; among the special squads of the LTTE, the phrase must be taken with new literalness. Suicide operations rely on a full range of actors: motivated individuals, small special units of naval, air or ground capabilities, and larger, more conventional combat forces. As part of this long effort, there were 168 suicide attacks before the year 2000 by LTTE. These killed more than 500 people in Sri Lanka and wounded thousands more. With these and other efforts, LTTE has fought the Sri Lankan government and armed forces to a standstill. The revolutionaries' leaders see their success, and it is yielding opportunities to bargain with the state of Sri Lanka. So they steer their activities more toward diplomacy. In such moments, suicide bombings and other attacks decline.[25]

Scholars and journalists are giving lavish attention to suicide bombings—another testament to the strategic success of this tactic. Familiar for several decades, it seems to be growing in use, not dwindling. There were 411 suicide car bombings in Iraq in 2005 alone,[26] but little attention is paid to the other development in terrorist bombings. Indeed, there is no settled name for the newest tactic. Scattered police or media reports use terms such as *staggered explosions* or *dual bombs*; *secondary device* is the most common. It is apparent, from repeated use, that the double-bombing is now well understood within the terrorist underground. It remains to be better planned for, and adapted to, by the victimized states, armies, emergency medical teams, and first responders.

IRA Provisionals may well have initiated the pattern, against British "Paras" at Narrow Water Castle near Warrenpoint in Ulster. Plotting took place on two tracks. As the Provos planned their first strike—via a bomb buried in a roadway—they made their best judgment of the likely British response and arranged to strike as well at that point where they expected other Paras to arrive. On August 27, 1979, the IRA bomb detonated under a passing convoy. When a Wessex helicopter bearing reinforcements arrived nearby, the second bomb detonated just there. Much later, the Provos used the same method, this time in an October 1996 strike against Thiepval Barracks in Lisburn. The targets were no longer only military. Two car bombs were brought onto a base used by Northern Ireland and Britain. The first car was blown up near a center for travel arrangements, wounding many civilians. As they were rushed away in a predictable direction to the base hospital, a second car bomb was waiting and blew up there. Some victims were literally thus bombed twice within minutes. Medical staff responding to the bloodshed of the first crisis were suddenly half-buried in the rubble that had been their clinic.[27]

In America, right-wing terrorist Eric Rudolph may have been among those paying attention. Certainly he soon made two attempts at double-bombings. In the first days of 1997, Rudolph's conviction that "Abortion is murder" brought him to blow up a family planning clinic in Atlanta, Georgia. Although no one died, the medical personnel, fire crew, and police who were first to respond were hit in the parking lot by a second hidden bomb, 45 minutes after the first. Five weeks later, Rudolph turned his moral distastes on an alternative-lifestyle nightclub, also in Atlanta. Again he combined dynamite and nails and steel plates to direct the blast—an "antipersonnel" weapon, but there, only the first half of his attack plan worked; police discovered the hidden secondary device.[28]

Double-bombings[29] require careful tactical planning, not elaborate technology. They were certainly not the invention of al Qaeda, although the organization likes them just as much as it does synchronized attacks at different locales. The devastating Bali Indonesia attacks of October 12, 2002 were managed by Jamaah Islamiya, a Bin Laden sub-set. The first detonation was minor by al Qaeda standards, but the blast was designed to drive bar patrons out into the street, where the "real" bomb awaited. There, packed into a large vehicle, was a full ton of explosives. Some two hundred died that day. As is usually the case, the victims included the unintended; a perpetrator named Mukhlas paused in his gloating over the carnage to confess that "I sought Allah's forgiveness because apparently there were some victims from the Muslim side."[30]

The Middle East's legacy of double-bombings may go back to Hezbollah practices of the 1980s, but it clearly is imbued into the Iraqi insurgents and terrorists of the present. In April 2005, there was a highly coordinated, three-phase attack in the town of Madain. Police investigating a first bomb were attacked by two suicides arriving from different directions. A day that August saw two bombs, ten minutes apart, at a Baghdad bus station. These explosions yielded many victims who, as at Lisburn in 1996, were rushed to the obvious place, the closest hospital. However, a third bomber awaited them there and blew up his vehicle, injuring many arriving in ambulances or awaiting help. Demoralization in the capital that day was one result; another was more than 100 dead and wounded souls. And, as 2005 moved to its close and national elections approached, the pattern came into play again, a week into December. There was a suicide attack on an Iraqi police academy. Survivors fled that scene for the shelter of blast walls nearby, but a second suicide ran along with them. Once the second terrorist had enough people around him in the refuge, he pressed his own trigger. The extreme lethality of such attacks was brought home to Iraqis—some thirty died, and another fifty were wounded. The technology behind such bombings is simple enough, but the lethality of such tactics is frankly devastating.[31]

9-11-01 was a complex attack that took several years to prepare and was stunningly successful and damaging. Yet it involved nothing commonly thought of, or previously designated, a "weapon of mass destruction." Indeed, its genius was in use of everyday things, owned and paid for by the future victims. There has been intense curiosity about whether anyone foresaw terrorists using commercial airliners as weapons of attack on U.S. strategic targets. The answer is both yes and no. On the one hand, prior to 9-11, there was apparently no one in a top political or law enforcement position in the United States who expected, or thought government must plan for, such usage of air carriers, civilian or military. The oversight, or lack of imagination, extended even to analysts and speculators in terrorism studies. They might conceive of it, but they did not expect it or warn of it publicly. On the other hand, hindsight indicates that by July 10, 2001, the date of agent Kenneth Williams' "Phoenix memo,"[32] the FBI at a low level was alert to the purposeful activity associated with the plan. The Bureau—and especially the Federal Aviation Administration, which has strangely escaped public irritation—should have taken steps that could thwart the prospect. Two that would have helped greatly and had been discussed for years were adding air marshals to flights and strengthening cockpit doors.

Those in public service in the national security reading message traffic in 2000 and 2001 knew, or should have known, about two major terrorist operations. The first was nearly realized, yet went largely ignored in America. In December of 1994, Algerians of the Armed Islamic Group seized an Air France plane in the air and brought it down in Marseilles, where they refueled and placed explosives in the cockpit. They apparently planned either to fly the jet into the Eiffel Tower or blow it up over "The City of Light," showering Paris with the embers of their "propaganda of the deed." The second prelude to 9-11 was "Operation Bojinka," a plan of Ramzi Youssef to use Muslim militants to simultaneously bomb eleven airliners over the Pacific. A partner to Youssef, Abdul Hakim Murad, reportedly told Philippine authorities he and Youssef discussed crashing a hijacked airliner into the CIA headquarters in Langley, Virginia. Unlike the GIA's actions, this was not attempted and did not even become public knowledge at the time. Finally, many years separated this pair of plots with 2001, but Bin Laden's organization would have known both incidents well and was connected to both groups of terrorists involved in these plots of the mid-1990s.

In the run-up to 9-11, most of the warnings by intelligence agencies (later exhumed by the 9-11 Commission and others) were limited or sketchy or from sources deemed unreliable. And some were foolishly ignored. Yet even the famous CIA warning in the daily intelligence summary of August 6, 2001, a document the Bush administration defended against release for some weeks before yielding, did *not* warn of an Al Qaeda plot to use an airliner as a bomb. It warned of Al Qaeda desires to attack inside the United States and it referred to an unconfirmed report that Al Qaeda may want to hijack an airliner. Here came a failure of imagination: The memo's authors said they expected, in accord with past practice, that such a hijacking would be used to lever from maximum security prison a desired comrade or leader—in this case Sheik Omar Abdel Rahman, spiritual head of the group that bombed the New York World Trade Center in 1993.

So, it was left to a few thoughtful "amateurs" to actually put words on paper that this tactic would work. A 1994 Tom Clancy novel, *Debt of Honor*,[33] was revisited often after the 9-11-01 attacks: The story has a Japanese rightist with a Samurai sword overtaking an airliner and crashing it into the U.S. Capitol during a joint session of Congress. More relevant was the admirable report of 1999 by Rex Hudson and the federal government's Congressional Research Service. Amid a general exploration of the question "Who Becomes A Terrorist and Why?" the report used a few spare lines to suggest dreadful options, including: "Suicide bomber(s) belonging to Al Qaeda's Martyrdom Battalion could crash-land an aircraft packed with high explosives (C-4 and Semtex) into the Pentagon, the headquarters of the Central Intelligence Agency (CIA), or the White House."[34]

After airliners—filled with gasoline and passengers—there are other mid-tech threats richly deserving attention. Not all have seen exploitation in recent years. These include hang gliders and ultralight aircraft. The former, especially, were for some years a central interest of the Popular Front for the Liberation of Palestine-General Command, the Ahmad Jibril faction that is still conducting operations today. Several attacks of decades past were only partially successful, although Jibril and his crew remain operative. The success of 9-11 can only have inspired other terrorists, such as the LTTE Tigers, to think anew about small aircraft as well as large.

Of remaining mid-tech threats, the most pressing is certainly the shoulder-fired missile, as readers of our first edition well recall. Militaries around the world have produced these—best known by the acronym MANPADS, for man-portable air defense system. The existence of some 500,000 such weapons testifies to their utility. They are light, portable, and easily hidden in a golf bag or a car trunk or behind a false panel in a ship or a house, and the like. Cost estimates for obtaining such a missile vary wildly from $5,000 to $100,000[35] but, given their desirability, even the higher figure would not be a serious bar to most well-entrenched terror organizations. And the states that make them and could supply them through secret services or through criminals with access to martial supplies include Pakistan, China, and North Korea. Nor are U.S. terrorists to be forgotten, for in past years many military weapons have been stolen or black-marketed and thus leaked into civilian hands. The weapons are not simple to operate, but Milt Beardon, in Afghanistan with the CIA when the agency was handing out Stingers to Afghan mujahideen fighting the Soviet Air Force, asserts that the basics of the weapon can be mastered in a few lessons.

Given the terrific backlash against those in authority for not foreseeing the 9-11 tragedy, the complacency about defending airliners against this other threat must be noted.[36] Officers serving in Iraq report that SAMS are often fired at airliners and transports leaving or arriving at Baghdad airport.[37] And the U.S. State Department published a September 2005 report that, worldwide and to date, twenty-four civilian aircraft had already been downed by MANPADS. Yet in that very month, with the new report just out, a commercial airlines spokesman rose at a Washington policy forum to say that America would be making a "multi-billion dollar mistake" to push forward with deployment of defenses. He did not insist that currently available technologies would fail; he argued on grounds of (1) high costs, (2) profiteering defense contractors' distortions of fact, and (3) the existence of other threats to air travel, and then insisted that (4) nearly all the past attacks had been in war zones or had failed.[38] A subsequent interview with an airline pilot and national security specialist confirmed that commercial airlines executives are indeed seated comfortably in this rhetorical position. They are defending the status quo, which is well short of defending their passengers.

Reports in Jane's defense publications—leaders in their technical fields—support the State Department's concerns and those of independent analysts,[39] fully justifying strong concern that terrorists do own and will attempt to use shoulder-fired missiles to explode civilian air liners. Two dozen groups have been reported to have or seek such missiles, including Hezbollah, the Kosovo Liberation Army, and FARC in Colombia. The FBI has repeatedly "busted" purchasers in the United States associated with terror groups. Some perpetrators were helping the IRA Provos. A January 2005 "sting" captured sellers in Nicaragua—given Soviet SA-7s during the Sandinista years—with buyers who pretended to be Colombian terrorists. That later became especially interesting in light of the November 2006 electoral victory of the Sandinistas' Daniel Ortega to the presidency. An August 2003 case linked an eager arms dealer with a Russian SA-7, St. Petersburg Russia, New Jersey, and the "buyer"—an officer posing as a Muslim extremist.[40] Media reports have begun emerging, alerting anyone who did not know of the public fear factors surrounding this weapon and making it all the more desirable to terrorists.

Aircraft over Russia, South West Asia, and Africa have not always been lucky. The military losses have been the most numerous, of course. In May 1997, the Kurdistan Workers' Party operators in northern Iraqi borderlands downed two Turkish helicopters with SA-7s, although no one was killed. Now, in the ongoing war in Iraq, insurgents have at least twice struck U.S. aircraft with missiles. Chechen rebels have repeatedly used Soviet-made missiles and others to attack Russian aircraft, downing a helicopter in August 2003 and several jets in 2000. A photo on the State Department's website shows Chechens displaying three different types of MANPADS.[41] The Tamil Tigers of LTTE have Indian training in use of MANPADS and have owned such weapons since 1994; they are acquired through the Tamils' sophisticated naval logistics force. One SAM consignment reached them from Cambodia via Thailand. Not only do the Tigers boast of their missiles, they have used them successfully, as in destroying a helicopter near Trincomalee Harbor in October 2000, a transport aircraft (An-26) that March, and other aircraft in 1996.[42] LTTE buyers were caught trying to acquire SAMS in the United States. in 2006.

Other attacks have been made on civilian aircraft. The first cases may have been a pair of attacks with Soviet-supplied ground-to-air missiles in southern Africa in the late 1970s. It appears that Air Rhodesia flight RH825 was downed with a Sam 7 on September 3, 1978, and then "ZIPRA" terrorists arrived at the crash site to shoot down surviving passengers, so that ten more died there. Then on March 3, 1979, flight RH827 was attacked. A witness saw a flare fired from the ground, which was later taken to be a ZIPRA signal to another such cell; the latter then fired a missile, causing the crash of a second aircraft, this time killing all fifty-nine aboard. A memorial was laid for the dead in 1998. UNITA rebels in Angola downed several United Nations planes at the end of the 1990s. The Democratic Republic of the Congo lost a Boeing 727 over national territory in 1998.[43]

The most recent attempt to get a commercial airliner in Africa failed. Arkia Airlines, an Israeli charter firm, flies frequently to Mombassa, Kenya, a seaside city. It was there that Al Qaeda carried out its first direct and coordinated assaults on citizens of the Jewish state, on November 28, 2002. A suicide vehicle was driven into a major hotel at a resort, demolishing the large structure accommodating many from Israel and killing twelve people. The murderers had counterparts; the other team included at least one Pakistani and one Somali, who would be captured at the scene, as would their weapon. They drove to the airport perimeter in a Mitsubishi automobile and used a Russian-made Strela missile tube. Five minutes after the explosions at the hotel, these men fired two missiles at departing flight 582 lifting off from Mombassa for Tel Aviv. A veteran pilot felt a "bump"; a passenger further back heard an explosion and saw a smoke trail by the blinking light on the tip of the left wing. All 272 people aboard escaped uninjured.[44] The tube was later found at the scene.

Worldwide, governments' vigilance on the SAM threat has been weak. The United States, having distributed such missiles to allies and to guerrillas in Afghanistan, Central America, and Angola in the 1980s, appears to have attempted some post–Cold War recovery operations. There was a publicized buyback program in South West Asia in the 1990s. 2005 brought news of the U.S. work with Nicaragua's government to remove unnecessary missiles from that country, and December of that year brought the most unusual of news items: Bolivia's President elect Evo Morales, an Indian, leftist, and former cocoa farmer, accused the United States of removing his nation's military stock of Chinese HN-SA shoulder-fired missiles. Acquired in 1995 and still very serviceable,

Box 4.3 Attacks by MANPAD missiles

In recent years, there have been many attempts by terrorist groups to acquire or use missiles to down aircraft. The "prize" is a spectacle and inevitably high death rates. The prospects are favorable, as judged by insurgents' successes with missiles against military aircraft of fixed-wing and rotary-wing types. Aggressive policing has stopped many missile acquisitions, as FBI actions have foiled IRA attempts in the Eastern United States. Some deployments on site have failed owing to technique or arrests, as when PFLP Palestinians tried to fire SAM-7s at an El Al plane in Nairobi in January 1976. However, in the following cases, it appears that non-state groups fired missiles at civilian aircraft.

Air Rhodesia. Flight RH825 was brought down with a Soviet-made "Sam 7," September 3, 1978. The Zimbabwe People's Revolutionary Army," ZIPRA, then sent gunmen to the crash site, where they shot ten survivors.

Air Rhodesia. Flight RH827 was shot down by ZIPRA, March 3, 1979. All fifty-nine on board were killed in the ensuing crash.

Angolan Airlines (TAAG). Two Boeing 737s crashed, on November 8, 1983 and on February 9, 1984. The first was claimed in a MANPAD attack by UNITA and killed all 130 on board. The second plane, hit climbing at 8,000 feet, still managed a crash landing without fatalities.

U.S. AID. On December 19, 1988, two Douglas DC-7 aircraft chartered to spray against locusts were hit while flying from Senegal to Morocco. POLISARIO terrorists supported by Algeria and operating in the Western Sahara fired the MANPADs. One plane crashed, killing five people; the other landed safely.

Private aircraft. The presidents of Burundi and Rwanda were shot down on April 6, 1994, as their Dassault Mystere Falcon executive jet flew over Kigali. All aboard died. A new book details the attack, in which two SA-16 missiles from a Ugandan arsenal were fired by the Rwandese Patriotic Front. The incident led to the fall of the capital and to the genocide. Today the RPF rules in Rwanda.

United Nations. Chartered C-130 Hercules transport planes were shot down over central Angola on December 26, 1998 and on January 2, 1999. Twenty-three people died. Presumed responsible is UNITA, the anti-communists who had been supplied with American "Stinger" missiles for the insurgency against Cuban troops.

Congo Airlines. On October 10, 1998, the Democratic Republic of the Congo (formerly Zaire) lost a Boeing 727. The attack, possibly by an SA-7 missile, was

Box 4.3 continued

admitted by Tutsi rebels, who were threatening any aircraft using Kindu airport in the eastern Congo. The missile struck a wing; the plane crashed in the jungle, killing all forty-one people.

Arkia Airlines. Flight 582 was attacked with two Soviet-made SA-7 missiles as it departed Mombassa Airport, Kenya, November 28, 2002. The airline is an Israeli charter firm and was attacked for that reason; Al Qaeda also bombed an Israeli-owned resort in the city.

DHL. Carrying mail, an Airbus A-300 was damaged by MANPADS as it flew off from Baghdad airport. Although a wing caught fire, the plane was able to return and land safely.

they had been a preoccupation of U.S. military attaches, according to former Bolivian defense minister Gonzalo Arredondo, and subsequently they disappeared, the Bolivians say.[45]

Al Qaeda, for its part, has a history of interest in MANPAD use. According to the leading English-speaking authority (Rohan Gunaratna), about 1992, during his Sudanese years, Bin Laden planned to transport Stingers from Peshawar to Khartoum and use them against U.S. passenger aircraft. It may only be coincidental that later a Sudanese member of Al Qaeda fired a SAM at a U.S. plane in December, 2001 at Prince Sultan military base in Saudi Arabia. However, a clear paper trail follows Al Qaeda's interest in killing airplanes. Within the 7,000 pages of the group's *Encyclopedia of the Afghan Jihad* are instructions on how to take down aircraft with Stingers. CNN recovered a second, printed al Qaeda manual for training on Milan missiles and Stingers. Dated October 11, 1990, this manual declares its dedication "to every Muslim mujahid taking up arms in the face of its every oppressor." A third training tool is a video, showing a Bin Laden group member demonstrating a SAM. A label on the film file attributes the work to "Abu Hafs," who is none other than military commander Muhammad Atef. Ironically, Atef would be killed by an aircraft—a U.S. Predator—in Afghanistan two months after the 9-11-01 attack on America.[46]

High-tech terrorism

High-tech threats are numerous, dangerous, and as fascinating to terrorists as they are to potential victims. We may never know whether the novel *Debt of Honor* gave ideas to the December 1994 Algerian hijackers or whether Velupillai Prabhakaran really said he came to the idea for a suicide vest by watching the movie "Death Wish II." However, both dramas were known to millions, as is the 1997 novel *The Cobra Event* by Richard Preston,[47] which reportedly motivated President William J. Clinton. It is clear that most terror leaders are alert, well informed, and often well educated.[48]

In December 1998, Osama Bin Laden declared it a matter of religious duty that he acquire a nuclear weapon. A letter of a few months later, April 1999, on the computer of Al Zawahiri, Al Qaeda's number 2, included this pair of remarks to colleagues—the second of which is as frightening as the first: "...the destructive power of these weapons is no less than that of nuclear weapons....we only became aware of them when the enemy drew our attention to them by repeatedly expressing concern that they can be produced simply."[49] Avid consumers of the press, they also study technical journals, field manuals, and the Internet for tradecraft. Al Zawahiri is a surgeon, well traveled, and fluent in English, French, and Arabic; even in his bleak ramshackle offices in Afghanistan, he had around him computers, diskettes, and access to the Internet, technical manuals, and foreign medical journals. Al Qaeda was also doing initial research on chemical weapons. At a camp called Al Farouk, they were seen to be doing experiments involving poisons. The CIA reportedly concluded that similar work was advancing at another camp, Derunta, which Bin Laden frequently visited. This prompted Ahmed Shah Massoud, a courageous Afghan guerrilla commander, to send guns on pack mules and shell the camp, though with unknown effects.[50]

Al Qaeda's proven interest in WMD demonstrates one of the oldest and most reliable patterns in terrorism: That is the presence within the leadership of academic degrees, specialized skills, and sometimes military training of varying levels. Carlos Marighella spelled out some lesser skill requirement in his 1969 *Minimanual of the Urban Guerrilla*. After varieties of physical preparation that the self-respecting guerrilla must make to strengthen himself, the terrorist-author enumerates more technical skills. "The guerrilla"—by which he seems to mean the group, must learn how:

> to drive, pilot a plane, handle a motor boat and a sail a boat, understand mechanics, radio, telephone, electricity, and have some knowledge of electronic techniques... A knowledge of chemistry and of color combination, and of stamp making...In the area of auxiliary medicine, nursing, pharmacology, drugs, elemental surgery, and emergency first aid... how to handle arms such as the machine gun, revolver, automatic, FAL, various types of shotguns, carbines, mortars, bazookas, etc. A knowledge of various types of ammunition and explosives...dynamite...incendiary bombs, smoke bombs...Molotov cocktails, grenades, mines, homemade destructive devices, how to blow up bridges....[51]

When such skills are developed and others more elevated are added by specialized recruiting or in-house training and when these talents are marshaled well and with patience, high-tech terrorism is possible. Indeed, many terrorist leaders dream of it and argue for it. The elaborate technical problems that would deter lesser terrorist planners only challenge and excite the more capable. This is especially true of those with global reach and access to the products of laboratories and industries and markets in high-tech regions. Such terror groups and insurgencies of the day include Lebanon's Hezbollah, the LTTE of Sri Lanka, FARC and also ELN in Colombia, and the Irish Republican Army.[52] Two terror groups have demonstrated a serious intention to acquire a nuclear bomb: Al Qaeda, and Aum Shinrikyo. It is fortunate that the former is now under the most intense scrutiny worldwide, whereas the latter has been dismantled in nearly all respects...save its website.[53]

These and many other groups have worked on plots involving less demanding technologies for mass killing. Cyanide and ricin plots may be the most common. Al Qaeda has demonstrated interest in both. Aum created cyanide gas and actually deployed it against the public at a subway station—Shinjuku—but alert authorities prevented death. Aum created at least small amounts of a half-dozen other gasses: tabun, sarin, VX, phosgene, mustard, and soman. Some were used in attacks, and in a few of these, people were injured or killed, including judges central to a court case involving Aum. The sarin attack on the Tokyo station was thus merely the last of many efforts by "Supreme Truth" scientists to deploy WMD.[54]

The gas weapons terrify, although plots to make lethal use of them have usually failed. Not far behind these toxins comes the "RDD" or radiological dispersion device; popularly called the "dirty bomb," the genre can also include silent ray-emitting devices that aim to do their harm inauspiciously. It is an irony about "WMDs" that plots involving them thus far have killed far fewer people than the diverse and murderous methods that are more familiar, including sinking oceangoing ships or downing airliners or killing with common weapons. 1985 and 1988 saw Canadian and Korean airliners destroyed and sunk in the seas, whereas Aum Shinrikyo's more sophisticated operations later with "Weapons of Mass Destruction" killed few people.

Defining WMD is difficult. Traditional usage references chemical or bacteriological or nuclear weapons or agents. In the United States, the problem has been visible in the requisites of law and punishment. Expansion in the definition is evident. U.S. Code (18 U.S.C. 2332a) and other legal sources make it evident that a WMD could be derived from a range of explosives, incendiaries, and poisons and from the traditionally feared weapons. "Chemical, biological, and nuclear" has, in many formal discussions, been superceded by the four-letter "CBRN," which adds "radiological" to cover the "dirty bomb" that uses conventional explosive to disperse nuclear waste or fuel.[55] The FBI considers a weapon one of "mass destruction" if its use overwhelms local responders. For its part, the Pentagon's definition of weapons of mass destruction advances a pair of points: a high order of destruction or an implement used to destroy large numbers of people.[56]

This means that a mammoth truck bomb such as the one used to take down the Murrah Federal Building in Oklahoma City can readily be classified as a WMD—and that in fact did occasion the first official use of the acronym by the FBI in domestic American circumstances. It also means that the greatest importance must attach to, say, an anthrax experiment by a small terrorist cell; its potential consequences are so enormous, and it may indicate the existence of parallel efforts by that or allied groups. Therefore, Aum Shinrikyo's little-publicized deployments of botulin toxin and anthrax around Tokyo may also be said to be cases of "WMD" under American guidelines. In everyday terms, there is agreement that successful deployment of one of these weapons could, under the right conditions, make a silent wilderness at the heart of a modern city.

Chemical weapons

Chemical war tools, such as phosgene and mustard, terrified, strangled, burnt, or killed soldiers on the Western Front in World War I. The grisly "field experience" of those times is well known, and Al Zawahiri's Afghan reading lists include a 1921 book titled *Chemical Warfare*.[57] Later deployments of chemicals came from such men as Saddam Hussein, who used them to kill some 5,000 Iraqi Kurds whom he deemed disloyal in 1988. A Dutch businessman has been convicted at The Hague for war crimes in supplying Saddam with chemicals necessary to make such weapons. [58] Chemical weapons also have many disadvantages, a reason they have been more often stored than used by governments. They are hard to deploy or apply, and the change of wind or other weather can weaken or neutralize the impact or even endanger the handler. Some chemicals loose their strength with exposure, as to sunlight, or they weaken merely with age: By one account, the sarin used in the Tokyo train stations by Aum was several weeks old, a reason why its physical effects were not more grave. On the other side are the evident advantages to these weapons, and the most evident is terror. Another is the range of damaging effects, such as brain damage, blindness, or nerve damage; far more lives were wrecked in Tokyo than the small death tally indicates. And some chemicals do not quickly lose potency in exposure; they may remain in an environment for long periods and continue to inflict damage.

Cyanide is the weapon behind some terrorist threats and plots. The United States saw a very early case of threatened use by right-wing religious zealots of the "Covenant, Sword, and Arm of the Lord" in 1986. The group hoped to contaminate city water supplies with cyanide, but the thirty gallons acquired was hopelessly inadequate. More often than not, plots to poison municipal drinking water have dissipated for that same reason.[59] Subsequent efforts to make use of cyanide, in its potassium or sodium forms, have followed. In 2003, in East Texas, a storage shed rented by white supremacist William Karr yielded pipe bombs and briefcase bombs and two pounds of sodium cyanide—allegedly enough to poison everyone in a large office building.[60]

Hydrogen cyanide gas was to be the key element in an Al Qaeda plot against the U.S. embassy in Rome in 2001. The Tunisian Combatant Group, perhaps in league with the Salafist Group for Preaching and Combat (GSPC), intended to enter maintenance tunnels beneath the embassy and release massive amounts of toxic gas upward into the building. When Italian authorities broke up the group, it had already acquired appropriate chemicals and maps of the underground. Police also recorded a conversation in which al Qaeda man and local group leader Sami Ben Khemais Essid said of an unnamed substance now taken for cyanide: "The produce is better. It's more efficient because this liquid, as soon as you open it, suffocates people." He was soon sentenced to eight years, and some North African cohorts were also in Italian custody.[61]

Ricin, garnered from castor plants, lies in the division between chemical and biological weaponry. Ricin has actually killed, though perhaps only once. In the infamous state-managed "umbrella" attacks on East Bloc defectors in London streets in 1978, Georgi Markov died, but the other stabbing victim's life was saved by fast-moving medical experts who had learned from the first case. Apparently there has never been another terrorist success with the toxin, but there endures a human fascination with poisons, there is a clear record of successful killings in all societies with poisons, and the interest

Box 4.4 The challenge of weapons of mass destruction

In September 2006, the White House released a new "National Strategy for Combating Terrorism," successor to a document of 2003. The new strategy includes language below, about WMD and the U.S. approach thereto. It is of course possible that the transition from the Donald Rumsfeld defense department to that of Robert Gates may have effects on the enunciated strategy:

> ... our comprehensive approach for addressing WMD terrorism hinges on six objectives...

- Determine terrorists' intentions, capabilities, and plans to develop or acquire WMD...

- Deny terrorists access to the materials, expertise, and other enabling capabilities required to develop WMD. We have an aggressive, global approach to deny our enemies access to WMD-related materials (with a particular focus on weapons-usable fissile materials), fabrication expertise, methods of transport, sources of funds, and other capabilities...

- Deter terrorists from employing WMD....Traditional threats may not work because terrorists show a wanton disregard for the lives of innocents and in some cases for their own lives. We require a range of deterrence strategies that are tailored to the situation and the adversary. We will make clear that terrorists and those who aid or sponsor a WMD attack would face the prospect of an overwhelming response to any use of such weapons. We will seek to dissuade attacks by improving our ability to mitigate the effects of a terrorist attack....

- Detect and disrupt terrorists' attempted movement of WMD-related materials, weapons, and personnel. We will expand our global capacity for detecting illicit materials, weapons, and personnel transiting abroad or heading for the United States or U.S. interests overseas. We will use our global partnerships [and] work with countries to enact and enforce strict penalties for WMD trafficking...

- Prevent and respond to a WMD-related terrorist attack. ...we will seek to contain, interdict, and eliminate the threat [and develop] capabilities to manage the range of consequences that may result from such an attack...

- Define the nature and source of a terrorist-employed WMD device...We will develop the capability to assign responsibility for the intended or actual us of WMD via accurate attribution—the rapid fusion of technical forensic data with intelligence and law enforcement information.

among terrorists is acute. American "sub-state actors" of several extreme rightist causes were caught in ricin plots during the 1990s. A Colorado native transplanted to Florida, James Kenneth Gluck, was the last of the arrests for that decade. He had made threats to "wage biological warfare" and threatened judges, and in his home were all the materials to make ricin, the celebrated *Anarchist's Cookbook*, and books on biological toxicology.[62]

It is the self-declared "jihadis" or "holy warriors" who dominate the news in ricin arrests outside the United States. In January 2003 alone, there were two finds. In Wood Green, London, police arrested a half-dozen Algerians after their apartments disclosed traces of ricin and relevant technical equipment. Some of these men were believed to have been trained in Chechnya or Georgia. Then a recipe for poisons, including ricin, was found by Russian Special Forces on the body of a Chechen insurgent they killed. About the same time came arrests in Spain: The 16 North Africans there had chemicals, equipment, and false passports. In March 2003, French police doing a routine sweep of the Gare de Lyon train station in Paris found a locker with two vials of ricin, in a nonlethal form, protected by a plaster mold, perhaps for travel. Some Chechen link was suspected.[63] French police—whose intelligence was crucial to earlier ricin arrests in Europe—also nabbed Menad Benchellali in 2004. He was known to associates as "the chemist" from his training in Bin Laden's Afghan camps. Between 2001 and late 2002, he was making ricin in France, experimenting with other poisons, and plotting an explosives attack on the Russian Embassy in Paris, according to press reports. In mid-2006 came convictions for Benchellali and another twenty-four homegrown Muslims. Police called them "the Chechens" because of their training in the Caucasus.[64]

As has so often been the case with the militant Muslim international, such law enforcement cases can be readily linked to published doctrinal and policy statements, training manuals, and the like. Terrorists and governments alike take seriously Osama Bin Laden's proclamation that acquiring weapons of mass destruction is a "religious duty," and he has threatened their use.[65] The training manual recovered in an Al Qaeda safe house in Manchester, England explains ways to make and deploy poisons: "It is a simple operation to extract ricin, and castor beans themselves can be obtained from nurseries throughout the country."[66]

Biological weapons

Biological instruments of mass killing[67] have been another point of terrorist interest for such advanced groups as Aum Shinrikyo and Al Qaeda. In the Afghan camp at Derunta, research and planning on poisons and chemical weapons began more than a year before Coalition forces arrived[68] in late 2001. Some of the attention was devoted to the very simple: how spoiled food could be used, as against American troops in their dining halls. "Yogurt" or "curdled milk" was the name on one computer file—"Zabadi" in Arabic. Given that al Qaeda targets both military and civilian targets, one top concern for any country aggressively pursuing terrorists abroad is the security of food in military "mess halls." They are vulnerable, especially as many use contract labor, workers who may or may not be well screened by security personnel. Simple methods or high-tech ones could both be effective sabotage. Methods of polluting food have already been demonstrated in cases of private hatefulness, as in Japan and Canada in 1970 and in a 1996 case in a Texas hospital. Flagrant terrorist cases of food poisoning have been rare. The most studied and successful poison plot within the United States was unfolded by the Rajneesh cult in The Dalles, a small town in Oregon. Several trained medical personnel were at work in a lab, led by "Ma Anand Puja," referred to as "Dr. Mengele" by those working for her. They poisoned open salad bars in restaurants, using spray from syringes. The result was an outbreak of salmonella, intended to affect elections.[69]

Anthrax, a devastating germ that can arise in nature and persist for generations, was used in one of the only other highly successful terror attacks with bioweapons: that of October 2001 in the Washington, DC area and Florida mails. Though much is now known of the attack, it remains unsolved—an astonishing fact given the tens of millions of dollars poured into pursuing the perpetrators, aiding victims, screening mail areas and post offices, and cleansing work places known to be poisoned. The mysteries surrounding the East Coast U.S. attacks lent special interest to all traces of the work Al Qaeda was doing to develop anthrax. Coalition forces capturing Al Qaeda compounds in Afghanistan found no connections to the anthrax attacks in America, but they found much that would disturb anyone aware of the lust for lethality of the Bin Laden organization. Documents found included letters from a Pakistani scientist with glittering credentials who appears to have been one of several direct liaisons to Al Qaeda in its efforts to weaponize anthrax. These letters (discussed in print in 2003 but released for the first time in October 2006) seem to show that Abdur Rauf, a member of the Society for Applied Microbiology, which is based in Britain, was hard at work on lethal anthrax and in direct communication on the matter with number 2 Al Qaeda boss, Ayman Al Zawahiri, himself a surgeon. In 1999, Dr. Rauf reportedly sent a formal letter in halting English to the terror leader boasting that he had "successfully achieved the targets," advanced work on many complex technical problems, and "finalized all the accessories required for the smooth running of our bioreactor." As correspondence between the two medical experts continued, Rauf sent along a hand-done plan for a bio-weapon lab.[70]

Then U.S. troops near Kandahar, Afghanistan in 2002 discovered an abandoned, unfinished laboratory that actually had traces of anthrax. They were so minute that they could be found in nature, so then Joint Chiefs of Staff Chairman Richard Myers was cautious with his words at the time. However, this changed when further al Qaeda documents on bio-war were captured along with Khalid Sheik Mohammed in Pakistan in March 2003. His whereabouts alone was frightening: the home of a bacteriologist, Abdul Quddoos Khan. Notes, plans, and computer files show advanced work on making salmonella and botulin and a plan to purchase bacillus anthracis. Al Qaeda's former chief of operations, Mr. Mohammed, is now in U.S. custody, but his bacteriologist host has disappeared.[71]

Botulism is another disease that invariably puts authorities on maximum alert— when even mere literature is found in a terrorist safe house. The Monterey Institute of International Studies has now shown that little hard evidence supports the 1980 reports of a brew of this bioweapon at the Paris safe house of German Red Army Faction members. However, creating the botulism germ is not difficult, and spreading it could be quite possible. Iraq had admitted to making a swimming pool–sized supply of botulinum toxin, enough, in theory, to kill tens of millions of people. Aum Shinrikyo not only made botulism in batches in a lab it ran in central Kyushu but repeatedly attempted to deploy it.

These attacks began in April 1990, and targets included central Tokyo, American naval facilities at Yokosuka and Yokohama, and Narita Airport—the large new station that, under construction, inflamed leftists and militants in Japan for years. Senior scientist Seiichi Endo continued work, including making research trips to Russia. He made a further release of botulinum toxin at the imperial palace in Tokyo, timed for the state wedding of Crown Prince Naruhito and diplomat Masako Owada. However, biological weapons are difficult to deploy, and all these attacks failed.

In the United States, debate over bio-dangers, their public handling, and censorship came during 2005. A research paper slated to appear in the respected *Proceedings of the National Academy of Science* and penned by Lawrence Wein, a Stanford professor, described how the milk production system in the United States could be contaminated with botulinum toxin by terrorists. The message: it would not be difficult. A government official asked the journal not to publish this article lest it be "a road map for terrorists."[72]

The other "germ" threats come from established states. Globalization and the hard indicators of recent years make it possible that groups—even of limited technical savvy—could be helped and coached and supplied by a rogue state or knowledgeable experts from a state. There are suspected biowar programs in a range of states today, including some dubious or known to traffic in dangerous materials: China, Cuba, Pakistan, and the Sudan. Libya's status is unclear; despite many improvements, its government cannot yet be presumed entirely benign. There are known biowar or biodefense projects ongoing in Iran and Syria,[73] two states deserving their reputations for making foreign mayhem. The old Soviet Union's creaking laboratories, which once housed the powerful "Biopreparat" complex, are a clear and present danger, given what might be stolen or sold from the labs. Motives for such theft are too many: The most likely include crime, calculated theft, and graft by lab employees who are notoriously underpaid. Another likely leak point would be certain lab managers who may be desperate for operating cash and fearful their institutions are collapsing for lack of state resources.[74]

Iran's presence on these lists is a special concern, given its brazen record of two and a half decades of exporting terrorists, money for terrorists, training for terrorists, and inspiration to terrorists. When the new president, Mahmoud Ahmadinejad, rhetorically spat on the country of Israel and on reflection then renewed his verbal attack, it further colored foreign perceptions. Certain Al Qaeda officers are now hiding in Iran—something Tehran finally admitted after U.S. accusations were supported by the UN's special envoy to Afghanistan.[75] This in turn is a reminder that Al Qaeda's demonstrated interests in WMD include agro-terrorism. Alleged "twentieth hijacker" Zacharias Moussaoui was found to have material on crop dusters in his personal computer, and many Americans will long remember the bizarre but true post-9-11 story of mission commander Mohammed Atta's attempt to secure a loan to buy a crop duster plane in the southern United States. General knowledge of agro-terror possibilities has spread in recent years. There were apparently photographs of pilotless versions of crop-dusting aircraft under testing in Iraq in the late years of Saddam's regime. At that time there were limited Al Qaeda contacts with Baghdad[76]—another reason for the White House's fears of a WMD attack. For reasons of both science and politics, it is thus relevant that today there are limited Al Qaeda relations with Tehran.

Terrorists' fantasies of making such horrid tools date back at least as far as the American leftists of R.I.S.E., a young small group that nonetheless acquired at least four different biological agents and came close to releasing typhoid bacteria into the Chicago water supply in January, 1972.[77] Such an attack would be more likely to succeed than would chemical poison in so large a reservoir. And the terror factor would outweigh the physical damage done. Two historical indicators of that postulate are useful to recall. The first is Thucydides' unrivaled description of a plague that struck Athens in 430 B.C. The second is our own distinct recollections of Tokyo, April 1995: There were actually not more than 5,000 sarin casualties, but tens of thousands more frightened persons swamped the medical system. The victimized nation entered a period of collective trauma. This prompts a reflection: Today, on the level of low psychology, many citizens might contemplate with resignation the instant death that could come in a terror group's nuclear bomb blast, almost as airline passengers calmly board aircraft every day unaffected by the clear hazards of flying. However, there could be wide and extreme terrors in a biological attack, fiendishly ugly and carrying medical and mathematical ambiguities. For ease of production, low cost, and obvious capability to do psychological and physical damage, biological weapons of mass destruction are the most dangerous of all terror threats today.

Nuclear weapons

Nuclear weapons and terrorism have been closely linked in a wealth of public speculation, in several new books, and in the imprudent boasts of terrorists, such as Al Qaeda. The Russian government, led by a former agent of the KGB, is widely suspected in the polonium 210 cases erupting in that country, Britain, and continental Europe as 2006 turned into 2007. *Nuclear* and *terrorism* are also terms that co-join in the more measured public efforts by governments around the world that seek to control proliferation.

There is little avoiding the ever-present risk of terrorists making a bomb, probably using conventional explosives, and distributing radioactive material. Either nuclear waste or a form of nuclear fuel could fulfill their purposes. Various prospects were detailed in our first edition[78] and include positioning nuclear fuel or waste in an air conditioning or water system or emplacing a barrel of nuclear waste in a high urban location where terrorists threaten to blow it up with conventional explosives and irradiate the area. This would maximize the psychological—as well as medical—concerns in terrorism.[79] There is another set of possibilities, of course, less imminent, more technically troublesome: terrorists acquiring a nuclear bomb. Even the smallest atomic detonation could cause a city to vacate, perhaps permanently, as occurred after the Chernobyl reactor failed. This greatest danger—an actual detonation—has recently and wrongly been dubbed "inevitable" by one authority.[80] It is not—any more than nuclear war has proven inevitable. But the stakes represented are so high that anyone can approve of the studies made of the risk and the global efforts to contain it by such persons as Senator Richard Lugar.

The declared intentions of terrorists with a record of attacks are at least as important as the views of analysts of terrorism. On this matter, Osama Bin Laden has spoken at least twice publicly. Both speeches came in 1998, eerily bracketing his devastating vehicle bombings of two American embassies, killing and wounding thousands of

Africans. In May of that year, Bin Laden exhorted "the Muslim nation" and especially Pakistan to prepare for jihad and said: "This should include a nuclear force."[81] Then in December, 1998 he went on camera with the Qatar-based station Al Jazeera. Speaking with customary logic, deadliness, and an absence of rhetorical riff-raff, the leader of al Qaeda announced that his organization was seeking weapons of mass destruction. The reporter had deferentially inquired about possible truth to any "accusations" by newspapers and American officials that Al Qaeda was pursuing nuclear, chemical, or biological weapons. "[T]his is not an accusation but a fact," Bin Laden replied. Al Qaeda must not be thought "backward and stupid" said the construction magnate. After all, he had already "congratulated the Pakistani people when God blessed them with possession of a nuclear weapon, because we consider it the Muslims' right to have it..." Perhaps surprised by the ease of this admission from Bin Laden, the reporter asked if this was "confirmation that you are seeking to acquire this weapon." Bin Laden replied: "There is a duty on Muslims to acquire them..."[82]

There is doubt, however, that his drive is nearing success. One report that Bin Laden had acquired a kilo of uranium when he was based in Khartoum in the early 1990s now seems baseless; Bin Laden may even have been hoodwinked in the deal by others as skilled in the underground as he; some suggest that he paid good money for fake material. A Bin Laden aide who later went under American witness protection has testified that his leader did authorize attempts to buy uranium to make a nuclear bomb, but the attempts failed.[83] And the next training and research locale—Afghanistan—saw much Al Qaeda work on CBRN but no tangible nuclear results, apparently.

If Bin Laden cannot build a bomb, he can build a "dirty bomb." As we noted in our first edition in 2000, the technology is undemanding. The results in fear, and economic and social dislocation, could be enormous, even if the physical destruction were minimal. It is possible that Bin Laden dispatched two different agents to create such a device in the months after 9-11. The first case—which would evolve considerably—involves Jose Padilla, an American Hispanic, Brooklyn-born, who was a Chicago street gang member until converting to Islam and taking the new name Abdullah Al Muhajir. He spent time in the Middle East and Afghanistan and entered the United States from Pakistan via Zurich. Customs officers held him up at Chicago's O'Hare Airport, and he was soon detained indefinitely as an "unlawful combatant" preparing "acts of international terrorism" against the United States as a member of Al Qaeda, itself at war with the United States. Though his legal status as an interned American citizen has been much disputed, some believe he plotted the destruction of apartment buildings in the United States, possibly via small bombs that would disperse radioactive material.[84] Ultimately, formal charges against him did not include any about a "dirty bomb." A second possible Al Qaeda man on a nuclear mission to reach Northern American territories was posing as a student at McMaster University, Hamilton, Ontario. A nuclear reactor for research purposes functions there. The FBI was seeking his arrest out of concern that he was part of an Al Qaeda cell planning a "dirty bomb" attack in the United States.[85]

In 1995, chiefly to frighten, Chechens buried radioactive material in a Moscow park and alerted authorities. Well demonstrating the power of a mere threat, it garnered enormous attention, including television footage of the recovery of the nuclear material and subsequent references in terrorism reports and books for a decade. In 1998, Chechens did something more dangerous; they built a radioactive bomb, which security forces discovered (and disarmed) it in a suburban area outside the Chechen capital of Grozny.[86] In neither case is much known of the perpetrators, but the Chechen insurgency is world-renowned for its skills and its ruthless usage of terrorism to include frequent mass murders and the taking of 1,100 children hostage at Beslan on September 1, 2004.[87]

In this new millennium, with an ongoing post-9-11 global contest, a bomb built to irradiate more than to blast remains a top concern. In his careful analysis of both U.S. border security and the availability of radiation weapons, scholar and former Coast Guard Commander Stephen Flynn has judged the odds and finds the math disturbing. There are some 130 laboratories in forty countries that use nuclear material. The United States and Canada alone license some 2,000,000 sources of radiation, including cobalt 60, cesium 137, americium, and plutonium. Three hundred of these are lost or stolen each year, half never to be recovered. The material could thus be stolen or bought within the United States, but smuggling[88] such material into the United States is just as possible. During 2002, some 60,000 vessels docked in U.S. harbors, and 8,000,000 maritime containers arrived. There are 95,000 U.S. shoreline miles, apart from long unguarded stretches of land borders, and 2,400,000 freight cars entered the United States that year, as did myriad trucks and vans. Air cargo, poorly monitored, is central to the economy as well.[89] There are, in short, many ways to move a dirty bomb and many advantages to using one. Use in the future is very likely.

Conclusions

From these discussions of technology, tactics, and trends in terrorism there emerge several conclusions. First, numerical levels are significant, and the majority of attacks are, and will be, of the low-tech sorts. Modest means suffice to make such acts successful and, if desired, lethal. Also, some urban terrorists and rural insurgents using terror must depend on inexpensive options. Myriad groups from European anarchists to Nepalese communists may not have ready access to sophisticated weapons or cash in quantity. Second, the promising "mid-tech" range has had close focus from terrorists and inadequate attention by governments. The dangers presented by shoulder-fired missiles and remotely detonated bombs are examples of dangers that loom over us presently and have already consigned many victims to hospitals or morgues. Third, highly elaborate plots requiring special skills in physics, biology, chemistry, or nuclear science remain a grave danger. Of these, terrorist success is most likely with a biological weapon or an enhanced radiation device, but wider, more lethal damage attends on the risks of use of all CBRN capabilities. Complex weapons might be homemade; they could be well provided by rogue scientists or governments; there is a chance of theft from badly protected military or scientific sites in unprepared advanced countries.

Modern terrorism is also reflecting the overall technological advance of the world. Classifying terror acts by their technical sophistication is thus a challenge. The standard of what is available "off the shelf," hard to acquire, or most difficult to find is changing. Insurgents practicing terror against civilian and security force targets in Iraq today may be indicative of a rising "learning curve" of armed groups in many countries. Double-bombings and shaped charges in a bomb used to be unusual in terrorism; in Iraq now they are frequent. Remote detonation of bombs was something on which IRA Provos labored for decades and used to signify a disturbing and marked advance by terrorists; now a half-dozen household technologies, such as the car door opener, can be a trigger for lethal purposes. Plastique was once a dramatic innovation; now it is common, and varied, and still far easier to hide and more powerful than older explosives. Using a GPS device to aid in an illegal border crossing was inconceivable ten years ago; now it is within reach of any professional gang of smugglers. A similar climb may be occurring in other areas important to terrorists, be they in explosives, guns, rocketry, gasses, or germs. In 1969, a reader of the new *Minimanual of the Urban Guerrilla* could be forgiven if he found unrealistic author Carlos Marighella's invocation to terrorists to master flying, special driving skills, counterfeiting, mechanics, underwater devices, and the like. Now, given the spread of education worldwide and the readiness of cadres often well schooled in science to work tirelessly for violent groups, Marighella's challenge has been met— and surpassed—by such groups as Colombian FARC, Japan's Aum Shinrikyo, and the international network Al Qaeda.

Notes

1 *Terrorism Today* (London, Frank Cass, 2000), p. 161 and following.
2 An Al Qaeda spokesman claimed credit, announcing that it was a protest against events in Palestine at a time there were "Jews cavorting in Djerba" Tunisia; BBC News, June 23, 2002. The incineration, and such words, are worthy of the Nazis, and may help explain our ch. 1 argument that anti-Semitism is a powerful link between two apparently disparate movements: the militant Muslims and the neofascists. Ch. 5 of the first edition explored this more deeply.
3 National Public Radio reports of July 31, 2004 and Nov. 12, 2005; the latter is the interview with Lakwena. A photo of Kony accompanies Martin Plaut's BBC profile of Feb.6, 2004, at http://news.bbc.co.uk/1hi/world/africa/3462901.stm The U.S. State Department *Country Reports on Terrorism: 2004* (Washington D.C., GPO, 2005) has a good profile which is all but copied on the Web site of the Federation of American Scientists. See also www. globalsecurity.org/military/world/para/Ira.htm On the ICC indictments, see the *International Herald Tribune* of 15-16 Oct. 2005.
4 *Washington Times*, Dec. 9, 2005.
5 M. R. Narayan Swamy, *Inside an Elusive Mind:Prabhakaran* (Delhi: Konark, 2003), p. 39.
6 *Washington Times*, Dec. 9, 2005; *New York Times*, Dec. 13, 2005.
7 Three bombings in Western Europe of that time are examined in Christopher C. Harmon, "The Red and the Black: Left-Right Terrorist Collusion in Italy," *Strategic Review* (Winter 1985).
8 *The Daily Star* (Dhaka), Dec. 14–20, 2005. *Star* clippings are courtesy of Joseph Goldberg, an expert on extremism and terrorism in Bangladesh, and professor, Industrial College of the Armed Forces, Washington, DC. More generally, on "The Rise of Islamist Militancy in Bangladesh," see Sumit Ganguly's *Special Report* 171 for the U.S. Institute of Peace (August 2006). And his sources include this promising title: Ali Riaz, *God Willing: The Politics of Islamism in Bangladesh* (Lanham, MD: Rowman and Littlefield, 2004).
9 Lashkar-e-Jhangvi is Sunni, Deobandi, and responsible for many violent actions in Pakistan. Formed in 1996, it was proscribed by Pakistan just before 9-11. The admirable South Asia Terrorism Portal carries a lengthy profile, including references to the Daniel Pearl case, on its Web site, accessed Nov. 12, 2006,at www.satp.org/satporgtp/countries/pakistan/terroristoutfits/lej.htm

10 The swift translation of terrorist brutality into video form for sale in the market place is standard pattern now in the Iraq insurgency as well. Lt. Col. John Nagl, a U.S. Army armor officer, tells of his partnership with an Iraqi battalion commander who was very effective at his work and thus targeted. This Iraqi was tempted to a meeting in a mosque, taken captive there, and beaten to death on tape. This tape was then sold in the streets as an advertisement against those considering supporting the new Iraqi government or its American partners. Dr. Nagl, "Learning to Eat Soup with a Knife: Counterinsurgency Lessons from Malaya and Vietnam," lecture, Army-Navy Club, Washington, DC, Sept. 7, 2006.

11 "Full Text of Terror Guide"/The Last Night, printed in the *New York Times* on Sept. 29, 2001; trans. by Capital Communications Group, accessed Feb. 25, 2004 for syllabi at the School of National Security Executive Education, National Defense University, Washington, DC.

12 See ch. 3 on "operations."

13 This was also a standard tactic of the FLN in the Algerian war against France.

14 Al Arabiya television (Saudi Arabia) as cited in the *New York Times*, Dec. 28, 2005.

15 *Washington Times*, Nov. 17, 2006.

16 *New York Times*, Dec. 24, 2005.

17 This anecdote was detailed by Iraq campaign veteran Lt. Col. W. Buhl and other officers at the Marine Corps War College, Quantico, VA, Dec. 8, 2005.

18 In an October 2006 visit to Iraq, I was walked through an outdoor course of mock IEDs (improvised explosive devices) by an officer of Marines who had set up the course to train his unit. He had recovered such a range of real detonators and bomb holders in Al Anbar Province that creations on his part were unnecessary. Some detonators were remarkably primitive; many were of the mid-tech sorts. See also a young officer's October 2006 article on IEDs in Iraq in that month's *Marine Corps Gazette*.

   A Pentagon official sent one newspaper a photo of a failed bomb (from Iraq) with a cell phone detonator. "The screen on the Nokia phone displayed "01 Call Missed." *Washington Times*, Dec. 23, 2005.

19 Christoph Reuter, *My Life is a Weapon: A Modern History of Suicide Bombing*, trans. by Helena Ragg-Kirby (Princeton, N.J.: Princeton University Press, 2004). He writes "Even Muhammad Khatami, acclaimed a decade and a half later as a reforming president, but at the time "cultural commissioner" at the military command center, was in the latter capacity one of those responsible for producing propaganda films in which actors on white horses, dressed as heavenly messengers, summon the children to come into Paradise." Page 48.

20 E.G., see the *New York Times* on both bombings, Dec. 13, 2005.

21 Maria A. Ressa, *Seeds of Terror* (New York: Free Press, 2003).

22 Swamy, *Prabhakaran*, pp. 155–6. "Miller" was chosen and destroyed a school house in use as a military headquarters.

23 Not all attacks succeed, of course. In early fall of 2006, the Navy claimed to have destroyed a dozen small "Tiger" naval craft in an odd sea battle in Sri Lankan waters. And during that October, the Navy claimed to foil attacks by five explosive-laden fishing boats at the Galle naval base, leaving some minor damage to Navy ships. There were several further sea combats that season, including one in mid-Nov. 2006 off the northwest coast of the island; reports include the *Hindustan Times* (India) of Nov. 9, 2006.

24 Author Travis Sinniah, Captain, Sri Lankan Navy, has granted permission to reference the early 2005 paper done for the "Global War on Terrorism" course I teach at National Defense University's SNSEE program, Fort McNair, Washington, DC.

25 C. Reuter, op. cit., pp. 156–7. Rohan Gunaratna writes that Prabhakaran came to the method that killed Rajiv Gandhi by watching a movie, "Death Wish II." At any rate, LTTE selected "Dhanu" (Thenmuli), a young woman, for that infamous attack. *International & Regional Security Implications of the Sri Lankan Tamil Insurgency* (Colombo: International Foundation of Sri Lankans, 2001), 3rd ed.; see photographs and text at pp. 68–9.

26 Michael E. O'Hanlon et. al., eds., *Iraq Index* (Washington, DC: The Brookings Institution, Sept. 5, 2006); www.brookings.edu/iraqindex. This is a superior resource, updated every few days.

27 D. J. Vassallo, et. al, "Shattered Illusions—The Thiepval Barracks Bombing, 7 October 1996," *Journal of the Royal Army Medical Corps* 143 (1997), pp. 5–11.

28 Press sources, and the detailed Department of Justice press release of Oct. 14, 1998: "Eric Rudolph Charged in Centennial Olympic Park Bombing," accessed Nov. 12, 2006 at www.usdoj.gov/opa/pr/1998/October/477crm.htm

29 *Secondary device* is a useful term of art for these. "Double-bombing" is my preferred term, in part because the second bomb may be "the main event." My article on "Double-Bombings" may be the only thorough general one on the subject as of 2006; *Journal of Counterterrorism and Homeland Security International* 11: 4 (Winter, 2005), pp. 42–7. My thanks for interviews to combat medicine specialists Josh Vayer and Cliff Cloonan (a former Army doctor); then-Colonel John Toolan, a regimental commander of Marines who survived a double-bombing in Iraq; and Lt. Col W. Buhl, USMC, for his knowledge of enemy explosives and tactics in Iraq.

30 Ressa, *Seeds of Terror*, p. 187.

31 Reports by the *Washington Post* and the *New York Times*, as on Dec. 7, 2005.

32 *CNN.com*, May 21, 2002. This memo about flight training by militant Muslims never reached the highest levels of the FBI or CIA before 9-11-01, apparently.

33 Published by Putnam.

34 Rex Hudson, ed., *Who Becomes a Terrorist and Why*, a 1999 report of the Congressional Research Service, reprinted by Lyon's Press, Guilford, CN., n.d. Page 15 received great attention, although analyst Jim Robbins, Ph.D., deprecates the significance of the passage in commentary for *National Review Online* in August 2004.

35 A Northrop Grumman expert and marketing director, Jack Pledger, offers estimates for a black market SAM as low as $5,000 and as high as 80,000. Former House Speaker Newt Gingrich asserted the systems can be had "for less than $100,000;" *Washington Times*, Sept. 24, 2003.

36 Among the NON-complacent, those in the U.S. Congress bringing deserved attention to the issue and proposals to the table are Sen. Barbara Boxer and Reps. Steve Israel and John Mica.

37 For example, Lt. Col. Mike Lawrence of the U.S. Marines, a helicopter pilot, says such firings are usually with SA7s. (They often miss, owing to low quality of seekers or poor batteries.) However, there are newer types coming into theater, and Lawrence reports the downing of a Cobra helicopter with an Iranian Strella, an Iranian copy of the U.S. Stinger. Interview of Dec. 29, 2005, in Quantico, VA.

38 A public event at the Heritage Foundation, Washington, DC, Dec. 8, 2005.

39 State had also published an earlier report on the problem: "MANPADS: The Potential for Use as a Terrorist Tactic," Bureau of Diplomatic Security, Feb. 1994. See also *Terrorism Today* (2000), pp. 162–3, and Web-published research papers by the Lexington Institute of Arlington VA. .

40 *USA Today*, Dec. 3, 2003; *New York Times Sunday Magazine*, Feb. 8, 2004, p. 36.

41 "The MANPADS Menace," a Fact Sheet of the Bureau of Political-Military Affairs and Bureau of International Security and Nonproliferation, Department of State, Sept. 20, 2005.

42 Gunaratna, *Implications of the Sri Lankan Tamils*, pp. 29, 82; Swamy, *Prabhakaran*, pp. 143, 255. Swamy writes that the LTTE's attacks on aircraft virtually crippled the "air corridor through which the government kept troops in the peninsula (of Jaffna) supplied with arms and food."

43 Information on incidents is from these sources, among others: "Viscounts in Africa: The Air Rhodesia Story, at http://home.iprimus.com.au/rob_rickards/vioscounts/umniati.htm, and a companion page, accessed Jan. 21, 2003. Thomas B. Hunter, "The Proliferation of MANPADS," *Jane's Intelligence Review*, Sept. 1, 2003, courtesy of Maj. Robert Stanford, USMC. State Department "Fact Sheet" of Sept. 20, 2005 (op. cit.). Lieutenant Abdul Ruzibiza, *Rwanda: L'Histoire Secrete* (2005); http://justworldnews.org/archives/ruzibiza.html

44 *Daily Telegraph*, Nov. 29, 2002; *Financial Times*, Nov. 29, 2002. The Israeli-owned resort is called Paradise Beach. It may or may not be relevant, for understanding how the plotters moved about in Kenya, to note that Muslims are a significant religious minority there.

45 *Washington Times*, Dec. 22, 2005. Dan Fisk, an official in the State Department's Bureau of Western Hemisphere Affairs, had mentioned U.S. concerns in a speech at the Center for Strategic and International Studies, Washington, DC, June 18, 2003; *The DISAM Journal*, Fall, 2003, p. 81.

46 See the scattered but telling references to SAMS in the 3rd edition of Gunaratna's *Inside Al Qaeda*, pp. xxxii, xxxix, 49, 93.

47 Random House, 1997.

48 See the author's ch. 5 in the first edition and "Propaganda at Pistol Point: The Use and Abuse of Education by Leftist Terrorists," *Journal of Political Communication and Persuasion* 9: 1 (Jan.–March, 1992), pp. 15–30.

49 Alan Cullison, "Inside al Qaeda's Hard Drive," *Atlantic Monthly*, Sept., 2004, pp. 55–70.

50 Steve Coll's book has, and deserves, a top reputation: *Ghost Wars: The Secret History of the CIA, Afghanistan, and Bin Laden, from the Soviet Invasion to September 10, 2001* (New York: Penguin Press, 2004), pp. 367; 411–2; 487–8. The 9-11 Commission would later establish that the group "has tried to acquire or make weapons of mass destruction for at least ten years;" p. 381.

51 Carlos Marighella, *Urban Guerrilla Minimanual* [1969] date and trans. not given, (Vancouver Canada: Pulp Press, 1974, pp. 7–8.

52 It is not only the "Provos" who have global reach. 2005 disclosures, including federal indictments, indicate a leader of the "Official" branch of the IRA was traveling widely throughout Europe and Eastern Europe while circulating fake U.S. currency.

53 Aum Shinrikyo tried to re-emerge from all the arrests of 1995 by renaming itself and resuming internet activity on an "Aleph" Web site. Leader Shoko Asahara remains in jail and is reported by his daughter to be psychologically sick. Many lesser members of this terror cult have served time and been freed.

   The Japanese group bought a ranch in Australia where there were uranium deposits, successfully extracted small amounts, and started a laboratory there. This effort ceased when Australian authorities paid too much attention. Asahara also had obsessions with the power of nuclear weapons—both wanting them and fearing them enough to tell disciples about the need for civil defense measures. Robert Jay Lifton, *Destroying the World to Save It: Aum Shinrikyo, Apocalyptic Violence, and the New Global Terrorism* (New York: Metropolitan Books, 1999), p. 200, and the like.

54 Ibid., pp. 40, 41, 141, 148, 179–86, and the like. Also an expert on Hiroshima A-bomb survivors, Lifton is Distinguished Professor of Psychology and Psychiatry, John Jay College, NY.

55 See for example Peter D. Zimmerman and Cheryl Loeb, "Dirty Bombs: The Threat Revisited," *Defense Horizons* (Washington, DC: National Defense University Press, Jan. 2004).

56 *Dictionary of Military and Associated Terms* (Washington, DC: Department of Defense).

57 Cullison, op. cit., p. 62. Al Qaeda's number 2 also refers to the books *Tomorrow's Weapons* (1964) and *Peace or Pestilence* (1949).

58 Reuters story about the conviction of Frans van Anraat, in the *Washington Times*, Dec. 24, 2005.

59 A colleague, Aaron Danis, expert on many aspects of WMD, tells me that a popular quip, "The solution to pollution is dilution," explains the inadequacies of many water-poisoning plots.

60 *U.S. News & World Report*, Aug. 22, 2005, referencing an uncompleted two-year old case.

61 Italian press reports, cited by the Department of State's *Patterns of Global Terrorism: 2001* (Washington, DC: GPO, 2002), pp. 38, 39, 66. The reality of the plot has been confirmed to me by an American engineer who helped in Italy with investigations.

62 At least one further American ricin plot was privately motivated, not political. An information technology expert thought to want his wife's death was exposed to authorities by fellow office workers in June, 2002. In the man's corporate office in Spokane Valley, Washington

were test tubes, castor beans, glass jars, and about one gram of the finished powder. The most recent scare from this potent weapon was a false-positive test on powder discovered on Feb. 2, 2005 in the mail room of then-U.S. Senate Majority Leader Bill Frist, a medical doctor who has written on bioterrorism.

63   *CNN* news reports of Jan. 13 and March 21, 2003.

64   The *Washington Post*, May 5, 2004, covered the arrests, but the report was later challenged, as in the *Seattle Times* in 2005. On the convictions in French court, the press includes John Lichfield's report for *The Independent* (London), June 15, 2006, which includes the remark by one of the defense lawyers, Isabelle Coutant-Peyre, that the defendants were "accused of being Muslims..." This woman met "Carlos the Jackal" in jail in France and became his lawyer and then his third wife. An interview published on March 25, 2004 by Britain's *Sunday Telegraph* makes it clear that Carlos, like so many others quoted in my preface, does not object to all applications of the term *terrorist* to himself. His wife says Carlos "...does not believe the terms 'terrorist' or 'terrorism' are pejorative when they describe acts committed to avoid something worse happening, or more people being killed...He is a political man, a freedom fighter, a revolutionary."

   Our first edition (ch. 5) discussed the problem courts face when lawyers are actual members or illicit allies of terror clients, acting beyond norms in a kind of guerrilla war against legal systems. There has been a subsequent conviction of a New York woman of the bar who was not content to defend a Muslim militant but served as a communications conduit for his terrorist conspiracies.

65   State Department, *Patterns of Global Terrorism: 2001* (Washington, DC: GPO, 2002), p. 66.

66   *Declaration of Jihad Against the Country's Tyrants* [hereafter, the Jihad Manual], undated and no publisher given, was recovered from an Al Qaeda safe house in Manchester and has been used in trials in recent years. It is a training book for guerrillas and terrorists of about 180 pages and includes discussions of poisons, firearms, torture, intelligence operations, and the like. Several chapters are on the U.S. Department of Justice Web site, and the full manual is also on the Web. I began using the manual in graduate school teaching in 2002. This Jihad Manual should not be confused with the 11-volume *Encyclopedia of the Jihad*, created about the time the Afghan resistance (with its Arab allies) was completing its victorious war against the occupying Red Army.

67   For a lengthy and helpful popular account of WMD, the *Washington Post* did a three-part series beginning Dec. 29, 2004.

68   Coll, *Ghost Wars*, p. 487.

69   W. Seth Carus, "The Rajneeshees (1984)," in *Toxic Terror: Assessing Terrorist Use of Chemical and Biological Weapons*, Jonathan Tucker, ed. (Cambridge, MA: MIT Press, 2000), pp. 115–37.

70   After the journal *Science* mentioned the letters in 2003, the *Washington Post* pursued the matter, publishing a long report by Joby Warrick on Oct. 31, 2006. Also discussed was Yazid Sufaat, said to be a member of Jemaah Islamiyah, involved in purchasing equipment for a lab doing biowar work in Kandahar. Sufaat is still in custody; Rauf is free in Pakistan, apparently. There is unfortunately no significant new information on the anthrax or ricin work of Al Qaeda in the long new book by Jonathan Tucker, *War of Nerves: Chemical Warfare from World War I to Al Qaeda* (New York: Pantheon Books, 2006); the volume focuses on traditional chemical weapons.

71   *Washington Post*, March 23, 2003.

72   This controversy was described by Malcolm Dando, "The Bioterrorist Cookbook," *Bulletin of the Atomic Scientists*, Nov./Dec., 2005, pp. 35–6. Though this article is thin, my terrorism books (2000; 2007) agree with its proposition that high-end attacks have received so great a share of publicity that the risks of lower-level attacks are not receiving much thought.

73   Most of these data are from Henry S. Parker's fine monograph *Agricultural Bioterrorism: A Federal Strategy to Meet the Threat,* McNair Paper 65 (Washington, DC: National Defense University, March 2002), p. 8. A second edition appeared in June 2003.

74 The Monterey Institute of International Studies, a leader in thinking about the problem, released much of a recent study of the old Soviet labs to the *Washington Post*; see the issue of Aug. 20, 2005. This long-time reader of the *Post* cannot recall many strong concerns, *at that newspaper* during the 1980s, about Soviet war preparations, but now the paper sometimes uses prose it then would have dismissed as "purple" when discussing the Soviets. In this *Post* issue, for example, the writer declares that Richard Nixon halted U.S. weaponization of biological materials and the Soviets signed The Biological Weapons Convention, but then, "Within the next two years, the Soviets secretly began to build a massive offensive weapons program….Biopreparat…put tens of thousands of scientists to work on bioweapons…."

75 Dr. Ali Farassati, "Iran and Al Qaeda," in the *Terrorism Monitor* of the Jamestown Foundation, Sept. 11, 2003. Farasatti holds a degree in geopolitics from the University of Paris and once taught political science in Iran.

76 Stephen Hayes, "Case Closed," *The Weekly Standard*, vol. 9 no. 19 (Jan. 26, 2004). Because it reprinted at length what was apparently an official and high-level Defense Department memo written by Douglas Feith for intelligence committees of Congress, this article has become famous and controversial.

77 W. Seth Carus, "R.I.S.E. (1972)," in *Toxic Terror*, op. cit., pp. 55–70.

78 *Terrorism Today* (2000), pp. 171, 185.

79 There is also, of course, a prospect of economically devastating contamination. When an abandoned or stolen industrial gauge using cesium was recovered from a scrap metal plant in North Carolina, a scientific group ran speculative exercises in which it was blown apart by TNT. As much as a mile-long swath of a city could be dangerously polluted, depending on weather.

80 Famed Harvard political scientist Graham Allison probably makes a fundamental error in social science by flinging about the term *inevitable* in his latest book, *Nuclear Terrorism* (New York: Times Books, 2004). The term frightens but does not help. Allison himself steps away from it in other parts of his book. The true depths and possibilities that term *inevitable* suggests are better considered in, say, Thucydides' *History of the Peloponnesian War*.

81 Attributed to Bin Laden by another al Qaeda member interviewed in September 2001; quoted by Rohan Gunaratna, *Inside Al Qaeda* (New York: Berkley Books, 2003), 3rd ed., p. 65.

82 *Messages to the World: The Statements of Osama Bin Laden*, ed. Bruce Lawrence, trans. James Howarth (London: Verso, 2005, p. 72. It has further been reported that Bin Laden requested and received a fatwa in 2003 from radical cleric Nasser al-Fahd, who complied by "authorizing" almost any weapon "if the infidels can be repelled from the Muslims only by using such weapons." Quoted by AP's Charles Hanley, from Amman, *Seattle Post-Intelligencer*, Oct. 29, 2005, with reference to authorities in the FBI's counterterrorism division.

83 Coll, *Ghost Wars*, p. 367.

84 Sources here include press materials of the time of arrest (May 8, 2002), and Dec. 2005, and a "Memorandum Opinion and Order" by Henry F. Ford, U.S. District Judge for the District of South Carolina, Feb. 28, 2005; www.humanrightsfirst.org/US_law/inthecourts/padilla_briefs/4th_circut/padilla-ruling-030105.pdf

85 *Washington Times*, Oct. 17, 2003, cited in a highly recommended paper on "Dirty Bombs: The Threat Revisited," by Peter D. Zimmerman, with Cheryl Loeb, Defense Horizons, #38 (Fort McNair, Washington, DC: National Defense University, Jan. 2004), p. 5.

86 This "dirty bomb" discovery is quietly mentioned in footnotes by Stephen Flynn: *America the Vulnerable: How Our Government is Failing to Protect Us from Terrorism* (New York: HarperCollins, 2004), p. 176.

87 In the absurd and tragic Russian state response, 331 hostages and many others were killed.

88 Flynn pp. 24–6. Countries worldwide are facing smugglers with considerable sophistication at moving stolen goods, drugs, weapons, and human beings across borders. Terrorists are integrated with such operators and operations, as has been recently documented by David E. Kaplan, "Paying for Terror," *U.S. News & World Report*, Dec. 5, 2005, pp. 40–54. The article does not broach nuclear issues.

89 Data from Flynn, *America the Vulnerable*.

5

COUNTERTERRORISM

It should not be forgotten that the norm of today—a U.S.-led coalition war against international terrorism—is an astonishing change from past practices. Not even during the Ronald Reagan presidency was U.S. policy and strategy so focused on terrorists or "sub-state actors." Perhaps never before in U.S. history, except in episodic fighting with Barbary Pirates between 1801 and 1816, has the country found itself so militarily preoccupied over many years with a problem not attributable to a sovereign state. Al Qaeda, a very original sort of enemy, has sparked this change.

Nor perhaps in world history has there been a *multinational* community so focused on trying to cooperate against violent political renegades. The closest parallels, demanding collaboration by past states in international assembly, may have been the impressive efforts orchestrated by the United Kingdom and other nations to suppress piracy on the seas and to end the slave trade. Both piracy and slaving are vicious and commercial enterprises, but both by nature are primarily nonpolitical. Far from challenging states directly, normally pirates and slave traders strive to disappear between the seams of international politics. They draw blood quickly and usually quietly, to avoid entanglements and exposure. They are by no means "revolutionary powers" or "revisionists of the world order," as a Henry Kissinger might call some states he has studied.[1]

In stark contrast, Al Qaeda and its networked allies are explicitly and overtly making continuous war. They place no credence in the international state system. Those under attack in this war by the Militant Muslim International[2] are allegedly "apostate regimes" in the Islamic Middle East and North Africa; Israel and its allies; North Atlantic Treaty Organization states that destroyed the terrorist presence in Afghanistan in 2001 or fight now in Iraq; and of course the United States of America.[3] This war, as both sides openly recognize, will be long. How could it not be when, despite the killing or capture of so many middle and senior Taliban and Al Qaeda officers thus far, the top three enemy leaders remain at large, still publishing and fighting, six years after 9-11?

This chapter reviews counterterrorism policies and practices of present and recent past, doing so under two rubrics. The first is about individual state efforts; the second covers multinational and United Nations efforts. The former have been the most important, historically. Multinational institutions of the twentieth century were new and weak in the period of the League of Nations (1920s through 1940s) and, in the latter decades of the century, multinational institutions still tended to act—or deliberate without acting—as states, *against other states* posing conventional threats. Until very recently, multinational institutions usually had special aversion to problems posed by "indirect aggression." That phenomenon—indirect aggression—is real and well known but undefined in the United Nations Charter and thus awkward each time it arises. In the Cold War, guerrillas and terror groups ranged about freely, unhindered even by the Security Council and occasionally supported by the General Assembly. Even today, the General Assembly is embarrassingly unable to define "terrorism." So its new denunciations thereof, while helpful, are underpowered in their effects. And yet a new spirit of enhanced cooperation against terrorism does indicate an improvement in the multinational realm and in prospects for eventual success against the Militant Muslim International.

Individual state responses to terrorism

Because terrorism is intensely political, its challenge to governments is profound, whether the challenge be internal to a country, foreign-based, or as multinational in character, as Al Qaeda. No state can be credible if it long ignores declarations of war against it by violent groups conspiring and acting in pursuance of such declarations. Nor can a state rightfully permit safe haven to such groups, so that the combination of violent words, preparations, and acts are flaunted from there, against *others.* This is a form of criminal negligence, or willful support to transnational terrorism; either way, it is a violation of the principles of sovereignty and encourages all violence-prone groups.

It is thus dangerous for a democracy, such as India, to permit decades of political organization, agitation, robbery, and terrorism by the "Naxalites." They take their name from a low-intensity conflict begun by the Communist Party of India (Maoist) in 1967 in Naxalbari, north of Calcutta. The group has flourished in such states as Chhattisgarh, and Naxalites now have a presence in as much as one-fourth of all of India's districts.[4] Neighboring Nepal, for its own part, takes immense risks when it allows indigenous Maoists to prosper in rural areas, to propagandize at will, and to take de facto control over great reaches of rural lands. The Communist Party of Nepal (Maoist) has grown to assume a cockiness that brings it to "negotiate" with normal political parties and has formally objected to being excluded from deliberations with the monarchy before the crown reinstated parliament in mid-2006.[5] Both these Asian states have failed their citizens in these respects.

It is just as dangerous for established Western powers, such as France or the United States, to bargain with terrorists who take hostages, as Iran and Lebanese Hezbollah did in the Middle East in the 1980s. To make deals with such entities was to shame the legitimate power of elected state governments, including that of Lebanon, and to bare such weaknesses to other potential extortionists. Yet governments submitted to such indignities at that time. Terrorism can also threaten and disrupt the normal legitimate functions of a state. That is, assassination of ministers and ambassadors, so damaging to international norms and principles and so encouraging to political extremists, also damages day-to-day government operations. It may be rare that a terrorist assassination threatens the very existence of a modern state—one would have to seek out examples from World War I: the killers of Archduke Franz Ferdinand of the Hapsburg Empire or of Nicholas II of Russia. However, any state may be thoroughly shaken and perhaps demoralized and weakened for months by even one illicit execution by terrorists. The damage was sensed deeply in Italy when kidnapped Christian Democratic Party leader Aldo Moro was murdered by the Red Brigades in 1978. Great staunchness has been required of Sri Lanka, which lost Prime Minister Ranasinghe Premadasa, murdered in 1993 by the Liberation Tigers of Tamil Eelam.

Though the seriousness of the terrorist challenge has often been apparent and the need for occasional force was evident well before 9-11, the will and ability of a state to respond have usually been less strong. Counter-force, often considered, has rarely been used (as our first edition concluded in 2000.) In the specifically American case, this conclusion was echoed after study of defense and national security documents of the United States by the University of Virginia's Timothy Naftali for his 2005 book, *Blind Spot.* [6] Naftali's views paralleled conclusions in the narrower study of the Pentagon's Joint Staff's deliberations and papers done by Richard H. Shultz Jr. and released in unclassified form early in 2004:[7] Even senior U.S. military leaders have usually opposed the force options in counterterrorism. In practice, states use a range of approaches, usually beginning with those least forceful. Capitals normally begin with moderation and conciliation; quite often they remain within that zone even when its available methods fail.

Concessions

Outright concessions to terrorists are not the norm in government either. Even a state that feels driven to make concessions will usually be cagey enough to demand negotiables in return. However, rank concessions do occur, and one or two states a year will make them. In this, nations are akin to families made desperate by the kidnapping of a loved one. Families usually pay the ransom demanded, or some part of it. So do corporations whose officers have been grabbed. Political or criminal hostage takers may receive several thousand dollars or much more in many parts of the world, and $30,000 is now the average ransom in Iraq.[8] Then there are the upper reaches, in the tens of millions; staggering sums have been paid to free executives, beginning in the 1960s when Latin American revolutionary "idealists" found they could also make their organizations wealthy. Some states will block such private payments for freeing a hostage. Usually, however, the state has no such power in practice. The family or a hired negotiator orchestrates the exchange quietly. Officially, U.S. posture long opposed such private settlements for American citizens, but the State Department liberalized its stance several years ago and though it still discourages deal making by bereaved families or businesses, it may look away if need be.

Complete concessions to terrorists also come, sometimes, at governmental levels. Consider states' behavior when armed parties seize airliners. The risks to numerous captive citizens can seem too high for stalling, let alone counterforce. In the 1960s and 1970s governments frequently gave in on all points—the aircraft, money, access to a "golden bridge" of escape for the terrorists. One might have hoped that such flat surrenders became passé, given the large number of state counterterrorist forces now on standby. Not so. India Air flight 814, with 155 persons aboard, was hijacked in December, 1999 and landed at Kandahar, Afghanistan. The Kashmiri Muslim militants inside the plane had much in common with the Taliban who quickly appeared in jeeps outside. The demand was for freedom of three Kashmir militant leaders jailed in India. New Delhi submitted. This doubtless exhilarated Taliban and the Kashmiri extremists; certainly it exhilarated the three released terrorists. For the world, the effects were sad and damaging. One of the men freed was Maulana Massoud Azhar, formerly a leader of the hijackers' larger group Harakat ul-Mujahidin, which means "Movement of the Holy Warriors." HUM was enabled to further its long record of terrorism; their camps in Afghanistan were among the many that had to be destroyed in post-9-11 air strikes by the Coalition. A free man, Azhar promptly returned to his terrorist work by founding a new Kashmiri group, Jaish-e-Mohammed, without interference from Pakistani authorities. Before 2001 was over, this new group was associated with two major attacks on parliaments—one in Kashmir and one in India proper—that left forty people dead. Another escapee in the Flight 814 deal was Ahmed Omar Sheik, convicted in the abduction and murder of U.S. journalist Daniel Pearl.[9] Yet, a month before this deal with terrorists, New Delhi had announced the establishment of a bilateral counterterrorism working group with the United States. And a few months later, New Delhi would introduce an international convention against terrorism at the UN General Assembly.[10] Such events encourage cynicism. Moreover, such events prompt states toward unilateralism that the international community may dislike.

For a time, 9-11-2001 makes it more difficult for a state to withstand the negative publicity accompanying drastic concessions to terrorists, but further such cases will occur. Some states—or perhaps any state when sufficiently challenged and overmatched in cleverness by gunmen—might incline toward concessions that make a crisis disappear, rather than supporting general moral and legal principles. Some governments have yet to create serious counterterrorist forces. Capitals may show allergies to any outside offers of armed help, for reasons religious, cultural, or emotional. Many citizens, and all those with any connection to the hostages, will warmly approve the settlement, despite the larger damage it may do. Finally, there are the victims: One can hardly expect hostages to think beyond their own captivity and fear toward deterring the next round of such terrorism. Thus, concessions to terrorists seem inevitable in some cases.

Negotiations

Another context in which a state may try to negotiate with terrorists is when they are integral to the activities of a major insurgency.[11] Colombia has been unable to free itself from internal violence for a half-century. Since the mid-1960s, the Revolutionary Armed Forces of Colombia (FARC) have festered and grown. Several of the state's recent presidents have made indulgent gestures to FARC but found their efforts unrewarded. In 1997, when Ernesto Samper opted for concessions, a foreign journalist took note of the irony that rebel movements all over Latin America were fading away while FARC was winning victories against the army and government and gaining strength. He quoted Carlos Conte, a government minister: "Historically in Colombia, each time the government makes announcements that it's trying to negotiate with the guerrillas, there has been an increase in terrorist actions, with the obvious purpose of obtaining a position of strength."[12] Samper's successor, Andres Pastrana, attempted a reckless[13] concession to kick-start negotiations: He effectively granted autonomy over a zone the size of Switzerland to the insurgents. That provided the FARC with security, unfettered training areas, and authority over the trapped Colombian citizens living in the zone. And it produced no serious concession by the FARC.

Madrid has been far more successful in negotiating with its major internal enemy: Basque Homeland and Liberty, or ETA, terrorists, who began their fight in 1959. The post-Franco constitution of Spain gave Basque political forces an opportunity to ask for unprecedented regional authority over their own affairs—although not over foreign policy or defense matters. Basques voted for this limited autonomy in 1979, and Madrid later approved the referendum and its arrangements for regional assemblies, local police forces, and the like. The concessions by the state ameliorated regional tensions enough to weaken the Basque political support for terrorism and gratify the more proper and pacific Basques favoring autonomy. The new status of semi-autonomy did not end ETA terrorism, but it did undermine it. Spain now hopes that its legal and administrative concessions have fatally weakened this entrenched movement. Indeed, given these political realities and the law enforcement methods resulting in legions of arrests, such hopes are not groundless. ETA's unilateral ceasefire, announced in April, 2006, even if it was also violated that December with a car bombing, could more generally last. It could last for years. It could develop into a firm peace protecting all of Spain. It is possible.[14]

Law enforcement

The law enforcement approach is the single most common one that states use when facing terrorism. If that seems an easy generalization, it is easily defended. The precedence of law—the existence of statutes, ready at hand—often suffices for punishing most aspects of terrorist operations. States normally do have in place legal barriers against, and punishments for, such common crimes as robbery, document fraud, illegal weapons possession, assault, and the like on which terrorism routinely depends. This fact has long made it possible for a government to punish terrorists or would-be terrorists who do of course have many political rights as citizens; when they transgress laws, vocal self-defense as "a political minority" and the like need not keep them at liberty. Terrorists are often tried and convicted as criminals. This law enforcement approach is in evidence even now, amid a "global war on terrorism."

There may be in the law insufficiencies that a government encounters when facing terrorism. These often prompt it to make legal changes—by fiat or after democratic debate. Within the United States after 9-11, some three dozen states reexamined and changed laws related to terrorism. Thoughtful lawmakers were doing the same worldwide. During 2005, for example, Ethiopia was strengthening its laws against terrorists' fund raising: banning money laundering and also *hawalas* (an informal money-transferring system), and requiring domestic banks to keep better intelligence on customers potentially involved in terrorism. Nearby, Kenya was toughening its relevant laws by broadening what is allowable as evidence in courts and by drafting a "Suppression of Terrorism Bill." Nigeria worked on its own antiterrorism bill that, if passed, would permit incarceration for up to thirty-five years. Current Nigerian criminal codes do not define terrorism as a crime.[15] That same gap was common to many countries in the late twentieth century.

"Conspiracy" and "membership in an illegal armed group" are prime examples of the sorts of additional crimes that governments write into law when pressed by terror groups. Criminalizing "conspiracy" troubles some civil liberties advocates, but without an ability to charge would-be terrorists with "conspiracy," there may be little real authority with which to preempt violent political crimes, such as the August 2006 airline bombing plot preempted by the British. Without such charges as "conspiracy to commit terrorism," a government may be left with no option but (1) awaiting the bloody results or (2) arresting suspects on such minor charges as lying to authorities or document fraud. It is true that an arrest based on interviews in which the suspect lies to an officer can be "useful in disrupting groups and their plans."[16] However, it sets up a very brief sentence and gives broad warning of police surveillance. So, a serious penalty for terrorist conspiracy is an important tool of counterterrorism.

A second issue with existing laws may be that "terrorism" charges are available to authorities but they are badly written, or too weak, or permit incarceration for periods far short of what justice would require given the heinous character of much terrorism today. Such legal "shortages" may dictate that suspects are not convicted or are given early release. This creates immediate problems of security and encourages cynicism among citizens or the country's allies—but it occurs. During June 2006, Indonesia released— for the second time—Abu Bakar Bashir, an overtly pro–Al Qaeda cleric. Widely seen as the spiritual head of Jemaah Islamiyah, he was released to a crowd of jubilant followers from his *madrassas*. He had served a mere 26 months for association with Bali bombings of October 2002, killing 200 people. There were other notable releases that year. In July 2006, Nikos Papanastasiou, a founder of the November 17 terrorist group in Greece, was freed after serving a mere four years.[17] One can only imagine what his victims' families felt.

Today, the world's parliaments are stewing with debates and initiatives on matters linking terrorism concerns to aliens' rights and citizenship, crime, financial fraud, immigration, subversion, and xenophobia. Such debates should be healthy; they are democracy in action; they may better define societal opposition to terrorism; they are an aide once a state begins the highly demanding, forcible activity that suppression of terrorists may take. Whatever other options a state may use—from illegal covert support to paramilitary forces to open appeals to the public for aid—the law enforcement options are nearly always both important and useful during counterterrorist campaigns.

The rubric of "law enforcement" is a broad one. Democracies have a way of responding too slowly to terrorism, and then, repeatedly prodded and bloodied, turning to harsh lawful measures. Few states might be deemed as liberal and gentle internally as Canada; in its external affairs, it only barely supervised its borders until the shock of 9-11-01, and even now its active armed forces number only some 60,000, far too few for so large a country. However, when separatists of the Quebec cause turned militant (after 1960) and then began killing and took ministers hostage (1970), Canada changed. Ottawa revived an early twentieth-century "War Measures Act" and allowed intrusive police practices, use of *agents provocateurs*, countless arrests, and detention for unusual periods before or without trial. Such measures were taken against fellow Canadian citizens; the problem was not one of aliens, let alone foreign terrorists captured abroad, such as those now detained by the United States at Guantanamo Bay, Cuba.[18] A hot issue since 9-11 has been how much Canada will permit intelligence work against indigenous threats. The stakes are high: In mid-2006, the government arrested seventeen radical Muslim suspects for plotting to destroy the Parliament and behead the prime minister. Nearly all the suspects were Canadians, apparently without formal ties to Al Qaeda, but citizens' discussions of surveillance "spiked" upward. A *New York Times* report on the patient police work leading up to the arrests was titled "Lessons from Canada: Snooping Works."[19]

Today, Europe offers multiple views of such change in one democratic horizon. Many states show belated or stronger determination. The United Kingdom struggled successfully with Irish separatism and is presently enjoying a "strategic pause"; that is fortunate, given the sudden new challenge of Muslim violence. Britain is long familiar with Arab faces, Southwest Asian identities, and foreign cultural groups in major cities; even a quarter-century ago, one could walk a London boulevard and feel closer to a United Nations convention than to an English town of old. Anti-Muslim spirit or anti-Arab racism were not the reasons why Britain has turned to urban camera surveillance; crime, hooliganism, and Irish radicalism were the reasons for that expensive innovation. However, some saw a strengthening politico-religious undercurrent, especially in the activism of several brutish clerics. In July ("7 / 7") 2005, the island experienced tragedy in its "tube" transit system. Another major plot two weeks later failed, leading to police sweeps and one shootout-forced entry at Dalgarno Gardens, West London, which wrecked an apartment but caused no deaths.[20] Thus, 2006 found the long-time prime minister and leader of Labour—hardly a British party known to denigrate the alien or oppress the poor man—calling for intensifying legal countermeasures against totalitarian "jihadis."

As remarkable are the political forces changing law enforcement in the famously liberal states of Holland and Belgium.[21] These countries have faced markedly increased illegal immigration and dealt with violence by fanatics adhering to a form of Islam. Parliaments are now reviewing the laws. This is true throughout Western Europe: In a late 2005 survey of current legislation, Britain's paper *The Guardian* found most states have tough laws permitting detention of terror suspects without trial or perhaps even without charges. France allows as much as four days of detention on a judge's order and up to four years' detention prior to trial, as will Spain. Greece is swift to levy a charge but can then hold a suspect as long as eighteen months before trial. Germany requires an appearance before a judge but then permits up to six months of detention. Britain could detain a suspect without charges for fourteen days; Mr. Tony Blair sought approval for expanding that to three months; Parliament ultimately allowed only a two-week increase, to twenty-eight days total.[22]

Australia is another country wherein the traditional welcome mat for immigrants has now been kicked about by some newcomers, making citizens wonder whether their welcome should be withdrawn. Formerly, when Australians faced critical foreign press stories, these usually focused on the rights and financial status of internal Aborigines; recently, critics are more likely to question policy and actions on immigration, including the temporary detention camps for those arriving without papers from abroad. Indignation and occasional violence characterize these immigrants' camps. Stays in such quarters are understood to be "temporary," but that concept is elastic. Meanwhile, Australia deals with real terrorist threats from a miniscule Muslim minority. The homeland was unnerved by losing more than eighty citizens vacationing in the nearby Bali Indonesia town of Kuta on October 12, 2002. French officials warned Sydney in the next year that a terrorist they were hunting was living and recruiting in their city and had been for five years. By 2005, intelligence was reported to be watching some seventy men known to have taken training in Pakistan or Afghanistan. Several authorities called for "draconian" laws to give the state the counterterrorist powers it needs.[23] Prime Minister John Howard signed a stiff new law, and police used it early in 2006 to pounce on twenty-three properties in Sydney and Melbourne and arrest nine men. It was gravely announced that police surveillance had permitted an inside view on two rival groups and each was racing to be first to register a major attack on Australia. Stockpiled chemicals and other property were seized in the skillful raid.[24] Thus far, Australia has suffered no direct "hit" on its own territory.

Private legal suits

There is a further, somewhat unusual form of the use of a country's legal codes to oppose terrorism. It occurs when a state allows, and perhaps enforces, a private legal suit against a foreign terrorist or terrorist state. In 1996, the U.S. Congress and Clinton Administration departed notably from past U.S. norms by stripping away a protection that foreign governments have—immunity from private suits—if such governments are formally classified as sponsors of terror. A New Jersey father took the initiative to file when his daughter, Alisa Flatow, was slain in a Palestine Islamic Jihad bus bombing. PIJ's money comes largely from Iran. This placed the Flatows' suit in the federal courts, where an American judge rendered a major cash award to the family. Today, there is a considerable line of similar federal judgments for other U.S. civilians, arising from attacks by Hamas or PIJ.

Because Iran has always supported Hezbollah militarily, diplomatically, and with tens of millions of dollars a year,[25] the family of Col. William Higgins was awarded a remarkable $57 million for his death under prolonged torture by that terrorist group— Lebanese Hezbollah killed Higgins while he served as a UN peacekeeper in troubled Lebanon. Another collective private suit against the Islamic Republic of Iran succeeded in Washington in December 2006. A federal judge apportioned awards totaling $254 million to survivors of American Air Force personnel killed and injured in a peacetime[26] bombing of Khobar Towers, Dhahran, Saudi Arabia, a decade before. The perpetrators, Saudi Hezbollah, were declared to be recruited, trained, inspired, and paid by the state of Iran, its interior ministry, and its Revolutionary Guards. The profligacy with which Iran supports Middle Eastern terrorists and thus makes new American victims of tourists, travelers, and students in Israel is now rivaled by the profligacy of the U.S. court awards. Some claimants, including successful ones, are unlikely to ever be paid; Iranian assets impounded in 1979 when the U.S. embassy was seized in Tehran are exhausted.[27]

Proscription

Proscription is an important form of legal barrier to the eruption of internal terrorist enemies. An act by which a state flatly bars the existence of a named party or organization, proscription is a difficult step for many countries to take and is thus not commonplace. Neither is proscription rare. There is almost no published analysis of the risks and advantages of proscription and the success rates of states proscribing a party. In one admirable article, John Finn[28] surveyed proscription legislation on the books in Austria, Chile, Estonia, France, Germany, Ireland, Israel, Portugal, Romania, Rwanda, and the United States. All these states claim the principled right but exercise it infrequently and with great care. Usually the state acts only because the organization in question openly denounces representative government or democracy as forms of government. Doing actual harm is not always required under these countries' laws for proscription to occur, but many parties are banned after providing a wealth of violent acts for examination. The banned have included fascists in Italy, the Communist Party in the United States in former times, the Kurdistan Workers Party in Australia, and fourteen groups in Northern Ireland, including loyalists of the Ulster Freedom Fighters and Ulster Volunteer Forces.[29] Bangladesh proscribed the terrorist group Jamaat ul Mujahedin Bangladesh (JMB) and renewed the ban in subsequent years, which proved useful in 2006 as the country captured several top suspected leaders: Abdur Rahman and Bangla Bhai.[30] Religious parties that appear antithetical to democracy have also been blocked from competing in elections by proscription; examples include several parties in Turkey and the American-Israeli extremists of Kach and Kahane Chai.[31]

Two challenges accompany a state's decision to proscribe a party it deems likely to engage in violence or terrorism. One is of principle; another is of practicality. Some believe that democratic principles make it logical, easier, and more effective to permit or license all parties, however radical, and restrain with state powers only when individual violent members break laws. However, there is greater wisdom in the principle visible in Abraham Lincoln's rhetorical question about the danger in protecting open rebellion with the law's majesty: "Are all the laws, but one, to go unexecuted and the government itself go to pieces, lest that one be violated?"[32] Concluding otherwise, he suspended the right of *habeas corpus* until the rebellion was ended. Britain and Prime Minister Winston S. Churchill did something similar in the first years of World War Two: An order under Regulation 18 B of defense laws allowed indefinite detention of British citizens who were members of enemy political organizations.[33] When published platforms and related actions give every indication of hatred of democracy, the prudent democracy will consider proscribing that narrow party.

A second, very practical problem is whether banning a group by name will inhibit terrorists. Certainly a barrier to public assembly, overt publications, and media appearances can dramatically weaken the success of a radical political party. However, what of a terror group whose life is clandestine? It may change its name when the state proscribes it, or it may ignore the ban, but that has disadvantages for the terrorists, and as our brief study of "fronts" (see ch. 2) indicates, the overt political work of a violent underground is a force-multiplier. Knowing this, few hard-pressed states give up their statutory power to ban a group dedicated to destroying the state or eliminating the state's authority in a given ethnic region, as insurgencies often seek to do. Critics of proscription advance a further argument. In the case of marginal political parties, some worry that proscription will drive extremists underground. In Britain, the Muslim Council of Britain—which has publicly deplored terrorism—opposes proscription of Hizb ut Tahrir, an offshoot of the Muslim Brotherhood, lest the ban drive extremism underground and intensify it. That concern might seem mainly to be one of civil liberties advocates, but in fact it is shared by Britain's Association of Chief Police Officers.[34]

Martial Law

When moderation or half-measures fail, there may be a regression into martial law. In this, the classic phrase "law and order" is cleaved and loses the first of those important words. Countries may, and do permanently or temporarily, give up most law and legality in favor of forceful restoration of public order. This is what occurred in Uruguay. Known to some as "the Switzerland of Latin America," and a sturdy edifice, Uruguay did fall to the hundreds of little hammer blows of the communist Tupamaros.[35] Those attacks began in earnest in 1965 and continued intensely for seven years, until they caused an April 1972 military coup. Something of the same came to the Turkish Republic, that daring enterprise in Muslim democracy now nearing a century old. After years of mounting terrorism, to a level at which there were almost a dozen murders a day by rightists, leftists, and others, generals stepped in during September 1980, made martial law, and suppressed terrorism. These two national stories have favorable endings in the restoration of democracy, but there is a long historical string dangling dozens of false charms, cases of glittering promises in which all powers were soon wrapped around the arms of despots. Some of these usurpers prove poor even at providing security. Some are merely replaced by others just as bad for the citizens.

The relative restraint of the militaries in these two cases cited is no norm and offers little reassurance to democratic peoples. Martial law can be a sham excuse by those in power to destroy critics and opponents indefinitely. In modern history, the cases in which rulers once deemed legitimate then turned tyrannical and imposed years of martial law include too many Latin American instances to mention; Ferdinand Marcos of the Philippines; and today Robert Mugabe. Once, Mugabe was a darling of many international political observers for his important role in changing Rhodesia. After a quarter century at the helm of the renamed state of Zimbabwe, he has become, or is exposed for, a racist demagogue who knows few limits and has fewer scruples. Since 2000, Mugabe has been exhorting mobs to drive white farmers off lands their families have worked for generations. This is an example of state-sponsored terrorism and of state-sponsored militias engaged in terrorism.[36] In July 2006, shortly before elections, the despot ordered the arrest of his chief political rival and many others, relatively easy to do under statutes that ban most forms of pacific political activity.

Intelligence

From policing and law enforcement topics it is natural to move on to intelligence. In conventional war, intelligence has a defined role and a duly appointed officer with a staff to manage the issues and flow of intelligence. In irregular warfare, intelligence has a far more central role. Counterterrorism turns on intelligence. It demands martial discretion and precision of the most unusual degrees.

Along with lack of will power, and concern for collateral damage, the most common reason that a state does not use military force in response to a vicious terrorist attack is lack of certain and prompt information. Terrorists bring this about by habitually veiling their personnel, logistical structure, and training areas. France's Judge Jean-Louis Bruguiere is famed not only for his will power and fearlessness in prosecution of terrorists but for the intelligence he helps to develop, collate, and deploy in the courtroom.[37] The William J. Clinton administration's success in rendering for trial South African citizen and Al Qaeda member Khalfan Khamis Mohamed, a perpetrator of the U.S. Embassy bombing in Tanzania, was a product of good intelligence. One of that president's possible failures, a missile-strike on a pharmaceuticals plant in Khartoum, Sudan the year before, as retaliation for the same Al Qaeda attack was due to poor intelligence about the target.[38]

This section will turn to four central and practical problems in the management of intelligence for counterterrorism. First, many states simply lack sufficient trained human assets to preempt or capture terrorists. Second, the effort by some states to create fresh intelligence channels also brings problems of hierarchies, bureaucracies, secrecy, and interagency coordination. Third, covert action, while utterly necessary to dealing with overseas terrorists, remains morally or legally troubling to many citizens. Fourth, difficulty in obtaining intelligence pushes police and military interrogators and the governments in charge of them to personal and legal limits and sometimes beyond.

One of the least palatable realities about terrorism is how it may drive a modern democratic society toward something most unnatural to it: spying, especially spying on one's fellow citizens. "The Open Society," as philosopher Karl Popper called it, is built on interlocking features of equality, freedom, and civility—which might be defined as the accommodation of differences in pacific manners. Would-be totalitarians—be they Bolsheviks, fascists, or neo-fascist Islamicists—have a qualified view of equality and openly disparage other features of liberalism. They quietly conspire against it, from within and without, as well as using overt violence. This combination is only successfully resisted by the government that gains superior intelligence, and it is best acquired today by varied technical means and above all by human agents.

Before satellites, radio receivers, computerized data mining and the like, human agents were the main collectors of intelligence. Ancient China's military theorist Sun Tzu taught that battle should not be risked without exact knowledge and even predictability; to get these, spies of all kinds must be hired. Indeed, he argued, the leader who declines to employ enough spies is inhuman. When willingly "ignorant of his enemy's situation" he is "completely devoid of humanity" because his refusal to spend gold on spies condemns soldiers and citizens to death needlessly.[39] Sun Tzu's advice for intensive "HUMINT" collection is something few democratic governments have been willing to take—absent full-scale war.[40] Of course, the Chinese theorist's agents might do more than listen and learn. Some were trained to proactively disturb, disrupt, or destroy enemy organizations. They might be, in effect, agents of influence. Here again, democracies have been very reluctant. The FBI appears to have used such methods successfully within the United States against white supremacists in the mid-to-late 1990s, without complaints from many citizens or activists. They appear to have done so again, in tandem with Florida police, in the June 2006 arrests of the "Miami Seven" who had pledged allegiance to Osama Bin Laden and discussed destroying the Sears Tower in Chicago. However, there is little to no evidence in print showing the CIA as successfully doing such hard-nosed work abroad before 9-11—even though legal constraints were considerably less than they are for the FBI.

Modern democratic states have often proven outright negligent about their own security—the theme probed by important books published during the 1980s under such titles as *Kingdoms of the Blind* and *How Democracies Perish*.[41] Just as today some states decline to raise a large army or navy, some deem distasteful the hiring of spies and write rules that prevent what spies they do hire from mixing with criminals and terrorists— precisely the people the spies most need to approach and to fool. In the inter-American inquiries and finger pointing after 9-11-01 about failures of intelligence, it was all but forgotten that not long before, Congressman (later Senator) Robert Torricelli of New Jersey was laboring to keep U.S. intelligence agents separated from killers who were also good intelligence sources in Guatemala.[42] He and some Capitol Hill colleagues devoted too little energy to improving U.S. intelligence-*gathering* capabilities. One might think the "Pearl Harbor" of 9-11 changed everything. However, after that tragedy, when angry about White House budget proposals on community development programs, Baltimore's mayor Martin O'Malley gave a fiery speech comparing this fiscal way of "attacking America's cities" with the Al Qaeda airplanes of September 11.[43] If there has been a Mayor O'Malley speech in similarly strong language and devoted to enhancing human intelligence assets against terrorism, to defend Baltimore—or all of America— this author is unaware of it.

It now appears that before 9-11, there was not a single language-qualified U.S. case officer living in Afghanistan and tracking Middle Eastern and foreign terrorists there in vast numbers. At any rate, there were almost no such experts in the entire directorate of operations at the Central Intelligence Agency. There was no program in the 1990s to insert reliable and convincing American spies into foreign Muslim terrorist organizations.[44] Large, important underworlds of Muslim militancy in the United States, United Kingdom, Germany, and elsewhere were largely ignored by official intelligence agencies in the West.

This left the United States partially blind to the personalities and general character of the growing threat—generally, in Afghanistan, or for the impending 9-11 plot. Up to late 1999, there was no American expert to liaise directly with such formidable nationalist commanders as Ahmad Shah Massoud, "The Lion of the Panshir Valley." A hero of the anti-Soviet guerrilla war and opposed by nature to the foreign-sponsored Taliban militia that later overtook most of his country, Massoud was murdered two days before 9-11 by a highly effective international plot, a damaging loss at exactly the moment the world would need him most. Another reason why the pre-9-11 dearth of American intelligence on Afghanistan still shocks is that open sources readily displayed the magnitude of problem of foreigners entering Afghanistan for guerrilla and terror training. In 1994— four years before Al Qaeda exploded two American embassies and six and a half years before the World Trade Towers were burned to the ground—*New York Times Sunday Magazine* reporter Tim Weiner drew attention to the tens of thousands in training there.[45] Other reports accumulated in the world media over subsequent years. When the news weekly magazine *Insight* asked in early 2001, "What terrorist hot spots should we be most concerned about?" one academic replied "Southwest Asia is probably the most dangerous part of the world right now. Start with Osama Bin Laden in Afghanistan...."[46] Central Intelligence Agency director George Tenet declared that the United States was "at war" with Al Qaeda...so why did CIA not station credible American officers in that country?[47]

A second issue of intelligence follows directly: new assets and new arrangements since 9-11. Here too, some believe that 9-11 changed everything. In fact, there has been an immense amount of movement and only some good change. Britain still only employs some 2,000 officers in its foreign intelligence service, MI 6,[48] and the scheduled increases for 2005–2008 involve adding only handfuls of new people. MI 5, the domestic service, will grow; MI 5 is hiring—while also fending off the terrorism supporters or infiltrators trying to apply.[49] The entire national intelligence complex in the United Kingdom has a surprisingly small budget: £1.3 billion, reportedly set to grow to £1.6 billion.[50] The United States spends twenty times as much; the intelligence budget is now publicly reported to be $40 billion. However, despite the evident shortages of human intelligence assets, growth after 9-11 was not rapid. There was institutional sluggishness, and there was the problem that hiring and training a skilled case officer takes five to seven years.[51] Certainly, some improvements in democracies' intelligence abilities have been made. Yet, the U.S. intelligence establishment grew less quickly than believed after that unforeseen tragedy. George W. Bush, after his 2004 reelection, felt compelled to call, and call publicly, for a 50 percent increase in "HUMINT" assets. September 2005 still found new CIA chief Porter J. Goss vocally criticizing the sluggishness of CIA's directorate of operations in getting new officers into good field positions abroad. Goss had been a former CIA agent, and his criticism must have stung. The number 2 executive in that directorate resigned. Later, Goss himself resigned.[52]

For the U.S. intelligence structure, the most notable changes have been two: mobilization of Defense Department assets and reorganization of the larger national apparatus.

The Department of Defense has a budget a dozen times the size of the U.S. intelligence services and is thought to control 80 percent of U.S. intelligence assets. Under the aggressive leadership of Donald Rumsfeld, secretary from 2001 through 2006, the department engaged in new efforts of its own to get actionable intelligence on Al Qaeda and its violent partners. Some in the department were and are for listening abroad; many were and are now for listening and then taking action.[53] Both are possible with Special Operations Forces, which experienced swift growth under Rumsfeld, and are most recently joined by once-withheld elements of the Marine Corps. Intelligence for these operators is enhanced with some twenty new military liaison elements, attached to U.S. embassies in certain locales thought busy with terrorist operations. Unlike traditional military attaches, they are reportedly there to track terrorists for the special operations command and become familiar with the operating environment and institutions, rather than file reports for the Defense Intelligence Agency.[54] Conversely, the program is small, and its officers have all the same challenges of acclimatization, mastering language, and moving within a foreign culture that any other American intelligence officer has.

Washington's larger tier of changes is in how it organizes to fight the intelligence battle. Many of the answers have turned on better interagency coordination. This was suggested in the first campaign of the global war on terrorism: the late 2001 invasion of Afghanistan. CIA operators went quickly into the country and were as quickly followed by special operating forces. The former reported to Langley, Virginia; the latter reported to special operations command and to central command, both sited in Tampa, Florida. The intelligence experts and the military specialists were critical parts of a team; they shared risks, with CIA losing the first man; their cooperation was exceptionally good;[55] each helped to liaise with indigenous Afghan guerrillas; the results they created were remarkable. CIA's performance in working directly with operating military units was the result of considerable planning and thought. After the first Gulf War of 1991, complainants had it underperforming in the struggle for Kuwait. The critique yielded a change of attitude, enhancement of the agency's Office of Military Affairs, and better cooperation between CIA's directorate of operations and partners in military special operating forces.

The American strategic-level reorganization accomplished thus far began with a twenty-two-month effort as the new director of national intelligence by Ambassador John Negroponte.[56] His office staff would grow to 1,700 persons. This formal position sits above that of the chiefs of the civilian and military sides of U.S. intelligence. That is, it directs and coordinates the efforts of Central Intelligence (Director Porter Goss, and now Michael Hayden). During his tenure,[57] Negroponte had similar authority over military intelligence, including Dr. Stephen A. Cambone (who was working directly for the defense secretary), and the individual service intelligence branches and the supervening Defense Intelligence Agency. DIA is also based in Washington, is much smaller than the CIA, and has a master's-level college and a strong cadre of analysts, interpreters, and, increasingly, experts on the sub-conventional side of military operations. Negroponte was succeeded at the beginning of 2007 by Admiral James M. McConnell; Dr. Cambone moved aside as well, succeeded by Lt. Gen. James R. Clapper.

Another key facility under the DIA is the new National Counterterrorism Center. Sited in McLean, Virginia, it is within hailing distance of (1) the CIA at Langley, Virginia, and (2) executors of political and military authority in the Washington, DC area. NCTC opened in June, 2005 and is charged with collection and fusion of intelligence on terrorists from sixteen relevant U.S. agencies, including the enormous Department of Homeland Security,[58] the tiny U.S. Capitol Police, and the obvious candidates of varying sizes, such as the Central Intelligence Agency, the Department of Treasury, the Federal Bureau of Investigation, and the Department of Defense.[59] The new center, though promising, is also part of the U.S. government's ongoing exertions—and occasional trauma—with intelligence reassessment and reorganization. In the sixth year after 9-11, many problems remain.

The Drug Enforcement Agency, like the FBI, was not folded into the new Department of Homeland Security but remains within the Department of Justice. DEA will be a considerable source of information about terrorism for the director of national intelligence. Because of the nexus between the drug trade and political terrorism, the DEA's work can and should be closely integrated with that of other U.S. and foreign agencies. Only such a partnership can best track and inhibit such problems as the Taliban connections to heroin markets of the eastern United States. After decades of fighting its own difficult "war on drugs," the Drug Enforcement Agency has wide-ranging and talented operatives in foreign locales and the continental United States. These personnel are apparently less restricted by domestic law as to whom they can meet with or learn from.[60] Their human intelligence capabilities and infiltration tactics have application as models for other agencies and non-U.S. security forces, as they get good results. The DEA's notable experience in such work will be better catalogued and enhanced by a new training establishment at Quantico, Virginia.

The Federal Bureau of Investigation has itself been a study in reformation. "The Bureau" had an impressive run in the 1980s and 1990s. It did much to suppress international terrorists coming to or operating within the United States. It disassembled the early 1980s incarnation of violent Puerto Rican nationalism and showed follow-through as late as September 2005, when bureau personnel had a gun battle with Filiberto Ojeda Rios, a top leader, killed in a safe house in Puerto Rico. The FBI infiltrated and took apart white power groups and anti-federal militias in many American states, in some cases preempting plots that promised broad and bloody consequences. Counterterrorism was a growing mission for the FBI of the 1980s and 1990s, and the shift of resources was apparent. Regular budget increases allowed growth overseas, not just growth at home. More than fifty foreign cities have resident FBI "LEGATS," or Legal Attachés, usually in consulates or embassies of the United States, and their work includes counterterrorism.

However, real problems and harsh critics have also bedeviled this powerful subset of the U.S. Department of Justice. Before 9-11, only a few FBI offices showed adequate interest in the developing problem of militant Islam, and barely a handful spoke or read Arabic. This was true even years after foreign Muslims directed the 1993 truck bombing of the World Trade Center in New York City, followed by plots against the Hudson River Tunnel[61] and other landmarks. Those investigations produced court convictions, but they also aroused other American officials in intelligence and national security affairs who felt the FBI was (1) clutching evidence so tightly that other U.S. agencies could not see it and (2) was obsessed with trial procedures in ways that prevented a broader understanding of the growing problem of the militant Muslim international.[62] Criticism of the bureau's handling of terror cases was inflamed after 9-11 in the ways just indicated[63] and in yet another way: how national officers manage the important discoveries of FBI field offices. A final—and one could say perennial—critique is that the FBI cannot seem to manage the transition from paper management and record keeping to electronic forms. In 1993, an otherwise favorable portrait of the Bureau spotlighted the information management problem for strong criticism; by 2006, the Bureau had spent as much as $170 million on contractor SAIC (Science Applications International Corporation, headquartered in San Diego, CA) and other options and still had no system that remotely satisfied the bureau or its overseers in Congress.[64] The new effort to create a cyber "Sentinel," as the system will be called, is expected to cost $400 million.[65]

The FBI has had success working with intelligence offices below its national level. That is to say, regional task forces on terrorism have strongly benefited from many years of Department of Justice and FBI development and attention. There are regional intelligence fusion centers, such as one in Northern Virginia, where national experts and local cops pool what they know and discuss threats to the area. Many localities that once lacked intelligence specialists now have them, and many liaise well with the Bureau. Major cities' "Special Weapons and Tactics" (SWAT) teams often have FBI training from its respected Hostage Rescue Teams.

There are additional ways in which U.S. cities are rethinking how they deal with intelligence for counterterrorism. New York, under Commissioner Ray Kelly, has led the way. Hiring on David Cohen, a CIA operations chief under President Clinton, the city created its own intelligence division, with some 500 analysts and translators and agents. "Secure" from public view in a nondescript building in the central city, the division is producing its own intelligence—not just sifting what may fall from higher authorities in Washington and Langley. Kelly and Cohen are "taking policing outside New York City…to protect against another terrorist attack." The division rushed a team to Madrid after hideous bombings there in 2003 to learn what it could of transit system security. Also, the New York City police have introduced small offices into relevant foreign cities: Toronto, Montreal, Tel Aviv, Singapore, London, and Lyon where Interpol is headquartered. The new Intelligence Division is a concept that is smart and original and is bringing New York queries from other U.S. cities, such as Los Angeles, Chicago, and Phoenix, all wondering if they too need their own intelligence divisions. For obvious reasons, though, the trend may be resented by some whose first thoughts are protecting the roles and "turf" of the FBI.[66]

Covert action

Covert action is difficult to separate from successful intelligence work; it uses, but also generates, intelligence. For that and other reasons, it is an established feature of statecraft from time immemorial. It survives intact in a modern, United Nations–affected global community, in part because of such phenomena as transnational terrorism. Terrorists create a shadow world on the margins of normal, healthy politics; they cannot be found and brought to justice without superior intelligence, including clandestine action. Governments have found that this rubric may include diversion of terrorists' black bank accounts; waylaying operational messengers; sabotage of their illicit weapons depots; disruption of their electronic or paper propaganda sources, as by jamming broadcasts; and direct action against encampments to preempt actions or disrupt training and planning. What follows concerns only two of the many kinds of covert action: state assassination and rendition.

Assassination

Most governments refuse to discuss a policy of assassinating certain terrorist leaders. Israel—which considers itself at war—is unusual in the frankness with which it overtly threatens terrorists with this ultimate punishment. Examples of deliberate assassinations include the deaths of two successive Hamas leaders, Sheik Ahmed Yassin and Abdel Aziz al-Rantisi. The United States was long typical of the democracies and well known for its self-imposed ban on assassinations. Set in regulations in 1976 and repeatedly renewed by later administrations, the prohibition is now known publicly as Executive Order 12333, but it appears to have changed, or stretched, such that the George W. Bush White House may now allow, in extreme cases, the planned killing of carefully-designated individual terrorists. That may well be fully appropriate in time of war; the U.S. government remains secretive about its own self-imposed guidelines.[68] It is now

Box 5.1 French 'CT' intelligence

France does not maintain an entirely centralized intelligence system—nor do many countries. If there are advantages to fully "centralized intelligence," there are also advantages to "competitive" intelligence by rival bureaucracies within one national government.

Internally, the **Direction Centrale des Renseignments Generaux**, or "RG," is the largest service, with some 3900 officers, and possesses powers greater than some democracies would allow. "Through aggressive HUMINT and wiretap operations, the RG has been able to recruit tens of thousands of informants and deeply infiltrate radical *salafi* networks in the cites, the suburban and poor neighborhoods in and around Paris, Lyon, Lille, and Marseille, where most of the French Muslim community is concentrated and which erupted in rioting in November [2005]."

Direction de la Surveillance du Territoire (DST) specializes in counter-intelligence. Known for close linkages to the French police, it is "the main coordinating agency for internal security." Personnel are "judicial" more than military and report to the Ministry of the Interior. DST has only 1,000-plus officers, but it has developed an elaborate network of informants, some of who doubtless hope to reduce or defer prison sentences. "Once highly controversial, the DST culture of aggressive intelligence and destabilization operations (including the wide use of phone taps) against subversives has been the cornerstone of the French counterterrorism apparatus since the early 1980s." Some 150 CT arrests are attributable to DST in the years 2000–2005.

Externally, the **Direction Generale de la Securite Exterieure**, or DGSE, is the main intelligence service. Its overseas operations are crucial and include such theaters as Northern Africa, from which dozens of terrorists emerge annually to infiltrate or act in France.

Much less known is DNAT, or **Division Nationale Anti-Terroriste**. The newest service, its specialty has become *salafi* militants, whose threat to the state far exceeds that of, say, separatists in Corsica or Basque lands. DNAT deals with interagency bureaucracy in part by its "privileged links with local police units" and good relations with DST.

Other relevant agencies that aid in collecting, sorting, and using anti-terrorist intelligence include, of course, local police and, less expectedly, a judicial office in Paris. The **Section Anti-Terroriste du Parquet de Paris** is run by Jean-Louis Bruguiere, who travels worldwide gathering information on terrorist enemies of France, liaising with foreign specialists on terrorism, and preparing cases for the national courts back home. This justice's reputation for integrity and courage has become enormous.

Quotations are from Alexis Debat,"Terrorism and the Fifth Republic" *The National Interest* Winter, 2005/2006 pp. 55–61[67] evident that even the Clinton Administration debated, and might have allowed, the idea of assassinating Osama Bin Laden. Since 9-11, the White House has successfully hunted down and killed at least three Al Qaeda figures, with missiles, fired by unmanned aerial vehicles: Mohammad Atef, the military commander, in October, 2001 in Afghanistan; Qaed al-Harithi, the leader in Yemen, in November, 2002; and a secondary operative Hamza Rabia, in December, 2005.[69]

There are many examples of past campaigns by individual states that involve killing known or suspected terrorists. Several are much less well known than the Israeli operations highlighted in the films "Sword of Gideon" (1986) and "Munich" (2005). France appears to have conducted clandestine counterterrorism by raising a "Red Hand" against suppliers of the Algerian FLN in that war of 1954–1962. The Red Hand developed quickly and mysteriously and enjoyed superior intelligence on how the FLN rebels' network in Europe worked to supply the revolution with weapons and funds. Red Hand seems to have carried out assassinations, sunk vessels, and used other forcible means.[70] Because it was apparently the work of a state, Red Hand was very separable than another phenomenon of the time, the OAS, or Secret Armed Organization.[71] The latter was a covert group of pro-French army officers and others who used terror to try to hold on to French privileges in North Africa and hold Paris to its earlier commitments to keep Algeria within French control. Arising early in 1961, OAS soon turned nihilist, relishing the damage bombs could do and foolish as to what the results would be. Ultimately, OAS was attacking the French government; by contrast, Red Hand may well have been a French state intelligence arm, expert at covert action.

Contemporary examples of such lethal state activity include that of socialist Spain, challenged by the ETA Basque killers. The aforementioned constitutional devolution, by which the Basques attained semi-autonomy within Spain, had already come about, but this alone had not ended ETA terrorism. Thus, some members of the Spanish security apparatus formed an unofficial death squad to assassinate ETA functionaries and leaders. The personnel included individuals from the Anti-Terrorist Unit, the Civil Guard (or national police force), and the Interior Ministry, with the latter's chief, Jose Barrionuevo, being the most important figure. With black humor, the assassins called themselves the Anti-Terrorist Liberation Group (GAL) and operated from about 1983 to 1987. It has been alleged that France quietly agreed to operations on its side of the international border, where the ETA had long enjoyed safe haven. However, even the consent of Paris could not prevent this covert project from running headlong into political problems in Spain. The illegal killing was exposed in 1995; Interior Minister Barrionuevo was jailed in 2002; the affair heavily damaged the legacy of Socialist Party leader Felipe Gonzalez. Apparently this activity did not resume, but Spain went on to defeat the Etarras in other and legal ways. This short counterterrorist campaign is little known outside Spain.[72]

As the OAS case suggests, state activities deserve to be analyzed separately from the independent, pro-state terror groups, which form to check the authority of terror organizations over their neighborhoods or to otherwise defend their "turf" against perceived threats. Aptly termed "preservationist" terror groups or insurgencies by analyst Bard O'Neill,[73] they by no means depend on state connections. Examples include the JVP (Janatha Vimukthi Peramuna) organizers and hit men of the Sinhalese majority in Sri Lanka in the 1970s, who imagined they were protecting majority rights vis-à-vis the minority Tamil population. Another example is the very-much-weakened Ku Klux Klan in the United States and Canada, "fighting for white rights." However, right-wing or "pro-state" terror groups might at times enjoy information conduits from friendly officers within the state apparatus, armed forces, policing services, or intelligence units. Central American death squads may have at times operated with such limited state help. There are rare and perhaps revealing glimpses into Loyalist terror groups in Northern Ireland in this respect; pro-IRA entities regularly allege such collusion. Loyalist groups by the late 1990s were killing more people a year than were the IRA "Provos," and the pattern probably continues now, with the IRA in its strategic pause. Leaks of state intelligence, or independent groups that might act with the part-time participation of state or military officers, are a profound problem where they have lethal results. The state's dignity and legality are compromised; so is the counterterrorist work of others on state payrolls; tragic mistakes are likely and perhaps are encouraged by the shady nature of the process of targeting and striking and the like.

Rendition

State covert action against terrorism includes different and unique forms, and one of these is rendition. Rendition often combines covert or semi-covert action with law enforcement. It means the removal, often by force, of a wanted fugitive from someplace overseas. The wanted terrorist may be a citizen of any country, wanted for crimes against the country seeking him by rendition. Israel famously "snatched" Adolph Eichmann from "A House on Garibaldi Street"[74] in San Fernando, near Buenos Aires, Argentina in 1960, brought him to Israel for trail, and convicted him for war crimes. In what may have been a "rendition with Sudanese foreknowledge,"[75] French authorities spirited Ilich Ramirez Sanchez, a.k.a. Carlos the Jackal, from the Sudan in August, 1994 when he was incapacitated while undergoing a medical procedure. He is now a convict, jailed in France for his many crimes in that country. U.S. presidents, both Democratic and Republican, have rendered wanted terrorists and subsequently convicted them in federal courts. The Clinton administration even boasted previously of using the tool more than Republicans had, claiming at least nine renditions during two terms, 1993–2000.[76] In a manner fully according with U.S. law and with international conventions damning terrorists to arrest anywhere and anytime by any legitimate state authority, these fugitives from justice were brought into U.S. courts, tried, convicted, and jailed for lengthy terms.

Proponents of rendition can well argue that in cases of hardened terror leaders or operatives, rendition is moral and better (legally and politically) than doing nothing (there should never be a statute of limitations on mass murder and terrorism offenses). Rendition is also better than targeted killing. Indeed, rendition is a useful and underemployed tactic against terrorists that should be encouraged.[77] Instead, it is now hobbled by the important charges of torture of detainees in non-U.S. prisons: Syria, Jordon, Morocco and Egypt have all been mentioned in open reports[78] as mistreating their own citizens after the United States delivered terrorism suspects to them. In principle, rendition is entirely and easily separable from torture[79]—see below—and also from the much-criticized detention centers offshore in Guantanamo Bay, Cuba. Individual countries will doubtless carry on the practice when reasons of state or the crimes of the fugitive are great enough. Where the justice system of the country carrying out this covert action and subsequent public trial is wholesome, such counterterrorism deserves international encouragement—the same type it would give a country that had deployed peace keepers abroad who trapped a well-known pirate or indicted war criminal. Any capital risks negative reaction from the second country wherein the "snatch" occurs, but it is just as true that the rare unilateral action of rendition may well prod the harboring state, and all states, to be more willing to extradite fugitives wanted on charges of mass murder in terrorist actions.

Torture

The fourth and final aspect of counterterrorism intelligence to be discussed here is torture. Foully inhumane, banned by a UN convention, torture is nonetheless sometimes used[80] in counterterrorism in the effort to crack open the secrets of a clandestine organization. An example of continuing strong interest is the practice by the French in Algeria after 1954. The press of the late 1990s, and that of the immediate postmillennium, too has often carried disclosures, news, and old photographs of the systematic abuse the French Army and police turned on the Algerian FLN, especially beginning with the Battle of Algiers in 1956.[81] A major in military intelligence, Paul Aussorresses, later a general, is among those to confess to the practices of torture and nonjudicial executions. He is among those who are certain the practice in the professional security forces was well known and condoned at high levels. There has been similar press and academic interest in Argentine behavior in the "dirty war" of 1976–1983. A naval mechanics' school, ESMA, is now infamous—and a museum—for its involvement in routinized interrogation and torture of the leftists whom the state wanted to "disappear."[82] Members or presumed members of such groups as the Trotskyite People's Revolutionary Army, the pro-Cuban Armed Revolutionary Forces, and the Montoneros were all candidates for extreme methods of interrogation or outright murder. Like the French Army "Paras" in Algiers, the Argentines successfully broke many enemies, but at unspeakable costs.

2005 and 2006 brought considerable world discussion of American practice of "third country renditions." In some cases, non-American terrorists, captured abroad, have been taken covertly to a third country—that of their citizenship—where authorities interrogate and imprison them. Egypt, Syria, and others states are said to be torturing their own citizens, the United States indirectly and illegally aiding them. Massachusetts Congressman Edward Markey actually tried to ban the "rendering" of these suspected terrorists to their home countries, but there is another vocal minority, one most odd: a lobby *for* torture—under certain circumstances and controls. Popularly associated with Harvard Law professor Alan Dershowitz,[83] these voices defend the practice, especially in a case that could include a "ticking bomb" of which the subject may have knowledge. Harvard's professor would allow a court to issue "a torture warrant," and interrogations would proceed accordingly in extreme cases. This conclusion is woven from three skeins: hatred of terrorism, fear of weapons of mass destruction, and the opinion that torture will yield actionable intelligence.

The logic is faulty; the conclusions are not defensible; the teaching in the argument is poisonous. Former Soviet dissident and torture victim Vladimir Bukovsky is among those to attack the "pro-torture school," penning a devastating editorial enriched by references to communist governmental practice.[84] What follows is something different:

the present author's own views of the issue,[85] developed in various considerations of logic and morals and study of the French experience in Algeria. Whatever France gained in horrific abuse from Algerian revolutionary prisoners it lost in multiples in moral, legal, and political terms. French behavior was a tragedy and a failure, and France knows it. It is remarkable that a tiny minority of Americans can persist despite such results.

First, prudence and law both teach that there is rarely certainty about a suspect. As an example, the American justice system offers extraordinary safeguards to defendants in capital cases and then elaborate appeals that take years; yet DNA evidence is today discrediting some earlier convictions of people waiting on death row. So the potential for error in the Dershowitz procedure is enormous. The suspect at hand may be the wrong person or he may be a terrorist but may not know a thing about the "ticking bomb," making his interrogation an exercise in useless sadism. The suspect may have boasted of such knowledge without having it, just as Saddam Hussein may have pretended to have stockpiles of WMD. The arrestee may think he knows of a ticking bomb but actually possesses outdated information; the plot may have failed or been cancelled by his superiors. The bomb itself may exist but for mechanical reasons or user incompetence fail to detonate; this *often* happens in terrorist attempts now,[86] and technical failure is much more likely with a WMD device than with simpler weapons. For all these reasons, torture of a suspect is foolish—as well as immoral. The argument's inadequacies are illuminated by the swift devolution to the most unusual example of circumstance: the ticking bomb. It is usually a bad idea to base one's arguments on the most extreme cases; normal ones may be the better guide; yet defenders of torture rely in a profligate way on rare ticking bomb scenarios.

Second, torture ruins as many possibilities to gather intelligence as it can possibly gain. The general knowledge that a state tortures its opponents enhances indignation and disgust among good citizens, who are thus less likely to help the government or approach the police to offer valuable information. By contrast, torture of suspected terrorists can only buttress morale and uniformity of convictions within a terrorist organization. The members know they have nowhere to turn, even if their allegiances are changing or they seek a way out.[87] The smarter approach would use public knowledge that *terrorists* torture their hostages while also using knowledge that a good government does *not* do so with prisoners. That underscores the moral and legal differences and suggests that the state will work with compliant prisoners to reduce sentences or trade special conditions in prison for special information. Reformed terrorists could well serve a government in intelligence roles or as translators and the like. By contrast, terrorists who refuse to reform can be locked up for decades, or permanently, or given hard labor, or even executed in some countries. All these are adequate replies to terrorism; it does not necessitate torturing suspects in a guessing game to find out whether they are terrorists or what they may know as terrorists.

More reasons present themselves: A third is that some experts in interrogation doubt the quality of information gained from torture. They report that abused prisoners may lie or say anything to stop the pain. This creates a practical problem: wastage of government resources on false leads. That wastage should especially trouble the advocates of the ticking time bomb–scenario; it is important for all cases wherein time may be critical.[88] Fourth, information extracted by torture is useless in most courts in the democratic world and may be undesired by allied governments as well. Fifth, there are practical alternatives to torture, including the trickery of a skilled interrogator. A sixth—albeit strange—reason against the practice is that it may psychologically harm those who administer and see torture. This, too, was discovered by the French in Algeria; Alistair Horne writes of it in his classic account, *A Savage War of Peace, 1954–1962*.[89] Some of those who use pliers or electric shock on helpless prisoners must later rely on psychotherapists or drugs to quell *their own* nightmares. This oddity underscores how sick and wrong torture is. Seventh, torture is a disaster for a state's public diplomacy.

Public diplomacy

Public diplomacy is an essential part of contemporary counterterrorism. In terms of political ideals, this art recognizes that, in affairs involving violence, there must be "a decent respect to the opinions of mankind," as the U.S. Declaration of Independence declared in 1776. There are practical channels in which information flows, and public diplomacy addresses the fact that in modern times classical diplomacy is no longer adequate. In the past, a state's business abroad could be done by skilled individuals who worked with or spoke to other individuals in other capitols. Today, a foreign government is but one "audience"; its citizens are another; a third are the other peoples of the world. Perhaps all these require different approaches, different mechanisms.

The United States has civility and reason on its side in the war with Al Qaeda, and was widely seen in that favorable light until several scandals related to the war in Iraq. However, even before those scandals, it was evident that the U.S. government was largely failing in its public diplomacy efforts. The disappointment is now widely shared in Washington, having grown year after year as the world's post-9-11 sympathies dissipated and ever-louder critics came to enjoy headlines and book sales. A budget of $600 million has not seemed to find results. The central problem is not media bias or leftist silliness. The central problem is the general poverty of good arguments in the Administration's rhetorical quiver. There have been a few exceptions, such as Mr. Bush's masterful speech to a joint session of Congress on September 20, 2001. More typical was a lost opportunity for the admirable Collin Powell, a proven public servant in both martial and state affairs: His 2004 article on terrorism in the prestigious journal, *Foreign Affairs*,[90] lacked moral power or innovative argument. In most other cases of administration speeches and publications, the best and strongest grounds for a moral offensive were neglected. Notable leaders were nearly silent or tended to return again and again to a few limited arguments hinging on self-defense, which can hardly appeal to foreign populations not then under attack. The White House *was* effective in pointing out many of the cases in which U.S. policy has directly helped Muslim populations: Afghanistan, Bosnia, Kosovo, Somalia, and the like. Few administration speeches of the years 2002–2005, in extended and effective form, enumerated good arguments against the Militant Muslim International. Meanwhile, the senior State Department post in public affairs went empty for long stretches or was inadequately filled, and the National Security Council, which might have helped, instead held to its tradition[91] of keeping "hands off" of the important business of coordinating the government's few efforts at public affairs and public diplomacy.

Box 5.2 **Arguments Washington has neglected**

1 Al Qaeda's leaders are not clerics, and most are not even deeply schooled in the subtleties of Islam. Thus they have no credibility when publishing "fatwas." It is astounding that a civil engineer who lost his Saudi passport (Bin Laden) or an Egyptian surgeon (Al Zawahiri) should pretend to tell Muslims how to be holy or whom to kill while on the path of holiness. Washington, correctly, does not try to explain the Koran, but Washington must vigorously deprecate these terrorists' impudence and posturing as religious interpreters.

2 Most attacks by "Muslim" zealots have killed or injured others of that faith. The dead range from Anwar Sadat of Egypt to the lowliest soul buying vegetables in a bazaar or seated with Arab friends at a pizzeria. Apparently the U.S. government declines even to count the Muslims murdered by self-described holy Muslims. Yet such a tally would be a compelling argument against terrorism, especially for those abroad who imagine that counterterrorism is nothing but an American or Western concern.

3 Innumerable terror attacks have been carried out by Shia against Sunni or vice-versa. These are unseemly invitations to a war within a civilization. Eventually, a Sunni terrorist, Abu Musab Zarqawi, stated openly his strategy for war on all Shia in Iraq. Such declarations should be held up to the cold light of shame and mentioned frequently in explanation of other but similar attacks by other Zarqawis of the world.

4 Purportedly aiming at "American and Jewish Crusaders," Islamic terrorists have murdered scores of non-Americans in third countries. In Eastern Africa, U.S. embassies were targeted but, overwhelmingly, the human damage was to Kenyans and Tanzanians. In Bali, Australian tourists were the main target, but many Indonesians and a mix of foreigners died from the Jemaah Islamiya–Al Qaeda double-bombing. How can terrorists justify such murders? "Collateral damage" is not a sufficient answer. Collateral damage is not a "risk" in terror bombings; it is a certainty. The real uncertainties in terror bombings are whether the chosen target(s) will actually be hit by the terrorists, and whether the person(s) targeted were actually culpable of any crime against the terrorists.

5 Some legitimate clerics of the Muslim faith have spoken out. The Islamic Commission of Spain, representing some 200 Sunni mosques in that country, has "roundly condemned" Osama Bin Laden and the Al Qaeda organization for terrorism. They published a fatwa against them, in mid-March, 2005. Early that July, the Muslim Council of Britain utterly condemned the indiscriminate terrorism of London by bomb plots. The clerics went so far as to call on the faithful in Britain to "unite in helping the police to capture these murderers." However, their bravery is barely noted by the Western press and hardly mentioned in Washington. The Spanish and British clerics'

Box 5.2 continued

declarations by themselves deserved a press conference by some senior White House official.

7 Senior U.S. spokesmen have too seldom appeared in foreign media during the years after 2001. This is the studied view of Robert Satloff, an expert in public diplomacy, who adds that those who do appear for the United States abroad are often not the best available. In November, 2005, a news story alleged that President Bush had considered bombing Al Jazeera TV; the true need is for skilled speakers to use Al Jazeera and other stations for what they are—media, media through which the United States reaches people abroad. The State Department's ambassador who coordinates counterterrorism should not be the only administration official known for such public diplomacy.

Multinational counterterrorism

There are three overwhelming reasons why counterterrorism should be a multinational concern. Terrorism is a transnational phenomenon. It has been so for several decades, as well as in earlier historical moments, such as the late nineteenth century and early twentieth century years of anarchists. A serious act of international terrorism may therefore be "a threat to international peace and security," in the formal language of the United Nations Security Council in a finding of 2001.[92] International terrorism is also a breach of all traditional international law; that is a second reason why the global community is compelled to care. As the UN recognized in another of its Security Council resolutions, (No. 1189, in 1998), "Every state has the duty to refrain from organizing, instigating, assisting or participating in terrorist acts in another State or acquiescing in organized activities within its territory directed towards the commission of such acts…"[93] Third, and quite simply, the largest and strongest enemy in the current global effort against terrorism is Al Qaeda, and it is distinctly international in its operations, targeting, and recruitment.

As suggested earlier in this chapter, states still find it easier and more direct to handle many counterterror problems themselves. Indeed, there are clear limits to what a sovereign state would wish from its international partners. Canada wants Sri Lankan help in interrupting the flow of Canadian dollars into Tamil Tiger hands, but there are limits to the amount of access to its national bank records Ottawa would allow inspectors from Colombo. Russia frequently calls for world support against Chechen terrorism, which has demonstrated excesses that could shock even a "Carlos the Jackal," but one cannot imagine Russia allowing in, say, Uzbeks and Turkmans to form an international peace-keeping force in Chechnya, which has long been an integral part of Russia. Yet, in spite of the inclinations of states to protect their sovereignty, states today are more than ever before prepared for exploration and resolution of mutual problems. It is need, not only ideals, that push them into cooperation. By going international, terrorism spawned international counterterrorism.

The United Nations

Slowly departing from its past reluctance to involve itself in issues of indirect aggression or counterterrorism, the United Nations has assumed a more active character. After the UTA flight 772 and Pan Am 103 airliner bombings, the early 1990s saw the UN pressing Libya to turn over two suspects, cooperate in investigations, and stop terrorism support. A Security Council Resolution (UNSCR 731) formalized that posture and was toughened by subsequent sanctions in Resolutions 748 and 883. The United States—and such directly involved American officials as Michael Sheehan of the State Department and Stephen R. Kappes of the CIA—had roles in coaching Tripoli away from its deep involvement in terrorism. However, the UN role cannot be overlooked—even if a cynic would say it merely legitimated the grievances of two Security Council permanent members, France and the United States. The larger body's moral and legal support was well worth while. In 1992 or 1995, who would have thought that the UN and the United States would both be removing sanctions from Tripoli? By 2005–2006, they were doing so; Washington's ban on many contacts with Libya expired on June 26, 2006, and the United States was preparing to resume formal diplomatic relations with its old adversary.[94]

The United Nations also passed resolutions and sanctions against Sudan's regime and the Taliban for their gifts of safe haven to Al Qaeda. After Egyptian President Hosni Mubarak was nearly murdered by a Sudanese plot in Addis Ababa in 1995, Cairo reportedly sought bilateral help from the Clinton Administration and did not get it. However, in the next year, the Security Council (including the United States) passed resolutions demanding the end of Khartoum's support to the international terrorists and requiring handover of three named terrorists. That helped to occasion Osama Bin Laden's reluctant departure from his established foothold in Sudan on the upper Nile.

When Bin Laden moved to Afghanistan, the Security Council "followed" him, with Resolution 1267, in November, 1999 and then with Resolution 1333 in December, 2000. The State Department took pride in how these "smart sanctions" were aimed at Taliban officials and their foreign travel, political organization, arms trade, and the like, without interrupting economic aid and commerce, seen to be crucial for a country wracked by a quarter-century of guerrilla wars.[95] Such efforts failed to move the Taliban or break their link to Bin Laden, demonstrating the limits of diplomacy and economic sanctions when the prospects for use of force are slender.[96] Free-world coalition forces accomplished both the destruction of Taliban's power and the expulsion, scattering, or killing of Al Qaeda's men in quick weeks at the end of 2001. Today, the UN Security Council is still engaged on the area's problems: Resolution 1617 of July, 2005 strengthened anti-Taliban and anti-Al Qaeda sanctions,[97] and the larger UN antiterrorist financing regime is of help as well.

The United Nations may also deal with grievous conflicts that result in "export" of terrorism by allowing, or mustering, forces under Chapter VII of the UN Charter. That language is sometimes referred to as "peace enforcement" and goes above and beyond a mere presence for peace keeping." Such UN work continues in Afghanistan, where Security Council resolutions have backed the coalition operations. Once led by the United States, these operations are more recently guided by other NATO fighting forces from Canada, Italy, Holland, the United Kingdom, and Germany.

Box 5.3 **UN sanctions against terror states**

The United Nations is sometimes derided for inaction, or for tardiness when it does act. This was especially true in past decades on matters of transnational terrorism. For example, a Security Council resolution against revolutionary Iran was blocked on January 13, 1980 by Soviet veto—despite the ongoing occupation of the U.S. embassy in Tehran and the terrorization of its personnel. Even today, Iran and Syria, prime sponsors of terrorism abroad, have never been sanctioned by the UN,

However, increasingly, the UN has inserted itself into situations wherein human rights violations are acute, especially genocide, and terrorism. Following are three cases of Security Council action against terrorism in recent years. Quotations are from U.S. State Department annuals.

Libya

Moammar Qaddafi's regime and international terrorism had been closely linked for two decades when Libyan agents were indicted in 1991 for their roles in the earlier Pan Am 103 bombing. The UN Security Council responded by passing Resolution 731. It ordered Tripoli to "turn over the two Libyan bombing suspects for trial in the US or the UK, pay compensation to the victims, cooperate in the ongoing investigation into the Pan Am 103 and UTA flight 772 bombings, and cease all support for terrorism."

UNSCR 748 followed in April of 1992, imposing "sanctions that embargoed Libya's civil aviation and military procurement efforts and required all states to reduce Libya's diplomatic presence. In November 1993 UNSCR 883 was adopted, imposing additional sanctions against Libya for its continued refusal to comply…" Also added: a limited freeze on Libyan assets and a ban on sales of some oil technologies Libya wanted. Thus, pressures mounted.

In 1999, Libya put the Palestinian "rejectionists" at arm's length and announced support for the Palestine Authority, increasingly recognized as a legitimate "statelet." The Abu Nidal organization was forced out, ending many years of safe harbor. In 2000, Libya finally paid damages for the 1984 shooting out of its London embassy, leaving twelve British casualties in the streets. And Libya made at least initial payments to some families for killing 171 persons in the bombing of France's UTA flight 772 over Niger in 1989.

More recently, and doubtless in part owing to the 2003 Coalition's invasion of Iraq—another state terrorism sponsor[98]—the regime in Tripoli has moved to further normalize foreign relations, it abandoned programs for building weapons of mass destruction, and it promised to allow in inspectors. By 2005, the United Nations had removed its sanctions, and the next year the United States removed most of the American sanctions as well.

Sudan

Lt. General Umar al Bashir seized power in a 1989 coup and soon surrounded himself with Islamic militants, especially cleric Hassan al Turabi. Terrorists of both secular and religious types gathered openly there, including Hezbollah, Egyptian Gama'at, and Palestine Islamic Jihad. Osama Bin Laden left Afghanistan to set up in Sudan, making this his international headquarters and training area, from 1991 onward. There is even evidence that two Sudanese diplomats where among those in a 1993 conspiracy to bomb the UN headquarters in New York City.

The Security Council imposed sanctions on Sudan in 1996. UNSCRs 1044, 1054, 1070 together "demand that Sudan end all support to terrorists… They also require Khartoum to hand over three Egyptian Gama'at fugitives linked to the assassination attempt in 1995 against Egyptian President Hosni Mubarak in Ethiopia."

Sudan denied all involvement with terrorism but, in fact, Bin Laden was prompted to move, and he returned to Afghanistan in 1996. The Muslim cleric who was a power behind the Sudanese throne, Hassan al Turabi, was demoted and spent the next years under house arrest, reportedly. What is more, some evidence indicates that Sudan is actually now assisting in the global war on terrorism.

Afghanistan

In the mid-1990s, the Taliban and its leader, Mullah M. Omar, were moving well and coming into control of 90 percent of the factionalized country. Two events of 1996 are vital: The Taliban set up an interim national government under strict *sharia* dictates, and Osama Bin Laden returned after five years in the Sudan. Al Qaeda fighters and officers were again housed and trained in Afghanistan and intertwined their organization with the regime.

The United States, with an Executive Order of July 1999, levied sanctions on the Taliban for harboring Bin Laden. The United Nations followed that November and "overwhelmingly passed Security Council Resolution 1267, which imposed a similar set of sanctions against the Taliban." That December, the General Assembly adopted a convention against financing terrorism, which several years later, when implemented, would have effect on Taliban and Al Qaeda resources. December, 2000 brought a further UN Security Council Resolution: 1333. Its "smart sanctions" targeted the regime and its weapons, foreign travel and missions abroad, etc, without foreclosing humanitarian aid or normal trade with Afghanis.

The Taliban was unmoved—by the outside world generally and by UN restrictions—and they refused to expel or hand over Bin Laden. However, one may argue that the sanctions were an important public effort and useful to legitimate war should that become necessary, as it did after September 11, 2001. The UN's financial sanctions remain in place, and the UN tracking teams remain at work. Also, their efforts were further tightened by the mechanisms of UNSCR 1617, passed unanimously by the Security Council in July 2005.

Regional efforts

A feature of the UN Charter, as conceived by such statesmen as Winston S. Churchill, was that it should never preclude useful *regional* efforts to keep the peace. Nor has it. The "special relationship" the prime minister hoped the United Kingdom and the United States would retain indefinitely has been kept—in security issues, intelligence exchange, and mutual training of military and counterterrorism forces. All this is also part of a much larger North Atlantic Treaty Organization effort. NATO has introduced its own multinational, integrated unit of commandos. Still new, they have thus far done more training and talking than "take-downs,"[99] but their proficiencies are much needed, and the availability of such forces was important during the Athens Olympics of summer 2004. The African Union—with grave responsibilities for a continent that has profoundly troubled countries, including Algeria, Liberia, Rwanda, and Sudan—has begun taking initiatives as well. The AU opened a new research facility in Algiers called the African Center for Study and Research on Terrorism. On a more important plane, the AU is in charge of United Nations duties in genocide-plagued Dharfur, central-western Sudan. Africa may also be seeing the rise of nascent regional organizations to deal with the specialized problems of transnational terrorism. With U.S. aid and encouragement, the Trans-Sahel Initiative has been a major step in linking the region together, including the countries of Niger, Mali, Mauritania, and Chad. A reputed commander of the Salafist Group for Call and Combat, Amari Saifi (a.k.a. Abderazak al-Para), was trapped in 2004 in Chad and turned over to Algerian authorities. Algeria may be a despotism, but there seemed to be few international complaints about handing over such a man as Al-Para to them, given that he had directed the 2003 kidnapping of nearly three dozen European tourists in Algeria.[100]

Financial sanctions

Financial sanctions and terrorist deterrence with economic tools have come to be among the UN's preferred forms of counterterrorist action. They inhibit "sub-state actors"—cases in which there may be few diplomats to bar or blame but many individuals, militias, or international terror groups. Conversely, money is fungible and easily hidden, and terrorist monies in circulation probably do not exceed a few billion dollars, whereas the world financial system is awash in trillions. This makes financial counterterrorism a useful but limited tool.[101]

The new UN regime to control terrorist financing is the creation of multiple decisions and actions. A Convention for the Suppression of the Financing of Terrorism entered into force in April, 2002. Now it is important, and more than three-fourths of the globe's 191 states are parties. The convention's language condemns terrorism as "criminal and unjustifiable, wherever and by whomever committed," and offers a useful definition of terrorism that is important because of failure thus far to reach a more universal UN definition. The new convention on financing proscribes any act "intended to cause death or serous bodily injury to a civilian, or to any other person not taking an active part in the hostilities in a situation of armed conflict, when the purpose of such act, by its nature or context, is to intimidate a population or to compel a government or an international organization to do or to abstain from doing any act."[102]

This United Nations effort is supported by another, UNSCR 1373, adopted in late September of 2001. The policy statement links the individual and collective right to self-defense—which all states possess—to a duty to prevent the crime of aiding terrorists financially. That is certainly a first for this body. The resolution reiterates 1998 language of the Security Council that ignoring such terrorist financing is impermissible: No state may acquiesce "in organized activities within its territory directed towards the commission" of terrorist financing actions. And indeed, the 2001 resolution invokes the powerful language of Chapter VII and decides that "all States shall: (a) prevent and suppress the financing of terrorist acts; (b) criminalize the willful provision or collection, by any means, directly or indirectly of funds…," refuse safe haven to terror financiers, and the like.[103] This is stout stuff, which can and will become the ground of action by states on their individual, regional, or other multilateral levels.

To make its resolutions against terrorist financiers effective, the Security Council created a "Counterterrorism Committee" with an executive directorate that became operational in 2005. Its objective is what the U.S. State Department calls "capacity-building work," (i.e., "facilitating technical assistance to member states and promoting closer cooperation and coordination with international, regional, and sub-regional organizations"). The committee can also pay unwanted visits to select countries deemed negligent. U.S. Treasury officers indicate that Washington has an important role in such forms of technical aid. The premise of capacity building is that some states may be quite willing to block terrorist financing but may not know precisely how to do so, given the demanding and arcane skill-sets involved. The United States thus trains bankers, accountants, customs officers, and other foreign professionals for counterterrorist work and has done so at least since the late 1990s, when Michael Kraft and others at State began running seminars.[104] Naturally, other capitals share this interest and take their own initiatives. Regionally based technical and political efforts at financial counterterrorism are ongoing through the Financial Action Task Force of the G-7.

Established in Paris in 1989, the Financial Action Task Force on Money Laundering is the product of a multilateral summit. The G-7 has been active, concrete in its recommendations, and growing in numbers of participants. In June 2003, the membership expanded to thirty-three states, with the addition of Russia and South Africa. Now the group not only sets world standards for efforts against money laundering—affecting both crime and terrorism—it may be said to have the active participation of "the major financial centers of North America, South America, Europe, Africa, Asia, and the Pacific."[105]

Results of the international efforts to stop terrorist financing have been limited but all to the good. For example, while individual governments often had offices specializing in foreign assets control, there is for the first time one sited at the UN: the "New Consolidated List of Individuals and Entities Belonging to or Associated with the Taliban and Al Qaeda Organization as Established and Maintained by the 1267 Committee." That specialized sanctions committee is a Security Council creation that tracks the Taliban and Al Qaeda remnants, listing by name hundreds of suspects, with data (as available) on their places of birth, known pseudonyms, and passports. During 2005, the list included noted Taliban leaders, such as Mullah Mohammed Rabbani of Kandahar, Chairman of the Ruling Council, and Mullah Mohammed Omar of Uruzgan Province, Afghanistan, formally recognized before (and since) 9-11 as the "Leader of the Faithful" Sunnis in his country. Further down on the list are now-infamous, once-obscure "charities": Al-Haramain and Al Masjed al Acsa Charity Foundation in Bosnia-Herzigovina; similarly named offices in Albania and Ethiopia; the Benevolence International Fund of Ontario, Canada; and the Benevolence International Foundation. The last had multiple addresses: Illinois and New Jersey in the United States; Ontario Canada; Baku, Azerbaijan; Maastricht in the Netherlands; Khartoum, Sudan; Peshawar, Pakistan; and so on. The list also includes financial facilitators, with such overtly corporate titles as Barahat Post Express and Barakat Banks and Remittances in Mogadishu, Somalia; Babita Trust in Lahore, Pakistan; the Barako Trading Company in Dubai, U.A.E.; and the Somali Internet Company, among many others.[106]

Legal designation

Another international approach to counterterrorism is through law, though it may carry financial impacts as well. Acting together—or individually—states sometimes formally designate organizations as "terrorist" in character. In 2006, the European Union and Canada each finally reached such a decision about the LTTE Tigers, after earlier judgments by Sri Lanka and the United States.[107] United States moves against Middle Eastern terror entities go at least as far back as January, 1995—when President Clinton used the International Emergency Economic Powers Act of the U.S. Code against groups he deemed damaging to his elaborate efforts at peace in the Middle East. Listed were two groups of American and Israeli Jews (Kach; Kahane Chai), a Lebanese insurgency and political force once known only for its terrorism (Hezbollah), secular Palestinians (PFLP; PFLP-GC; Palestine Liberation Front), and other Palestinians with religious ideologies (Hamas; Jihad; Palestine Islamic Jihad–Shiqaqi Faction). Refinements and additions followed in subsequent Executive Orders by the White House—aiming at Osama Bin Laden on August 20, 1998, the Taliban on July 4, 1999, and many other groups in later actions by President George W. Bush.[108] Such individual state actions may lead to more effective multilateral counterparts, as the example of the E.U. and the LTTE Tigers seems to show.

Intelligence cooperation and exchange

Specialists and police officials at the national level do cooperate on transnational intelligence and exchange information. This effort, which demands continuous renewal and improvement, is key to multinational counterterrorism. As an example, the month of May, 2006 found Russia engaged in various related actions. It signed a counterterrorism agreement envisaging exchange of intelligence and facilitating extradition with Egypt. It announced that a joint operation with the Kazakhs had yielded an armed Chechen separatist wanted for shooting up a ministry. Russia also announced that its Federal Security Service has amassed "over 200 agreements on cooperation in the border sphere with foreign colleagues," according to Director Nikolai Patrushev. One sub-set of this work was a Collective Security Treaty Organization linking Russia with Kazakhstan and Kyrgyzstan. The anti-smuggling and terrorism fight was also reaching into the Northern

Pacific and the Black and Baltic Seas. The European Union is among Moscow's many partners. "We are cooperating even with those states, with whom we have no borders, but have air or sea communications," Patrushev said.[109]

The continuous problem with secret intelligence, of course, is that governments strive to keep it secret, and that means reluctance to share. Consider that Al Qaeda used Western Europe— as our first edition [ch. 3] suggested terrorists do—as a commodious land of stable living quarters, accessible ethnic diasporas, easy communications and transit points, access to banks and to weapons manufacturers, and the like. After 9-11, the Al Qaeda linkages between Spain, Belgium, Germany, and the United States were combed out finely but, before a catastrophic event, such cooperation can be impossible to get. Indeed, even after the year's mass murders, as Berlin proved again that it is an admirable ally to Washington, there were frequent concerns that the United States was not sharing enough intelligence with Germany. Such things matter deeply—not just to prettify a political climate. International terrorism court cases often require international help in building a case. Shockingly few Al Qaeda cases have been successfully concluded by convictions and jail, anywhere in Europe[110] (or the United States, for that matter). Each trial is seen as a test of the evidence and of the system of justice. Failure to share adequately can mar both. In mid-2006, it was the United States' turn to be irritable. A standing agreement of two years with the European Union had caused the latter states to forward full data on all air passengers destined for U.S. airfields. Thus, passengers arriving in the United States were prescreened, which is efficient and safe but, because of privacy issues, the European Court of Justice annulled the accord at the end of May, 2006.[111] That was the very season in which Muslim militants with British and Pakistani links were preparing their attacks on ten airplanes bringing people from Heathrow Airport to the United States.[112]

Jordan and the United States enjoy active collaboration in intelligence matters, reportedly. Jordan is just the sort of moderate Arab partner the Americans need, at many times and especially in the current war on terrorism. The Kingdom also wants allies and has had hard experiences over many years with terrorists who hate the mild and secular monarchy even more than they hate distant Western powers. Jordanian counterterrorist forces, including the elite "Battalion 71," proved themselves skilled in a four-part preemptive operation in April, 2004. They seized three trucks carrying many tons of explosives and chemicals and driven by Syrian nationals in Irbid, near the Syrian and Lebanese borders. This led them to understand an unfolding suicide attack operation aimed at three buildings in their capital. They then made raids—two of which required gun battles—thaat collected alive nearly all the essential participants. Closing a circle by which outstanding experience may be harvested by an ally, a commander of this successful operation then enrolled in a program at the National Defense University in the United States where he could teach fellow students, and study, counterterrorism.[113] In 2005, a terrorist leader based in Iraq, Abu Musab al Zarqawi, blew up luxury hotels in his native Jordan, underscoring the need for Amman to work abroad. Reportedly, the Kingdom moved covert intelligence agents into Iraq, and this extra effort led them to a Zarqawi lieutenant, whose revelations in turn helped U.S. ground and air forces surround and bomb the house in which the terror mastermind was meeting group members. The best success thus far against "Al Qaeda in Iraq" was a result of bilateral cooperating in intelligence.[114]

Training security forces

Just as states may cooperate on intelligence, they may also cooperate on formal training of police and military forces with the aim of bettering their mutual counterterrorist capabilities. This is an area in which the U.S. government organized itself early and well and has extended a hand to friends and allies for two decades. 1985 was the year in which the State Department's Office of the Coordinator for Counterterrorism established a secret arm called "FEST," the Foreign Emergency Support Teams. In a leaflet released only recently,[115] the department describes this now-veteran organization as "the government's only interagency on-call short-notice team poised to respond to terrorist incidents worldwide." Deployable within four hours from Washington to go abroad for a crisis, the teams can render valuable advice, communications, and other support to a U.S. ambassador or the requesting foreign government—which has a pre-established accord with the Department of State. Scores of countries are quietly partnered in this way. FEST team deployments have been to East Africa (after the Nairobi and Dar es Salaam embassy attacks) in August, 1998 and to Yemen (after the *USS Cole* was boat-bombed) in October, 2000, for example. Other State Department teams have had the lead from Washington in liaison work with Sydney, Turin, and Athens for the Olympic Games of 2000, 2004, and 2006, respectively—for which security preparations were elaborate, expensive, and entirely effective.

Such teams hint at the extent of bilateral work by the United States abroad. An Anti-Terrorism Assistance program active for two decades has touched more than 140 countries and 52,000 foreign civil servants, police, military personnel, disaster experts, and the like. Jointly run by the ambassador who is counterterrorism "Coordinator" and by the department's Bureau of Diplomatic Security, the program helps to enhance the antiterrorism skill levels of men and women around the world. For example, Indonesia's elite antiterrorist team, called Task Force 88, included some men with American training as it tracked down or killed several of those wanted for mass murders in terror actions in Indonesia.[116] Around the world, in Colombia, which is plagued with kidnapping of both criminal and political sorts, U.S. aid has made possible special working teams of police and military personnel called GAULAs, an acronym meaning Unified Action Groups for Personal Liberty. These small, specialized forces have made some impressive rescues and delivered some hostage takers to jail or to their deaths.[117] There is a wider picture as well of less direct counterterrorism training by the United States: The country's departments and military schools educate thousands of foreign officers, abroad and in the United States each year.[118] There are International Law Enforcement Training Academies run by the State Department's Bureau of Narcotics and Law Enforcement, and by the FBI, in Budapest, Hungary and in Bangkok, Thailand.

Negotiations

The final section of present discussions of multinational counterterrorism concerns one of the less concrete but nonetheless important political roles of state governments: negotiations. It has become common to see independent-minded, helpful governments step in between foreign belligerents in "low-intensity conflicts" and quietly attempt to mediate peace. Sometimes the government selects and dispatches a particular individual, as the White House did with former Senate Majority Leader George Mitchell to Northern Ireland. Sometimes there is a larger delegation. On occasion, a state will welcome onto its own soil representatives of the two combative sides, hoping that a new environment and the suasion of the hosting officials will relax a bitter and tense atmosphere. This was why William J. Clinton invited Palestinian and Israeli leaders to a secluded resort in Wye River, Maryland in 1998 and why Malaysia has hosted talks between rebels in Mindanao and the central government authorities from Manila, Republic of the Philippines.

Finns have taken the lead in the once-desperate situation in Aceh, at the northern tip of Indonesia, where some inhabitants sought independence and it led to 2,000 deaths per year.[119] The GAM, or Free Aceh Movement, was brought together for talks with Jakarta's representatives. It is unclear how much progress they were making, but when the 2004 tsunami crushed so much of the area, aiding the population leapt ahead of political differences. Soon GAM agreed to leave the path of war and lay down arms— or keep them insofar as individual fighters would integrate into the Indonesian Army. Twice in recent years the East Timorese have shown just how ruthless and protracted such separatist struggles may be; in this case, the people of Indonesia were happily spared the worst of what separatist struggles may bring.[120]

As lead negotiator, Norway had a considerable success in shaping the Oslo Accord for the Middle East. Unfortunately, there has been a failure in similar talks aiming to salve the wounds of Sri Lanka. Norway has made immense efforts to reach out a hand of peace and interpose itself between the Tamil Tigers and the democratic government. Peace was decided on in December, 2001 and formalized three months later. However, four years on, the peace was shattered. LTTE was making regular attacks, and a pro-Tiger website declared the Tamil minority "ready for the war." Norway's top diplomat, Eric Solheim, admitted in May, 2006 that five to ten deaths were coming each day. "There is a major crisis looming," he said, and called out to both sides: "Come back to the table." Norway's multifaceted efforts included transmitting Indian messages from New Delhi to the LTTE, urging restraint. But India's earlier and disastrous armed intervention on the island has left an enduring, ugly legacy....the dark side of "peace-enforcement." Absent especially creative statesmanship, the oversized northern neighbor, India, is unlikely to much affect the thirty-year old war on the little island across the Palk Strait. Its most useful power may be a subtle type—demographics; there are 60,000,000 Tamils in India proper and fewer than 4,000,000 in Sri Lanka.

It cannot go without saying that the global community must beware of frauds in international mediation as well. Sub-state actors, as well as states, will engage in such chicanery. During the 1985 crisis caused by Shia hijacking TWA flight 847, Algeria postured as a helpful neutral, despite having been a preferred destination for hijacking teams for some two decades. Also, when the plane was on the tarmac at Beirut International Airport, Lebanese Minister of Justice Nabih Berri played negotiator as well, if not more credibly than the FLN government of Algiers. Mr. Berri, an official and a Shia militant, may well have allowed Hezbollah to reinforce the hijacking crew by putting new men into the plane as it lay in trauma in Beirut. This was one of several ways in which the Lebanese state's inaction directly created a much worse situation. Today, Nabih Berri is Speaker of the Lebanese parliament.

The same year, 1985, saw an Italian cruise ship in the eastern Mediterranean snatched by terrorists of the Palestine Liberation Front. PLF leader Abu Abbas, who was not aboard the ship, had the nerve to pop up in the role of would-be negotiator, seeking to "defuse" the situation. He largely escaped ridicule—in this ridiculous role—because he raised questions about whether the PLF team might have planned to act against a different target, after the cruise ship docked. He alleged that the gunmen were "surprised" in their stateroom when cleaning their weapons and thus had to act precipitously. Any such ambiguity is largely irrelevant; Abu Abbas was entirely responsible for the terrorism, as the gun team was entirely his. Abu Abbas was arrested in Iraq when the coalition invaded in 2003; he later died there.

A more recent case of the phony negotiator was worked with unexpected skill by Colonel Mommar Qaddafi of Libya. That country had long welcomed "Moros" from the militant underground in the southern Philippines (e.g., Mindanao). Sometimes the operatives and leaders came to Libya for conferences; sometimes they went home to the Philippines bearing material aid. In the very midst of a multiyear campaign to alter his image as a paymaster for terrorists, the Colonel found a new way to continue Libyan support for these distant Muslim militant brethren. Abu Sayyaf—one of whose leaders used the name "Khadaffy" Janjalani until his recent death—was also an Al Qaeda ally and a proven Pacific-region problem. When they seized twenty foreign hostages in April, 2000, Libya's chief interposed, promising to 'resolve the crisis.' He did so by paying some $20 million to Abu Sayyaf.[121] The group quickly turned some of its new capital into stores and weapons and then took more than thirty additional hostages. Yet, because of the timing of each step, remarkably few voices were heard criticizing Libya for state sponsorship of terrorism—although that is what it was.[122]

Conclusions

The foregoing chapter covers individual state actions and multinational actions against terrorism. Both varieties emerge with their advantages and shortcomings. For example, it is easily seen that multinational and UN action are as yet immature in some respects. Even as they improve, it remains evident why, when the UN charter was drawn, some delegates insisted on including language making it clear that the individual state's right of self-defense against foreign threats must be assured beyond question. At the other extreme lie the tragic—or absurd—actions of Russia in two recent cases involving Chechen hostage-barricade situations. The Moscow theater catastrophe of October, 2002 was followed by the Beslan school slaughter of September, 2004, and each is a crude tutorial on how force may fail.[123] As every graduate of a military staff college learns, when force is applied, it must be done with a good plan, discipline, and skill. To this must be added a modicum of restraint when those deploying force are not warring against attackers so much as trying to save their citizen-brethren.

Among the conclusions based on the foregoing analysis, the first and foremost is that terrorism is about power—acquiring it or keeping it. And terrorism is always political, even when other motives, such as religion, are involved. Therefore, terrorism is a direct challenge to the state's legitimacy and authority and often merits a forceful response.

Terrorism presents a moral, political, and legal challenge to the legitimate state. Normally this challenge cannot be ignored or minimized. Past years of U.S. policy are one example of how often careful people in the National Security Council or phlegmatic advisors to U.S. presidents counseled that the White House should take a "hands off" approach to a given crisis or subordinate counterterrorism to most other interests of government. Such an approach is ill-advised. The state that will protect its citizens and well serve its allies must fight back in ways that involve morals, the law, law enforcement, and measures that are politically astute. This should be done in an integrated manner becoming of the concept of "grand strategy."

Economic power is often underrated. The economic and diplomatic sanctions of the United Nations and of individual strong states, and ongoing use of banking law, data systems, and national treasuries to hunt for and cut off terrorist financing, form a limited but much-needed tool in counterterrorism.

Information and public diplomacy are essential tools in any counterinsurgency or counterterror campaign. The immense skill of the Web masters and video makers used by Al Qaeda are merely the latest reminder of this. Governments without an information strategy—or governments whose information strategies are failing—find themselves at a decisive disadvantage against terrorists, whose attention to publicity is pervasive and instructive.

Counterterrorism decisions are complex. At the national level, they include the requirements for making the nation and government secure; the character of the national leadership; the mood and character of the people; the proper balance between force and other aspects of national power; and questions of how the enemy will react.

At the tactical level, when force is involved and police, military personnel, or allied forces are included, decision making and execution will be affected by all the classical problems that Carl von Clausewitz described: friction, doubt and hesitation, fear, unclarity of purpose, and the fact that each action may well provoke the terrorists to reform, respond, or retaliate. Recent years offer failures to study. They also offer proof that brilliant operations can destroy the morale, and perhaps even the structure, of prominent terrorist organizations. Today's headlines from Peru are always of new elections or old scandals in past governments, including those of Alberto Fujimori. One must also take note of the sounds of silence—the near disappearance, after years of terrorism, of the two successful Peruvian communist organizations Sendero Luminoso and of Tupac Amaru. Skillful use of intelligence and force in the 1990s destroyed them.

In democratic governments, the interagency process is a prime feature of success or failure in counterterrorism. One may mock the failures of the bureaucracies to "connect the dots" before an attack or to respond well after one, but in a large, complex, and human institution like a national government, coordination takes immense effort by hard-driving public servants. They function best when they show breadth of understanding of other departments' needs and "bureaucratic cultures." Five and six years after 9-11 and a completed "tour" as Secretary of State by the country's former senior military officer, Collin Powell, how well do the American State and Defense Departments cooperate and understand one another? Many challenges remain. Such intramural differences can grow cavernous when they begin to include work with distant and different allies abroad. Yet the latter, international counterterrorism, is of the essence in the current struggle.

A state will do well to address its partners and allies maturely—according to their self-interests, as well as their ideals, the particulars of their circumstances, and their bilateral relations of the past. Mutual self-interest is much underrated by students of counterterrorism. If citizens of France and the United States are polled on attitudes toward the other, many citizens' replies would include indications of hostility, lack of understanding, and resistance. However, Paris and Washington are cooperating exceedingly well in counterterrorism in the post-9-11 world. For this reason, of course, France is a prime target of Al Qaeda and its network.

Work of an allied kind is particularly important not just in diplomacy but in intelligence. Washington must take notice when Germany repeatedly complains of inadequate U.S. sharing with respect to Al Qaeda matters. Israel has occasionally let Washington know that it puts limits on what sensitive information will arrive from Tel Aviv because in Washington it is too often leaked to the public, jeopardizing secret operations or tradecraft.

The centrality of intelligence to effective counterterrorism cannot be overstated, but that precept does not permit torture, which is not only immoral but can be stupidly counterproductive. Much is allowable in interrogation of suspected terrorists, and skill and swiftness (acting while information is fresh) are vital. More generally, good intelligence is acquired by hard work, sufficient personnel, the support of the polity, analytical training and focus, explicit effort by military organizations not perhaps used to unconventional operations, and systems that guarantee interagency "fusion."

Notes

1 Henry Kissinger, *Diplomacy* (New York: Simon & Schuster, 1994).

2 *Militant Muslim International* is my preferred term for Al Qaeda and its diverse allies. I used the term testifying to the House of Representatives' Committee on Government Reform, 20 Sept. 2001.

3 This "roster of enemies" is not prioritized. It reflects my understanding based on the actions and documents of the revolutionary terrorists, including the "Jihad Manual" found in Manchester and scores of communiqués of the Bin Laden organization. Michael Scheuer touches on all these as well but places least emphasis on the allies of the United States and the most emphasis on the United States–Israeli axis, in his own judgment about what Al Qaeda most seeks to destroy; *Through Our Enemies' Eyes: Osama Bin Laden, Radical Islam, and the Future of America*, 2nd ed. (Washington, DC: Potomac Books, 2006).

Another way to distinguish Al Qaeda enemies is separating the "Near" and the "Far," with the former being the secular and Arab regimes, as well as Israel, and the latter representing powerful Western states, especially the USA.

4 *New York Times*, 13 April 2006, and a 16 Dec. 2005 assessment by "Stratfor.com" appearing on the "New Noise" website, accessed 5 June 2006.

5 During several years when many media showed no interest in the conflict in Nepal, the *Washington Times* frequently published lengthy and valuable stories; the article referenced in the text was on 27 May 2006.

6 Timothy Naftali, *Blind Spot: The Secret History of American Counterterrorism* (New York: Basic Books, 2005).

7 Richard H. Shultz, Jr., "Showstoppers: Nine Reasons Why We Never Sent Our Special Operations Forces After Al Qaeda Before 9/11," *Weekly Standard*, 26 Jan. 2004, vol. 9, #

19. Dr. Shultz has coauthored a new book with Andrea J. Dew: *Insurgents, Terrorists, and Militias: The Warriors of Contemporary Combat* (New York: Colombia University Press, 2006).

8 Materials from the Hostage Working Group at the U.S. Embassy, Baghdad, in the *New York Times*, 17 May 2006.

9 British press accounts and the U.S. State Dept. annuals on international terrorism covering the years 1999, 2000, and 2002.

10 U.S. State Department, *Patterns of Global Terrorism: 1999* (Washington, DC: Government Printing Office [hereafter, GPO], April 2000), pp. 7–8.

11 My first edition explicitly included in its treatment of terrorism those insurgents who make regular use of terror. To not do so seemed artificial; nothing about the nature of a terrorist group means that it must be small. This same methodological approach was taken at the same time by Paul Wilkinson, coeditor of the Frank Cass book series on terrorism. His volume in that group well handles the similarities and differences of terrorists and insurgents; see *Terrorism vs. Democracy: The Liberal State Response*.

12 *Washington Post*, July 27, 1997. Samper was in office from 1994 to 1998, whereupon Pastrana assumed the presidency.

13 The word *reckless* may seem harsh, but there is a difference between that which is good yet bold and that which is reckless. Military planners sometimes make a similar distinction, asking whether a proposed operation is a "risk" and thus acceptable or even normal, or a "gamble," which is usually unacceptable.

14 One example of pessimism has appeared in the *Financial Times*, June 24–5, 2006. When Spain arrested a dozen ETA extortionists, the organization demanded that the government "dismantle" its "repressive" organs or face resumption of hostilities. Mr. Paris Michaels of the Institute of World Politics also reports that citizens of Spain show skepticism about ETA's cease-fire.

Ireland's Sinn Fein has been working with ETA front Batasuna on negotiation strategies, according to the January 2007 issue of *Smithsonian* magazine.

Concessions by any state also have their price, even when producing peace. The autonomy given the Basques appeals to other regions, and now Catalonia is driving for even greater independence, as indicated by Dr. Evelyn Farkas of the U.S. Senate Armed Services Committee professional staff, in an interview of Jan. 20, 2006. Her Fletcher School Ph.D. dissertation evolved into the book *Fractured States and U.S. Foreign Policy* (New York: Palgrave/Macmillan, 2003).

15 The three states' laws are discussed in ch. 5 of the U.S. State Department's *Country Reports on Terrorism: 2005* (Washington, DC: GPO, April, 2006).

16 An observation of American foreign service officer Leonard Hill, who kindly reviewed a draft of this chapter in August 2006. Mr. Hill has seen cases of effective use of the charge of "lying to a federal officer" who is carrying out official duties. The author further appreciates Hill's insights on Canada's War Measures Act.

17 AP wire story, July 19, 2006, "Convicted Greek Terror Group Head Paroled," courtesy of Mr Larry Cosgriff, an expert on maritime terrorism.

The past releases frustrating to counterterrorists included the way in which Italy let slip the PLF gunmen who hijacked the ship *Achille Lauro*. Front chief Abu Abbas was never jailed, and his subordinates served relatively short sentences and were quietly and individually released, disappearing abroad. Noted in our first edition, p. 253.

Other times, releases may disappoint but are strictly necessary. The same day's newspapers covering the Indonesian release of Bashir also noted that British authorities had to cut loose two Bengali-born Muslims arrested in a highly publicized raid in London during which one suspect was shot. No charges resulted; authorities had erred, the civic damage was obvious; an August 13, 2006 news story on the incident treated it as a bungle.

18 E-mail exchange with then Consul-General for the United States in Halifax, Canada, Leonard Hill, Jan. 2006, and "Why Terrorism Subsides: A Comparative Study of Canada and the

United States," by Jeffrey Ian Ross and Ted Robert Gurr, *Comparative Politics*, vol 21, no. 4 (July 1989), pp. 405–26.

According to Dr. Daniel Pipes, Quebec's international relations minister, Monique Gagnon-Tremblay, is not favorably inclined toward (Muslim) immigrants "who want to come to Quebec and who do not respect women's rights or who do not respect whatever rights may be in our Civil Code." "New Message for Islamicists," *New York Sun,* Aug. 30, 2005.

19 Eric Lipton's essay, *New York Times*, June 1, 2006. That paper, about that time, was notably criticized for leaking secret information about some forms of intrusive antiterrorism directed in the United States by the George W. Bush administration.

20 *Times Online* (London), July 29, 2005. A mile away in a park another bomb was found, identical to the devices of the failed second tube attack. Police snipers and other officers also made arrests at a residence on Tavistock Crescent. All three sites are near one another in central west London, just north of the Thames River.

21 Germany's case underscores the point. The people and government have been generous to foreigners in some respects, and the current climate of tightening is not due to a rise in neo-fascism but to the sheer numbers of immigrants and the clandestine character of their ingress and the pain of knowing that Hamburg's hostels directly contributed personnel to 9-11-01, including commander Mohammed Atta (killed in the plane) and current U.S. detainee Ramzi Binalshibh and two others still on the run: Said Bahaji and Zakariya Essabar; BBC News, Aug. 19, 2005, accessed on http://newsvote.bbc.co.uk. On French intelligence and the new counterterrorism issues, see Alexis Dodbat, "Terror and the Fifth Republic," *The National Interest*, no. 82 (Winter 2005-2006), pp. 55–61.

22 "British Police Powers Toughest in Europe," *The Guardian*, Oct. 13, 2005. The datum about twenty-eight days is confirmed by the *New York Times*, Aug. 13, 2006.

23 *New York Times*, Sept. 29 and Nov. 3, 2005.

24 *The Times* (London), on *www.timesonline.co.uk* on Nov. 8, 2005. The *Militant Islam Monitor* covered the story that same day, supplied other details, and noted an earlier (June 2005) raid on some of the same locations; *www.militantislammonitor.org*. Both were accessed May 22, 2006.

25 Past estimates have usually ranged from $30 million to $60 million a year for Iranian aid to Hezbollah. The war of mid-2006 caused revisions upward in many estimations; *NBC News* claimed the subsidy had become $40 million per *month*.

26 Judge Royce Lambert was clear that while the victims were uniformed personnel, the attack was terrorism, because the men and women were not at war but part of a peacetime deployment to a friendly country at that capital's request; *Michael Heiser, Millard Campbell, et. al. v. Islamic Republic of Iran*, U.S. District Court for the District of Columbia, Dec. 22, 2006.

27 There are legal and media reports since 1996 on cases named for such victims as Flatow, Ben Haim, Higgins, Barnea, and the like, including the *New York Sun* story of April 3, 2006. I am grateful to Peter Leitner, a legal expert on these cases, a representative of The Higgins Foundation, and a professor at George Mason University in Virginia, for lecturing to my "Counterterrorism" class at Command & Staff College, Marine Corps University, Quantico, VA, in May of 2006.

28 John Finn, "Electoral Regimes and the Proscription of Anti-democratic Parties," *Terrorism and Political Violence* 12: 3 & 4 (Autumn/Winter 2000), pp. 51–74.

29 Australia's late 2005 action against the PKK or Kurdish Workers Party was covered by the UPI on Dec. 16. Proscribed groups in Northern Ireland are listed on the Home Office website: Continuity Army Council; Cumann na mBan; Flanna na hEireann; Irish National Liberation Army; Irish People's Liberation Organization; Irish Republican Army; Loyalist Volunteer Force; Orange Volunteers; Red Hand Commando; Red Hand Defenders; Saor Eire; Ulster Defense Association; Ulster Freedom Fighters; Ulster Volunteer Force. That website is: http://security.homeoffice.gov.uk/counter-terrorism-strategy/legislation The author thanks the Marine Corp Research Center's Kimberley Adams for these articles.

30 Dr. Joseph Goldberg of the Industrial College of the Armed Forces (Fort McNair, Washington, DC) kindly supplied press items from Bangladesh on the arrests. Notes: Bangla Bhai is a *nom de guerre*, and Mr. Rahman is *not* the same man who, on behalf of Muslim militants in Bangladesh, was an original cosigner of the Feb. 1998 Bin Laden *fatwa*.

31 The American-Israeli extremists of Kach and Kahane Chai were formed by Meir Kahane and his son, both now deceased. Each group had its lethal moments, and they remain listed today in some annuals, including the October 2005 issue of *Military Balance* by the International Institute of Strategic Studies.

32 President Abraham Lincoln, in a message to Congress of July 4, 1861 that explained his temporary wartime withdrawal of the civil liberty called *habeas corpus*. Mr. Dennis Teti located this for me.

33 More specifically, the order allowed government to detain any members of any organization if "the persons in control of the organization have or have had associations with persons concerned in the government of, or sympathies with the system of government of, any Power with which his Majesty is at war." Churchill disliked the breadth of this permission, but it was enacted under his premiership and rescinded before 1945, when the internal threat was deemed manageable. Martin Gilbert, *Winston S. Churchill*, vol. 6, *Finest Hour: 1939–1941*. Boston: Houghton Mifflin, 1983, p. 616 and fn 2.

34 Two relevant articles dealing with proscription and with Hizb ut Tahir are "UK Terror Laws Face Legal Challenges," UPI, April 13, 2006, and "The Feeble Helping the Unspeakable," by Dean Godson, *The Times* (London), April 5, 2006.

35 Though Uruguay has long been calm, a new organization calling itself "Tupamaros" and looking back fondly to Tupac Amaru has arisen recently elsewhere, in Venezuela. As many as 2,000 may be organized. Their graffiti includes a "T" inside a star, and they make demonstrations, sometimes disguised in red and black bandanas, according to an interview with a former U.S. Army specialist on Venezuela, in Washington, DC Nov. 3, 2006. The MIPT Terrorism Knowledge Base lists the group as "terrorist," saying it grew from vigilantes in the "23 January" neighborhood of Caracas and then swung leftist in its politics. The "Tupamaro Revolutionary Front of January 23" organization now overtly supports the Hugh Chavez presidency; www.tkb.org/Group.jsp?groupID=3543, accessed Nov. 18, 2006.

36 There were only 4,000 white farmers anyway; now there are 400; many of the farms taken over by mobs or militias are now failing; *U.S. News & World Report*, June 12, 2006, pp. 34–5.

37 The judge is not unerring. In 1997, he arrested 131 suspects but had to release 100 of them. There have been several profiles on Bruguiere (e.g., Henri Astier for BBC News, July 1, 2003, at *http://news.bbc.co.uk*)

38 An adjunct professor for the SNSEE program at National Defense University in Washington, DC, advises me that former U.S. officials involved in the strike on the Sudanese plant are less vocal in defending their actions now. The plant owner, who had business connections to important Saudis and the name of Salah Idris, filed suit against the United States; his suit failed but has been renewed more recently. By one published account, the Al-Shifa plant had been sold in March, 1998, months before the attack, to Mr. Idris, yet CIA was unaware of this.

39 Sun Tzu, *The Art of War*, trans. and ed. by Samuel B. Griffith (Oxford: Oxford University Press, 1963), p. 144.

40 A recent example of unwillingness to adapt is the resistance to a new approach to human intelligence suggested by experts who studied some of our allies' successes abroad in counterinsurgency. See "Intelligence Dominance: A Better Way Forward in Iraq," by Richard H. Shultz Jr. and Roy Godson, *The Weekly Standard*, vol. 11 # 43; see also the critics' remarks at the end.

41 The first, by Harold W. Rood, was published in 1980 by Carolina Academic Press; Rood is now on the adjunct faculty of Missouri State University's graduate program in Defense & Security Studies (Fairfax, VA). The second title, by Jean Francois Revel, appeared from Doubleday in New York in 1984; Revel died in May 2006.

42 Details may be found at p. 26 of Ronald Kessler, *The CIA At War* (New York: St. Martin's Press, 2003). Then Director of Central Intelligence John Deutsch reportedly agreed with Torricelli and signed a directive that sharply inhibited U.S. agents' contacts with sources who were believed to have committed certain violent crimes.

43 The Mayor O'Malley speech was to the National Press Club; *Washington Post*, Feb. 9, 2005. He became governor of Maryland in early 2007.

44 Reuel Marc Gerecht, "The Counterterrorist Myth," *The Atlantic Monthly* 288: 1 (July-Aug. 2001), pp. 38–42. Gerecht is challenged in Ronald Kessler's book on *The CIA At War*, op. cit., but is supported as to the weakness of CIA HUMINT on the Militant Muslim International by another retired CIA operative, Robert Baer, *See No Evil* (New York: Three Rivers Press/ Random House, 2002).

45 Tim Weiner, "Blowback from the Afghan Battlefield," *New York Times Sunday Magazine*, March 13, 1994. The numbers of foreigners then going through Afghan training camps was rather frightening.

46 I was interviewed in January 2001 in Alexandria, VA by Stephen Goode for *Insight on the News* (Feb. 5, 2001), pp. 36–8.

47 Reuel Marc Gerecht's article in the *Atlantic Monthly* just before 9-11 is important (see above), and its conclusions are echoed by another retired CIA officer, Robert Baer, op. cit.

48 By coincidence, a similar number is cited for officers in Iran's foreign intelligence directorate: 2,000 persons; in the larger service, called VEVAK, or Ministry of Intelligence and National Security, there are some 15,000 Iranian officers and support staff, according to Mahan Abedin, "The Iranian Intelligence Services and the War on Terror," *Terrorism Monitor* 2: 10 (May 20, 2004), reprinted in *Unmasking Terror: A Global Review of Terrorist Activities*, eds. Julie Sirrs et. al. (Washington, DC: Jamestown Foundation, 2004), p. 407.

49 British officials are keen to hire speakers of Arabic, Bengali, Urdu, Somali, and the like for new posts in MI 5, the domestic intelligence service. They believe their six- to eight-month vetting process is weeding out the Al Qaeda types who apply, reports Reuters wire service from London, July 3, 2006. My copy is courtesy of Mr. Larry Cosgriff.

50 Like the United States, Britain is increasing the number of its intelligence officers. MI 5 (the domestic service) is adding 3,000 officers in the years 2005–2008. The foreign service, MI 6, is reported to have 2,000 on its staff and to be growing only slightly; *The Guardian*, Oct. 13, 2005.

51 Tim Weiner, *New York Times*, May 14, 2006.

52 The highly capable investigator Bill Gertz covered the story for the *Washington Times*, which titled the article "CIA Chief Placing More Spies Abroad," Sept. 24, 2005. See also "Seeking Spies: Why the CIA is Having Such a Hard Time Keeping Its Best," *U.S. News & World Report*, Feb. 13, 2006.

53 One report declares that, as a former head of central intelligence in the early 1990s, Robert M. Gates had "tried to rein in Pentagon activities" in intelligence and may well do so now, in 2007, as he begins in his role of Secretary of Defense; Walter Pincus, the *Washington Post,* Nov. 14, 2006. Pincus reported on Ambassador Negroponte's departure amid the ongoing challenges of reordering U.S. intelligence, in the *Post* on Jan. 21, 2007.

54 *New York Times*, March 8, 2006.

55 Andrew Koch, "US Central Intelligence Agency Forces: Covert Warriors," *Jane's Defense Weekly*, March 19, 2003, repr. in Roger Z. George and Robert D. Kline, eds., *Intelligence and the National Security Strategist: Enduring Issues and Challenges* (Washington, DC: NDU Press, 2004), pp. 509–15.

56 Reports on the new office include an estimate that the director's budget may near $1 billion; *Washington Post*, April 20, 2006.

57 *U.S. News & World Report* did a cover story on Negroponte's challenges and efforts on Nov. 13, 2006. However, in a larger and unfortunate pattern of change at the top levels of U.S. intelligence bureaucracies, the ambassador has left, returning to the State Department in early 2007. Similarly, the relatively new Ambassador for Counterterrorism at the State Department, Henry Crumpton, announced his resignation as 2007 began.

58 Homeland Security, as conceived, was to have a major intelligence capability in-house, but this conceptual structure was pared away as the department came online, and today it heavily relies on intelligence other agencies produce.

This massive new department also has a parallel, miniscule organization within the White House. For the department itself, there is a useful Web site at *www.dhs.gov/dhs* There is also a published national strategy for the organization, although it is verbose and heavy with platitudes.

59 See the U.S. government's websites *www.nctc.gov* and *www.dni.gov* as well as Kevin Whitelaw, "The Eye of the Storm," *U.S. News & World Report*, Nov. 6, 2006, pp. 48–52.

60 Interview with a U.S. official, June, 2006, Washington, DC.

61 This same target has continued to attract the militant Muslims with its promise of flooding a major traffic arterial; see the U.S. press of July 8, 2006 (e.g., the *Washington Times*, "FBI Foils New York Terror Plot").

62 See for example Dr Laurie Mylroie, "The World Trade Center Bomb: Who is Ramzi Yousef? Why It Matters," *The National Interest* (Winter 1995–96), pp. 2–15, and her subsequent book *Study of Revenge: Saddam Hussein's Unfinished War Against America* (Washington, DC: AEI Press, 2000).

63 Anonymous [Rita Katz], *Terrorist Hunter* (New York: HarperCollings/Ecco, 2003). In latter sections, this author's voice becomes intense as she criticizes the FBI for taking over intelligence developed by others and confining it—instead of fully exploiting it.

Tom Hastings, a career State Department counterterrorism expert now working for the FBI, notes that "Every FBI field division now has a joint terrorism task force and a field intelligence group…in all the 56 field offices." Correspondence of August, 2006.

64 Ronald Kessler, *The FBI* (New York: Pocket Books, 1993), pp. 368–372.

65 The failures of the "Virtual Case File" system were widely reported in 2005 and 2006 (e.g., *InformationWeek,* Sept. 1, 2006). Lockheed Martin is the contractor for the new effort on FBI's behalf.

66 Laura Sullivant, "Intelligence Gathering: New York-Style," broadcast on National Public Radio, May 3, 2005. The facts of her report were confirmed for me in an interview by a specialist with knowledge of this new division, May 2005.

The new division was important in the conviction of a Pakistani terrorist who plotted against the city's Herald Square subway station—one of the busiest. The *New York Times* noted that "The trial was the first time that a federal terrorism investigation was largely conducted by the department's Intelligence Division, rather than the F.B.I." See the issue of May 25, 2006 about convict Shahawar Matin Siraj.

67 For another approach to the French antiterrorist intelligence structure, see pp. 10–1 of "Defense Against Terrorism: A Top Priority of the Ministry of Defence," an excellent report in multiple languages, 48 pages long, published by Michele Alliot-Marie, Minister of Defense, April 2006.

68 One recent source is the Congressional Research Service attorney Elizabeth B. Bazan, "Assassination Ban and E.O. 12333: A Brief Summary," *CRS Report for Congress*, Jan. 4, 2002. Her sources include W. Hays Parks, a U.S. Army legal authority on laws of war and a specialist of help to the present author as he dealt with this difficult subject in the first edition.

69 Our first edition (p. 263) raised the complex question of assassination of known terrorists—an option on which there was a minimum of public discussion or literature—outside the case of Israel. See also Caspar Weinberger, "Can We Target the Leaders?" *Strategic Review* (Spring 2001), pp. 21–4. After the tragedy of 9-11-01, there has been more to read. Among the most thoughtful examinations is Daniel Byman's "Do Targeted Killings Work?" *Foreign Affairs*, vol. 85 no. 2 (March–April 2006), pp. 95–111.

Pakistan confirms the killing of Hamza Rabia, so important to Al Qaeda that some think he was the new number three leader. And it apparently occurred in Pakistan, but the United States. has avoided saying so, as has Mr. Byman's article, though it twice mentions the lethal strike. See "Evidence Suggests U.S. Missile Used in Strike," NBC News, Dec. 5, 2005; www.msnbc.msn.com/id/10303175 accessed Aug. 12, 2006.

An example of further reading is Andrew McGregor, "The Assassination of Zelimkhan Yandarbiyev: Implications for the War on Terrorism, in *Unmasking Terror: A Global Review of Terrorist Activities*, op. cit., pp. 117–21.

70 Joachim Joesten, *The Red Hand: The Sinister Account of the Terrorist Arm of the French Right-Wing "Ultras"—in Algeria and on the Continent* (London: Abelard Schuman, 1962).

71 Bard O'Neill of the National Defense University would classify this kind of group as "preservationist"—a sub-state group determined to retain its particular place or interest as against a revolutionary group or even state force seeking to challenge it. His valuable rubric for analysis appears in his book *Insurgency and Terrorism: Inside Modern Revolutionary Warfare* (Washington: Brassey's, 1990; repr. by Potomac Books, 2005). Other examples of this kind of terrorists are the Ku Klux Klan in the United States and Canada and Sinhalese thugs of "JVP" in Sri Lanka in the 1970s.

72 One portrait of GAL action is by Richard H. Ward et al., eds, *Extremist Groups: An International Compilation of Terrorist Organizations, Violent Political Groups, and Issue-Oriented Militant Movements*, 2nd ed. (Huntsville, TX: Institute for Study of Violent Groups, Sam Houston University, 2002), pp. 451–53. Ch. 1 of my first edition, and fn. 84, offer a few earlier mentions.

73 O'Neill, *Insurgency and Terrorism*, pp. 27–8.

74 Isser Harel, *A House on Garibaldi Street* (New York: Viking Press, 1975). The author, a Hagana member, later rose to lead Mossad.

75 John Follain, *Jackal: The Complete Story of the Legendary Terrorist, Carlos the Jackal* (New York: Arcade Publishing, 1998), ch. 12.

76 U. S. State Department, *Patterns of Global Terrorism: 2001* (Washington, DC: GPO, April 2002), p. 131. FBI statistics show eight rather than nine renditions during the Clinton Administration. CIA's George Tenet has testified in open session that seventy terrorists were rendered or brought to justice before 9/11.

77 We encouraged rendition in our first edition, ch. 6. To that time it had not been publicly connected with either third countries or with torture—nor must it be.

78 Media reports of recent years, and Ronald Kessler, *The CIA At War: Inside the Secret Campaign Against Terror* (New York: St. Martin's Press, 2003), p. 277.

79 For a strong and searching critique of most or all renditions by the United States—which however shows no concern for the appalling crimes of those sought—see Jane Mayer, "Outsourcing Torture; Annals of Justice," *The New Yorker* 81: 1 (Feb. 14, 2005).

80 Days before the first publicity on the Abu Grahib prison scandal in Iraq, I raised the question of torture-for-information in a seminar of military officers (from diverse countries). The foreign professionals discussed the problem. One Asian said that as a brigadier general, he found that suspects expected rough handling so he could surprise them and get more with politeness than he might by abuse. Eventually I closed the discussion with strongly expressed opposition to torture for intelligence purposes, pointing especially to the French experience in Algeria, a strategic disaster. However, the majority view, quietly stated by one foreign officer, was that 'Whatever we might say here, out in the field everybody does it.'

81 Press on the torture problem and France includes a cover story of Nov. 30, 2000 in *L'Express*, pp. 56–61. Some important individuals have concluded that torture by the French was at least as much a result of deliberate unwritten policy and a new approach to counterinsurgency as it was a product of accident or circumstance.

82 Paul H. Lewis, *Guerrillas and Generals: The "Dirty War" in Argentina* (Westport, CN: Praeger, 2002). The *Christian Science Monitor* in late June 2006 produced a series of articles on trials for the perpetrators.

83 Alan Dershowitz is the author of a book promoting the idea of a legal "warrant for torture" in certain cases and has for several years expounded this position publicly, as on National Public Radio in the Washington DC area in late June, 2006. The radio host asked Dershowitz if he was mockingly offering "A Modest Proposal" in the tradition of Jonathan Swift, but

the Harvard professor said no. The "Publisher's Introduction" to Paul Aussaresses' book, op. cit., also describes Mr. Dershowitz's advocacy role.

84 Vladimir Bukovsky, "Torture's Long Shadow," *Washington Post*, Dec. 18, 2005. A well-published author, Bukovsky is also a member of the (U.S.) President's Council on Bioethics.

85 My arguments here are not a defense of terrorists, nor a suggestion that they deserve the same rights as legitimate belligerents fighting under the Geneva Accords, nor even advocacy of a ban on placing under stress persons suspected of terrorist murders. My arguments here are against torture.

86 Bomb failure is common. So is premature detonation, which the IRA, in a black humor reference to a footballer's error, calls an "own goal." In July 2006, when Vladimir Putin claimed "an operation" had blown up Chechen Shamil Basayev (thought to have masterminded the Beslan school massacre of 2004), others speculated that the truck full of explosives that killed him may have been owned by his group and an accident occurred in a transport operation.

87 Albert Camus said that "...torture has perhaps saved some at the expense of honor, by uncovering thirty bombs, but at the same time it has created fifty new terrorists, who, operating the some other way and in another place, would cause the death of even more innocent people." Quoted in Alistair Horne, *A Savage War of Peace: Algeria 1954–1962* (New York: Viking Press, 1978), p. 205. *Washington Post* military correspondent Tom Ricks knows this book well and wrote of it in a story April 28, 2006 covering counterinsurgency discussions at the School of Advanced Warfighting, Marine Corps University, Quantico, VA. I am appreciative of the visit and a brief exchange of messages on Horne's book.

88 Ibid. French torture in interrogation yielded a "mountain" of false information, Horne writes.

89 Ibid. On torture, see Horne, pp. 195–207. French self-hatred is discussed at 200-1, 206, and 233. In a 1960 poll by a Catholic publication that asked soldiers what their worst Algerian experience was, 6 cited their wounds, but 132 cited atrocities *by the French*.

90 Colin L. Powell, "A Strategy of Partnerships," *Foreign Affairs*, Jan-Feb. 2004.

91 When public diplomacy expert Dr. Juliana Pilon wrote several years ago to the NSC about lost possibilities a senior officer wrote back, "We don't do public diplomacy here." This confuses "going public"—which the NSC should not do, given its advisory and coordinating roles—with taking care of the business of public affairs or telling America's story abroad—which the U.S. government is indeed supposed to do. The exchange is mentioned in Dr. Pilon's forthcoming book, *Why America is Such a Hard Sell: Beyond Pride and Prejudice*. I appreciate her willingness to grant access to the manuscript and to comment on my draft list of "Arguments Washington Has Neglected," in this chapter's text.

I made my own brief inquiry to the NSC on the matter of public diplomacy, at the end of 2006, and came away discouraged.

92 UN Security Council Resolution 1373; downloaded Feb. 10, 2005 at http://domino.un.org/

93 Ibid; the 1998 document is quoted within the 2001 document. The traditional doctrine of "state responsibility" is notably missing from today's conversations about counterterrorism, when it should be a central argument in many State Department and non–U.S. government statements. It is the fundamental and essential counterpart of the principle of "state sovereignty." An old and useful reminder of this principle of international law is in an award-winning monograph by then Lt. Col. Richard J. Erickson of the U.S. Air Force: *Legitimate Use of Military Force Against State-Sponsored International Terrorism* (Maxwell, AL: Air University Press, July 1989), ch. 3.

94 Mr. Sheehan of the Department of State spoke of this priority when I met him in his offices during his tenure as Coordinator for Counterterrorism. Of Mr. Kappes, the *New York Times* reported May 30, 2006: He "played a pivotal role in the secret talks with Libya that culminated in December 2003 in the agreement in which Col. Muammar el Qadaffi agreed to give up his chemical and biological weapons program."

95 U.S. Department of State, *Patterns of Global Terrorism: 2000* (Washington, DC: GPO, April 2001), p. 7.

96 One of the better treatments of this unsatisfying effort to restrain Taliban is by Richard Miniter, *Losing Bin Laden* (Washington, DC: Regnery Publishing, 2003).

97 U.S. State Department, *Country Reports, 2005*, p. 28.

98 Debate over Iraq's relations with Al Qaeda is one matter; another, quite beyond debate, is Baghdad's long clear record of sponsoring international terrorists, such as Iranian Mujahedeen Khalq and secular Palestinians Abu Nidal and Abu Abbas.

99 Author's interview in May 2006 with Avanulas R. Smiley, a U.S. Army Lt. Col. with relevant service in Europe. See also David C. Gompert and Raymond C. Smith, "Creating a NATO Special Operations Force," *Defense Horizons* (Washington, DC: National Defense University) no. 52 (March 2006) as well as "Special Operations Forces Discover Common Ground, Goal at Conference," U.S. EUCOM, press release of May 30, 2006.

100 Author's conversations with Sahel country military officers at National Defense University and U.S. Department of State, *Country Reports on Terrorism: 2004* (Washington, DC: GPO, April 2005), p. 28.

101 When speaking at the Department of State on Oct. 22, 2001, the first question I fielded, by forum host Alan Lang, concerned whether pursuit of terrorists' monies would pay. It was and is an excellent question; the Department of State recognizes the utility of financial counterterrorism and pursues it but without overstating what it can achieve—which in my view is exactly the right posture to take.

102 International Convention for the Suppression of the Financing of Terrorism (Dec. 9, 1999; April 2002), pp. 2–3.

103 UN Security Council Resolution 1373, adopted Sept. 28, 2001, and referencing UNSCR 1189 of Aug. 13, 1998 as well. Accessed Feb. 10, 2005 at http://domino.un.org

The same principle of obligation of states to act could be the basis for demands that Syria, Iran, and the like stop training international terrorists. However, incredibly, neither has ever been sanctioned by the UN for such ongoing activity. It may be hoped that the special UN report of 2005 on the Syrian involvement in the murder of Lebanese statesman Rafiq Hariri will become a basis for UN action against Damascus.

104 The U.S. Departments of State, Treasury, and Justice all help to fund these programs. My sources here include informal interviews with Treasury officers in the fall of 2005 and discussions with Michael Kraft. Now a frequent contributor to the public prints and to "*Counterterrorismblog.org*," Mr. Kraft served for eighteen years at the Department of State. He discussed financial counterterrorism in a lecture at the Institute of World Politics, a Washington DC graduate school, on March 27, 2004, shortly after his retirement.

105 Informal discussions with Treasury officers, fall of 2005, and (including the quotation) U.S. Department of State, "International Narcotics Control Strategy Report, 2003," released March 2004, p. 3; www.state.gov/g/inl/rls/nrcrpt/2003/vol12/html/29915.htm

106 This list was accessed Sept. 29, 2005 at www.un.org/Docs/sc/committees/1267 UNSCR 1617 was discussed by E. Anthony Wayne, Assistant Secretary of State for Economic and Business Affairs, before the Senate Committee on Banking, Housing, and Urban Affairs, Washington, DC, April 4, 2006. I am also thankful to Mr. Gene Fisher for his understanding of U.S. House of Representatives legislation on financial controls on terrorism; interviews of 2005.

107 The Canadian action came with the change of government to the Conservatives and was reported by the *Washington Times*, April 11, 2006.

108 U.S. Executive Orders 12947, 13099, 13129, by Mr. Clinton. George W. Bush followed these with number 13224, naming twenty-eight groups and individuals, and number 13268, focused on Taliban and Al Qaeda. Such Executive Orders may be found in the *Federal Register* and often on the Internet.

The many indicators of how slowly such sanctions take effect and work include *Washington Times* accounts of the efforts. In 1997, Bill Gertz found that the State Department was too slow in publishing a list of foreign entities raising terrorist funds within the United States, and House International Relations Committee Chair Henry Hyde was writing to Secretary Madeleine Albright to prompt action in line with Congressional requirements. According to "State Slow to Publish List for Terrorists," the FBI was aware of money raising within the United States by Hamas, the Irish Republican Army, Hezbollah, Gamma'at al-Islamiya, the Palestine Islamic Jihad, Jammat ul-Fuqra, the Islamic Salvation Front, Kach, Kahane Chai, and En-Nahda, a Tunisian group; Aug. 8, 1997. Then see Betsy Pisik, Dec. 2, 2003, "108 Nations Decline to Pursue Terrorists."

109 From the May 30, 2006 news summaries by A. N. Pratt and the Graduate Support Office of the George C. Marshall European Center for Security Studies. The sources were *AXIS*, May 29, and *Itar-Tass*, May 28.

110 There have been several disappointments in Germany's cases based on the plots for 9-11. Also, Spain's supreme court threw out a conviction of the only person that country had found guilty of involvement: Imad Eddin Barakat Yarkas did get twelve years for leading a terrorist group, but his longer sentence was overthrown because of lack of proof, according to the *Washington Post*, June 2, 2006.

111 *Agence France Press*, May 30, 2006.

112 An example of difficulties with intelligence sharing between even good allies appeared after this latest aerial bombing plan was preempted. The *New York Times*, in background reporting, noted how a year before when the FBI had teams in London to help investigate the tube plots, U.S. personnel irritated their British counterparts by being too public with what investigations were uncovering: "Tracing Terror Plots, British Watch, then Pounce," Aug. 13, 2006.

113 Though the Jordanian officer was a valued student of mine, it would be unwise to publish his name.

114 See "Jordon Emerges as a Vital U.S. Ally," *Wall Street Journal*, June 10–11, 2006, and "Inside the Takedown: Intelligence Work Guides Bombs to Zarqawi," *U.S.A. Today*, June 9, 2006. Jordan has also been vocal and active in condemning Muslim terrorism.

115 Once the program became a public one, my copy of the leaflet came from Mr. Tom Hastings, the program's leading action officer within the Department of State.

116 U.S. Department of State annuals *Patterns of Global Terrorism: 2003* (Washington, DC: GPO, April 2004), pp. 162–3; and *Country Reports, 2004*, pp. 10, 36.

117 See the display on the ATA program in *Patterns of Global Terrorism: 2003*, pp. 162–3.

118 The U.S. Marine Corps alone educates or trains some 500 foreign personnel a year in varied military matters, in part through the work of teams in at least forty-five countries. The author appreciates this information from Capt. Alex Hult, then of the staff of Marine Corps University, as I prepared a speech on "Partnerships in Counterterrorism," later printed in *Vital Speeches*, Sept. 15, 2005, pp. 721–5.

119 "Chart of Conflict: 2005," an insert in *The Military Balance: 2005/2006* (London: International Institute for Strategic Studies, Oct. 2005; courtesy of Dr Paolo Tripodi.

120 For relevant clippings on how the militancy ended (at least for now) in Aceh, I am appreciative to Professor Aaron Danis.

121 One of several open statements on this transaction is by Dr. C. H. Briscoe, "Rescuing the Burnhams: The Unspoken SOCPAC Mission," *Special Warfare* 17: 1 (Sept. 2004), p. 46.

122 The U.S. State Department, then openly hoping to "moderate" Libyan actions, downplayed this chain of events in a skeptical account of Libya's "high-profile" negotiations role with Abu Sayyaf; see *Patterns of Global Terrorism: 2000* , p. 34.

123 The *Washington Post* and *New York Times* were among the papers on Oct. 25 and 26, 2002 detailing the tragedy in Moscow, which ended in a CT gas attack. For the Beslan school disaster, which featured all manner of oversized weapons when the object was rescuing school children, see retrospectives by the *New York Times* printed a year later: Aug. 26, and Sept. 1, 2005.

6

HOW TERROR GROUPS END

How is it that terrorist groups decline or disappear?[1] Social scientists, government analysts of terrorism, and law enforcement specialists show great interest in the origins of violent political groups. They have shown the same interest in the origins of terrorist bands, no matter how small, but no parallel body of literature has tracked, and treated of, the end of these same groups. Only a few articles,[2] and no books, delimit and plumb this subject. Yet it is especially important now, given the engagement of many governments in a protracted "global war on terrorism."

Many terror groups lodged strongly in recent memory have indeed come to an end. Any glossary or encyclopedia of the 1970s or 1980s[3] covering sub-state violent organizations that use killing to advance a political cause yields dozens of names no longer in the news. The many that have expired include the Armenian Secret Army for the Liberation of Armenia; the Breton Liberation Front in France; Belgium's Communist Combatant Cells; the Liberation Front of Quebec; and the like. El Salvador's Farabundo Marti National Liberation Front, a coalition of small guerrilla and terror groups, once imagined that they were going to conquer and communize El Salvador; now they have gone. Not far away, in Peru, the spring of 1997 brought disappearance of the once-proud organization Tupac Amaru—MRTA. Across the oceans, in Greece, arrests of 2003 swept up the miniscule Revolutionary Organization November 17th, which had frequently assassinated NATO officials.[4] Never once had November 17 suffered an arrest, let alone a conviction. Greece never caught any of them in a quarter-century, while, every year, they struck and killed at least once. Now they are apparently all jailed; the silence is what is now striking.

History's lessons on how terrorism ends are varied, though not usually contradictory. The group's strategic choices and internal fissures are involved, but the action of governments in opposition is usually central. Terror groups are usually defeated by public determination over many years, good leadership, systematic police work, excellent intelligence, adequate resources, and occasional operations by SWAT (Special Weapons and Tactics) or military units. This chapter illustrates six of the most common ways in which terror groups have been defeated or have declined.

Military force

The option of force was often derided as "simplistic" before September 11. Studied views—as well as intellectual fashions—were critical or disdainful of recommendations for highly forceful methods. Surprisingly, such reservations about forcibly responding to terrorist attacks extended even into the centers of power in the Pentagon. Dr. Richard Shultz, a Defense Department insider and a professor at the Fletcher School of Law and Diplomacy, has detailed the many categories of "Showstoppers"[5] that inhibited the Pentagon's Joint Staff and senior military officers from approving dozens of plans or proposals for using U.S. weapons and special forces to attack training camps and other terrorist installations. It hardly needs to be added that among academics, journalists, and politicians, a long list of well-known figures counseled caution about military force— before 9-11.

Ironically, the same sort of writer who deprecated or declined to discuss the use of force—even within a larger strategy for counterterrorism—often began his or her terrorism article with mention of "The Assassins." Colorful prose surrounds this movement's origins in the eleventh century in northern Iran, its lethal clandestine character, the legend of use of hashish and "heavenly beauties" to persuade young men of what awaits them after their martyrdom while killing, and so on. Our writers almost never say how the story ended for this organization of terrorists—variously called Isma'ilis, Nizaris, and Fatimids. There were several reasons for the defeat of this unusual Shia cult, including schism and continuous pressure by mainstream Sunni Muslim rulers in what today are Syria, Iran, Iraq, and Egypt. However, the most important reason these terrorists met their end was the army of the Mongols. In the mid-thirteenth century, they systematically reduced the Assassins' fortresses along the Caspian Sea and points south. The Mongols killed or dispersed the sect's adherents and properties. The Assassins' deft, sly individual fanatics with knives were overmatched by big, determined, heavy-handed armies led by Genghis Khan. The fortified headquarters was taken and then, by 1270–73, the cult was crushed.[6]

No one fails to see that the political and moral parameters of counterterrorism for the latter twentieth and early twenty-first centuries differ from those of the Mongol Age. States and their behaviors are constrained by political limitations, by conceptions of international law, by the United Nations, by prudent or reluctant statesmen, and by powerful public media, but that is not to say that force has been banished. Modern states are permitted self-defense by the United Nations Charter. Many are actually bound to defend against aggression by their own current arrangements, such as Article Five of the North Atlantic Treaty Organization, activated immediately after 9-11. There are other reasons why force is still used. Despots act as they will. Democratic governors may do what defense of the polity, or public opinion, seems to require. So if harsh military offensives against terrorists are less usual than in historic times, they do still occur.

The Cambodian communists called the Khmer Rouge were at once revolutionaries, insurgents, and terrorists. Their years of calculated and well-integrated efforts were crowned with victory, and they were thus able to rule, and even to rename, Kampuchea. It was not public disgust or international revulsion at their genocide or a new revolutionary organization that unseated them. It was instead a war, waged by another formerly guerrilla army, that of Vietnam. The Vietnamese destroyed and dislodged the Khmer Rouge regime in 1978.

Half a world away and several years later came a different sort of example of overwhelming use of force. Brutish power was one state's rejoinder to the Muslim Brotherhood in 1982. The Brotherhood are a long and sometimes respected international association with a history approaching a century in length. They promote religion and also involve themselves in politics. However, these ranks also include many extremists and, with some regularity, the Muslim Brotherhood yields up its hardest members into terror organizations. A close look at the personal biographies of terrorists convicted in the Middle East region during the last generation will sometimes locate a man's past in the Muslim Brotherhood. In the early 1980s in Syria, the brethren were too troublesome for dictator Hafez al Asad, so he reduced them. He did so under what later became known as "Hama rules," literally bombing and shelling that Syrian city for almost two weeks. The massacre was not stopped by public outcry or media coverage—what is today called "The CNN effect." The many reporters who seemingly document every artillery wound in the Levant were not in Hama or were not allowed there. Asad suffered little long-term disrepute for killing more than 10,000 fellow Syrians. Nor did this aggression prompt rebellion against his 30,000 to 40,000 troops occupying Lebanon, including the Bekaa Valley, an international terrorist haven. Indeed, on his death in 2000, the Syrian dictator who wrecked the lives and property of so many fellow countrymen was lionized. His son succeeded him to power. A range of British newspapers—thought to be more discriminating than some world media—recalled his regime accomplishments in friendly or laudatory tones; it was difficult to find a paragraph about Hama or about a career spent exporting terrorism. Successor Bashar al Asad and those around him have carried on using state terrorism against the Lebanese, even as Syrian troops have been withdrawn.

Military force in those two modern cases was used rather indiscriminately to crush and destroy a hardened political enemy. Military force more narrowly and wisely directed has been a part of many successful governmental campaigns in contemporary times.

An exemplary case is that of the de facto end of MRTA, or Tupac Amaru, a Peruvian Marxist-Leninist organization, sometimes called Castroite. By 1996, the small but determined group had revealed certain inadequacies and suffered some reversals at the hands of Peruvian police. Many members, including their leader, Victor Polay Campos, were in jail. Following the age-old pattern, the other terrorists resolved to spring their comrades form prison. To do so, they boldly took over the Japanese Ambassador's residence in Lima on the occasion of an evening dinner attended by hundreds of foreigners. However, after months of planning, Peruvian commandos—with U.S. technical advice—recaptured the complex. The quick resolution came in minutes on a day in April, 1997; both the story and the film of the "takedown" are dramatic. All but one of the seventy hostages lived; fourteen terrorists were killed, including mission leader Nestor Cerpa Cartolini. No "martyr complex" brought about national longing for the terrorists. Apparently, most Peruvians thought that the gunmen who took civilian hostages were terrorists, not martyrs. With the recapture of so many hostages, MRTA collapsed. For a decade, virtually nothing of Tupac Amaru made its way into foreign newspapers—long a hallmark of any group's success. Only now is the group appearing to stir again, as remnants attempt to reform in an accommodating Bolivia and perhaps link up with FARC of Colombia.[7]

Still more recently, military efforts were the key to the immense success against the Taliban in Afghanistan. That regime, sponsored by Pakistanis and also far more extreme than most political or religious entities in the region, then became intertwined with Osama Bin Laden. The result was as close a mix of despotic politics and international terrorism as anywhere in modern memory. Literally, only by destroying the Taliban state could the training and export of terrorists be solved and the Afghan nation given a fair chance at liberty. And yet, all knew Afghanistan to be a difficult place to occupy, and most experts thought it nearly impossible to fully conquer and change. Only the coalition's entry and success in combination with indigenous Afghans during the last months of 2001 broke the Taliban–Al Qaeda arrangement. These military operations bought the country an historical fresh start and a full two-year respite from most political terrorism. In Afghan history, two years of peace is an impressive interval.

Since 2003, terrorism has been creeping back. The Taliban regrouped; the U.S. National Security Council deemed an insurgency active again by the beginning of 2005;[8] the Taliban was staging limited offensives by mid-2006.[9] Central government in Afghanistan will be challenged, as it always has, to control its territory and administer its programs. Meantime, the national reconciliation process sponsored by elected President Hamid Karzai makes limited strides. By early 2006, some fifty senior Taliban officials and six times as many from the rank and file, had stepped forward and formally reconciled to the new democratic order.[10] Unfortunately, Pakistan still allows Taliban leaders to live in Quetta, according to senior Afghan officials, and Taliban operations are now frequently staged from Pakistani territory, apparently with acquiescence of authorities.[11]

Capturing or killing the leaders

A second way in which a terror group may fail is when its leader of singular importance is arrested and irrevocably jailed. Some terror groups and broader insurgencies would easily survive such an arrest; no "decapitation" of the revolution may even be possible. However, other groups, more personality-driven or despotically led, are vulnerable to metaphorical decapitation. They risk much by preferring their own "cult of personality" to development of a broad leadership cadre. An accident, an arrest, an extradition can thus mean doom for the group.

That fate befell the egoistic and gifted Abimael Guzman, creator of Shining Path, or Sendero Luminoso. The holder of two doctoral degrees, Guzman was a teacher. His writings were sometimes deemed dull, but an acquaintance testifies that the professor was a magnetic speaker and easily attracted women and men to his cause.[12] After years of careful planning and cadre building, especially in Peru's outlying universities and high schools, Guzman turned the Shining Path to overt violence in 1980—the very moment when reform and elections were restoring democracy in Peru. Sendero Luminoso had different ideas, including the ideas and fervor of Mao Tse Tung in the 1920s and 1930s. With dynamite, machetes, and single-shot weapons, in the countryside and to a lesser degree in slums and cities, Sendero intimidated, organized, and butchered other Peruvians.

Several tens of thousands died, and many more suffered tragedy, injury, or despair. The ruin of the state economy was also extensive, while the "shadow government" of the rebel communists effectively controlled considerable parts of rural Peru.

However, this protracted social struggle and its terrorism and guerrilla war all but ended, and quickly, with the arrest of the principal. This came about owing to steady, patient police work, especially that of a secret unit within DINCOTE, the national counterterrorist division of police. Major Benedicto Jimenez reportedly commanded the small unit, emphasizing forensic science and hard work while strongly opposing torture and other human rights abuses. His office veiled its efforts and actually hid some parts of the investigative work from Vladimiro Montesinos and other top Peruvian security officials. By "tailing suspects, cultivating informants, poring over captured documents," and other old-fashioned methods and with the reported advantage of some CIA funds and technical advice,[13] the Jimenez unit found Sendero safe houses, identified top operatives, and eventually captured Abimael Guzman himself in September of 1992.[14]

This achievement by the police and government stunned Shining Path. Oscar Ramirez, a.k.a. "Comrade Feliciano," tried to carry the torch of leadership but could not; he was trapped by Peru's army. The women and men around the famed founder were mostly arrested; they may not have lost their faith, but they did lose their power and momentum. Only a few hundreds of Sendero remain active now. In an early 2006 incident, SL made a successful attack on a government patrol. A hooded "Comandante Artemio" appears in a video, threatening larger attacks. Peru closely tracks movements by the militants in the central valleys. But the group that once dominated more than half the national territory of Peru is a shadow of itself, rather than a light shining on the national future. Abimael Guzman remains in jail.[15]

Another celebrated militant movement of the 1980s was the PKK, or Kurdistan Workers Party. This group developed from its founding days in the mid-1970s into a capable terrorist organization and a credible combat force for guerrilla action against the Turkish armed forces. PKK also proved a special enemy of the Federal Republic of Germany, linked to the Turks by military contracts and by partnership in NATO. Abdullah Ocalan built the Kurdistan Workers Party with an eye to creating an independent state centered on ethnic areas of southeastern Turkey. The organization's strengths were communist doctrine, thousands of qualified gunmen, and a closely managed reign of terror. The latter involved terrorizing other Kurds, in Turkey, adjacent countries, and in Western Europe, to gain support in manpower and materiel. PKK also deployed suicide terrorists, including women, before most Middle Eastern groups dared to do so. Its operational "signature"—rarely recalled now—was a string of simultaneous bombs aimed mostly at doing property damage in several cities. PKK grew through extortion, drug trafficking, and killing, while its leader gave press interviews from safe haven in Syria.

However, after a quarter-century in the field, Abdullah Ocalan was caught. "Rendition" removed him from temporary hiding at a Greek diplomatic residence or facility in Kenya and returned him to Turkey for trail in February, 1999.[16] Formally speaking, PKK passed from the scene in the year 2003.

A new organization called KADEK (Kurdish Freedom & Democracy Congress) arose in April, 2002; it was more political than violent. A successor to that, called the

---

Box 6.1 The evolution and end of the Kurdistan Workers Party

1974   Kurdish activist Abdullah Ocalan founds PKK, which is overtly Marxist-Leninist, nationalist, and secular, working for a Kurdish state based in southeastern Turkey.

1970s and 1980s   Numerous operations of a terrorist and guerrilla character—against Turkish government employees, other Kurds, and Turkish security forces. Rapid growth, given Syrian safe haven and training facilities in Lebanon's Bekaa Valley.

1990   Syria continues providing safe haven for cadre, including a comfortable residence for Ocalan. The organization also enjoys help from Iraq and Iran.

1993   PKK terrorism within Turkey includes a campaign against tourism, with attacks and the kidnapping of Westerners. This continues for several years, as does PKK's growth and enrichment.

1994   U.S. analysts estimate that the Kurdistan Workers Party fields 10,000 to 15,000 guerrillas and can call on at least four times as many part-time militants. There are also thousands of civilian supporters and a financial network in Western Europe. Attacks and activity in Germany are commonplace.

1996, 1997   Abdullah Ocalan lobbies the German government to lift its ban on PKK, negotiating with a promise to end attacks within Germany. This succeeds. Germany withdrew its international arrest warrant on Ocalan in 1998.

1998   Having left Syria (perhaps owing to Turkish pressures), Ocalan drifts about, visiting Italy, Russia, and other countries in search of a new home base.

1999   In February, Turkish authorities "snatch" Ocalan in Nairobi, Kenya, where he had been offered a protected residence by Greek diplomats. He is bundled aboard an airplane and flown to Turkey for trial. Press accounts stressed his submissiveness in captivity. August 1999 brought announcement of a peace initiative from Ocalan. Lesser PKK leaders focus on political activism in Western Europe, directed at Turkey's treatment of the Kurds.

2000   At a January congress, PKK activists promise to follow Ocalan's lead on a peaceable political route. This confirms a new era of political maneuvering, leadership questions, the rise of groups with new names, and so on—but most Kurdish activists abstain from terrorism for the next years. Ocalan remains in jail today.

Kurdistan Society Congress, Kongra Gel, then emerged as national activism's next step and as formal successor to PKK, on November 12, 2003. Kongra Gel is ostensibly a political party, and its demands include "constitutional recognition to all ethnic identities including Kurdish identity." The overriding fact is that after February 1999, terrorism in Turkey fell off dramatically, as did Kurdish terrorism in Germany. There are instances of terrorism each year in Turkey, and these numbers began growing in 2004.[17] However, tens of thousands had died in the PKK wars, and now a full decade of relative peace was enjoyed by this modern Muslim republic. The Turks, with a characteristic stroke of boldness, had bought their country relative peace.

A turn toward democratic ways

As certain activists in the ranks of the Kurds have now shown, some members of terrorist groups will turn away from violence or toward democratic ways, or both. Though their sincerity in this may be suspect or challenged, it is a fact that some terrorists do outwardly and convincingly reform, reentering normal society and pacific political life. When made by an organization, this constitutes a major strategic choice—the reversal of the initial choice the group had made to depend on terror or to add terror to other strategies, such as clandestine political organization or guerrilla war against a state's armed forces.[18]

The imprisoned Nelson Mandela was the most esteemed man in the African National Congress. ANC held firmly to anti-apartheid ideals while working systematically in politics and all too frequently conducting hideous terror attacks. The latter were most often performed on black South Africans who dared to take a differing view of the future of the country or adhere to some political rival to the ANC, such as Zulu chief Buthelezi and his Inkatha party. A signature practice of the African National Congress' thugs was "necklacing"—placing a gasoline-filled automobile tire around the neck of a bound victim and then igniting it, burning him to death. However, when Mr. Mandela was released, he quickly replaced acting leader Oliver Tambo and led the ANC to power in a new way, through elections. This made him not just president of a new republic; it made him a hero to much of the world.

For an example of the turn away from terrorism in the Western Hemisphere, one may consider Colombia's M-19. The April 19th Movement was a small Castroite organization. It helped introduce the contemporary problem of narcotrafficking—by furthering the export of Colombian cocaine to pay for its guns and operating expenses. However, this group overplayed its hand in a spectacular seizure of the national justice building in Bogota in November, 1985. Thirty-five men and women of M-19 stormed the place, killed guards, and took masses of hostages, including many supreme court justices. Some of the terrorists raced directly to the fourth floor where drug traffickers were on trial or facing extradition to the United States—the group leader had proclaimed opposition to such extradition. Ultimately the whole building was burned down (which of course destroyed most of those government. records), but the M-19 attack drew well-armed Colombian police, and most of the terrorists did not survive. Some time later, the group remnants entered the democratic process. Laying down guns in Colombia's environment can be dangerous, and the personal disarmament cost some former terrorists their lives to assassins and old enemies. However, the others, the survivors of this demobilization, took well to honest politicking. M-19 men ran for, and won, public office.

The same has happened with certain of the old Salvadoran guerrillas of the FMLN front. Joachim Villalobos is among those to have done well at folding into postwar democratic life. This extremist had shot his way into a leadership post of the Revolutionary People's Army (ERP) while ridiculing his opponents and victims for "excessive liberalism… and bourgeois tendencies."[19] When the Sandinistas of Nicaragua prompted the five Salvadoran groups to meld, Villalobos emerged as a top field commander. Today, El Salvador's many brutal years of war lie in the past, gone though not forgotten. One-time revolutionary Joachim Villalobos married a millionaire Salvadoran woman and they live safely behind substantial walls in a wealthy area of San Salvador. Modestly active in politics, Villalobos also speaks abroad on occasion. He does so with ease, carrying an Oxford Ph.D. earned in postwar studies. Some old comrades from the bush are also proving their adaptiveness, serving as members of Parliament in El Salvador.[20]

One prominent politician in Germany is another part of this pattern, the turning to nonviolent political work. Germany's foreign minister through 2005, Joschka Fischer, had a personal past association with terrorists suggested in photographs. It is not crucial that these show him kicking a policeman in a street brawl on April 7, 1973 in Frankfurt-Mein. That was embarrassing, but the photos show something more important: He was fighting alongside a close associate, Hans Joachim Klein, an infamous German terrorist associate of "Carlos the Jackal" (Ilich Ramirez Sanchez). Nor was any escape for the eminent German politician possible via reference to tampering with the photographs or computer rerenderings, because the photos came from none other than the daughter of Ulrike Meinhof, a founder of the German terrorist movement of that time. Nonetheless, the real point is the passage of such forms of political action into the past and the current public service—which all hold to be good and credible—that Joschka Fischer did for many recent years while serving German democracy.[21] Later he announced retirement from politics now and took a professorship at Princeton University.

Certain American terrorists of the same era have surfaced from the underground to become influential again though in quieter ways. It is striking how many have emerged as educators.[22] Mark Rudd, student leader turned Weatherman, has been teaching in the Southwest United States. One of those who led the Weatherman after Rudd did, Billy Ayers, is now "Distinguished Professor of Education, University of Illinois, Chicago" and author of a book about child education. Ayers is married to former Weatherwoman Bernardine Dohrn, also a children's rights advocate and a professor of law at Northwestern University. In 2003, she authored an article against the Patriot Act entitled "Homeland Imperialism: Fear and Resistance." Husband Billy Ayers makes few (and weak) apologies for Weathermen bombings. His recent memoir, *Fugitive Days*, could have reflected wisdom or at least deep change; instead, he renounces little and, like so many others of those violent days, merely suggests that "other strategies are more appropriate now." The paperback received an indulgent review from the *New York Times* two days before 9-11-01.[23] Some two years later, the same newspaper followed up with many of the principal Weather Underground leaders, yielding the headline: "Lives of 60's Revolutionaries Have Quieted, but Intensity of Beliefs Hasn't Dimmed." Many of those interviewed struck militant tones but avow they are nonviolently active in such causes as the environment, AIDS, or prisoners' rights. A professor observed that the Weathermen "sustain certain kinds of ideological and ethical commitments" but have moved "beyond the armed struggle."[24] That suffices, in its way, and may be as much as American democracy can expect of former terrorists.

Good grand strategy

A fourth way in which terrorists end—and this has happened many times in the post–World War II era—is with opposition by a strong national effort under good grand strategy. Sober government leadership and all major aspects of national power, from the political and military through the economic and informational, are deployed with focused energy and adequate resources. Democracies are often at their best in these struggles: rallying after initial inaction; demonstrating adherence to principles, yet taking temporary exceptional measures, and drawing on little-used internal and external resources. Confronted with terrorist crisis, a country is thus saved by remaining united and acting with prudence and appropriate force.

One of the historical figures most impressive for such conduct is the brilliant Filipino, secretary of defense and then president, Ramon Magsaysay. In the World War II years, he was a guerrilla against the foreign occupation of Japan. When his country was liberated and then formally freed by U.S. authority in 1946, he made a modest living in work for a bus company. Gradually, Magsaysay's interest in the new opportunities of the postwar world led him into politics and then into the Cabinet. There he began to lead his Filipino people in beating a communist guerrilla movement that freely used terrorism: These were the *Hukbo ng Bayan Laban sa Hapon*, or simply Huks. They arose as the 1940s turned into the 1950s, and the victories of Mao over the Koumintang Nationalists were sparkling in the air like fireworks. Other insurgents, too, were winning in other Third World theaters. Under Luis Taruc, the Huks developed and advanced, especially on the island of Luzon.

However, the government rallied. Ramon Magsaysay's leadership combined well with U.S. military aid that was notable for its limits and with the subtle and gentlemanly counsel of American advisor and intelligence professional Edward Lansdale. The Republic of the Philippines attacked the insurgency from all sides. Magsaysay purged corrupt army officers, altering the bad image of the army among the people. Citizens had felt like prey; now they felt protected. They created a new citizens organization, NAMFREL, which would become famous anew in Mrs. Cory Aquino's 1986 election, and revitalized confidence in polling and democracy. Relief works were initiated to begin to address landlessness; the best-known project was small but a potent symbol of a new era. In making war, the Filipino security forces focused on superior intelligence, and they got it because now citizens were willing to offer information to them. The Army was taught to avoid destructive major operations and favor small-unit tactics; these succeeded and did not create the human refugee swarms that demoralized citizen and counterinsurgent alike during the loss in South Vietnam. Police were improved with training and were better paid. They also emphasized intelligence, carefully mapping the enemy's human organization, not just its military presence. Police by definition lived locally and knew much. As they learned, their intelligence assets directly supported military operations. That was assured by the two forms of security services—police and army—liaising closely and continuously. Ultimately, the government side wore out and defeated the Huks. The rise and fall of this challenge spanned no more than eight years. The rebel leader surrendered in 1954, and Secretary of Defense-become-President Ramon Magsaysay enjoyed shining success.[25]

From a broad-based Asian rural movement freely employing terrorism, one may turn to a remarkably small European and urban sect of Marxist-Leninism, Germany's Red Army Faction. Each supplies a good illustration of governmental victory via grand strategy.

The Baader-Meinhof cells, under the name RAF, were led by strong individuals who complemented one another well. There was a bold man, good at planning, Andreas Baader, and several gifted intellectuals who were better than he at creating propaganda: Gudrun Ensslin and Ulrike Meinhof. From 1968 onward, this band robbed and shot a pathway across West Germany. Few among 60,000,000 West Germans actually stood up and followed the tiny self-proclaimed "vanguard," but that only underscored a much-neglected point: Terrorists may aim at popular support, but at least initially, popular support may not be necessary. It was enough that RAF could find protection, safe houses, a few guns, and borrowed cars. Individuals helped them from mixed reasons: militant leftism, or liberalism, or generosity, or odd brands of religious sympathy, such as also influenced Central American revolutionaries of later years.

Popular support did not deepen, but police attention did, so gradually the gun holders were cornered, one by one, and jailed. Law enforcement attrition was the reason the first Baader–Meinhof wave subsided, in mid-1970. However, then comrades sprung Andreas Baader from jail, and the Red Army Faction began a stronger, second wave of actions. This would not break until 1977. How? The answer was good grand strategy and an emphasis on law enforcement. Germany wore out RAF with effort and self-discipline. When there was no bloody overreaction to soil their methods, this foiled the terrorists' hope to "expose the latent fascism" of the postwar republic. The Germans did require some new laws and new efforts at policing and intelligence. Most notable was a revolutionary approach to computerization of data by a police specialist named Horst Herold, later called a father of computer profiling. Shown a room-sized computer used to calculate civil service pay, Herold considered how such calculating power might help find fugitives. He established a small new office to mine through commonplace data by the ton and kept at it until there slipped out, in the sieving process, little nuggets… banal facts…modest patterns. Germany's government learned how bank accounts were managed, what automobiles were the most often stolen, what kinds of apartments RAF were likely to rent, and how they paid for things. Such data mining and profiling led the painstaking police to the right doorsteps, where they made one arrest after another.

With a sense of relief, Germans also came to feel a sense of new nervousness. Once a democracy feels a danger is behind, it may gain a troubled conscience. The special computer unit raised civil liberties concerns in a country so self-conscious of its past and so liberal in the present. There were worries that Bonn was turning citizens into "glass people" whose secrets were visible to authorities. Terrorists had became visible and were caught, but there was a price paid in fear of the state. BKA—the Federal Crime Office—disbanded the special computer unit and pushed its founder out. After 9-11, the

Wall Street Journal located Horst Herold, nearly eighty years of age, living in obscurity in a broken down pre-fab on a German Army base. He had been given the house there for security reasons a quarter-century before and could never afford to move to a better civilian residence.[26]

However, modern democracies need more than sleuths to deal with modern criminals and terrorists, as even many pistol-carrying British "Bobbies" now admit. Gunpowder also helped to defeat the Red Army Faction. There was need of GSG 9, the formidable border guard unit created in response to the bloodshed in Munich in 1972 at the Olympic Games. A brilliant commando raid on October 18, 1977 by these specialized police liberated a hijacked Lufthansa airliner taken to Somalia by German and Palestinian terrorists. Bonn's well-judged risk, and the tactical success of GSG 9, had crushing psychological effects on the little RAF. Three Baader-Meinhof leaders took their own lives in their cells (Jan-Carl Raspe, Andreas Baader, and Gudrun Ensslin). A fourth also attempted suicide but failed. Because only a year before that Ulrike Meinhof had taken her own life in jail (May 9, 1976), the Red Army Faction became almost impotent. There was a last-gasp effort of remnants to reorganize, and these clung to political life through about 1982. A decade later, and very formally, RAF quit. They announced in an unusual statement that they were disbanding and admitted their ideological naiveté and their political failure to create popular support.[27]

Some terrorists succeed

A fifth way in which terror groups may end is in winning. History since 1945 has shown that some terrorists attain local, regional, or even national power without undergoing any political softening, liberalization, mellowing, or reform. At that point, they may regard their experiment to be complete or choose other more popular strategies or carry on as before. Despite the attempts of certain scholars to argue that terrorism always fails,[29] it is evident that the strategy of using violence to create general fear, when combined with political organization and often with guerrilla warfare, may succeed at even the highest strategic level: capture of state power. Examples of such victories include Lenin's Bolsheviks, Maoist communists, the Sandinistas of Nicaragua, and Yasser Arafat's Palestinians' acquisition of their own statelet, the "Palestine Authority." In the case of the latter, few literate adults who have observed Middle Eastern events for the last twenty years would argue that the "PA" would have come into being without the frequent use of terror.

Such groups may prove to be rough masters as they take state power. Today, Hamas and Fatah frequently fight in the streets and even shoot each other inside government buildings, each side claiming exclusive authority over the Palestinians. One still blanches at what the Khmer Rouge did while in power. For the past half-decade, up to today, there is frequent news of Cambodian and international attempts to try the remaining Khmer Rouge leaders for war crimes before they die of old age; a few of the guilty still live openly. More often, terrorists-turned-rulers restore outward calm—something despotisms do well. They aim to govern by clever spying, quiet coercion, and selective brutality. They more often tend toward the model of the efficient East German police state of 1980 than the upheaval-prone Soviet Union of the mid-1930s. The Sandinistas

---

Box 6.2 A Red Army Faction communiqué of April 1992

"In 1989, we, the RAF, began to apply more thought and discussion to the understanding that, for us and for all of those who have a record of resistance in the FRG [Federal Republic of Germany] things cannot go on as they have done.

"...we were all facing a completely changed situation regarding the international balance of power—the dissolution of the socialist state system, the end of the cold war. We were faced with the fact that we had failed to accomplish our objective: to achieve a breakthrough in the joint international struggle for liberation. The liberation struggles were generally too weak to hold their own...The collapse of the socialist states, which was essentially caused by internal inconsistencies, has had a disastrous effect on millions of people...Many of our comrades from the Tricont [Tricontinental: a Third World movement founded in Havana, 1966] have repeatedly said as much in our discussions...

"We ourselves were confronted with the fact that the policy we pursued in the years before 1989 had not strengthened us politically but weakened us. For the most varied reasons we no longer managed to attract people here...a situation in which we, the guerrillas, make all the decisions ourselves, while the others have to follows us, cannot go on.

"We very much reduced our policy to attacks against imperialist strategies, failing to look for immediate positive objectives and to show how an alternative was able to exist here and today.

"...attacks by us against top officials of the state and the economy with the intent to kill cannot advance the process that is now necessary because they will result in an escalation of the whole situation.

"WE HAVE DECIDED TO PREVENT SUCH ESCALATION....WE WILL SUSPEND ATTACKS AGAINST LEADING REPRESENTATIVES OF THE ECONOMY AND THE STATE." [28]

---

ruled Nicaragua without much overt internecine violence after their victory in 1979. They enjoyed power for a decade until risking it in elections, which they lost.

An instructive case of attaining victory by successful combination of terrorism, guerrilla war, and superior political organization is the Algerian FLN, or National Liberation Front. Their beginning came on November 1, 1954 and, in accord with a published program, they emphasized politics and sporadic guerrilla war against French soldiers. However, almost two years on, the FLN decided that its progress was too slow and its internal disputes too common. At a strategic conference in the mountains of Soummam in the late summer of 1956, they resolved on a change. Soon came the *plastique* bombings in Algerian cities, killings in mainland France, and "café wars" in Paris. Throughout the eight years of Algerian war, the FLN was consistent in using terror freely against their own Algerian countrymen, especially those accused of collaborating with the French. They ultimately paraded into the capital in victory in 1962. Terrible purges awaited Algerians who had opposed their movement.

Not the worst of despotisms, the FLN clung to power in their single-party state and also advanced many third-world revolutionary causes. Ironically, by the early 1990s, the FLN was fiercely repressing another revolution—by their own Muslim countrymen, more religious than themselves and just as political. The new revolutionaries used terror; doubtless the FLN was quite shocked but resisted violently. In that decade, as many as 150,000 Algerians died.[30]

When doctrines end

The cases above in which terrorism succeeded illustrate the high stakes of the current global war on terrorism. But our natural interest in all past cases—whether terrorism triumphed or lost—may be weakened by a concern for the utility of history. Excepting states embroiled in fierce nationalist wars within their borders, such as the Sri Lankans and the Indians watching over Kashmir, the most pressing threat of the present for most states is that of the Militant Muslim International. These terrorists are much influenced by doctrine and ideology. May such things be defeated? Is al Qaeda a movement too amorphous to get hold of or a hydra with too many heads to cut off with swords? Whatever the answer may be about al Qaeda, it is evident that doctrines that spawn terrorism may decline or be defeated. Two cases in recent history prove the possibility.

First, Soviet communism has failed. It rose like a shooting star and dominated horizons for decades; then it fell just as silently and quickly. Analysts and academics continue arguing about why bolshevism failed, but surely the following form parts of a reasonable answer. Soviet communism was contained by explicit U.S. and NATO political and military strategies. The doctrine lost because, in time, its limited idealism failed and left only stark tyranny. Bolshevism failed because of the obvious contrast between the spirited leaders of free peoples, from Ronald Reagan to Lech Walesa to Pope John Paul II, and conversely the aged or will-sapped bosses of Warsaw Pact states. The Soviets failed because the democracies were willing to support limited wars in Central America, Africa, and Asia, where indigenous peoples rejected Soviet ways and the Bolshevik model for political life. Whatever the mix of reasons, it was a stunning victory—an example of what Sun Tzu would have admired as a victory without a war. No state, including China or Vietnam, adheres to the Bolshevik model. No new movement of significance looks back longingly to Soviet history. Bolshevism has lost.

Second, though less familiar and little studied today, is the failure of the world anarchist movement of a century ago. The doctrine spawned thought, new social ideas, hundreds of crimes, such as armed robbery, and terrorism. Anarchist terrorism is most unusual in that it can be described as "political" or "antipolitical." Nineteenth-century adherents believed that that government is inherently dictatorial, that any government crushes man's best instincts and ideals, and thus that no government can be good. Many heads of state in the West and Russia were murdered by anarchists in the years leading up to World War I. The movement's thinkers and killers ranged freely from country to country, teaching, writing, and practicing the "propaganda of the deed." Their passions and their ideas mattered completely to them; they cared little for their places of origin. They could be as happily employed at a press in Geneva as they might be writing for an Italian anarchist newspaper in Rome. The doctrine was internationalist and potent, drawing on both ideals and resentments. In short, they had some of the qualities that make al Qaeda feared today. Yet anarchism's terrorists perished, leaving mostly safe residues, such as pamphleteering.

Symbolically, given the character of anarchism, the reasons for its decline and end as a violent movement are indistinct. It is likely that the anarchists' assassinations, which inspired headlines and some adherents, also alienated millions of decent people, including some tradesmen and unionists whom the anarchists said they were fighting for. It is possible that the doctrine for which anarchists robbed, killed, and bombed lost its newness and its intellectual curiosity, after a time. It is certain that governments had a profound effect. In general, they had not been fiercely repressive, despite what their accusers said, but they came to be so under direct and prolonged provocation. Governments did not even consider buckling under the ideological and tactical attacks; their wills proved far stronger than the violent minorities crying, "Away with all Government and all Rulers." Governments used their police forces, customs officers, and intelligence networks to harass anarchism's militants. Individual leaders of anarchism were pursued resolutely, at the cost of much state manpower. Peter Kropotkyn, Russian prince and talented geographer as well as sponsor of anarchism, studded his memoirs with references to intrusions and arrests of his comrades by Tsar Alexander's "Third Section" of police. Russian dissidents, anarchists, and students possessing the "wrong" books were all at perennial risk of being swept up by state authorities. When the Soviet Union replaced the Russian Empire, it quickly jailed or killed anarchists. In a vivid passage in his book about *The Aftermath* of World War I, Winston S. Churchill describes how quickly the new Bolshevik authorities dealt with all domestic rivals after securing power in November, 1917. Liberals, reformers, and radical politicians in Russia were all "cast into outer darkness," wrote Churchill:

> Social Revolutionaries, Mensheviks, many smaller groups of Socialists; all, especially, the most extreme, those nearest in opinion to the Bolsheviks, were marked for destruction. The doctrinal left flank had been turned, and every gradation of political opinion known to men crumpled up almost simultaneously. One sect alone made a momentary stand. The anarchists, strong in the traditions of Bakunin, conceived themselves unapproachable in extremism. If the Bolsheviks would turn the world upside down, they would turn it inside out; if the Bolsheviks abolished right and wrong, they would abolish right and left. They therefore spoke with confidence and held their heads high. But their case had been carefully studied in advance by the new authorities. No time was wasted in argument. Both in Petrograd and in Moscow they were bombed in their headquarters and hunted down and shot with the utmost expedition.[31]

Methods were far less ruthless in the other states of the northern hemisphere. Yet in the great democracies, too, the police work was systematic. In Europe and America, such anarchist leaders as Italian Errico Malatesta, Russian immigrants to America Emma

Goldman and Alexander Berkman, and Ukrainian Nestor Makhno were all jailed or deported, or both.[32] Sovereign states recognized, under pressure of assassinations, how direct a challenge was this new and strange doctrine.

States began by refusing entry to these agitators with simple acts, such as denying visas. That may seem self-evident, but liberal states prize the idea of unrestricted passage between countries. For example, as soon as the Cold War ended, the United States repealed the McCarran Walter Act that since 1962 had barred entry to any who loudly propounded revolutionary doctrines of anarchism or communism. These same United States, at the beginning of the twentieth century, had resorted to such barriers to anarchists. The United States deployed an array of political and legal defenses, up to and including execution in rare cases wherein doctrine and violent action had combined in a fighting personality. Western European states acted similarly, combining in what became international law enforcement against international anarchists. Ultimately these combined pressures by victimized countries discouraged the assassins and bomb throwers. Their leaders aged. Potential followers could no longer count on indulgent judges to avoid jail. The movement died.[33] Today, a century later, there are adherents to anarchist doctrines, but they normally lack the lethal edge.[34]

Conclusions

Terrorism's history does not support what is implied by occasional commentators or politicians that "these movements have a natural life span of 10, 12 or 14 years." Such talk relies on a statistical artifice, making an average out of wildly differing time spans. In point of fact, some terrorist gangs of diverse kinds have been born in spectacular headlines only to meet suppression or disintegration in two or three years: The Secret Armed Organization (Algeria and Western Europe); the Symbionese Liberation Army (California); The Order (the West Coast of the United States); the Hoffman Military Sports Group (West Germany); and the Communist Combatant Cells (Belgium). Many other modern political groups with heavy reliance on terrorism have shown great resilience, more than a few lasting more than three decades and alive at present: the Popular Front for the Liberation of Palestine (founded by George Habash); Mr. Arafat's Fatah; the Liberation Tigers of Tamil Eelam (Sri Lanka); the Ulster Freedom Fighters (Northern Ireland); and the National Liberation Army (Colombia).[35]

However, the history of terrorism and lines of argument in this chapter do point to ways in which the self-described *jihadis* may be defeated or forced into decline. First, international cooperation of a resolute kind explains some of today's successes and is the key to many more tomorrow, if those are to come. As terrorism is international, so must be counterterrorism. Second, the Coalition's 2001–2002 martial campaign in Afghanistan destroyed a valuable training area—which was a body blow to Al Qaeda and a major setback to their ally Taliban. Loss of training zones and safe havens can badly injure movements, as when the Iranians of "People's Mujahiden e Khalk" were quarantined within Iraq in 2003. Third, persistent, worldwide law enforcement effort is causing attrition in Bin Laden's second tier of leaders. Good policing—intelligence and a pattern of steady arrests—wrecked France's Direct Action, which is now completely gone. Fourth, a clever combination of intelligence, high-tech observation, small-unit infantry tactics, and determined political leadership, and foreign military help has decimated many cells of Abu Sayyaf in the Philippines. This key Al Qaeda ally saw yet another top leader killed in December, 2006; DNA tests have confirmed the passing of Khadaffy Janjalani at the very time evidence appears that his successor, Abu Sulaiman, is also dead.[36] Similar patterns of effort by the military, the police, and a political leadership willing to be firm—not just to negotiate—helped Northern Irish authorities to prevail. Few were confident of such an outcome for Ulster a decade ago, but now the British and the Northern Irish authorities have demonstrated their superiority vis-à-vis Irish "republican" terrorism. After three decades of consistent low-intensity conflict, peace enjoys a lengthy stay; it is the economy that is booming on the island. These cases, and others, show that progress is possible in the world community's current struggle against those who purposefully destroy the innocent to create a new caliphate. Such an entity would be governed as the Taliban ruled the Afghans, and few in the world—indeed, relatively few Muslims—long for such a thing.

Counterterrorism against an international force such as Al Qaeda must be insistent, persistent, and truly worldwide. Counterterrorism fell short of that standard, until 9-11; now it has improved notably. On September 8, 2006, the United Nations General Assembly took yet another step in this direction by publishing a seven-page resolution setting out objectives for counterterrorism. Such U.N. initiatives, once rare, have become common, and some are having considerable effects.

Notes

1 This chapter carries fewer endnotes than the others, as it grew from lectures. These were developed and then offered frequently from 2004 through 2006, including a speech at Sandhurst, a talk in the Office of Net Assessment in the Pentagon, a Web cast from the Woodrow Wilson Center in Washington, DC in early 2006, and many lectures at U.S. universities. Certain of the ideas appeared in Spring 2006 in my chapter "What History Suggests About Terrorism and its Future," *The Past as Prologue: The Importance of History to the Military Profession*, eds. Williamson Murray and Richard Sinnreich (Cambridge: Cambridge University Press, 2006), pp. 217–46. I am grateful to Dr. Murray, and to the Heritage Foundation's Jim Phillips, for their early interest in what in those years was a very obscure subject.

2 It will surprise no one familiar with her fine work that Prof. Martha Crenshaw of Wesleyan University, Middletown, CN, *has* worked in this neglected area. Her article "How Terrorism Declines" is the most useful of its kind; *Terrorism and Political Violence* 3: 1 (Spring 1991), pp. 69–87. Later, with Paul Wilkinson and others, Crenshaw produced a paper for The United States Institute of Peace: "How Terrorism Ends," May 25, 1999. She has been kind enough to show me a further unpublished paper. "Pathways Out of Terrorism: A Conceptual Framework."

In 1999, the Congressional Research Service's Rex Hudson released an edited work, *Who Becomes a Terrorist and Why*, with a half-dozen pages on "How Guerrilla and Terrorist Groups End" (Lyons Press, Guilford CN.). See also Jeffrey Ian Ross and Ted Robert Gurr, "Why Terrorism Subsides," with a focus on Canadian and U.S. groups, in *Comparative Politics* (July 1989), pp. 405–26. David Tucker and Aaron Danis kindly pointed me to one or two of the above.

3 Among the best is Peter Janke, with Richard Sim, *Guerrilla and Terrorist Organizations: A World Directory and Bibliography* (New York: Macmillan, 1983).

4 The author appreciates the research done in the summer of 2003 to expand our picture of Revolutionary Organization Nov. 17th by Paris Michaels, who completed his master's degree at the Institute of World Politics, an accredited graduate school in Washington, DC, headed by former National Security Council staffer and State Department officer John Lenczowski, Ph.D.

5 Richard H. Shultz Jr., "Showstoppers: Nine Reasons Why We Never Sent our Special Operations Forces after al Qaeda before 9/11," *The Weekly Standard*, Jan. 26, 2004, pp. 25–33.

6 Bernard Lewis, *The Assassins* [1967], pprbk ed. (New York: Basic Books, 2003), and M.G.S. Hodgson, "The Ismaili State," in *The Cambridge History of Iran*, vol. 5: *The Saljuq and Mongol Periods*, ed. J. A. Boyle, pp. 422–82.

7 Dr. Michael Radu noted the definitive power of the Peruvian operation of 1997 on the *Jim Lehrer News Hour*: "This group was moribund before; now it is buried." His credits in the terrorism field include co-authorship of *Latin American Revolutionaries: Groups, Goals, Methods* (Washington, DC: Pergamon-Brassey's, 1990). The news of MRTA attempts to regather, outside Peru, have been noted in prominent Peruvian newspapers and reported by Martin Arostegui in the *Washington Times*, Dec. 30, 2006.

8 Briefing given in the Old Executive Office Building to the author and his students from the National Defense University's SNSEE program, June, 2005. Arrangements were kindly made by Jim Kelly, whose public service includes a career with the Coast Guard.

9 As one of many guests of General James Jones, EUCOM commander, I visited Afghanistan in February, 2006. It was quiet, but the experts expected trouble as the spring came, and they were correct. Later, at a September 2006 conference, I was on a panel with a well-known analyst who announced that the United States "lost the war" in Afghanistan. That seems foolish; the victory of late 2001 was a remarkable one; it produced the country's first democracy, and if it bought only two years of total peace, well, in Afghanistan that is a small miracle.

10 *New York Times*, Jan. 15, 2006.

11 Afghan ministers informed us of the Quetta factor in Taliban's strength during briefings in Kabul, Feb. 2006. The *New York Times* covered more recent evidence in a page-one story of Jan. 21, 2007, noting Pakistani insistence that Taliban leaders are in country but "come and go."

12 The source was a Marxist colleague of Guzman, identified as a "future Congressman" of Peru, quoted by Simon Strong in *Shining Path: The World's Deadliest Revolutionary Force* (New York: HarperCollins, 1992), p. 31.

13 Published reports in the United States and Peru have often claimed, or hinted at, U.S. secret aid; see especially "'Superman' Meets Shining Path: Story of a CIA Success," by Charles Lane, *Washington Post*, Dec. 7, 2000. His report also points to the help of a Scotland Yard expert at disguise.

14 This was an achievement of intelligence and law enforcement, rather than the army. A cloud over its success, of course, is that capture of the chief terrorist came during the "self-coup" by the Fujimori presidency, which closed the Congress and took dictatorial powers. This national experience bears a resemblance to that of Uruguay twenty years before, when democracy failed to defeat the Tupamaros, a military coup did so, and only then did democracy resume.

15 In the calm that followed 1992, with the leisure to debate, Peruvians have reopened the cases of the 1980s. Hundreds of jailed personnel of MRTA and Sendero Luminoso are to be retried. The expense and recrimination will be extensive, and then some may well be released, given how time and the passing of witnesses may erode a prosecutor's case. Said differently, the United States was compelled to move from viewing terrorism as a peacetime law enforcement issue to recognizing the need for powerful defense and active military offense; in the same generation, Peru could be following a reverse course.

On the hopes of Sendero to revive and suggestions that some members are reforming in Bolivia, see Martin Arostegui's story in the *Washington Times*, Dec. 12, 2006.

16 Several authors suggest the Turks accomplished this "snatch" with U.S. intelligence help; see, for example, Mia Bloom, *Dying to Kill* (New York: Colombia University Press, 2005).

17 By one count, there were thousands of PKK attacks each year up through early 1999, but the millennium year that followed saw only forty'five acts in its first eleven months. Good notes on Kurdish Workers Party actions are in the State Department's past annuals on *Patterns of Global Terrorism* and pages of Rex Hudson, op. cit. Extensive notes provided by Dr. Michael Radu were the most useful of all.

18 Dr. Crenshaw's scholarship has emphasized the element of strategic choice by terror groups and her own conclusions about "How Terrorism Declines" (op. cit.) name this as one of three determinative factors. Her other two are physical defeat of the organization by government, and organizational disintegration.

19 Radu and Tismaneanu, op. cit., p. 210.

20 Telephone interview of an expert on the Central American violence of the 1980s, Prof. Michael Waller, Institute of World Politics, Washington, DC, 2005.

21 See the Nov. 27, 2005 *New York Times* review of Paul Berman, *The Power and the Idealists: The Passion of Joschka Fischer and its Aftermath* (Soft Skull Press, 2005). Another example for study might be Euro-celebrity Daniel Cohn-Bendit. "Danny the Red" was at the center of the militancy in France in 1968, but now he serves Germany in the European Parliament as a Green Party and Free European Alliance copresident.

22 Readers interested in the relationship between liberal education and many well-schooled terrorists may consider pp. 206–12 in our first edition.

23 This coincidence—a "puff piece" on a terrorist's memoirs appearing in the *New York Times* two days before 9-11—prompted Dr. Macubin Owens to reflect on a possibility: Among the many people in the offices or coffee shops of the World Trade Towers on the fateful morning could well have been some who were reading the Sunday *Times'* indulgent article on a terrorist…when the first airplane struck.

24 *New York Times*, Aug. 24, 2003. The professor quoted was Jeremy Varon of Drew University, Madison, N.J. Radicals interviewed included Jeff Jones, Cathy Wilkerson, and Brian Flanagan. One former Weatherman actually does repudiate the group—as a "cult of leftist cynicism and violence." His feature article appeared in the *Washington Post Magazine* during 2002.

25 Edward G. Lansdale, *In the Midst of Wars: An American's Mission to South East Asia* (NY: Harper & Row, 1972); Maj. Lawrence M. Greenberg, *The Hukbalahap Insurrection: A Case Study of a Successful Anti-Insurgency Operation in the Philippines —1946–1955* (Washington, DC: U.S. Army Center of Military History, 1986).

26 Ian Johnson, "A Top German Cop who Pioneered Profiling in the '70s sees Methods Make a Comeback," *Wall Street Journal*, Dec. 10, 2001.

27 The 1992 communiqué, quoted at length in ch. 6, is to me the decisive document, but six years later, in 1998, RAF made a public show of disbanding—and that later date is often cited as important.

28 Excerpts from a longer communiqué published in the *Frankfurter Rendschau*, April 15, 1992, translated by the Foreign Broadcast Information Service, and reprinted in Yonah Alexander and Dennis Pluchinsky, *Europe's Red Terrorists: The Fighting Communist Organizations* (London: Frank Cass, 1992), pp. 85–7.

29 Moderately but consistently, the important scholar Walter Laqueur has argued that terrorism fails. Immoderately, and at intellectual levels far below Laqueur's, is the argument by Caleb Carr, whose thin book, *The Lessons of Terror*, announces that terrorism has always failed and always will.

30 A common number in the media has been 100,000 Algerian victims of guerrilla war and terrorism during the 1990s, but some authorities say the number is twice as high. I use 150,000 as a compromise and after an interview with a military officer who served there as an attaché in the period in question.

31 Winston S. Churchill, *The World Crisis,* vol. 5, *The Aftermath* (London: Thornton Butterworth Ltd, 1929), p. 80.

32 Two sources on the turn-of-the-century anarchist movement are James Joll, *The Anarchists* (New York: The Universal Library ed., 1966), and Paul Avrich, *Anarchist Portraits* (Princeton, N.J.: Princeton University Press, 1988).

33 I have argued that government action was most influential in suppressing anarchist violence, not that it was the only factor. In a thoughtful lengthy article of Aug. 2005, *The Economist* argued that the movement aged and simply wore itself out. Of course, fatigue can be understood as a product of government resistance, as well as leaders' ages, fate, or other causes.

34 See ch. 1 for its section on contemporary anarchism, which seems dominated by discussion, demonstrations, international networking, and sometimes rioting or sabotage.

35 Colombia's ELN was in peace talks during 2006; that does not imply the group's end or the end of its terrorism. Colombia's larger Castroite group, FARC, is as old, more powerful, and more lethal, yet it has long had a secondary diplomatic track of operations and has often been involved in peace talks or other negotiations with governments.

36 *New York Times*, Jan. 21, 2007.

GLOSSARY OF
TERRORIST GROUPS

From scores of terrorist groups, the following are selected on the basis of current international significance, activity since 2000, or multiple references in this text. Bold print and alphabetical ordering show the most common name(s) used in English language sources.

Abu Nidal Organization (ANO; Fatah: The Revolutionary Council)   Responsible for some 900 casualties over a quarter-century of activities. With Iraqi state patronage, Sabri al Banna (who's *nom de guerre* is Abu Nidal) broke from Yasser Arafat's Fatah guerrilla-terrorist group in 1974. Unlike most factions, ANO began killing its former comrades, perhaps including Abu Iyad, a senior Fatah executive who headed Black September (see **PLO**). Nidal's group carried out terrorist spectaculars on many continents, including attacks on airlines and aircraft and their crews in Asia in the late 1980s. The leader had few admirers; to the nouns "nihilist" and "murderer," some would add "alcoholic," "sociopath," "paranoid." However, Syria, Libya, and Lebanon all gave his organization places to train at various times. Saddam's Iraq was a faithful patron almost to the end; Nidal was shot and died in Iraq in November, 2002, just before the Coalition invaded. Today ANO should be considered moribund.

Abu Sayyaf   In the fragmented "Moro" movement in the southern Philippines, this group has had the most terrorist spectaculars. Once a close ally of **Al Qaeda** in East Asia but today perhaps less so. Operations include snatching numbers of foreign hostages from tourist resorts; after one such job, they collected millions of dollars in Libyan help. Abu Sayyaf was living in the limelight until 1998, when its founding leader, Abdwajak Abubakar Janjalani, was killed. In recent years, the group has been weakened by relentless Filipino army pursuit, often with U.S. training or aid. Khadaffy Janjalani (a brother) led until his death in late 2006, probably from the island of Jolo. His successor, Jainal Antel Sali Jr (Abu Sulaiman), was probably killed by the Philippine Army in a January 16, 2007 firefight. Critics think the group has lost its ideological edge in a slide into mere gangsterism. There may now be fewer than a hundred armed members. Contrast with **New People's Army**.

AIAI   Al-Ittihad al-Islami; **Islamic Courts Union**; Conservative Council of Islamic Courts) Arose in the 1980s seeking a Salafist, pan-Somali state in the Horn of

Africa. Thus some early attacks were in Ethiopia. Never developed coherence but never went away either, remaining as inchoate as Somalia itself. Known for social, religious, and education activities, not only for terrorism. Its attacks on relief workers in the 1990s were a grim hallmark of a new era: Such abuse of aid givers is now a worldwide terrorism problem. AIAI conducted more attacks on relief workers after 2003. The group's manpower numbers are unknown. It does have connections to **Al Qaeda**, including the new leader, Hassan Dahir Aweys, who spent four years in hiding after 9-11-01. The man took boldly to the world stage in June, 2006 working with others in the Islamic Courts Union and seizing power in Mogadishu. That left the stumbling UN-backed government adrift in Baidoa. This new ruling entity then changed its name within days to the Conservative Council of Islamic Courts. Aweys alleged that AIAI no longer exists. He pledged a new state based on the Koran, and Osama Bin Laden quickly "answered" with a video supporting the new government in Somalia, but Ethiopian intervention swept aside the militiamen and their new government in days as 2007 began.

Al Gama'at (Islamic Group)   Active for a quarter-century and seeks an Islamicized state in Egypt. Killed Egypt's President Anwar Sadat and has attacked Egyptian security officials, Coptic Christians, and embassies (in Islamabad in 1995 and Tirana, Albania in 1998) and massacred sixty-two people at the Luxor Temples. That attack produced a schism in 1997. In Egypt, has not conducted further major attacks. A primary leader and revolutionary author of a book endorsing mass terrorism, Rafa'I Taha Musa, has disappeared. Perhaps feeling the group has passed its prime, Egypt released 1,500 members in 2003–2004. Spiritual leader Umar Abd al-Rahman, "The Blind Sheik," had a career in terrorism in Egypt, then the Sudan, and finally the United States. American authorities fatuously allowed him entry, despite Cairo's counsel. Al Rahman reciprocated by forging a violent clan around a New Jersey storefront mosque and trying to knock down the World Trade Towers with a truck bomb. That 1993 attack partially failed, and a subsequent plot to blow in and flood the Harbor Tunnel under New York City was preempted by policing. "The Spiritual Leader" has been in maximum security prison; as warnings flooded in before 9-11 and "the system was blinking red," some authorities expected a plot to liberate the Sheik. In August, 2006, an Al Zawahiri videotape said remnants of Al Gama'at would be folding into his **Al Qaeda** organization, but an IG spokesman denied that.

Al-Jihad (Egyptian Islamic Group; EIJ)   Leader Ayman al-Zawahiri wed this group to **Al Qaeda** at the end of the 1990s. Dr. Zawahiri was personal physician to Bin Laden and then top lieutenant, and their partnership became literally important to world events on 9-11-2001. Zawahiri's long memoir, *Knights Under the Prophet's Banner*, appeared shortly after the 9-11 attacks and has since circulated on the Internet. His narrative videos have since been released at frequent intervals. Al-Jihad should today be considered a global terror organization rather than one focused on Egypt; its several hundred operatives are distributed around Afghanistan, Pakistan, Lebanon, Yemen, and the United Kingdom.

Al Qaeda (The Base) Sunni Muslim group, founded as the Soviets were withdrawing from Afghanistan, by the Saudi civil engineer Osama Bin Laden and the Palestinian Abdullah Azzam. It began as the "Bureau of Services," Maktab Khadamat al-Mujihideen, in Pakistan. There is debate now whether this group is best described as a worldwide insurgency, a loose network of affiliates, or an international terrorist organization—as this author prefers. Authority Rohan Gunaratna declares Al Qaeda to be the most international of all terror groups. Egypt's **al Jihad** leader, Dr. Ayman al Zawahiri, joined Al Qaeda but before 9-11-2001, and **Taliban** chief Mullah Omar is another close partner. Of these four men, only Azzam has died (by a bomb in 1989), and Bin Laden has sons active in the movement. Many members have been arrested, but tens of thousands of others were trained in Al Qaeda camps in the Sudan and Afghanistan, and most are at large. Infamous for simultaneous attacks, patient planning, diverse weapons, and a claimed "religious duty" to acquire weapons of mass destruction. Recent actions include naval operations and firing two SAM missiles at an Israeli airliner in 2002.

Al Qaeda in Mesopotamia (Al Qaeda in Iraq; Al Qaeda in the Land of Two Rivers) Abu Musab al Zarqawi was a Jordanian crook who became a fundamentalist Sunni. He was present and active in Iraq before Saddam's regime fell, wisely organizing for the war or postwar phases. With the Coalition came opportunities. Zarqawi conducted a growing campaign of terrorist threats, individual attacks, and horrific bombings and guerrilla attacks on Coalition troops. Used foreigners, recruited from Syria, Iraq, the wider Middle East, and Western Europe. The leader declared allegiance to the international **Al Qaeda** terror organization in October., 2004 but may have had certain strategic differences. Worked hard for full-scale civil war between the Sunni extremists he loved and the Shia he despised. Died in a Coalition air strike in June, 2006 and apparently is replaced by Abu Ayyub al Masri, a forty-year old Egyptian, explosives expert, veteran of the training camps in Afghanistan which **Al Qaeda** ran, and an outstanding recruiter of foreign fighters.

Al Qaeda Organization in the Islamic Maghreb   see **GSPC**.

Armed Islamic Group (**GIA**; Al-Jama'ah al-Islamiyah al-Musallah) Algerian Muslim zealots, fighting for more than a decade against the secular Algerian government. Two main theaters have seen activity: northern Algeria, especially rural communities, and the streets of French cities. The initial campaign was in the Algerian villages, where massacres with simple bladed weapons recalled the work of **Shining Path** in the 1980s in Peru. A later campaign focused on foreigners living in Algeria. Donors in Europe supply some funding. As described in our first edition, GIA staged an imaginative Dec. 1994 prelude to the 9-11 attacks by capturing a French air liner, loading it with explosives, and threatening to slam it into Paris; the operation was defeated on the ground in Marseilles by French commandos. Unlike the other notable Muslim terrorist group, **FIS**, they never came to an accord with the government and so remain "at war," although in reduced fashion. It is unknown whether there are connections to, defections to, or coordination with the newer Algerian player on the international stage, the **Salafist Group for Preaching and Combat**.

Aum Shinrikyo   (Supreme Truth) International religious cult, founded by a half-blind Japanese eccentric and con-man named Shoko Asahara. Well funded by a variety of commercial enterprises that drew on the high skill levels and educational degrees of many members. Aum failed at early attempts in electoral politics. They gradually began preparing for apocalyptic war against that government and nation, acquiring Russian arms, experimenting with biological weapons, hunting for uranium, and making stocks of chemical agents. The group made chem-bio attacks in Japan, some of which failed. The successes include the 1995 use of sarin nerve gas on subway cars converging at the political center of downtown Tokyo, killing commuters and sickening or maiming thousands. A new era of concern over WMD began there. Arrests dismantled but did not entirely destroy Aum, which tried to reform as Aleph and has a Web site in that name. Asahara and several other leaders remain in prison, but many more were released in recent years.

AUC   (Autodefensas Unidas de Colombia; United Self Defense Forces of Colombia) A pro-state or right-wing paramilitary, formed in 1997 with grass roots support to combat **FARC** and **ELN**. Long led by Carlos Castano, who wrote a widely discussed autobiography; in early 2004, he disappeared. The self-defense militias obtained their revenues from land-owning patrons and businesses and especially from drug traffickers—something Castano admitted. That, and the open blame the Colombian government placed on AUC for massacres, cost the paramilitary its repute as a popular defense force. U.S. interests are not attacked by AUC, but Washington has designated the group "terrorist." AUC was strong the day it declared a cease fire in Dec., 2002. Subsequent negotiations with the Colombian government led many thousands to demobilize, disarm, or both. Some thousands of others remain active; some have become, or have remained, brigands.

Cambodian Freedom Fighters   (Cholana) This small but enduring group has dual origins: in the obstructive power of former Khmer Rouge politicians who still dominate Cambodia and in the Cambodian exile community in the United States, particularly California. Some CFF organizers felt they were kept from power in Cambodia in the late 1990s and so formed this armed group. The largest single attack came from seventy men armed and uniformed as guerrillas on Nov. 24, 2000, in the capital. Government installations and a fuel depot outside Phnom Penh have been among the targets. Charges against the group for an April 2004 ferry bombing—a tactic popular in Asia—that injured three have been dropped, however. For planning or executing various attacks within Cambodia, dozens of members have now been convicted in Cambodia, and the talkative leader, a Long Beach, California accountant named Chhun Yasith, has been arrested by the United States on charges of conspiracy to kill in a foreign country. Members have operated in Thailand as well as these other two countries, and funding is from the Cambodian-American community. Remains unknown to most Americans, despite profiles in *Time Magazine* (2001) and the *New York Times Sunday Magazine* (2004).

Communist Party of India (Maoist)   Often called "Naxalites," as the West Bengal and Darjeeling-area town of Naxalbari was the scene of early rebellion. Marxist and Maoist communist parties took form in the 1970s, as did the armed People's

War Group, and their influence spread into parts of eastern and central India: Andhra Pradesh, Bihar, Chhattisgarh, West Bengal, and other states. Greater political unity was achieved in September, 2004, and the next month the movement issued a directive renewing "armed agrarian revolutionary war" and the drive for national power. Indian Maoists have limited connections to, and are not dependent on, **CPN(M)** in Nepal. This Indian group is designated as terrorist by New Delhi and Washington. It employs Maoist rhetoric about surrounding the cities from the countryside and the classic menu of Maoist methods: abducting or killing landlords, political assassinations, attacking police, "revolutionary taxes" at will, and so on. On the strategic level, they have successfully created "liberated areas" within India wherein they run Maoist "shadow governments." According to the South Asia Terrorism Portal, these many pockets are to be consolidated into one "Compact Revolutionary Zone" running from Nepal through Bihar and including forested areas of Central India and Andhra Pradesh in the south.

Communist Party of Nepal (Maoist)   CPN(M) Nepal, the world's only Hindu kingdom, is under hard challenge from this broad communist insurgency. Orthodox Marxist-Leninists were participating in the parliamentary process when, in 1996, these Maoists broke away forcefully, denounced their former comrades, and went to war. In the following decade, they slowly and steadily built a large and credible political-/military organization. Now presume to conduct formal negotiations with other political parties and the central government. Their rise is due in part to the weakness of those other institutions. The top two Maoists are Pushpa Kamal Dahal (Comrade Prachanda) and Baburam Bhattarai, an Indian-educated PhD in urban planning and head of the political front, "United People's Front." Dedicated cadre are said to number "several thousand" by the U.S. State Department, but the numbers must be higher. There appears to be no aid from Beijing, but this group's international links do include RIM, the Revolutionary Internationalist Movement, with its Turkish groups, Peru's **Shining Path**, and the like. In many "liberated zones," the CPN(M) are de facto governors; the common symbols of Nepal's government, such as post offices and police stations and local councils, are shuttered or under perennial threat. In mid-2006 negotiations, the Nepalese Maoists actually promised to dismantle their shadow governments in rural areas while joining the open political process, but any such pledge must be treated skeptically.

Corsican National Liberation Front   (FLNC; National Front for the Lib. of Corsica) Despite a dearth of press notice in recent years, this group has been working for three decades to secure Corsica's independence from France. Uses terrorism against French and other European interests, attempting to "internationalize" the struggle. Banks and government buildings are targets, on the island and occasionally in Paris; so are elements of the tourism industry. Attacks are usually nonlethal but numerous and persistent. The FLNC has been less active than it was in the 1990s, and the U.S. State Department no longer lists this—or any other—Corsican terror group. However, FLNC remains, and the leader of its political front, *A Cuncolta Nazionalista*, told the French newspaper *L'Humanite* in June, 2006 that there was no intention of lowering arms; Charles Pieri declared the role of his front to be supplying "a place of debate to impel actions on the ground." The citizens of Corsica voted on autonomy within French rule in mid-2003, rejecting the offer on a narrow margin.

Dev Sol (Devrimci Sol; Revolutionary People's Liberation Party/Front) Turkish, Marxist-Leninist, anti-NATO. Seasoned and effective at assassinations and now deploying bombs as well. Made its reputation targeting conservative Turks, among others. The group has a history, consistent with its ideology, of attacks on foreign military personnel. This was evident during the first Gulf War of 1991 and continued with recent attacks on U.S. targets in apparent response to Operation Iraqi Freedom and a June, 2004 NATO summit in Istanbul. Funding has come from Western Europe and from donations, robberies, and extortion. The U.S. State Department reports a general belief that Dev Sol has facilities in Syria and Lebanon. Given a wave of arrests and trials in 2004, the group may now have only a score of hard-core gunmen, plus numerous supporters in Turkey and elsewhere in Europe.

ELN; National Liberation Army A Colombian group with second-rate status behind **FARC**, but it is larger than most terror groups, and wealthier, and has held on despite decades of opposition from the government, death squads run against it in the 1990s by Carlos Castillo's **AUC**, and now a revivified and professionalized Colombian army enjoying U.S. aid under "Plan Colombia." ELN has limited help, including the medical sort, from Cuba. Venezuela newly indulges the group's many cross-border activities. Money supplies are substantial and steady, given the creativity with which the group diversified: cattle rustling; extortion from mine operators; narcotics; theft from corporations; a schedule of revolutionary "taxes" from wealthy individuals; kidnappings for ransom, and the like. Membership may have dropped to 1,000 armed members, but there are far more active supporters. When reelected to a second term as Colombian President, Alvaro Uribe began preliminary talks with ELN (mid-2006).

ETA (Euzkadi to Askatasuna; Etarras; **Basque Fatherland and Liberty**) After IRA, Europe's oldest terror group; nearly a half-century has passed since its formation in 1959, and one need not believe the early 2006 declaration of a unilateral and permanent cease fire. ETA has killed some 850 people. Primary targets are security force personnel, but the bombings usually kill and wound many bystanders. The group's political front, Herri Batasuna, has been weakened by declining Basque support for violence and also affected by Spanish government legal actions against it for encouraging terrorism. It dropped the first half of its name, retaining "Batasuna." Arrests of ETA suspects in France (e.g., October, 2002) and Spain have become a regular feature of recent years, including the capture of seventy-one in 2005 alone. 2006 brought arrest of many who carry out extortion to finance ETA operations and of the presumed top leader of the entire organization. However, several hundred members remain at large, and ETA claimed a lethal Dec., 2006 car-bombing. Cadre have taken training in Nicaragua, Lebanon, and Libya in past years, and others are among the fugitives living protected lives in Cuba. Despite a few initial stories, there has never been any evidence ETA contributed to the catastrophic March, 2003 Madrid train bombings, which were the work of pro-**Al Qaeda** Muslims from North Africa and Spain.

196

FARC (Revolutionary Armed Forces of Colombia) The more successful of the two "Castroite" groups created in Colombia in the 1960s (see **ELN**) and one of the world's three or four strongest sub-state organizations. In Maoist parlance, FARC grew into "phase two" efforts—mobile warfare including large units—in the mid-1990s, but it was beaten back into "phase one" operations—guerrilla war and terrorism. FARC still has limited Cuban contacts; its ideology is unchanged but perhaps weakened; grizzled leaders Manual Marulanda and Raul Reyes remain in charge. Fund sources include kidnappings, expropriations, "revolutionary taxes" on peasants and corporations, and no less than $600 million a year in narcotics income alone. Armed membership is about 12,000, plus unarmed supporters. International activities include liaison with IRA bomb experts and a presence on the Venezuelan border. A commander, Ricardo Palmera, was arrested in Ecuador in January, 2004. FARC has shown some skills at diplomacy and once exercised authority over thousands of square miles in one zone of Colombia under accord with President Pastrana. The main threats to this power and resilience have been the much-improved Colombian Army and popular self-defense militias, **AUC**. The latter are dissolving, so July, 2006 saw FARC driving to take a town in Choco province that has been under AUC control.

FATAH (acronym for Palestine Liberation Movement) By far the largest of the armed components within the Palestine Liberation Organization. Led personally by Yasser Arafat until his death in November, 2004. With thousands of well-drilled members, many with formal military training in supportive countries, Fatah could handle semi-conventional warfare if need be. Provided regular security for the political operations of the PLO, and its internal security men of "Force 17" also conducted terrorism. Fatah manpower on other occasions could be used in specialized violent details, including in succession Black September, the Hawari Group, the Fatah Hawks, and probably also the Al Aqsa Martyrs' Brigade that appeared with the second intifada in 2000. As the Palestine Authority (or PA) formed, Fatah became a state security organization. It became comfortable in that role and fiercely resisted the takeover of Hamas authorities after the surprising elections of January, 2006. FATAH and **Hamas** have frequently battled in the streets, and even within Palestinian buildings, in 2005 and 2006.

Fatah al Islam Sunni Arabs who claim links with Al Qaeda. Leader Shaker Abssi had ties to Abu Musab al Zarqawi, the Al Qaeda leader who died in Iraq. In November 2006, this splinter group broke away from a larger Syrian-sponsored organization called Fatah al Intifada. They have claimed bus bombings in eastern Beirut. Its hundreds of members opened war with Lebanese security forces in May 2007 after the latter pursued bank robbers from the terrorist group back into their home base, the Palestinian refugee area Nahr al-Bared. The same Lebanese government that all but ignores Hezbollah appears to be at war with this far smaller sub-state group.

Front for Islamic Salvation (FIS; Islamic Salvation Front) One of modern terrorism paradoxes: hyper-violent groups seeking democratic political power. When it performed well in late 1991 regional elections, FIS was promptly banned by Algeria's secular government. The front and its "Islamic Salvation Army" went to war on government personnel and other civilians, carving a swath through the nation. Rival **GIA** shares many of its political objectives and contributed strongly to the bloodshed; well more than 100,000 Algerians died. FIS came to an accord with the government in Algiers in October, 1997. Thereafter, what violence it caused was described as the work of dissidents, and an amnesty had been offered by Algiers as of 1999. FIS is now a largely political force—much as it was before 1992. U.S. State Department no longer lists this group in its terrorism rosters.

GSPC; Salafist Group for Preaching and Combat (alt: "…for Call and Combat") Several hundred Algerians with operations in Canada, much of Western Europe, and Algeria. One commander operating in the Sahel was captured. The disruptions of the Algerian civil war of the 1990s produced several very violent groups, especially **FIS** and **GIA**. GSPC set up later, at the end of the decade. Its strength is not in numbers but in operating skill and, above all, in its alliance with **Al Qaeda**. Has recruited in Europe for fighting in distant Islamist theaters, such as Chechnya. GSPC does its greatest damage in France. Algerian reporter Mohamed Sifaoui moved to Paris and infiltrated and exposed them in a 2004 book, *Inside Al Qaeda*. GSPC announced in January 2007 that it was joining Bin Laden under a new name: The Al Qaeda Organization in the Islamic Maghreb.

Hamas (Islamic Resistance Movement) Its founding in December, 1987 is linked to the origins of the first Intifada (uprising). The Hamas charter declares it to be a direct offshoot of the Muslem Brotherhood. An anti-British hero of the 1930s gives his name to the military wing, Izz al-Din al-Qassam Brigades. Hamas are hard-line, Palestinian nationalist, and Sunni. Ideology posits a new Islamic state in "all of Palestine," pitting them against secular Palestinians, moderates, and any willing to make a deal with Israel or Palestinians, such as Yasser Arafat (d. 2004) and President M. Abbas. **FATAH** and Hamas fight in the streets regularly. Hamas has social and political wings as well, and the three are intertwined closely, lending each other legitimacy. A leading council or *shura* makes decisions, and political authorities appear to closely control the terrorist actions. Hamas tactics escalated in lethality quickly and, by 2000, they had murdered some 200 people and wounded six times as many. Car bombs, suicide attacks, and rocket attacks are now features. For this reason, Jordon, many European states, and the United States condemn the organization. Yet it triumphed over **FATAH** in January, 2006 elections and is making headway in the effort to take control of the Palestine Authority's areas.

Harakat ul-Mujahedin (HUM; Harakat ul-Ansar; Jamiat ul-Ansar; Al-Faran) A collection of Kashmiris, Pakistanis, Afghans, and Arabs fighting for Muslim control of Kashmir and a world-wide "Righteous Caliphate." Training camps in Afghanistan and Pakistan. Financial aid from the region as well as Saudi Arabia, other Gulf States, and other Islamic countries. Responsible for a December, 1999 hijacking of an Indian airliner that sprang three convicted terrorists. Two became even more important when free: Ahmed Omar Saeed managed the abduction/ murder of journalist Daniel Pearl in 2002; Maulana Masood Azhar founded **JEM**. HUM's chief until 2000 was reportedly Maulana Fazlur Rehman Khalil, who signed on to Bin Laden's "Front for Jihad Against Jews and Crusaders." At least twice he has been detained and then freed by Pakistani authorities. He was replaced by Dr. Badr Munir. In 2005, al Qaeda suspects arrested in California said they had trained in a Khalil camp, prompting another Pakistani scramble to find him, but he had disappeared. Operated under the name "Group of Helpers," or Jamiat ul-Ansar during 2003. JUA is strongly akin to **JEM**.

Hezbollah   (alt: Hizballah; "Party of God") A terrorist innovator of the early 1980s, these Lebanese Shia then grew into an adept guerrilla force that even the Israeli Defense Force found hard to handle; the Summer War of 2006 was merely the largest example of the new proficiency. With **LTTE** and **PKK**, shares "honors" for developing suicide bombing tactics and technologies. Takes Israeli and other hostages; murdered UN observer Lt. Col. William Higgins; staged the lethal TWA 847 hijacking in 1985—which made Hezbollah intelligence chief Imad Mughniya one of the FBI's "most wanted." Led by a council of Shia clerics, whose general secretary since 1992 has been Hasan Nasrallah. Has long enjoyed massive state aid from Iran, which ramped it up in 2006; *NBC News* estimated it to total $40 million a month. Champions Shia authority in the region, conducts relief and education programs, runs its own television station in Beirut, and has long held a dozen or more seats in parliament. Not only does Lebanon not act against Hezbollah; the government considers it a "legitimate resistance force" because of its old battles with the former occupation forces of Israel. Membership numbers are unclear, but its armed strength is surely greater than the U.S. State Department's April, 2006 estimate of "several thousand."

IRA, Irish Republican Army Provisionals   ("Provos") The main military and terrorist force dedicated to driving the British out of Northern Ireland's six counties (Ulster). A 1969 incarnation of the original group founded in 1916. Adept, flexible, powerful. The Provos are intimately connected to Sinn Fein ("Ourselves Alone"), the political arm directed by Gerry Adams—a former IRA boss. IRA now appears only on a lesser, secondary terrorism list of the U.S. State Department because of (1) an absence of attacks on Americans, (2) participation in the peace process, and (3) gestures toward demilitarization overseen by an inadequate team of international observers. The Provos retain several hundred hardened gunmen, many more in prisons, and legions of veteran supporters. But support in the Irish Republic to the south is shallow, the economic boom in Ireland is bad for terrorist causes, and 9-11 has weakened American interest. IRA has also experienced defections to splinter groups and a run of bad publicity after a 'routine' murder of 2005 and two bank heists of 2004. Other IRA funding comes from gaming, smuggling, drug sales and, of course, donations by Americans. The current strategic pause in operations has a few observers imagining IRA is "finished," but if the planned Northern Irish parliament concept fails or Sinn Fein is seen by harder men to be failing to deliver, dominance may well return to the secret Army Council, and another campaign of violence could ensue, in a pattern a century old.

Islamic Movement of Uzbekistan   Led by Tohir Yoldashev, alias Tohirjon Yuldeashev. Militants from Central Asia—as many as 500. Formal affiliation with Al Qaeda. Apart from major urban bombings and abduction of foreigners, the group has engaged in guerrilla war with Pakistan and with Coalition forces in Afghanistan. Their policy object is to crate an Islamic republic in Uzbekistan. The present government is a special irritant, as it permits Coalition forces air over-flight, and so on, for the low-intensity war in Afghanistan. This is one group security analysts are worried about regarding the Ferghana Valley, which is half-Uzbek in its population and where large numbers of Muslim militants are in training.

Jamaat ul Mujahedin Bangladesh (JMB) By one account, JMB emerged out of the Alhe Hadith Movement, funded by an Islamicist revival organization based in Kuwait. In recent years, more than 10,000 dedicated members have been preparing an Islamic insurgency against the still-new democratic culture of Bangladesh. For years, most terrorism reports in the West said next to nothing of Bangladesh, but one of the five signatories of Bin Laden's famous 1998 fatwa claimed to represent that country. A *Far Eastern Economic Review* cover story of late 2001 warned of the rise of Muslim militants. Their day in the full sun was August 17, 2005, when several hundred small bombs detonated around the country nearly simultaneously. Government responded to this test: The late 2005–early 2006 period brought capture of three top JMB leaders. Subsequent months have been much quieter in Bangladesh, but one expects that the movement will regroup.

Jaish-e-Mohammed (JEM; Army of Mohammed; Kuddam e Islami) A new group among those fighting for the Islamicization of Kashmir and its subordination to Pakistan rather than to India. Members include Afghans, Arab veterans of the war in Afghanistan, Pakistanis, and indigenous Kashmiris. Founder Maulana Masood Azhar was sprung from Indian prison by a December, 1999 hijacking. The group's political partner is Jamiat Ulema-i-Islam. There are ties to the **Taliban**, and many members come out of previous groups with the same objectives, including **HUM**. Jaish-e-Mohammed claimed "credit" for killing a policeman in Srinagar in late May, 2006 during a wave of attacks that left twenty-one others wounded.

Jemaah Islamiya Seeks to create a caliphate in the region now including Indonesia; Malaysia; southern Thailand, where there has long been separatist fighting; Singapore; Brunei; and the southern Philippines. Well funded and highly motivated, JI has been a loyal and effective **Al Qaeda** ally in southeast Asia. Trains international terrorists, as in its camps in the southern Philippines. Recent bombings, very lethal, include the Marriott Hotel and the Australian Embassy in Jakarta. Singapore preempted a major bomb plot in that country, and JI has struck churches and other targets in the Philippines. After the devastating year 2002 bombings of Bali, JI followed up with another round of attacks there on October 2, 2005. This involved four synchronized suicides carrying backpack bombs of some twenty-two pounds. Plans were done in a thirty-four-page document later found on a computer. Despite many police successes against the group, important leaders are free. Mohammed Noordin Top is at large, despite his role in the latest Bali blasts. And the founder, Abu Bakar Bashir, who some implicated in the original (2002) Bali carnage, served a short jail term on one terrorism charge before being released to rapturous followers in June 2006. He returned to his mosque and his *madrassa*.

Lashkar e-Tayyiba   (LET; Army of the Pure) An exemplar of three problems in transnational terrorism: the ongoing fighting over Kashmir; the former propensity of Pakistan's government to indulge Muslim militants making attacks abroad; and the connection between terrorism and activist religious schools, called *madrassas*. Nearly all LT members are Pakistanis trained in madrassas in that country or Afghanistan and then given physical and military training in those countries. The founder and leader is Hafiz Muhammad Saeed—called "Professor Saeed" for his background in engineering at Punjab University. Several thousand LET militants operate against the Indian Army in Kashmir or carry out attacks on civilians—especially Hindus and Sikhs—sometimes in disguise as Indian Army personnel. Of the suspects India seized after the horrific attacks on Mumbai trains in July, 2006, six had been trained in LET camps. The record of years of transnational attacks connects it to **Taliban** and **Al Qaeda** and, in June, 2006, a Pakistani living in the United States (Ali Asad Chandia of the "Virginia Jihad" cell) was convicted of providing material support to Lashkar. Has been headquartered in Munridke (near Lahore) and in Muzaffarabad—a large town damaged by an earthquake in October, 2005. That disaster was alleviated in part by Jamaat ul-Dawa, an LET charity on the spot but one that Pakistan had placed on its "terrorism watch list" under American pressure. Pakistan also was persuaded to ban LET after Washington did so in 2001. The United Nations declared the group terrorist in 2005.

Lord's Resistance Army   A cult-like militia of Ugandans, centered in but not limited to the Acholi people. The two leaders are Joseph Kony and, at a distance in Kenya, his mother. LRA aims to establish rule of the ten commandments of the Christian Bible in Uganda and argues that its leadership is divinely inspired. Meanwhile, the human damage in Uganda is considerable. Mutilation of victims is common. Another feature of LRA is its abduction of thousands of children and enforcing their bondage: Most boys become porters or warriors; most girls become concubines of the males, camp cooks, and so on. The group has had sanctuary in Sudan. Five commanders were indicted for crimes against humanity by the International Criminal Court in 2005. 2006 brought peace talks with regional authorities; results were unclear as 2007 began.

Los Macheteros   (Machete Wielders) Communist and nationalist, these are political grandsons of gunmen who in the early 1950s tried to kill President Harry Truman and shot up the House of Representatives. They are political sons of the gunmen of FALN who blew up a New York City tavern in 1974 and undertook dozens of acts of violence in the eastern United States and in Puerto Rico. Voters on the island always turn down the independence option, but terrorism still has supporters and apologists, on and off the island. Many Macheteros were convicted and jailed in the latter 1980s. Now, violent actions occur in Puerto Rico only, and most have been minor, such as pipe bombings. In late 2005, a top long-time leader, Filiberto Ojeda Rios, hiding in a house in Hormigueros (PR), died in a gunfight with the FBI. The $7 million he helped to steal from a Connecticut armored car company is still missing; some of it, and the "inside man" in that crime, Victor Manuel Gerena, may be in Cuba. Late in his presidency, William Clinton pardoned several

Macheteros and reduced the sentence of another, Harvard-educated terrorist Juan Segarra-Palmer.

Moroccan Islamic Combatant Group   North Africans emerged in the mid-1990s to take a prominent role in worldwide terrorism, and Moroccans have been a large component. This group has a hazy origin, but many members trained in Afghan camps, and there is evident internationalism and Muslim revolutionary spirit in its activities. Some members have lived in Europe. The group was apparently one of those involved in the May, 2003 gas bomb attack on targets in Casablanca, claimed by "Salafiya Jihadiya." Spain implicated Moroccan Islamic Combatant Group members in the mass murders in Spanish trains on 3-11-2004, and when police on the investigation opened a Madrid apartment, seven suicides therein were also Moroccans. For good demographical analysis of this particular group, consult Marc Sageman, *Understanding Terror Networks*.

Mujahedin-e Khalq   (MEK; People's Mujahedin e Khalq) Iranian Marxists opposed to the Mullahs' regime. A resilient organization four decades old and one uniquely led: The chiefs are Massoud and Maryam Rajavi, husband and wife. Some security experts are still unfamiliar with the organization, and many U.S. and U.K. politicians have supported official letters of indulgence or approval or Khalq initiatives, only to find the organization has a place on the State Department's terrorist list. Iraq long gave MEK support, safe haven, and even artillery and armor. In the second Coalition war against Iraq, MEK voluntarily surrendered arms to the Americans, and several thousand were confined to their Camp Ashraf, north of Baghdad. Mrs. Rajavi has operated for more than a decade from Auvers sur Oise, in northern France, giving press interviews and planning diplomatic trips. Ten thousand people appeared for an MEK march in July, 2006 in France. The group also spreads its message via large expensive newspaper adds. One report of 2005 had it that Iran is dangling the number 3 **Al Qaeda** commander, Saif al-Adel (now in Iran) in hope of a deal that gets the United States to give them MEK members sequestered in Iraq. And one 2006 report had it that many MEK personnel were about to reenter Iran on arrangement with that government.

New People's Army (NPA)   Military wing of the Communist Party of the Philippines. Once described as "the new Khmer Rouge" and seemingly unstoppable, NPA has lost much popular support and decreased violent activities. The three-fold reasons are the replacement of dictator Ferdinand Marcos by elected President Corazon Aquino, the accompanying rise in optimism about democracy, and loss of a beloved NPA propaganda target: the U.S. naval bases. NPA, a classical Maoist organization, is in a building phase emphasizing propaganda, infiltration, and perhaps front activities. Luzon and the Visayas and a few parts of northern Mindanao are the usual operating areas, and there is doubtless an underground in Manila. There was an up-tick in terrorist actions in 2001 and 2002 with attacks on civilian, commercial, and government targets, but this was answered by the armed forces. So despite its large size, NPA has fallen off the horizon of many international security analysts. A strategic choice by NPA could become a dramatic reminder of its seasoning and its political punch. Aging leader Jose Maria Sison remains in exile in Holland; not until 2002 did that government freeze his bank assets and block his social benefits. Sison controls the party structure and the army of some 9,000 women and men. Meanwhile, former NPA member, defector Victor Corpus, is newly appointed as head of the republic's national military intelligence service.

Palestine Islamic Jihad   (PIJ; Islamic Jihad; Al Quds Brigades) Al-Jihad Al-Islami fi Filastin had roots in Cairo and the interests of Fathi Shiqaqi, a leftist, medical doctor, Palestinian nationalist, and member of the Muslem Brotherhood. Expelled by Egypt, Shiqaqi returned to his native Gaza, made the formal step of founding PIJ, and opened war against Jewish civilians and Israeli soldiers under such banners as the "Jerusalem Brigades." Headquarters has been near Damascus Syria since 1988. Shiqaqi was assassinated in Malta in October, 1995. Iran funds this organization—early, often, and today. PIJ is notably less socially active and engaged in welfare projects than is Hamas, preferring violent operations, such as its five suicide bombings of 2005. Fought the Oslo peace process and shares Hamas' objectives of driving Israel out of existence and creating a new and holy Palestinian state. Thus, the two groups have sometimes collaborated and at others been rivals. Further reading: Mathew Levitt's *Hamas: Politics, Charity, and Terrorism in the Service of Jihad* (2006).

Palestine Liberation Front   (PLF) One of the PLO factions that generally remained loyal to Yasser Arafat and worked within the PLO umbrella. Founded and led continuously by Mouhammad Abbas (a.k.a. Abu Abbas). A cynical and articulate defender of terrorism by his own group, as in the ***Achille Lauro*** ship-jacking of 1985, he denounced Al Qaeda terrorism in a year 2002 interview. Like **Abu Nidal**, Abbas was a perpetual reminder of the role Iraq has had in secular Palestinian terror. Living in a villa in Baghdad, the PLF chief was caught by the coalition in 2003. He died of natural causes in April, 2004. Not all his group's activities died with him; there is a presence in Lebanon and the West Bank, and a few PLF members have been involved in the second (Al Aqsa) intifada.

Palestine Liberation Organization (PLO)   Notable for beginning as a terrorist and guerrilla war group and evolving into a successful "statelet," the Palestine Authority. The child of collective leadership but especially Yasser Arafat ("Abu Ammar"), the PLO was born in 1964 in complex political and martial forms. Negotiated its way among small and great powers influencing the Middle East and enjoyed Soviet bloc aid. With the Algerian FLN as one of its diplomatic models, the PLO was determined to become "the sole representative of the Palestinian people" and deployed information officers, cultural ambassadors, relief workers, and financiers to that end, as well as terrorists. Black September (of Munich, 1972) and Force 17 (an internal security force also given external killing missions) were among the tools of PLO terrorism. The U.S. State Department ceased listing the PLO as a "Foreign Terrorist Organization" many years ago. Arafat died in November, 2004. His successor as leader of secular Palestinian political forces is Mohamed Abbas (Abu Mazen), formerly ambassador to Moscow and secretary-general of the PLO Executive Committee. See **FATAH**.

Popular Front for the Liberation of Palestine (PFLP)   A radical Palestinian group that was sometimes inside the PLO umbrella, sometimes outside. PFPL literally brought air piracy to Western Europe in 1968–1970. Operations director Wadi Haddad (d. 1978) had foreign collaborators and was an innovator in using multinational teams; these included Venezuelan communist "Carlos the Jackal" and German terrorists. Founder and "General Secretary" George Habash, also a medical doctor, led the group until 2000 before stepping aside. Successor Abu Ali Mustafa was soon killed in an Israeli rocket attack, yielding the post to the current Secretary General, Ahmed Sa'dat. However, that man, and his deputy, Abdel Rahim Mallouh, are both in Israeli jails. Recent PFLP terror strikes have included the murder of Israel's tourism minister and several suicide bombings. An explosion in November, 2006 wrecked the house of a Gaza City PFLP commander named Talal Abu Safiyah.

PFLP-GC   (Popular Front for the Liberation of Palestine—General Command) Once within the PLO umbrella, Ahmad Jibril went independent in 1968, so his organization turns forty in 2008. He was a captain in the Syrian army, and his group has been known for its mix of terrorism and conventional military tactics. Conducted innovative attacks, such as infiltrations into Israel in hang gliders and other aircraft. Rather quiet now. Headquartered in Damascus and has bases in Lebanon. Mentioned for a role in reconnaissance in Lebanon leading up to the murder of former Prime Minister Rafiq Hariri in February, 2005, an action consistent with the view of PFLP-GC as a protégé of the Syrian state. An April, 2006 report indicated Lebanon might finally take steps against the organization, but that is unconfirmed. Iran continues to aid PFLP-GC; these Palestinians are one of several terror groups aided both by secular Syria and the Shiite regime in Tehran.

PKK; Kurdistan Worker's Party   (Kongra Gel) Once among Europe's most stable terrorism fixtures, Partiya Karkeren Kurdistan had the broad base of a Kurdish insurgency and the sharp sting of skilled terrorists. Their old hallmark was a string of simultaneous bombings; later they helped to pioneer suicide bombings, occasionally using women. Finances derive from extortion and the narcotics trade throughout Europe. PKK has undergone many changes since the day in 1999 when Turkish authorities snatched founder Abdullah Ocalan out of Africa and jailed him. There was relative silence for some five years—apparently encouraged by meek sounds from the jailed leader. Then a new organization was established and called democratic: KADEK, or Kurdistan Freedom and Democracy Party. This was superceded by Kongra-Gel, a new organization. In June, 2004, it put the cease-fire behind it, declared against disarmament and for Kurdish separatism, and promised armed actions "in self-defense." Terrorist strikes, including lethal bombings, began again and have grown in number. By 2006, Turkey was pressing for U.S. help against the group—especially as several thousand armed PKK are at liberty just over the Turkish border in Iraq (which Ankara expects Washington to control). There is now no clear PKK leader; Ocalan's son is among the important principals.

Real IRA   (Real Oglaigh Na Heireann) As various international peace efforts of the late 1990s slowed down IRA "Provo" militancy, splinter groups have tried to keep up with publicized attacks and the fight for Irish liberty and unity. Even with its founder, Michael McKevitt, in jail and calling for truce, some followers refuse to renounce terrorism. U.S. State Department sources note that forty members are jailed, with 100 or fewer others still out and at large. Responsible for very deadly August, 1998 Omagh bombing. There are continuing successes in actions, recruiting, and training. Some support doubtless comes from traditional IRA members and donors. The group was found to be manufacturing explosive devices in Limerick in 2004. Real IRA works in tandem with a political front, the 32 County Sovereignty Movement.

Revolutionary Organization 17 November (17 November; *Epanastatiki Organosi 17 Noemvri*) A Marxist-Leninist group that operated for more than a quarter-century in Greece. Named for a day of protest in 1973. Periodically killed Greeks, Americans, or NATO personnel, often with the same pistol. Also targeted multinational corporations and published rhetoric-filled Marxist denunciations of capitalism. Familial connections among some members and the group's miniscule size helped to ensure security, and no member was ever arrested. However, the Greek government's mood about the militants may have changed as Athens contemplated the 2004 Olympic Games. Then a November 17th man was wounded by his own bomb as he prepared for an attack in June, 2002; apparently he talked; subsequent arrests of November 17 members left few to none at large. Fifteen were convicted in December, 2003. The group may be considered finished, even though leftist terrorism is not gone from Greece.

Shining Path (Sendero Luminoso) Abimael Guzman, a Peruvian with a university post, organized this insurgency for a decade and then took it onto the warpath in 1980. The economic and political damage done in Peru in the subsequent decade was extraordinary, and some 20,000 died. More important, great swaths of the countryside were under the control of Shining Path. The government of President Fujimori defeated *Sendero*, jailing thousands of its cadre and imprisoning the leader—the self-described "Fourth Sword of Marxism." A regional leader, Oscar Alberto Ramirez Durand ("Feliciano"), tried to assume the reins but was not a strong leader and was captured in 1999. However, the corruption of Fujimori's powerful director of intelligence, Vladimir Montesinos, roiled the nation. Montesinos was arrested abroad in June, 2001, and many of the convicted terrorists of Sendero and **Tupac Amaru**/MRTA are being given new trials. Even Guzman himself was to get a new trial, but this stalled quickly.

Taliban An insurgency, turned state, that reverted to insurgency. "Taliban" comes from the Arabic word for "students." This movement emerged from Pakistan-supported *madrassas* in the early 1990s. Given Afghanistan's disarray, the readiness of thousands of Afghan refugees in Pakistan to return home, and heavy foreign support, the Taliban grew and conquered territory quickly, often fighting conventionally. They came to control 90 percent of the country from their capital in Kandahar. Analyst James Phillips says Taliban turned the phrase "state-sponsored terrorism" on its head by becoming a government dependant on terrorists. Only three countries recognized the government (all Muslim). Osama Bin Laden poured money into government hoppers, undertook civil engineering projects, and merged many **Al Qaeda** members into the Taliban-controlled Afghan army. The Taliban's grip on power was destroyed quickly in late 2001, but its leader, Mullah Mohammed Omar—senior imam in Afghanistan since 1996 clerical elections—survived. He even appeared in a June, 2006 video. So, after a two-year pause, the Taliban has returned to the offensive. Their insurgency emphasizes terrorism: shootings, car bombings, suicide bombings, and beheadings of opponents. Influential and growing in southern and eastern areas of Afghanistan, especially where opium is grown. **Al Qaeda** may not be in the narcotics business today, but Taliban is; at least two were indicted in U.S. federal courts in 2005 for trafficking heroin and opium into the United States. Afghan opium production broke records in 2006. Afghan authorities state that Taliban's leaders live in Quetta, Pakistan, and a captured Taliban leader, Mohammad Hanif, said as much in January, 2007.

Tamil Tigers; Liberation Tigers of Tamil Eelam (LTTE)   Founded in 1972 and still led by Vellupillai Prabhakaran. The Tigers destroyed their rivals in the Tamil militant movement, grew into a force of some 2,000 armed fighters in the mid-1980s, and today boast a force as much as ten times that size. Apart from the "Black Tiger" suicide units, LTTE is highly capable in conventional ground operations and sinks Sri Lanka Navy vessels—as in May, 2006. Possesses SAM missiles and has shot down Sri Lankan aircraft. The political infrastructure is secure and well-represented by spokesmen and a presence on the World Wide Web. LTTE's intelligence system is known for its accuracy and transnational reach. Funding is from the Tamil diaspora—especially Canada and Western Europe—and more money flows in from narcotics, smuggling, and the like. LTTE faces one factional split that has included fighting. A truce between LTTE and the government of Sri Lanka, formalized in February, 2002, broke down in 2006 and was formally renounced by a LTTE spokesman. Seven hundred Sri Lankans died in attacks in the first half of 2006. One example of recent LTTE actions is a motorcycle suicide bombing that killed Parami Kulatunga, deputy chief of staff of the country's army, in the streets of Colombo. More innovative—and more horrible—was the detonation of two landmines that LTTE suspended in trees over a road in Kabithigollewa; they blew through a passing city bus, killing fifteen school children and several score of adults.

Tupac Amaru (MRTA)   Named for an eighteenth-century Indian rebel executed by the Spanish. This modern group spawned in 1983. While **Shining Path** developed in the universities and in rural Peru, MRTA focused on the cities (and the universities). They have several thousand hard core militants and a sprinkling of foreign allies, such as New Yorker Lori Berenson, now in a Peruvian jail. Tupac Amaru's leader (Victor Polay Campos) was in prison in 1996 when Nestor Cerpa Cartolini and comrades staged an oversized hostage-taking effort at the official residence of Japan's Ambassador in Lima. Months later, Peruvian counterterrorist forces recaptured the residence and killed all of the fourteen MRTA gun holders, male and female. MRTA all but disappeared. Might it return? The leading prospects would be (1) a jail break frees founder Victor Polay Campos, a.k.a. Comandante Rolando, recently reconvicted, or (2) the ongoing retrials process permits many MRTA to evade the remainders of their jail terms.

Turkish Hezbollah   Turkey's Muslim and democratic cultures still unsettle many citizens, and left, right, and religious factions have marred this impressive polity and staunch member of NATO. Turkish Hezbollah, no relation to the Lebanese fixture, is a Kurdish and Sunni-based organization in southeastern Turkey. It is a quarter-century old. Authorities arrested many in the group in early 2000 and discovered a mass grave of the terrorists' victims. Typical terrorist actions include kidnapping; torture and murder of businessmen of Turkish and Kurdish origins; attacks on vice dens and "un-Islamic" establishments; and assassinations of journalists. The group also has a lengthy record of attacks on Kurdish militants of **PKK**, natural enemies for being both separatists and Marxists. Given that, and a lack of attacks on security forces, some allege Turkish Hezbollah is a tool of Turkey's government. Officials deny that and point to Iran as the group's financier. Turkish Hezbollah has been quiet since 2002.

Ulster Defence Association/Ulster Freedom Fighters   Formed in 1971 to promote British rule of Northern Ireland and continued integration of the United Kingdom. The largest "Loyalist" group, with several hundred armed men and several thousand other active members. The militants enjoy the support of a formal political front—first the Ulster Democratic Party and now the Ulster Political Research Group, which the United States designated as terrorist in December, 2001. Like the other Irish militias on both sides, this group is deeply embroiled in extortion, robbery, narcotics dealing, smuggling, and the like to pay its bills. The group is thought to operate only in Northern Ireland, not in England. At times it feuds with the rival **Ulster Volunteer Force**.

Ulster Volunteer Force (UVF)   Founded before, but smaller than, the **Ulster Freedom Fighters**. The Volunteers are a militia with a long record of violence in the border areas and Belfast, including kidnappings, assassinations, and extortion. Recent attacks include shootings of rivals from the **Ulster Freedom Fighters** in east Belfast. A governmental commission found UVF guilty of four killings during 2005, further evidence of a pattern of many recent years by which loyalists are killing as many as are "republican" militants. UVF is also reportedly linked to the Red Hand Defenders, another loyalist terror group. Most long-standing terror groups are paired with political activists: Ulster Volunteer Force works with the Progressive Unionist Party, and this team has been involved in some past peace talks and cease-fires. In early May 2007, UVF announced that it had placed its weapons "beyond reach" and was ending recruitment and military training.

SELECT BIBLIOGRAPHY

In addition to the interviews, journals, newspapers, Web sites, and special reports quoted in the endnotes to each chapter, the following have proven valuable:

Court documents

U.S. District Court. District of Colombia. Judgment: Shaul Stern et. al. vs. Islamic Republic of Iran, [undated].

U.S. District Court. Hartford, Connecticut. Indictments against certain members of Los Macheteros, 1987.

U.S. District Court. New Jersey. Affidavit, briefs, and sentencing memorandum against Yu Kikumura of the Japanese Red Army, 1988, 1989.

U.S. District Court. New York City, New York. Proceedings on Pan Am 103 claims [undated].

U.S. District Court. Sacramento, California. Journal and Letter Exhibits to Sentencing Memorandum against Theodore John Kaczynski, 1998.

U.S. District Court. Southern District of New York. Papers re. members of "Republic of New Africa", 1988.

U.S. District Court. Southern District of New York. Indictment of Usama Bin Laden, 1998

U.S. District Court. Southern District of New York. Indictment of Baz Mohammad and Bashir Ahmad Rahmany, 2005.

U.S. District Court. District of Columbia. Judgment in the case of Heiser, Campbell, *et al.* v. Islamic Republic of Iran, 2006.

Recurring U.S. Government reports

Congressional Research Service reports

Department of Justice, Federal Bureau of Investigation. *Terrorism in the United States.* [Until 2000]. Washington, DC. Terrorist Research and Analytical Center.

Department of State. *Patterns of Global Terrorism,* and then *Country Reports on Terrorism*

Department of State. *Annual Report on Human Rights*

The White House. *National Security Strategy*

The White House. *National Military Strategy*

The White House. *National Strategy for Combating Terrorism*, 2003 and 2006.

Monographs and short works

Aboul-Enein, Youssef H. *Ayman Al-Zawahiri: The Ideologue of Modern Islamic Militancy.* Counterproliferation Papers, Future Warfare Series, no. 21. Maxwell Air Force Base, AL: USAF Counterproliferation Center, March 2004.

Al Qaeda. *The Al Qaeda Training Manual* ["Military Studies in the Jiahd against the Tyrants"] ed. Jerrold Post. Maxwell Air Force Base, AL: U.S. Air Force Counterproliferation Center, 2004.

Eisenstadt, Michael, and White, Jeffrey. *Assessing Iraq's Sunni Arab Insurgency.* Policy Focus No. 50. Washington, DC: The Washington Institute for Near East Policy, Dec. 2005.

Godson, Roy and Wm. J. Olson. *International Organized Crime: Emerging Threat to U.S. Security.* Washington, DC: National Strategy Information Center, 1993.

Guzman, Abimael. *Interviews with El Diario.* July, 1988, repr. Berkeley, CA: Committee to Support the Revolution in Peru, 1988.

Hamas. *The Charter of Allah: The Platform of the Islamic Resistance Movement (Hamas).* Introduced and edited by Raphael Israeli. *The 1988-89 Annual of Terrorism.* Yonah Alexander and H. Foxman, eds. Netherlands: Kluwer Academic Publishers, 1990.

International Crisis Group. *In Their Own Words: Reading the Iraqi Insurgency.* Middle East Report No. 50. Washington, DC.: ICG, Feb. 15, 2006.

Irish Republican Army. *Handbook for Volunteers of the Irish Republican Army: Notes on Guerrilla Warfare.* Ireland: The Irish Republican Army, General Headquarters, 1956.

Jacobsen, Michael. *The West at War: U.S. and European Counterterrorism Efforts, Post-September 11.* Washington, DC: Washington Institute for Near East Policy, 2006.

Jenkins, Brian M. *Embassies Under Siege: A Review of 48 Embassy Takeovers, 1971–1980.* Santa Monica, CA: RAND, 1981.

[Kaczynski, Theodore John]. *Industrial Society and Its Future.* Washington, DC: *The Washington Post*, September 19, 1995. [Supplement].

Kilcullen, David. *Twenty Eight Articles: Fundamentals of Company-level Counterinsurgency.* Unpublished paper courtesy of author. Ed. of March, 2006.

Kramer, Martin. *Hezbollah's Vision of the West.* The Washington Institute Policy Papers Series, no. 7. Washington, DC: The Washington Institute for Near East Policy, 1989.

Marighella, Carlos. *Urban Guerrilla Minimanual.* [1969] Vancouver: Pulp Press, 1974 .

Marks, Thomas A. *Insurgency in Nepal.* Carlisle Barracks, PA: Strategic Studies Institute, Dec., 2003.

McGurn, William. *Terrorist or Freedom Fighter? The Cost of Confusion.* United Kingdom: Institute for European Defense and Strategy, 1990.

Metz, Stephen. *The Future of Insurgency.* Carlisle Barracks, PA: Strategic Studies Institute, Dec. 1993.

Moran, Sue Ellen, ed. *Court Depositions of Three Red Brigadists.* Santa Monica, CA: RAND, February, 1986. RAND Note, N-2391-RC.

Ness, Cindy D. *et al. Women and Terrorism.* A Special Issue of *Studies in Conflict & Terrorism.* Vol 28, No. 5. Philadelphia, PA: Taylor & Francis, 2005.

Parker, Henry S. *Agricultural Bioterrorism: A Federal Strategy to Meet the Threat*, Rev. ed. Washington, DC: National Defense University Press, 2003.

Pisano, Vittorfranco S. *The Terrorist Threat to the U.S. Army in Western Europe.* Carlisle Barracks, PA: U.S. Army War College, February 16, 1988. Unpublished Military Studies Program Paper.

Republic of France, Ministry of Defense, *Defense Against Terrorism: A Top Priority...* Paris. April, 2006.

Ryan, Chris B. *Tourism, Terrorism, and Violence.* Conflict Studies no. 24. London: Research Institute for the Study of Conflict and Terrorism, September, 1991.

Shultz, Richard H. et. al. *Armed Groups: A Tier-One Security Priority.* INSS Occasional Paper #57. Boulder, CO: U.S. Air Force Academy, September, 2004.

Southern Poverty Law Center. *False Patriots.* Montgomery, AL, 1996.

U.S. Army and U.S. Marine Corps. *FMFM 3-24: Counterinsurgency.* Pre-publication draft, 2006.

U.S. Department of Defense. *Terrorist Group Profiles.* Washington, DC: U.S. Government Printing Office. n.d. [1988].

Books

Abbey, Edward. *The Monkey Wrench Gang.* New York: Avon Books, 1976.

Adams, James. *The Financing of Terror.* New York: Simon and Schuster, 1986.

Alexander, Yonah, and Dennis Pluchinsky. *Europe's Red Terrorists: The Fighting Communist Organizations.* London: Frank Cass & Co. Ltd., 1992.

Allison, Graham. *Nuclear Terrorism: The Ultimate Preventable Catastrophe.* New York: Times Books, 2004.

Anonymous [Rita Katz]. *Terrorist Hunter: The Extraordinary Story of a Woman Who Went Undercover to Infiltrate the Radical Islamic Groups Operating in America.* New York: Ecco, 2003.

Anti-Defamation League. *Danger: Extremism: The Major Vehicles and Voices on America's Far-Right Fringe.* New York: Anti-Defamation League, 1996.

Asprey, Robert B. *War in the Shadows: The Guerrilla in History.* Vol. 2. Garden City, New York: Doubleday & Company, Inc., 1975.

Aussaresses, Paul. *The Battle of the Casbah: Terrorism and Counter-Terrorism in Algeria, 1955–1957.* [2001] Trans. Robert L. Miller. New York: Enigma Books, 2002.

Ayers, Bill. *Fugitive Days.* New York: Penguin Books, 2003.

Baer, Robert. *See No Evil: The True Story of a Ground Soldier in the CIA's War on Terrorism.* Rev. ed. New York: Three Rivers Press, 2002.

Baumann, Michael [Bommi Baumann]. *How It All Began.* Vancouver: Pulp Press, 1977; reprint, *Terror or Love? Bommi Baumann's Own Story of His Life as a West German Urban Guerrilla.* New York: Grove Press, Inc., 1978.

Becker, Jillian. *Hitler's Children: The Story of the Baader-Meinhof Terrorist Gang.* New York: J.B. Lippincott Company, 1977.

Bergen, Peter L. *Holy War Inc.: Inside the Secret World of Osama Bin Laden.* New York: The Free Press, 2001.

Betancourt, Ingrid. *Until Death Do Us Part: My Struggle to Reclaim Colombia.* Trans. Steven Rendall. New York: HarperCollins, 2002.

Bin Laden, Osama. *Messages to the World.* Compiled, edited and translated by Bruce Lawrence. London: Verso, 2005.

Bloom, Mia. *Dying To Kill: The Allure of Suicide Terror.* New York: Colombia University Press, 2005.

Brackett, D.W. *Holy Terror: Armageddon in Tokyo.* Uncorrected proof. New York: Weatherhill, Inc., 1996.

Buford, Bill. *Among the Thugs.* New York: W.W. Norton, 1991.

Byman, Daniel, et. al. *Trends in Outside Support for Insurgent Movements.* Santa Monica, CA: RAND, 2001.

Carafano, James Jay and Rosenzweig, Paul. *Winning the Long War: Lessons from the Cold War for Defeating Terrorism and Preserving Freedom.* Washington, DC: Heritage Books, 2005.

Cigar, Norman. *Genocide in Bosnia: The Policy of 'Ethnic Cleansing'*. College Station, TX: Texas A&M University Press, 1995.

Ciment, James. *The Kurds: State and Minority in Turkey, Iraq and Iran*. New York: Facts on File, 1996.

Clark, Robert P. *The Basque Insurgents: ETA, 1952-1980*. Madison, WI: The University of Wisconsin Press, 1984.

Clarke, Richard A. *Against All Enemies: Inside America's War on Terror*. New York: Free Press, 2004.

Cline, Ray S., and Yonah Alexander. *Terrorism as State-Sponsored Covert Warfare: What the Free World Must Do to Protect Itself*. Fairfax, VA: Hero Books, 1986.

—— *Terrorism: The Soviet Connection*. New York: Crane Russak, 1984.

Coll, Steve. *Ghost Wars: The Secret History of the CIA, Afghanistan, and Bin Laden...* New York: Penguin Press, 2004.

Connelly, Matthew. *A Diplomatic Revolution: Algeria's Fight for Independence and the Origins of the Post-Cold War Era*. Oxford: Oxford University Press, 2002.

Coogan, Tim Pat. *The IRA, A History*. Niwot, CO: Roberts Rinehart Publishers, 1993.

Corcoran, James. *Bitter Harvest: Gordon Kahl and the Posse Comitatus: Murder in the Heartland*. New York: Viking Penguin, 1990.

Corum, James S. & Johnson, Wray R. *Airpower in Small Wars: Fighting Insurgents and Terrorists*. Lawrence, KA: University Press of Kansas, 2003.

Crenshaw Hutchinson, Martha. *Revolutionary Terrorism: The FLN in Algeria, 1954–1962*. Stanford, CA: Hoover Institution on War, Revolution, and Peace, 1978.

Crenshaw, Martha, ed. *Terrorism in Context*. University Park, PA: Pennsylvania State University Press, 1995.

Debray, Regis. *Revolution in the Revolution?* Librarie Francois Maspero, 1967; New York: Grove Press, Inc., 1967.

Dees, Morris, with James Corcoran. *Gathering Storm: America's Militia Threat*. New York: HarperCollins Publishers, Inc., 1996.

Dees, Morris, and Steve Fiffer. *Hate on Trial: The Case against America's Most Dangerous Neo-Nazi*. New York: Villard Books, 1993.

Dillon, Martin. *25 Years of Terror: The IRA's War against the British*. London: Bantam Books, 1997.

Dobson, Christopher, and Ronald Payne. *The Carlos Complex: A Study in Terror*. New York: G.P. Putnam's Sons, 1977.

—— *The Terrorists: Their Weapons, Leaders and Tactics*. New York: Facts on File, 1979.

Douglass, Joseph D., Jr. *CBW: The Poor Man's Atomic Bomb*. Philadelphia: Institute for Foreign Policy Analysis, 1984.

Douglass, Joseph D., Jr., and Neil C. Livingstone. *America the Vulnerable: The Threat of Chemical and Biological Warfare*. Lexington, MA: Lexington Books, D.C. Heath and Company, 1987.

Drell, Sidney D., Sofaer, Abraham D., & Wilson, George D., eds. *The New Terror: Facing the Threat of Biological and Chemical Weapons*. Stanford, CA: Hoover Institution Press, 1999.

Duncan, Stephen M. *A War of a Different Kind: Military Force and America's Search for Homeland Security*. Annapolis, MD: Naval Institute Press, 2004.

Ehrenfeld, Rachel. *Funding Evil: How Terrorism is Financed—and How to Stop It*. 2nd ed. Chicago: Bonus Books, 2005.

—— *Narco-Terrorism: How Governments Around the World Have Used the Drug Trade to Finance and Further Terrorist Activities*. New York: Basic Books, 1990.

Emerson, Steven, and Brian Duffy. *The Fall of Pan Am 103: Inside the Lockerbie Investigation*. New York: G.P. Putnam's Sons, 1990.

Emerson, Steven, and Cristina Del Sesto. *Terrorist: The Inside Story of the Highest-Ranking Iraqi Terrorist Ever to Defect to the West*. New York: Villard Books, 1991.

Erickson, Richard J. *Legitimate Use of Military Force Against State-Sponsored International Terrorism*. Maxwell, AL: Air University Press, 1989.

Esposito, John L. *Unholy War: Terror in the Name of Islam*. Oxford: Oxford University Press, 2002.

Fanon, Frantz. *A Dying Colonialism*. [1959] Trans. Haakon Chevalier. New York: Grove Press, 1965.

—— *The Wretched of the Earth*. With a preface by Jean-Paul Sartre. 1961; New York: Grove Press, Inc., 1968.

Farah, Douglas. *Blood from Stones: The Secret Financial Network of Terror*. New York: Broadway Books, 2004.

Farkas, Evelyn. *Fractured States and U.S. Foreign Policy: Iraq, Ethiopia, and Bosnia in the 1990s*. New York: Palgrave/Macmillan, 2003.

Farrell, William R. *Blood and Rage: The Story of the Japanese Red Army*. Lexington, MA: Lexington Books, D.C. Heath and Company, 1990.

Fernandez, Ronald. *Los Macheteros: The Wells Fargo Robbery and the Violent Struggle for Puerto Rican Independence*. New York: Prentice Hall Press, 1987.

Flynn, Stephen. *America the Vulnerable: How Our Government is Failing to Protect Us from Terrorism*. New York: HarperCollins Publishers, 2004.

Fontaine, Roger W. *Terrorism: The Cuban Connection*. New York: Crane Russak & Company, 1988.

Foreman, Dave. *Confessions of an Eco-Warrior*. New York: Harmony Books, 1991.

George, Roger Z. and Kline, Robert D. *Intelligence and the National Security Strategist: Enduring Issues and Challenges*. Washington, D.C.: National Defense University Press, 2004.

Gertz, Bill. *Breakdown: How America's Intelligence Failures Led to September 11*. Washington, DC: Regnery Publishing, 2002.

Goren, Roberta. *The Soviet Union and Terrorism*. Edited by Jillian Becker. With introduction by Robert Conquest. London: George Allen & Unwin, 1984.

Guevara, Che. *Guerrilla Warfare*. With prefatory note by I.F. Stone. New York: Vintage Books, 1969.

—— *The Diary of Che Guevara*. Ed. Robert Scheer. Introduction by Fidel Castro. Ramparts Magazine, 1967; New York: Bantam, 1968.

Gunaratna, Rohan. *Inside Al Qaeda: Global Network of Terror.*, 3rd ed. New York: Berkley Books, 2003.

—— *International & Regional Security Implications of the Sri Lankan Tamil Insurgency*. 3rd ed. U.K.: International Foundation of Sri Lankans, 2001.

Hammes, Thomas X. *The Sling and the Stone: On War in the 21ˢᵗ Century*. St. Paul, MN: Zenith, 2004.

Hanson, Victor Davis. *An Autumn of War: What America Learned from September 11 and the War on Terrorism*. New York: Anchor Books, 2004.

Hasselbach, Ingo, with Tom Reiss. *Fuhrer-Ex: Memoirs of a Former Neo-Nazi*. New York: Random House, 1996.

Hearst, Patricia Campbell, with Alvin Moscow. *Every Secret Thing*. 1982; reprint, *Patty Hearst: Her Own Story*. New York: Avon Books, 1988.

Henze, Paul. *The Plot to Kill the Pope*. New York: Charles Scribner's Sons, 1983.

Hewitt, Gavin. *Terry Waite and Ollie North: The Untold Story of the Kidnapping – and the Release*. Boston, MA: Little, Brown and Co, 1991.

Hiro, Dilip. *War Without End: The Rise of Islamist Terrorism and Global Response.* Rev. ed. London: Routledge, 2002.

Hitler, Adolf. *Mein Kampf.* Trans. and ed. by John Chamberlain *et al.* New York: Reynal & Hitchcock, 1939.

Holland, Jack. *The American Connection: U.S. Guns, Money, & Influence in Northern Ireland.* New York: Viking Penguin, 1987.

Howard, Russell D. & Sawyer, Reid L. *Defeating Terrorism: Shaping the New Security Environment.* Guilford, CN: McGraw-Hill, 2004.

—— *Terrorism and Counterterrorism: Understanding the New Security Environment.* 2nd ed. Guilford, CN: McGraw-Hill, 2004.

Hughes, Matthew, & Johnson, Gaynor, eds. *Fanaticism and Conflict in the Modern Age.* Abingdon, Oxon: Frank Cass, 2005.

Hyun Hee, Kim. *The Tears of My Soul.* New York: William Morrow & Co., 1993.

Jacquard, Roland. *In the Name of Osama Bin Laden: Global Terrorism and the Bin Laden Brotherhood.* Rev. ed. Durham, NC: Duke University Press, 2002.

Janke, Peter with Richard Sim. *Guerrilla and Terrorist Organizations: A World Directory and Bibliography.* New York: Macmillan, 1983.

Jeffreys, Diarmuid. *The Bureau: Inside the Modern FBI.* Boston: Houghton Mifflin Company, 1995.

Joll, James. *The Anarchists.* New York: The Universal Library, Grosset & Dunlap, 1966.

Jonas, George. *Vengeance: The True Story of an Israeli Counter-Terrorist Team.* [1984]. Rev. ed. *New York: Simon & Schuster Paperbacks*, 2005.

Kaplan, David E. & Marshall, Andrew. *The Cult At The End of the World.* New York: Crown Publishers, 1996.

Katz, Samuel M. *Israel Versus Jibril: The Thirty-Year War Against a Master Terrorist.* New York: Paragon House, 1993.

Kessler, Ronald. *The CIA AT War: Inside the Secret Campaign Against Terror.* New York: St. Martin's Press, 2003.

—— *The FBI.* New York: Pocket Star Books, 1993.

Kinsella, Warren. *Web of Hate: Inside Canada's Far Right Network.* Toronto: HarperCollins Publishers Ltd., 1994; HarperPerennial, 1995.

Klein, Aaron J. *Striking Back: The 1972 Munich Olympics Massacre and Israel's Deadly Response.* Trans. Mitch Ginsburg. New York: Random House, 2005.

Kleinknecht, William. *The New Ethnic Mobs: The Changing Face of Organized Crime in America.* New York: The Free Press, 1996.

Kushner, Harvey W., ed. *The Future of Terrorism: Violence in the New Millennium.* Thousand Oaks, CA: SAGE Publications, Inc., 1998.

Laqueur, Walter. *The Age of Terrorism.* 2nd ed. Boston: Little, Brown and Company, 1987.

Laqueur, Walter, and Yonah Alexander, eds. *The Terrorism Reader.* 2nd ed. New York: Meridian Books, 1987.

Lenin, V.I. *'Left-Wing' Communism, An Infantile Disorder: A Popular Essay in Marxian Strategy and Tactics.* 1920; New York: International Publishers, 1940.

—— *State and Revolution.* 1917; New York: International Publishers, 1932, 1974.

—— *What Is To Be Done?* 1902; Beijing: Foreign Languages Press, 1975.

Lesser, Ian O. et. al. *Countering the New Terrorism.* Santa Monica, CA: RAND, 1999.

Levitt, Matthew. *Hamas: Politics, Charity, and Terrorism in the Service of Jihad.* New Haven, CN: Yale University Press, 2006.

Lewis, Paul H. *Guerrillas and Generals: The "Dirty War" in Argentina.* Westport, CN: Praeger, 2002.

213

Lifton, Robert Jay. *Destroying the World to Save It: Aum Shinrikyo, Apocalyptic Violence, and the New Global Terrorism*. New York: Metropolitan Books, 1999.

Lodge, Juliet, ed. *The Threat of Terrorism*. Boulder, Colorado: Westview Press, 1988.

Macdonald, Andrew [William Pierce]. *The Turner Diaries*. 2d ed. Hillsboro, WVA: National Vanguard Books, 1978.

MacDonald, Eileen. *Shoot the Women First*. New York: Random House, 1991.

MacGinty, Roger, and Darby, John. *Guns and Government: The Management of the Northern Ireland Peace Process.* Houndmills, U.K.: Palgrave, 2002.

McGowan, William. *Only Man is Vile: The Tragedy of Sri Lanka*. New York: Farrar, Straus and Giroux, 1992.

Mao Tse-Tung. *Selected Military Writings of Mao Tse-Tung*. 2d ed. Peking: Foreign Languages Press, 1963.

—— *Mao Tse-Tung on Guerrilla Warfare*. Edited by Samuel B. Griffith. Washington, DC: United State Marine Corps, Department of the Navy, April 1989.

Marenches, Alexandre de, Comte, and Christine Ockrent. *Dans le Secret des Princes*, Editions Stock, 1986; updated, adapted, and reprinted, Count de Marenches, and David A. Andelman. *The Fourth World War: Diplomacy and Espionage in the Age of Terrorism*. New York: William Morrow and Company, Inc., 1992.

Marks, Thomas A. *Maoist Insurgency Since Vietnam*. London: Frank Cass & Co. Ltd., 1996.

Martinez, Thomas, with John Guinther. *Brotherhood of Murder*. New York: McGraw-Hill Book Company, 1988.

McRaven, William H. *Spec Ops: Case Studies in Special Operations Warfare: Theory and Practice.* Novato, CA: Presidio, 1996.

Melman, Yossi. *The Master Terrorist: The True Story Behind Abu Nidal*. New York: Adama Books, 1986.

Merkl, Peter H. and Leonard Weinberg. *The Revival of Right-Wing Extremism in the Nineties*. London: Frank Cass & Co. Ltd., 1997.

Miller, Judith. *God Has Ninety-Nine Names: Reporting From a Militant Middle East*. New York: Simon & Schuster, 1996.

Miniter, Richard. *Losing Bin Laden: How Bill Clinton's Failures Unleashed Global Terror.* Washington, DC: Regnery Publishing, 2003.

Mizell, Louis R., Jr. *Target U.S.A.: The Inside Story of the New Terrorist War*. New York: John Wiley & Sons, 1998.

Mockaitis, Thomas Ross. 'The British Experience in Counterinsurgency, 1919–1960.' Ph.D. diss., University of Wisconsin, 1988. Ann Arbor, MI: UMI Dissertation Information Services, 1990.

Moore, Robin. *The Hunt for Bin Laden: Task Force Dagger.* New York: Random House, 2003.

Murakami, Haruki. *Underground: The Tokyo Gas Attack and the Japanese Psyche*. Trans. A. Birnbaum & P. Gabriel. New York: Vintage Books, 2001.

Nagl, John A. *Learning to East Soup with a Knife: Counterinsurgency Lessons from Malaya and Vietnam*. 2nd ed. Chicago: University of Chicago Press, 2005.

Netanyahu, Benjamin. *Fighting Terrorism: How Democracies Can Defeat Domestic and International Terrorists*. New York: Farrar Straus Giroux, 1995.

—— ed. *Terrorism: How the West Can Win*. New York: Farrar Straus Giroux, 1986.

O'Ballance, Edgar. *Islamic Fundamentalist Terrorism, 1979–95: The Iranian Connection*. New York: New York University Press, 1997.

O'Callaghan, Sean. *The Informer.* London: Bantam Press, 1998.

O'Neill, Bard E. *Insurgency & Terrorism: Inside Modern Revolutionary Warfare*. [1990]. Reprint. Washington, DC: Potomac Books, 2005.

Paret, Peter. *French Revolutionary Warfare from Indochina to Algeria: The Analysis of a Political and Military Doctrine*. Princeton Studies in World Politics No. 6. New York: Frederick A. Praeger, 1964.

Pillar, Paul L. *Terrorism and U.S. Foreign Policy*. Washington, DC: Brookings Institution Press, 2001.

Pipes, Daniel. *Syria Beyond the Peace Process*. Washington, DC: Washington Institute for Near East Policy, 1996.

Potts, Mark, Nicholas Kochan and Robert Whittington. *Dirty Money: BCCI*. Washington, DC: National Press Books, 1992.

Powers, Thomas. *Diana: The Making of a Terrorist*. New York: Bantam Books and Houghton Mifflin, 1971.

Ra'anan, Uri, Robert L. Pfaltzgraff, Jr., Richard H. Shultz, Ernst Halperin and Igor Lukes. *Hydra of Carnage: The International Linkages of Terrorism and Other Low-Intensity Operations: The Witnesses Speak*. Lexington, MA: Lexington Books, D.C. Heath and Company, 1986.

Radu, Michael. *Dilemmas of Democracy & Dictatorship: Place, Time, and Ideology in Global Perspective*. New Brunswick, NJ: Transaction Publishers, 2006.

Radu, Michael, and Tismaneanu, Vladimir. *Latin American Revolutionaries: Groups, Goals, Methods*. Washington, DC: Pergamon-Brassey's, 1990.

Rashid, Ahmed. *Taliban*. New Haven CN: Yale University Press, 2001.

Rood, Harold W. *Kingdoms of the Blind: How the Great Democracies Have Resumed the Follies That So Nearly Cost Them Their Lives*. Durham, N.C.: Carolina Academic Press, 1980.

Rotella, Sebastian. *Twilight on the Line: Underworlds and Politics at the U.S.–Mexico Border*. New York: W.W. Norton, 1998.

Sageman, Marc. *Understanding Terror Networks*. Philadelphia, PA: University of Pennsylvania Press, 2004.

Satloff, Robert. *The Battle of Ideas in the War on Terror: Essays on U.S. Public Diplomacy in the Middle East*. Washington, DC: Washington Institute for Near East Policy, 2004.

Scheuer, Michael. *Through Our Enemies' Eyes: Osama Bin Laden, Radical Islam, and the Future of America*. Rev. ed. Washington, DC: Potomac Books, 2006.

Schmidt, Michael. *The New Reich: Violent Extremism in Unified Germany and Beyond*. New York: Pantheon Books, 1993.

Schweitzer, Glenn E., with Carole Dorsch Schweitzer. *A Faceless Enemy: The Origins of Modern Terrorism*. Cambridge, MA: Perseus Publishing, 2002.

Seale, Patrick. *Abu Nidal: A Gun for Hire: The Secret Life of the World's Most Notorious Arab Terrorist*. New York: Random House, 1992.

Shultz Jr., Richard H. and Dew, Andrea J. *Insurgents, Terrorists, and Militias: The Warriors of Contemporary Combat*. New York: Colombia University Press, 2006.

Sifaoui, Mohamed. *Inside Al Qaeda: How I Infiltrated the World's Deadliest Terrorist Organization*. New York: Thunder's Mouth Press, 2004.

Simon, Steven, & Benjamin, Daniel. *The Age of Sacred Terror: Radical Islam's War Against America*. New York: Random House, 2003.

Singular, Stephen. *Talked to Death: The Life and Murder of Alan Berg*. New York Beech Tree Books, 1987.

Sirrs, Julie, et. al., eds. *Unmasking Terror: A Global Review of Terrorist Activities*. Washington, DC: Jamestown Foundation, 2004.

Stanton, Bill. *Klanwatch: Bringing the Ku Klux Klan to Justice*. New York: Grove Weidenfeld, 1991.

Stern, Jessica. *Terror in the Name of God: Why Religious Militants Kill*. New York: HarperCollins Publishers, 2003.

Strong, Simon. *Shining Path: The World's Deadliest Revolutionary Force*. London: HarperCollins, 1992.

Sun, Tzu. *The Art of War*. Translated and with an introduction by Samuel B. Griffith. With a foreword by B.H. Liddell Hart. Clarendon Press, 1963; reprint, London: Oxford University Press, 1963.

Swamy, M. R. Narayan. *Inside an Elusive Mind: Prabhakaran*. Reprint. Delhi: Konark Publishers, 2003.

—— *Tigers of Lanka: From Boys to Guerrillas*. 6th ed. Colombo, Sri Lanka: Vijitha Yapa Publications, 2005.

Tangredi, Sam J., ed. *Globalization and Maritime Power*. Washington, DC: National Defense University Press, 2002.

'Tayacán', with Joanne Omang and Aryeh Neier. *Psychological Operations in Guerrilla Warfare*. New York: Vintage Books, 1985.

Taylor, Peter. *States of Terror: Democracy and Political Violence*. London: BBC Books, 1993.

Thomas, Timothy L. *Cyber Silhouettes: Shadows Over Information Operations*. Fort Leavenworth, KS: Foreign Military Studies Office, 2005.

Thompson, Jerry. *My Life In The Klan*. With introduction by John Seigenthaler. New York: G.P. Putnam's Sons, 1982; reprint, Nashville, TN: Rutledge Hill Press, 1988.

Thompson, Robert. *Defeating Communist Insurgency: Experiences from Malaya and Vietnam*. Chatto & Windus, 1966; reprint, London: Macmillan Press, Ltd., 1987.

Tierney, John J. *Chasing Ghosts: Unconventional Warfare in American History*. Washington, DC: Potomac Books, Inc., 2006.

Timmerman, Kenneth R. *Countdown to Crisis: The Coming Nuclear Showdown with Iran*. New York: Crown Forum, 2005.

Trotsky, Leon. *Dictatorship vs. Democracy*. 1920; New York: American Communists (Workers Party), 1922; reprint, *Terrorism & Communism: A Reply to Karl Kautsky*. With a foreword by Max Shachtman. Ann Arbor, MI: Ann Arbor Paperbacks for the Study of Communism and Marxism, The University of Michigan Press, 1961.

Tucker, David. *Skirmishes at the Edge of Empire: The United States and International Terrorism*. Westport, CN: Praeger Publishers, 1997.

Tucker, Jonathan B., ed. *Toxic Terror: Assessing Terrorist Use of Chemical and Biological Weapons*. Cambridge, MA: MIT Press, 2000.

U.S. Department of the Army. *Human Factors Considerations of Undergrounds in Insurgencies*. Washington, DC: Special Operations Research Office, The American University, 1966.

U.S. Government Accounting Office. *Combating Terrorism: Interagency Framework and Agency Programs to Address the Overseas Threat*. Washington, DC: GPO, May, 2003.

Volkan, Vamik. *Blood Lines: From Ethnic Pride to Ethnic Terrorism*. Boulder, CO: Westview, 1997.

Von Clausewitz, Carl. *On War*. Edited and translated by Michael Howard and Peter Paret. With introductory essays by Peter Paret, Michael Howard and Bernard Brodie. Princeton, N.J.: Princeton University Press, 1976.

Ward, Richard H. et. al., eds. *Extremist Groups: An International Compilation of Terrorist Organizations, Violent Political Groups, and Issue-Oriented Militant Movements*. 2nd ed. Huntsville, TX: Institute for Study of Violent Groups, Sam Houston University, 2002.

Wardlaw, Grant. *Political Terrorism: Theory, Tactics, and Counter-measures*. 2nd ed. Cambridge: Cambridge University Press, 1989.

Weinberg, Leonard B., ed. *Political Parties and Terrorist Groups*. London: Frank Cass & Co. Ltd., 1992.

Weinberg, Leonard B. and Paul B. Davis. *Introduction to Political Terrorism*. New York: McGraw-Hill, Inc., 1989.

Wilkinson, Paul. *Terrorism and the Liberal State*. New York: New York University Press, 1979.

—— *Terrorism versus Liberal Democracy: The Liberal State Response*. London: Frank Cass, 2001.

INDEX